OXFORD EARLY CHRISTIAN STUDIES

General Editors

Gillian Clark   Andrew Louth

THE OXFORD EARLY CHRISTIAN STUDIES series includes scholarly volumes on the thought and history of the early Christian centuries. Covering a wide range of Greek, Latin, and Oriental sources, the books are of interest to theologians, ancient historians, and specialists in the classical and Jewish worlds.

Augustine's Commentary on Galatians

Introduction, Text,
Translation, and Notes

ERIC PLUMER

OXFORD
UNIVERSITY PRESS

OXFORD

UNIVERSITY PRESS

Great Clarendon Street, Oxford OX2 6DP

Oxford University Press is a department of the University of Oxford.
It furthers the University's objective of excellence in research, scholarship,
and education by publishing worldwide in

Oxford New York

Auckland Bangkok Buenos Aires Cape Town Chennai
Dar es Salaam Delhi Hong Kong Istanbul Karachi Kolkata
Kuala Lumpur Madrid Melbourne Mexico City Mumbai Nairobi
São Paulo Shanghai Taipei Tokyo Toronto

Oxford is a registered trade mark of Oxford University Press
in the UK and in certain other countries

Published in the United States
by Oxford University Press Inc., New York

British Library Cataloguing in Publication Data
Data available

Library of Congress Cataloging in Publication Data
Augustine, Saint, Bishop of Hippo.
[Expositio epistulae ad Galatas. English & Latin]
Augustine's commentary on Galatians / introduction, translation
(with facing Latin text), and notes by Eric Plumer.
p. cm – (Oxford Early Christian studies)
Includes bibliographical references and index.
(alk. paper)
1. Bible. N.T. Galatians–Commentaries. I. Plumer, Eric Antone. II. Title. III. Series.
BR65.A792 E5 2002   227'.407–dc21   2002070192

ISBN 0–19–924439–1

1 3 5 7 9 10 8 6 4 2

Typeset in Ehrhardt
by Regent Typesetting, London
Printed in Great Britain
on acid-free paper by Biddles Ltd,
Guildford and King's Lynn

To my mother
and to the memory of my father

Ad astra per aspera

Preface and Acknowledgements

Of all the voluminous writings of Augustine, few are so little known as his *Commentary on Galatians*. Written during a brief period of his life—that of his priesthood—which has never received even a fraction of the attention that has been lavished on his episcopate or on the years leading up to his conversion, this work stands none the less as Augustine's first and only complete commentary on any book of the Bible. It deals, moreover, not with some obscure biblical book—as does Jerome's first commentary, on the Book of Obadiah—but with one of the most decisive and influential texts in Christian history. Yet apart from recent articles by the distinguished Italian scholar M. G. Mara, the attention it has received has been limited almost entirely to passing references in footnotes. Equally surprising to me was the fact that no one had ever published an English translation of the *Commentary*, and so I decided to make that my first goal. As a translator I aimed at both accuracy and readability but often found it necessary to compromise between the two. In such cases I gave preference to readability but added a footnote wherever I thought the reader should be aware of the literal meaning. My translation retains Augustine's gender-specific language (e.g. 'sons of God' rather than 'children of God'), partly because his meaning would often have been obscured otherwise, partly because Augustine's world was nothing if not patriarchal.

This book also contains an Introduction to Augustine's *Commentary* that is nearly twice as long as the *Commentary* itself. In view of the ancient axiom that 'a big book is a big bore' (μέγα βιβλίον ἴσον τῷ μεγάλῳ κακῷ), some justification for the excessive length of my Introduction is in order. In his magisterial commentary on Augustine's *Confessions* J. J. O'Donnell remarked, 'The late fourth century was a great age for reading and debating Paul in the Latin church, and a fuller study of those movements would be most welcome' (ii. 477). My second goal was to offer a contribution to that 'fuller study' by comparing Augustine's *Commentary* with the other Latin commentaries on Galatians from this period. As it happens, Galatians is the only letter of Paul's for which commentaries have survived from all the other Latin commentators of the time: Marius Victorinus, Ambrosiaster, Jerome, Pelagius, and the anonymous commentator whose work was recently brought to light by H. J. Frede. I have compared Augustine's *Commentary* with all the others, chiefly with a view to tracing lines of influence, and have discovered a complex network of interconnections among them.

I have devoted a disproportionate amount of space to the question of Victorinus' influence on Augustine's *Commentary*, and this too requires justification. Having read a number of scholars who claimed that Augustine either had or had not read Victorinus' *Commentary on Galatians* but who offered little or no support for their claims, I felt there was need for a systematic investigation of the question, even if it produced no definitive results. My method was to begin not with a line-by-line comparison of the two commentaries but rather with what Newman called 'the argument from antecedent probability'. In other words, I began with the question: What is the likelihood, based on what we know about Augustine and Victorinus—and especially what Augustine himself says about Victorinus in the *Confessions*—that Augustine would have turned to Victorinus as a model for the interpretation of Paul? After examining all the evidence that seemed relevant I concluded that the likelihood was very great. This conclusion then became the hypothesis for the next stage of the investigation, which involved comparing the two commentaries for evidence of direct, verbal dependence. A small amount of such evidence was all that would be needed to confirm the hypothesis, which was fortunate given Augustine's well-known tendency to transform his sources beyond recognition. The comparison of the two commentaries yielded three instances of what appeared to be direct, verbal dependence, and the hypothesis was therefore confirmed. Further confirmation came later when the hypothesis cast new and unexpected light on a celebrated passage in the *De doctrina christiana*—the list of famous men in 2. 40. 61—which could now be seen as a passage of great personal significance for Augustine and not a mere rhetorical flourish. For these reasons I felt the extra attention given to Victorinus was justified. If I could have used the same method with Ambrosiaster I would have done so, but in the case of Ambrosiaster Augustine provided nothing like the sort of invitation that he did in the case of Victorinus when he wrote so memorably about him in the *Confessions*. In fact, it would appear that at the time Augustine wrote his *Commentary* the identity of the author we call 'Ambrosiaster' was as unknown to him as it is to us now. Hence, although I present evidence that bears on the relation between Augustine's *Commentary* and Ambrosiaster's, I make no attempt to draw firm conclusions from it.

Closely related to the question of sources and influences was the question of Augustine's purpose in writing, and comparison of his *Commentary* with the others brought both his purpose and theirs into sharper focus. All the other commentators, in addition to interpreting Paul's teaching on law and grace, levelled harsh criticism against specific heresies, and so I decided to see who had been targeted by Augustine, even though he did not refer to any false teachers by name. I began with the presumption that Augustine would certainly have wanted to counter the views of his former co-religionists, the Manichees. This proved to be a fruitful path to take. There is indeed implicit polemic against the Manichees in Augustine's *Commentary*, and not only against them, but also against the Donatists, the Arians, the pagans, and even a future Doctor of the Church—Jerome. In fact the implicit polemic against Jerome is extremely important because Jerome's explanation of the clash between Peter and Paul at Antioch (Gal. 2: 11–14) as mere play-acting had, in Augustine's view, called in question the authority of the entire Bible. The famous correspondence between Augustine and Jerome on this subject has tended to eclipse whatever light their commentaries might have to shed on their positions, yet as I have tried to demonstrate, their commentaries provide insight into the dispute that is simply unavailable from the correspondence alone.

Although Augustine's *Commentary* contains many polemical elements, I felt increasingly dissatisfied with the idea that its main purpose was polemical and so began looking elsewhere for fresh insight. One of the subjects I decided to explore was Augustine's monastic rule, which dates from roughly the same time as the *Commentary*. Augustine's monastic rule has probably suffered even more neglect from modern scholars than his *Commentary*, in part because the problem of its authenticity seemed insoluble. Tarsicius van Bavel made a notable contribution towards a solution when he offered a list of parallels he had found (amazingly, without the aid of computer technology) between the monastic rule and Augustine's undisputed writings. The parallels he found with the *Commentary* were very faint, but the more I considered them the more I became convinced that their very faintness showed not that they were insignificant but that the monastic rule was in fact being presupposed in the *Commentary* both by Augustine and by his audience, who could then be identified unmistakably as his fellow monks at Hippo.

This discovery in turn shed crucial light on Augustine's purpose: he was reading Paul's letter as a model of how to build community, both within the narrower circle of his fellow monks and within the wider circle of the Catholic parishioners he was serving. (This text supplies some of our most vivid glimpses of Augustine's life as a parish priest.) Central to building community as Augustine saw it was the difficult and delicate task of Christian correction. He viewed Galatians as a model of how to give and receive correction, not only because Paul corrected Peter at Antioch and, by means of his letter, was correcting the Galatians, but also because Paul taught the Galatians how they ought to correct one another (Gal. 6: 1). By focusing on this theme Augustine highlighted an aspect of the letter that has often and undeservedly been neglected.

The *Commentary* also reflects a significant moment in Augustine's personal development. The ideal of the contemplative life that his earlier reading of the Neoplatonists had inspired in him was undergoing transformation by being linked more closely to the ideal of active involvement in the world. Faith in things invisible must express itself visibly in love of neighbour, or, in the words of Paul that are almost a leitmotif in Augustine's *Commentary*, what matters ultimately is *faith working through love* (Gal. 5: 6). This self-giving love of neighbour is what Christ commanded in his teaching, exemplified by his death on the cross, and bestowed upon believers by his grace. Thus Augustine saw the closest possible connection between Paul's theology and his ethics. It is notable as well that it is in this monastic and pastoral context, rather than in any overtly polemical context, that we find the earliest form of Augustine's famous principle 'Love and do what you will' (cf. *exp. Gal.* 57. 4).

The Introduction goes on to examine Augustine's theory and practice of biblical interpretation as evidenced by his *Commentary* and to compare them with what he says in the *De doctrina christiana*. Having argued in earlier parts of the Introduction that, in addition to Victorinus, Augustine used Cyprian, Optatus, and Hilary as important though unnamed sources for his *Commentary*, I argue that the naming of these four authors in *De doctrina christiana* 2. 40. 61 (a passage written not long after the *Commentary*) is deeply significant. This connection, combined with others, demonstrates that the *Commentary* furnishes a practical example of the theory of interpretation set forth in the *De doctrina* and indeed paves the way for that theory.

The Latin text reprinted here is that produced by Johannes Divjak for Corpus Scriptorum Ecclesiasticorum Latinorum in 1971. Where I have followed a variant reading in my translation I have indicated the fact and given my reasons for doing so in a footnote. My discussion of the transmission of the Latin text is, admittedly, less than adequate. The examination of manuscripts was beyond the scope of this project (there are at least sixty-five manuscripts containing the text, together with very extensive quotations in medieval authors). Divjak himself appears not to have had the transmission of the text as part of his brief when he was asked to introduce the text for CSEL 84, and although a paper he gave at Oxford in 1971 supplies additional information concerning the manuscripts of the *Commentary*, it is still not enough to enable the reader to understand his rationale for discriminating among them and establishing the text that was published. In this regard, therefore, much work remains.

In addition to indicating departures from Divjak's text, the footnotes to the translation are also (and primarily) intended to indicate significant agreements and disagreements between Augustine and the other Latin commentators, parallels with Augustine's other writings (chiefly those from the same period), important points in the development of Augustine's thought, and, of course, points of ancient history and culture that may throw light on the text. The footnotes are intended to meet the needs of both seasoned scholars and beginning students. I will therefore count it as a success if the average reader thinks that half my notes are hopelessly pedantic and that the other half simply state the obvious.

Biblical references abound in Augustine's *Commentary*. This came as a surprise, since I had presumed (partly on the basis of Augustine's own testimony) that at this early stage in his career he hardly knew the Bible at all. Looking over the range of his biblical quotations and allusions now, I think he was already steeped in Scripture even at this early date. In order to help anyone who is under the same misapprehension I was under, and also generally to help anyone who lacks Augustine's familiarity with the Bible (including myself), I have gone out of my way to identify biblical quotations and allusions. As a further aid to the reader, biblical quotations have been printed in italics.

Before taking its present form this book was a doctoral dissertation submitted to the Graduate School of the University of Notre Dame, and I would like to thank the members of my dissertation board—Harry Attridge, Dan Sheerin, and Blake Leyerle—for their expert guidance. Special thanks are due to my advisor, John Cavadini, whose constructive criticism and warm encouragement enhanced the quality of my work immeasurably. While working on her own dissertation at Notre Dame, Jody Vaccaro Lewis took time to read mine and offer valuable suggestions. Conversations with Robert Markus and Karlfried Froehlich at the outset of my research were catalytic. In the final stages of that research the linguistic expertise of Chris and Silvia Dupont saved me untold hours of labour when I no longer had untold hours to spare. I would also like to thank those who supported my original decision to pursue doctoral studies, especially Edward Yarnold, SJ, John P. McIntyre, SJ, and Petroc Willey.

After the dissertation was finished it was read with great care by Robert Markus and Henry Chadwick. I am deeply grateful for the trouble they took and for the unforgettable lesson in kindness they have given me. I would also like to express my gratitude to Andrew Louth and Gillian Clark, General Editors of the Oxford Early Christian Studies series, to Hilary O'Shea, my commissioning editor and publisher, to Enid Barker and Lucy Qureshi, my assistant editors at Oxford University Press, and to Sylvia Jaffrey, my copy-editor. I could not have asked for a group of editors more helpful or more pleasant to work with.

With such a dazzling array of wise counsellors one might have expected this to be a work of impeccable scholarship, but—alas!—as Augustine himself would have said: impeccability is not to be hoped for in this lifetime. And so for the many shortcomings that remain in this work I have the dubious honour of thanking myself. I particularly regret that I was unable to consult the edition of Augustine's *Commentary* recently published by Augustinus-Verlag, with an introduction, German translation, and notes by Thomas Gerhard Ring, OSA.

For permission to reprint the Latin text from CSEL 84 I would like to thank öbv & hpt Verlagsgesellschaft, Vienna. Professor Johannes Divjak was kind enough to give me the Latin text in electronic form, which made the final preparation of the manuscript much easier than it would otherwise have been. Much of the rest of the manuscript was prepared by Margaret Jasiewicz, and I am grateful for her excellent work. I must also mention that it is by kind permission of Peeters Publishers that I have been able to use material from my paper on 'The Influence of Marius Victorinus on Augustine's *Commentary on Galatians*', which was published in *Studia Patristica*, 33 (1997), edited by E. A. Livingstone.

Additional thanks are due to the librarians and staff of the Hesburgh Library and the Medieval Institute of the University of Notre Dame, St Mary's College, the Catholic University of America, and the Dominican House of Studies (Washington, DC). I would also like to thank all the graduate students I had the pleasure of working with, and from whom I learned so much, during my year as Visiting Assistant Professor at the Catholic University of America.

Finally, I would like to thank my family and friends for their love and support over the many years that have gone into the research and writing of this book.

E.P.

Contents

Abbreviations

Abbreviations and Latin titles are given in the form and in the order in which they appear in *Augustinus-Lexikon*, i. pp. xlii–xliv, except for ep./epp. and s./ss. English titles are given in the form in which they appear in this book. Where a specific translation has been used for quotations, it will be found in the Bibliography under 'English Translations'.

Acad.	*De Academicis libri tres* (*Against the Academics*)
c. Adim.	*Contra Adimantum Manichei discipulum liber unus* (*Against Adimantus, a Disciple of Mani*)
c. adu. leg.	*Contra aduersarium legis et prophetarum libri duo* (*Against an Enemy of the Law and the Prophets*)
agon.	*De agone christiano liber unus* (*On the Christian Struggle*)
an. et or.	*De anima et eius origine libri quattuor* (*On the Soul and its Origin*)
bapt.	*De baptismo libri septem* (*On Baptism, against the Donatists*)
beata u.	*De beata uita liber unus* (*On the Happy Life*)
breuic.	*Breuiculus conlationis cum Donatistis libri tres* (*A Summary of the Meeting with the Donatists*)
cat. rud.	*De cathecizandis rudibus liber unus* (*On the Instruction of Beginners*)
ciu.	*De ciuitate dei libri uiginti duo* (*City of God*)
conf.	*Confessionum libri tredecim* (*Confessions*)
cons. eu.	*De consensu euangelistarum libri quattuor* (*On the Harmony of the Evangelists*)
cont.	*De continentia liber unus* (*On Continence*)
Cresc.	*Ad Cresconium grammaticum partis Donati libri quattuor* (*To Cresconius, a Donatist Grammarian*)
diu. qu.	*De diuersis quaestionibus octoginta tribus liber unus* (*Eighty-three Different Questions*)
doctr. chr.	*De doctrina christiana libri quattuor* (*On Christian Teaching*)
duab. an.	*De duabus animabus liber unus* (*On the Two Souls*)

en. Ps.	*Enarrationes in Psalmos* (*Expositions of the Psalms*)
ench.	*De fide spe et caritate liber unus* (*Enchiridion on Faith, Hope, and Love*)
ep. / epp.	*Epistula / Epistulae* (*Letter / Letters*)
ep. Io. tr.	*In epistulam Iohannis ad Parthos tractatus decem* (*Tractates on the First Letter of John*)
c. ep. Man.	*Contra epistulam Manichei quam uocant fundamenti liber unus* (*Against the Foundation Letter of Mani*)
c. ep. Parm.	*Contra epistulam Parmeniani libri tres* (*Against the Letter of Parmenianus*)
c. ep. Pel.	*Contra duas epistulas Pelagianorum libri quattuor* (*Answer to the Two Letters of the Pelagians*)
ep. Rm. inch.	*Epistulae ad Romanos inchoata expositio liber unus* (*Unfinished Commentary on Romans*)
exp. Gal.	*Expositio epistulae ad Galatas liber unus* (*Commentary on Galatians*)
exp. prop. Rm.	*Expositio quarundam propositionum ex epistula apostoli ad Romanos* (*Propositions from Romans*)
c. Faust.	*Contra Faustum Manicheum libri triginta tres* (*Reply to Faustus, a Manichee*)
c. Fel.	*Contra Felicem Manicheum libri duo* (*Against Felix, a Manichee*)
f. et symb.	*De fide et symbolo liber unus* (*Faith and the Creed*)
c. Fort.	*Acta contra Fortunatum Manicheum liber unus* (*Debate with Fortunatus, a Manichee*)
gest. Pel.	*De gestis Pelagii liber unus* (*The Deeds of Pelagius*)
Gn. litt.	*De Genesi ad litteram libri duodecim* (*The Literal Meaning of Genesis*)
Gn. litt. inp.	*De Genesi ad litteram liber unus inperfectus* (*Unfinished Book on the Literal Meaning of Genesis*)
Gn. adu. Man.	*De Genesi aduersus Manicheos libri duo* (*On Genesis, against the Manichees*)
gr. t. nou.	*De gratia testamenti noui ad Honoratum liber unus* (= *ep.* 140) (*On the Grace of the New Testament* (*Letter 140*))
Io. eu. tr.	*In Iohannis euangelium tractatus CXXIV* (*Tractates on the Gospel of John*)
c. Iul.	*Contra Iulianum libri sex* (*Answer to Julian*)
c. Iul. imp.	*Contra Iulianum opus imperfectum* (*Unfinished Work in Answer to Julian*)
lib. arb.	*De libero arbitrio libri tres* (*On Free Will*)

c. litt. Pet.	*Contra litteras Petiliani libri tres* (*Answer to the Letters of Petilianus*)
loc.	*Locutionum libri septem* (*Sayings in the Heptateuch*)
mag.	*De magistro liber unus* (*The Teacher*)
mend.	*De mendacio liber unus* (*On Lying*)
mor.	*De moribus ecclesiae catholicae et de moribus Manicheorum libri duo* (*The Catholic and Manichean Ways of Life*)
nat. b.	*De natura boni liber unus* (*The Nature of the Good*)
op. mon.	*De opere monachorum liber unus* (*On the Work of Monks*)
ord.	*De ordine libri duo* (*On Order*)
pat.	*De patientia liber unus* (*On Patience*)
perseu.	*De dono perseuerantiae liber ad Prosperum et Hilarium secundus* (*On the Gift of Perseverance*)
praed. sanct.	*De praedestinatione sanctorum liber ad Prosperum et Hilarium primus* (*On the Predestination of the Saints*)
ps. c. Don.	*Psalmus contra partem Donati* (*Psalm against the Donatists*)
qu.	*Quaestionum libri septem* (*Questions on the Heptateuch*)
reg. 3	*Regula: Praeceptum* (*Rule*)
retr.	*Retractationum libri duo* (*Retractations*)
c. Sec.	*Contra Secundinum Manicheum liber unus* (*Reply to Secundinus, a Manichee*)
s. / ss.	*Sermo / Sermones* (*Sermon / Sermons*)
c. s. Arrian.	*Contra sermonem Arrianorum liber unus* (*Against an Arian Sermon*)
s. dom. m.	*De sermone domini in monte libri duo* (*The Lord's Sermon on the Mount*)
Simpl.	*Ad Simplicianum libri duo* (*To Simplicianus*)
symb. cat.	*De symbolo ad catechumenos* (*On the Creed, to Catechumens*)
trin.	*De trinitate libri quindecim* (*The Trinity*)
uera rel.	*De uera religione liber unus* (*On True Religion*)
un. bapt.	*De unico baptismo contra Petilianum ad Constantinum liber unus* (*On the One Baptism, against Petilianus*)
util. cred.	*De utilitate credendi liber unus* (*The Usefulness of Belief*)
util. ieiun.	*De utilitate ieiunii* (*The Usefulness of Fasting*)

GENERAL ABBREVIATIONS

ACW	Ancient Christian Writers
BA	Bibliothèque Augustinienne
BP	Biblioteca Patristica
CCSL	Corpus Christianorum, series latina
Comm.	*Commentary*
CSEL	Corpus Scriptorum Ecclesiasticorum Latinorum
FC	Fathers of the Church
GCS	Die griechischen christlichen Schriftsteller der ersten drei Jahrhunderte
LCC	Library of Christian Classics
LXX	Septuagint
MS, MSS	manuscript, manuscripts
NBA	Nuova Biblioteca Agostiniana
NPNF	Nicene and Post-Nicene Fathers
OL	Old Latin (i.e. pre-Vulgate) version of the Bible
OLD	*Oxford Latin Dictionary*
PL	Patrologia Latina, Cursus Completus, ed. J.-P. Migne
pr.	praefatio
SC	Sources chrétiennes
trans.	translator or translation
TU	Texte und Untersuchungen zur Geschichte der altchristlichen Literatur
Vg.	Vulgate
WSA	The Works of Saint Augustine: A Translation for the 21st Century, ed. John E. Rotelle

Part I
Introduction

1

Date of Composition

Augustine's *Commentary on Galatians* can be dated within a relatively narrow compass. Augustine himself tells us in his *Retractations*[1] that towards the end of his priesthood he undertook three expositions of Paul: in chronological order, the *Propositions from Romans*, the *Commentary on Galatians*, and the *Unfinished Commentary on Romans*.[2] He explains the origin of the first exposition thus: 'While I was still a priest, we who were together in Carthage at the time happened to read the Apostle's Letter to the Romans, and after some of the brethren asked me certain questions which I answered to the best of my ability, they wanted to have my answers set down in writing rather than merely spoken.'[3] In the following chapter he describes his *Commentary on Galatians*: 'After this book [sc. *Propositions from Romans*], I explained the same Apostle's Letter to the Galatians, not in part, that is, omitting some portions, but in a continuous fashion and in its entirety.'[4] If, as is highly probable, the occasion of his visit to Carthage was the Council of 26 June 394,[5] then we have an earlier limit for the dating of the *Commentary on Galatians*. Since this work was written while Augustine was still a priest, his ordination as coadjutor bishop of Hippo,[6] which took place in either 395 or 396,[7] provides a later limit. Within these limits

---

[1] *retr.* 1. 23 (22)–25 (24).

[2] For the Latin titles of these three expositions see the list of Abbreviations of Augustine's Works under *exp. prop. Rm.*, *exp. Gal.*, and *ep. Rm. inch.* respectively.

[3] *retr.* 1. 23 (22). 1 (my trans., based on that of Bogan, 96; CCSL 57: 66. 3–67. 7: 'Cum presbyter adhuc essem, contigit ut apud Carthaginem inter nos qui simul eramus ad Romanos apostoli epistula legeretur, et quaedam interrogabar a fratribus; quibus cum sicut poteram responderem, voluerunt scribi potius quae dicebam quam sine litteris fundi').

[4] *retr.* 1. 24 (23). 1 (Bogan, trans., 101 (modified); CCSL 57: 71. 2–4: 'Post hunc librum exposui eiusdem apostoli epistulam ad Galatas non carptim, id est aliqua praetermittens, sed continuanter et totam').

[5] Thus Perler, *Les Voyages*, 162–3.

[6] As distinguished from his becoming sole bishop of Hippo following the death of Valerius. On Augustine's being made coadjutor bishop see Possidius, *Vita* 8. 2. Our earliest evidence of Augustine's acting as sole bishop of Hippo is his signature, dated 28 August 397, affixed to the Acts of the Third Council of Carthage (CCSL 149: 49). On this last point see Verheijen, *Saint Augustine's Monasticism*, 48, and Lawless, *Monastic Rule*, 62 n. 106.

[7] The date 395, which long held sway in scholarly circles (see e.g. Perler, 'Das Datum'),

an earlier rather than a later date is desirable in order to keep the first two expositions as near to each other as the arrangement and wording of the *Retractations* imply. The *Commentary on Galatians* should therefore be dated 394/5.

derives from Prosper of Aquitaine's *Epitoma chronicon* (mid-fifth century). But Prosper's accuracy has been vigorously challenged by Trout ('Dates'), who has argued instead for 396. Trout's revised dating has won wide but not universal assent. For a dissenting opinion see Dolbeau, 'Sermons inédits de saint Augustin', 48 n. 19.

2

Augustine in Relation to the Other Latin Commentators on Paul in Late Antiquity

As has often been noted,[1] during the last half of the fourth century an extraordinary and indeed unprecedented interest in the letters of Paul arose in the Latin West. Its specific causes are numerous, complex, and partially hidden, so that to this day they have never been fully explained.[2] For the moment, however, the question of causes may be put to one side; it is sufficient for our purposes to take note of the phenomenon itself as evidenced by a host of authors both within and without the Catholic Church[3] and writing in a variety of genres, including treatises, letters, homilies, and commentaries. Perhaps the most remarkable of these genres is the commentary, for although it had enjoyed a long history in the Greek church, in the Latin church it was largely unknown. Yet once taken up as an

---

[1] See e.g. Peter Brown, *Augustine of Hippo*, 151; Bernhard Lohse, 'Beobachtungen zum Paulus-Kommentar', 351–3.

[2] M. G. Mara, however, offers helpful reflections: 'Several things are not irrelevant to the phenomenon: *1)* the doctrinal maturity that the Christian community must have attained and which is witnessed by the fact that now, in anti-heretical polemic, they had recourse to the *corpus paulinum* . . . ; *2)* the rise of a marked interest by Jews and Christians in mutual proselytism: once more a rereading of P., particularly of Romans, could clarify the problems born from this circumstance; *3)* the changed political situation, which saw the proscription of paganism by the empire and the consequent conversion to Christianity of multitudes of pagans: P.'s epistles became a reference-point both for those who stressed the sufficiency of faith and those who dwelt on mankind's sin and man's consequent responsibility from the ethical point of view; *4)* the monastic ascesis that institutionalized in the new historical situation the longing for witness of life to be borne, with emphases that varied according to the intensity with which preference was given to grace or free will, mercy or merits; all themes that found full development in P.' ('Commentaries', 659). Mara discusses these points in detail in 'Il significato'. And see now the fine article on Pauline commentaries by Thomas Martin in Fitzgerald, *Augustine*, 625–8.

[3] In addition to the authors referred to in this paragraph one may mention, for example, Ambrose (*De Iacob* 1. 4. 13–16), Priscillian (*Canones in Pauli apostoli epistulas*), and Tyconius (*Liber regularum* 3). I should explain that I have omitted Tyconius from my discussion of Augustine's predecessors partly because he did not write a commentary on Galatians, partly because clear evidence of his influence on Augustine does not emerge until after *exp. Gal.*, in *Simpl.* 1. 2 (see TeSelle, *Augustine*, 180–2).

instrument for the interpretation of Paul, the Latin commentary was utilized again and again. So far as we know, the first Latin commentaries on the letters of Paul were those of Marius Victorinus, written not long after 362.[4] His commentaries on Galatians, Philippians, and Ephesians are extant but internal evidence from them suggests that he also wrote commentaries on Romans and 1 and 2 Corinthians.[5] Victorinus was followed by an anonymous author whom we call 'Ambrosiaster', who wrote commentaries on all thirteen Pauline letters between 366 and 384.[6] In 386 or shortly thereafter[7] Jerome wrote commentaries on Philemon, Galatians, Ephesians, and Titus. Augustine's three expositions of Paul were written between 394 and 395. A second anonymous author, writing between 396 and 405,[8] commented on the entire Pauline corpus, as did Pelagius between 405–6 and 410.[9]

Apart from any further considerations, the coincidence of subject and convergence of time should caution us against investigating any one of these commentators in isolation from the rest. In the case of Augustine's *Commentary on Galatians* the search for interconnections is facilitated by the fact that Galatians is the one text commented upon by all the authors mentioned above, and therefore the one text in which differences and similarities in interpretation may most readily and reliably be discerned, measured, and evaluated.

---

[4] Hadot, *Marius Victorinus*, 285–6; Erdt, *Marius Victorinus Afer*, 82–5. Editions of the extant Latin commentaries on Galatians from Late Antiquity are listed in the Bibliography. At this moment, none of these commentaries has been published in English translation, so that Augustine's will be the first, to be followed closely by that of Victorinus, which has been translated for this series by Stephen Cooper.

[5] The internal evidence is given by Hadot, *Marius Victorinus*, 287 nn. 10–12. External evidence for Victorinus' commentary on Romans may be found in Ambrosiaster, *Comm. on Rom.* 5: 14 (CSEL 81. 1: 177. 24–6): 'Nam hodie quae in Latinis reprehenduntur codicibus, sic inveniuntur a veteribus posita, Tertulliano et Victorino et Cypriano.'

[6] Souter, *Earliest Latin Commentaries*, 42–3.

[7] For 386 as the date see Nautin, 'La Date des commentaires'. Kelly (*Jerome*, 145) proposes 387/8.

[8] Frede, *Ein neuer Paulustext und Kommentar*, i. 215–17.

[9] De Bruyn, *Pelagius's Commentary*, 11. Finally, mention should be made of Rufinus of Aquileia's translation *c.*405–6 of Origen's commentary on Romans, on which see Bammel, 'The Last Ten Years', 403–6.

A. MARIUS VICTORINUS

The Problem

Although many have written on the relation between Victorinus and Augustine in the last hundred years or more,[10] the need for further work remains. In 1970 Almut Mutzenbecher wrote specifically of the urgent need for a thorough investigation of the relation between the Pauline exegesis of Victorinus and that of Augustine.[11] A generation later that need has still not been met.[12] The root of the problem has been pointed out by J. J. O'Donnell: 'One aspect of A.'s relation to V. requires emphasis: the lack of quotation or otherwise direct use anywhere in A.'s canon, of any of Victorinus' theological works.'[13] Despite the great successes that the search for verbal parallels has had in so many areas of Augustinian studies,[14] in considering Augustine's relation to Victorinus we are reminded forcibly of its limitations as a method for uncovering sources: its relative lack of subtlety and flexibility, its inability to move beyond fixed verbal forms, its liability to become mechanistic and reductionistic, and its tendency to look at points in isolation rather than to comprehend works as a whole. In such circumstances it is worth seeking an alternative method of approach—not that the search for verbal parallels should be abandoned, but rather that it should not be made the starting point or the sole standard of judgement. One alternative method of approach is to use the kind of argument found so often in the writings of Newman[15]—the argument from antecedent probability.[16] As applied in this case, the method involves beginning with

---

[10] e.g.: Gore, 'Victorinus Afer', 1137–8; Harnack, *History of Dogma*, v. 35 n. 1; Schmid, *Marius Victorinus*; van der Lof, 'De invloed van Marius Victorinus Rhetor op Augustinus'; Somers, 'Image de Dieu'; Hadot, 'L'Image de la Trinité'.

[11] In her edition of Augustine's *Simpl.* (CCSL 44: p. xxv n. 2).

[12] But see now Cipriani, 'Agostino lettore'. (For discussion of Cipriani's work see the references under his name in the General Index.)

[13] *Augustine: Confessions*, iii. 15.

[14] The work by O'Donnell just cited furnishes a splendid example.

[15] See e.g. Newman's *Essay on Development* (7th edn.), pt. I, ch. III. How highly Newman regarded this method can be gauged from a statement he made in a letter dated 12 June 1853: 'If I have brought out one truth in any thing I have written, I consider it to be the *importance of antecedent probability* in conviction' (*The Letters and Diaries of John Henry Newman*, ed. C. S. Dessain *et al.*, xv (London: Nelson, 1964), 381 (italics original)). I owe this reference to a note by I. T. Ker on p. 388 of his edition of Newman's *Essay in Aid of a Grammar of Assent* (Oxford: Clarendon Press, 1985).

[16] One of the teachers from whom Newman learned this method, Richard Whately, once gave the following example of antecedent probability: 'If a man who bore a good character

the question: Apart from any direct evidence that might be gleaned from a comparison of their commentaries on Galatians, what is the likelihood that Augustine would have consulted Victorinus' commentary? To estimate this likelihood we need to draw upon all we know about Augustine and Victorinus, and especially upon what Augustine himself tells us about Victorinus in the *Confessions*. If this likelihood can be estimated, even roughly, then it will provide an interpretative framework in which to view whatever direct evidence can subsequently be adduced from the commentaries themselves.

This is not the first time that the issue of antecedent probability has been raised in this regard. In 1927 Alexander Souter wrote: 'Nothing is more antecedently probable than that Augustine . . . consulted [Marius Victorinus'] commentaries on the Pauline Epistles in the course of his own work.'[17] But when his research yielded only two verbal parallels, neither of which he deemed telling, he concluded that Augustine's extraordinary independence of mind was likely to render doubtful any attempt to establish verbal dependence.[18] Charles Gore, on the other hand, writing some forty years before Souter, discerned in the writings of the two men not verbal but conceptual parallels, most notably (for our purposes) in their interpretations of the Pauline notions of predestination, the unity of Christ and the Church, and above all justification by faith.[19] In general, however, even where verbal and conceptual dependence can be established,[20] it is unlikely to be a satisfactory measure of one author's indebtedness to another. Often there will be more subtle and pervasive influences at work, such as the influence of an author's general approach to analysing and solving problems. Yet even this does not entirely capture the elusive notion of influence. We need to begin by considering the broadest type of influence

---

were accused of corruption, the strongest evidence against him might avail little; but if he were proved to be of a covetous disposition, this, though it would not alone be allowed to substantiate the crime, would have great weight in inducing his judges to lend an ear to the evidence' (Whately, *Elements of Rhetoric*, 81–2, quoted in Selby, *The Principle of Reserve*, 77).

[17] *Earliest Latin Commentaries*, 199.

[18] Ibid. The first parallel, Victorinus' frequent use of *liberatio* in the sense of 'salvation' and Augustine's frequent use of *liberator* in the sense of 'saviour', is too weak to be of value, as Souter himself recognized. The second parallel, their closely similar interpretations of Gal. 3: 1, is vitiated by the fact that they share the same reading of *proscriptus* (as opposed to Jerome's *praescriptus*, for example). (This second parallel will, however, be re-examined later in 2. A under 'Direct Evidence'.)

[19] 'Victorinus Afer', 1137–8. Gore's view was strongly endorsed by Harnack, *History of Dogma*, v. 35 n. 1.

[20] Pincherle, *La formazione teologica* (118 and esp. 132 n. 17), attempts to do this specifically for the Galatians commentaries of Augustine and Victorinus, but I find his arguments quite unconvincing.

identifiable: in this instance, that of Victorinus as he is presented in the *Confessions*—as a spiritual exemplar. For as Peter Brown has noted, the late classical world was marked by an 'overwhelming tendency to find what is exemplary in *persons*'.[21] Only when we have examined Victorinus' personal influence on Augustine as a spiritual exemplar will we have a meaningful context in which to raise the narrower issues of verbal, conceptual, and other forms of dependence in regard to their commentaries on Paul.

Victorinus in Augustine's *Confessions*

Although the autobiographical element in the *Confessions* is subservient to the author's devotional and pastoral intentions, on one level Books 1–9 may be read as an autobiographical narrative of Augustine's quest for wisdom, and it is in the context of such a narrative that I wish to situate the story of Victorinus' conversion.[22] To prevent that narrative from becoming obscured by the introduction of extraneous material, I will so far as possible avoid reference to other primary and secondary texts, except occasionally in footnotes, and instead rely on an analysis of the internal argument of the *Confessions* themselves. For Augustine never loses sight of the place of logic in the art of persuasion, and intends for us to understand what he himself has come to understand through faith: that the story of his conversion is an intelligible process.[23]

Although the theme is present from the beginning,[24] the quest for wisdom as a conscious undertaking in Augustine's life does not emerge until Book 3. As an 18-year-old student at Carthage, Augustine was living licentiously, not only in the narrow sense of illicit love (3. 1. 1) but also in the wider sense of breaking God's law (3. 3. 5).[25] But during the course of his studies he read Cicero's *Hortensius* and was at once filled with a desire to

---

[21] 'The Saint as Exemplar in Late Antiquity', 2 (italics added).

[22] In using the *Confessions* as a historical source I have tried to bear in mind the wise and richly suggestive remarks of J. J. O'Donnell on the 'garden scene' (*conf.* 8. 12. 29), of which the following provides a brief sample: 'There are differences of tone and emphasis between this narrative and the dialogues from Cassiciacum, but many signs of continuity and consistency as well. There is no convincing reason to doubt the facts of the narrative of this garden scene as A. presents them, and so we should depart from Courcelle; but at the same time, we should firmly believe (with Courcelle) that the presentation of those facts is marked by an artistry of selection and arrangement that gives the text here much, surely most, of its unique character and texture' (*Augustine: Confessions*, iii. 60). I offer my own apologia for drawing upon the *Confessions* as a historical source in Appendix 3.

[23] This is a basic premise of Starnes's *Augustine's Conversion* (see esp. pp. xi–xiii), and he fully vindicates it.

[24] Especially in Augustine's questions about knowing God (*conf.* 1. 1. 1).

[25] And cf. the reference to 'false liberty' (*falsa libertas*) in 3. 8. 16 (CCSL 27: 36. 52).

lead the 'philosophic life' in pursuit of truth. He speaks of the experience as a conversion, marking the beginning of his return to God (3. 4. 7).[26] But although Cicero's exhortation to philosophy moved him deeply, its omission of 'the name of Christ'—the name his mother had taught him from childhood to revere—left him dissatisfied (3. 4. 8). So he turned hopefully to Scripture, only to be repelled by its style: the Bible, he disdainfully concluded, was 'unworthy in comparison with the dignity of Cicero' (3. 5. 9).[27]

When he encountered Manicheism he was attracted both by its profession of Christ's name and by its presentation of itself as a sophisticated and superior form of Christianity (3. 6. 10–10. 18). In particular it raised and seemed to offer the only credible answers to three great problems: the origin of evil; the anthropomorphic portrayal of God in the Old Testament; and the morality of the Old Testament patriarchs (3. 7. 12).

Owing partly to Manicheism's claim to take all knowledge as its province, partly to his own unbridled curiosity, Augustine devoured writings on the liberal arts and philosophy, most memorably Aristotle's *Categories* (4. 16. 29–31).[28] The most influential of his readings, however, were those in astronomy. There he found arguments based on experience and number that were both persuasive and at variance with Manichean claims. Ironically, it was now the Manichees' appeal to authority and disregard of reason that led to their devaluation in Augustine's eyes: 'I did not notice any rational account of solstices and equinoxes or eclipses of luminaries nor anything resembling what I had learnt in the books of secular wisdom. Yet I was ordered to believe Mani' (5. 3. 6).[29] Not even Faustus, the Manichean wise man *par excellence*, was able to satisfy Augustine's importunate demands for answers.

Augustine's disaffection from Manicheism was accompanied by a growing attraction to scepticism (5. 10. 18–19), a sign that his quest for truth had in effect been grounded. In such a frame of mind he turned his attention to his teaching career, soon to culminate brilliantly in his appointment to the

[26] Cf. 6. 11. 18; 7. 1. 1; 8. 7. 17.

[27] Chadwick, trans., 40; CCSL 27: 31. 7: 'indigna, quam Tullianae dignitate compararem'. Hereafter when the *Confessions* are quoted in English the translator is always Henry Chadwick.

[28] Also memorable from this period was his writing of a work entitled *De pulchro et apto* that unintentionally revealed much about his spiritual state at the time: after a pretentious dedication to the Roman orator Hierius, it proceeded to the conclusion (among others) that 'our mind [is] the supreme and unchangeable good' (4. 13. 20–15. 27; quotation at 4. 15. 24 (trans., 67; CCSL 27: 53. 21–2: 'ipsam mentem nostram summum atque incommutabile bonum').

[29] trans., 75; CCSL 27: 60. 61–4: 'non mihi occurrebat ratio nec solistitiorum et aequinoctiorum nec defectuum luminarium nec quidquid tale in libris saecularis sapientiae didiceram. Ibi autem credere iubebar.' Cf. 6. 5. 7.

chair of rhetoric at Milan (5. 12. 22–13. 23). There he learned of Bishop Ambrose's great reputation for eloquence and out of curiosity went to hear him preach. In time, however, he found himself listening not to the style but to the content of the preaching, particularly Ambrose's figurative exegesis of the Old Testament and his commendation of authority as the fulfilment rather than the negation of reason (5. 13. 23–14. 24; 6. 3. 4–5; 6. 11. 18). In both respects Ambrose was overturning Manichean objections. Nevertheless, Augustine was still operating essentially at the level of understanding rather than at the level of faith (5. 14. 25; 6. 3. 3; 6. 4. 6).[30] Thus his encounter with Ambrose did not result in his assent to Catholic Christianity but merely in his recognition that it was at least as plausible as Manicheism, and when he turned his attention once again to Manicheism, it was in the hope of disproving it intellectually. When that hope failed, the influence of scepticism led him to the view that the science of the astronomers, while not conclusively demonstrable, was yet more probable than Manichean mythology, which he was now poised to abandon. But as he could not embrace scepticism, since it lacked the name of Christ, he decided for the sake of his soul to renew his status as a catechumen in the Catholic Church (5. 14. 24–5).

While Augustine had in principle abandoned Manicheism and no longer regarded Catholicism as a superstition at variance with reason (6. 5. 7–8), he was still beset by intellectual difficulties that resisted the most strenuous efforts of his mind to overcome them, chiefly: how to conceive of God in spiritual as opposed to material terms, and how to account for the origin of evil (7. 1. 1–7. 11). Both difficulties were resolved when, perhaps inspired by Ambrose's Platonizing readings of the Bible, he turned to certain 'books of the Platonists'[31] and discovered a God beyond all space and time, the transcendent source of everything that is (7. 10. 16–11. 17), and learned that evil is not a substance but rather a relative privation or corruption of the good (7. 12. 18–13. 19; 7. 16. 22). The knowledge and insight into the transcendent Creator that the Platonists enabled Augustine to gain (7. 9. 14) was necessary but not in the event sufficient. Although he had attained mystical union with God 'in the flash of a trembling glance' (7. 17. 23),[32] he soon realized that he was powerless to sustain it. He knew that he required the aid of a mediator.

At the same time, however, he was proudly confident that he could find

[30] Cf. Burns, 'Ambrose Preaching to Augustine', 376.

[31] The precise identity of these books has been the subject of vigorous but inconclusive debate among scholars. For discussion see O'Donnell, *Augustine: Confessions*, ii. 421–4.

[32] trans., 127. CCSL 27: 107. 27–8: 'in ictu trepidantis aspectus'.

the mediator by his own unaided efforts, but these efforts only led him to the Photinian view[33] that although Christ was truly human he was not truly divine. It followed that Christ could not be the true Mediator. With this result and with his pride still strong, Augustine was brought to the verge of despair (7. 19. 25–20. 26). But at this point he was prompted to turn back to the Scriptures and especially to St Paul, where he discovered that he had been mistaken after all: Christ is indeed the true Mediator, but this truth cannot be grasped and experienced as genuinely life-giving apart from God's healing grace (7. 21. 27). In Christ he found 'the way of humility' of the Word made flesh (7. 9. 13),[34] who *humbled himself* (Phil. 2: 8)[35] in order that we might know, love, and follow him (7. 18. 24).

By the beginning of Book 8 of the *Confessions* Augustine had undergone a conversion of the intellect and attained a kind of certitude (8. 1. 1), but he still needed to undergo a conversion of the will: 'I was attracted to the way, the Saviour himself, but was still reluctant to go along its narrow paths' (8. 1. 1);[36] 'I had discovered the good pearl. To buy it I had to sell all that I had; and I hesitated' (8. 1. 2).[37] Specifically, he hesitated to take on the life of continence that baptism implied.[38] Then God inspired in him the thought that he could learn how 'to walk in [God's] way' (8. 1. 1)[39] from Simplicianus, the very priest who had prepared and baptized Ambrose (8. 2. 3). So Augustine went and told Simplicianus of his 'wanderings in error' (8. 2. 3)[40] and of his reading of the Platonists in Victorinus' translation. Then, 'to exhort [Augustine] to the humility of Christ' (8. 2. 3),[41] Simplicianus told him the story of Victorinus' own conversion. It had begun with Victorinus' reading of the Scriptures and other Christian writings, to which he gave internal assent. Yet when he reported this to Simplicianus he was told that this was not enough: an external, sacramental commitment to the Church was also necessary. Though held back by fear and pride for a time, eventually Victorinus found the courage to proclaim

---

[33] The view associated with Photinus, bishop of Sirmium, who was synodically deposed for heresy in 351.

[34] trans., 121. CCSL 27: 101. 3–4: 'uia humilitatis, quod uerbum tuum caro factum est et habitauit inter homines'.

[35] *conf.* 7. 9. 14, where Phil. 2: 6–11 is quoted in full.

[36] trans., 133. CCSL 27: 113. 13–14: 'et placebat uia ipse saluator et ire per eius angustias adhuc pigebat'.

[37] trans., 134. CCSL 27: 114. 46–8: 'Et inueneram iam bonam margaritam, et uenditis omnibus, quae haberem, emenda erat, et dubitabam.'

[38] Cf. O'Donnell, *Augustine: Confessions*, iii. 7–8.

[39] trans., 133. CCSL 27: 113. 21–2: 'ad ambulandum in uia tua'.

[40] trans., 135. CCSL 27: 114. 3: 'circuitus erroris mei'.

[41] trans., 135. CCSL 27: 114. 9–10: 'ut me exhortaretur ad humilitatem Christi'.

his faith publicly and receive baptism (8. 2. 4). Thus one of the great champions of paganism and the most celebrated rhetor in Rome at the time 'was not ashamed . . . to bow his head to the yoke of humility' (8. 2. 3).[42] On hearing this story Augustine 'was ardent to follow his example' (8. 5. 10),[43] as Simplicianus had hoped he would be. Simplicianus added that later on, after the promulgation of the emperor Julian's edict prohibiting Christians from teaching literature and rhetoric, Victorinus resigned his post, preferring 'to abandon the school of loquacious chattering rather than [God's] word' (8. 5. 10).

Simplicianus thus considered Victorinus a fitting model for Augustine to follow, and the parallelism between the two is indeed uncanny. Both were men of learning with a passion for philosophy who as rhetoricians had attained the highest eminence in their profession, Victorinus at Rome and Augustine at Milan.[44] Victorinus had received the supreme honour of a statue in the Roman forum (8. 2. 3); Augustine had prospects of a provincial governorship (6. 11. 19). Both had influential patrons in the Senate to aid them in their ambitions.[45] For both, ambition and honour had gone hand in hand with superstition; indeed their very skills in rhetoric had been used to promote superstition.[46] The course of their conversions was also strikingly

[42] trans., 135. CCSL 27: 115. 25–7: 'non erubuerit esse puer Christi tui et infans fontis tui subiecto collo ad humilitatis iugum'. Cf. the language Augustine uses of himself in 9. 1. 1: 'quod subderem ceruicem leni iugo tuo' (CCSL 27: 133. 12–13).

[43] trans., 139. CCSL 27: 119. 2: 'exarsi ad imitandum'. Cf. 9. 2. 3: 'The examples given by your servants whom you had transformed from black to shining white and from death to life, crowded in upon my thoughts. They burnt away and destroyed my heavy sluggishness, preventing me from being dragged down to low things. They set me on fire' (trans., 156). O'Donnell notes that Victorinus should be numbered among the 'servants' alluded to here (*Augustine: Confessions*, iii. 78).

[44] Two further parallels, not mentioned in the *Confessions* but undoubtedly significant in Augustine's eyes: both men were Africans who had found fame far from their homeland and at the centre of civilization; both had been grammarians as well as rhetoricians. (That few rose from the position of grammarian to that of rhetorician is implied by Kaster, *Guardians of Language*, 129. On Augustine's having been a grammarian (i.e. teacher of literature) see Possidius, *Vita* 1. 2.)

[45] For Victorinus see 8. 2. 3; for Augustine see 5. 13. 23 (Symmachus) and cf. 6. 11. 19.

[46] Victorinus had defended certain cults 'with a voice terrifying to opponents' (*conf.* 8. 2. 3; trans., 135; CCSL 27: 115. 24–5: 'ore terricrepo'). His tongue had been used by the devil 'as a mighty and sharp dart to destroy many' (*conf.* 8. 4. 9; trans., 139; CCSL 27: 119. 24–5: 'Victorini lingua, quo telo grandi et acuto multos [diabolus] peremerat'). As a Manichee Augustine had 'disturbed many untrained minds with many trivial questions' (*conf.* 3. 12. 21; trans., 51; CCSL 27: 39. 10–11: 'nonnullis quaestiunculis iam multos imperitos exagitassem'); he describes his entire time with the Manichees as one of 'being seduced and seducing, being deceived and deceiving' (*conf.* 4. 1. 1; trans., 52; CCSL 27: 40. 2–3: 'seducebamur et seducebamus falsi atque fallentes'). He loved engaging Christians in debate and vanquishing them (*duab. an.* 9. 11). He swayed an unnamed friend from Catholicism to Manicheism (*conf.* 4. 4. 7) and may have had a similar influence on Alypius (*conf.* 6. 7. 12). Cf. also *Acad.* 1. 1. 3

similar: for both the 'books of the Platonists' served as a preparation for the gospel; for both the last great obstacle, the goad against which they kicked, was full sacramental initiation into the Church. Finally, both needed to learn humility and were fortunate to find so skilled a teacher of it as Simplicianus, who thus became their spiritual father.

Such parallelism as the text implies presumably had its psychological origin in the mind of Simplicianus, but the fact that it is here reproduced and highlighted means that Augustine not only recognizes it but whole-heartedly ratifies it. The following evidence of Augustine's artistic enhancement may be noted: both men convert suddenly after long years of searching; both are transformed by a single passage from Scripture;[47] both are greeted with joy and thanksgiving when they announce what has taken place;[48] and both let go of worldly ambition in the aftermath of con-version.[49] As if that were not enough narrative emphasis, Augustine goes still further by setting the story of Victorinus at the forefront of this crucial book. And yet the very artistry with which all this is done raises the question of the evidential value of this narrative in determining the real historical influence of Victorinus on Augustine. As has often been noted, there is an irreducible tension in the *Confessions* between incident and interpreta-tion,[50] yet in the case of the material on Victorinus we are fortunate in having a number of safeguards against uncontrolled speculation. On the one hand, there are external safeguards: first, when the *Confessions* were published, Simplicianus was still alive; next, the feelings of gratitude towards Simplicianus that Augustine displays in the *Confessions* are also displayed elsewhere in his writings;[51] and finally, against the view that Victorinus' real historical role in Augustine's conversion was as a model of

---

(Romanianus) and *util. cred*. 1. 2 (Honoratus). For Manicheism as a *superstitio* see *conf*. 4. 2. 3, 6. 7. 12, and 8. 7. 17 (CCSL 27: 41. 27–8, 82. 49, and 124. 24–5).

[47]   For Augustine it is, of course, Rom. 13: 13–14 (*conf*. 8. 12. 29 (CCSL 27: 131. 33–6)). For Victorinus it appears to be Luke 12: 8–9 (*conf*. 8. 2. 4 (CCSL 27: 115. 42–116. 1)). On the latter cf. O'Donnell, *Augustine: Confessions*, iii. 22: 'The position of this quotation suggests that this was V.'s "tolle lege".'

[48]   Van Fleteren analyses the *Formgeschichte* of the conversion stories in the *Confessions* in 'St. Augustine's Theory of Conversion' (see esp. 69 and 72).

[49]   It is true that worldly honour had already lost its appeal to Augustine even before he visited Simplicianus (cf. 8. 1. 2), but that does not mean he no longer felt his secular career to be a terrible burden (cf. 8. 1. 2, 8. 5. 10–6. 14, 8. 7. 18, and above all 8. 12. 30: 'The effect of your converting me to yourself was that I did not now seek a wife and had no ambition for success in this world' (trans., 153–4; CCSL 27: 132. 52–3: 'Conuertisti enim me ad te, ut nec uxorem quaererem nec aliquam spem saeculi huius')).

[50]   Cf. O'Donnell, *Augustine: Confessions*, iii. 3–4; Mohrmann, 'The *Confessions* as a Literary Work of Art', 377–81. See also n. 22 above.

[51]   Cf. *ep*. 37 and *Simpl*. 1. pr.

the merging of Neoplatonism and Christianity, with no awareness of any
real separation between them, there is clear evidence that in spite of (or
perhaps because of) Simplicianus' favourable disposition towards Neoplatonism, he perceived that separation very clearly—a perception for
which Ambrose himself praised him.[52] This last point leads to an important
internal safeguard, for the main didactic point that the story of Victorinus'
conversion is designed to make in the *Confessions* is that assent to abstract
truth, however lofty, is not what makes a person a Christian, but rather total
union with Christ made concrete in the sacrament of baptism.[53] Thus we
are brought back to the incarnational theology that underlies so much of
Books 7 and 8.

Augustine presents Simplicianus' story about Victorinus as an oracle and
Victorinus himself as a model offered to him by God for imitation.[54] The
stature of Victorinus in this narrative is therefore immense, inviting
comparison with that of Simplicianus and Ambrose.[55] And we should,
moreover, recall that Simplicianus is ultimately the 'father' not only of
Victorinus and Augustine[56] but of Ambrose as well, as Augustine himself
tells us.[57] The influence of Simplicianus and Ambrose in Augustine's
life is generally acknowledged; that of Victorinus has been largely and
undeservedly passed over in silence.

The story of Victorinus' conversion illuminates earlier portions of the
narrative, for in recounting it Augustine mentions that it was in Victorinus'

[52] Ambrose to Simplicianus, *ep.* 65. 1 (Maurist): 'With remarkably brilliant intellect you
have embraced all objects of the understanding, so that you are able to show how the works of
the philosophers have deviated from the truth' (Beyenka, trans., 308, where the letter is
numbered 56; Latin text in CSEL 82. 10. 1: 15. 10–14). I owe this reference to Starnes,
Augustine's Conversion, 217.
[53] The point is doubly emphasized by Augustine since, as we have seen, he indicates that it
was baptism with its moral commitment that brought him to an impasse.
[54] Cf. Augustine's statement concerning Victorinus in 8. 4. 9: 'Those who are known to
many are to many a personal influence towards salvation' (trans., 139; CCSL 27: 118. 8–9:
'Quod multis noti, multis sunt auctoritati ad salutem').
[55] For Augustine's veneration of Simplicianus cf. *ep.* 37. For Augustine's veneration of
Ambrose cf. *c. Iul.* 1. 3. 10, where he speaks of 'another of God's excellent stewards, a man
whom I revere as a father, for he gave me birth in Christ through the gospel, and by him as
Christ's minister I received the bath of rebirth. I am speaking of blessed Ambrose' (Teske,
trans., *Answer to Julian*, 272; PL 44: 645), and *c. Iul.* 1. 9. 44, where he calls Ambrose 'my
teacher' (*doctor meus*) (PL 44: 671).
[56] Augustine addresses Simplicianus as *pater Simpliciane* in *Simpl.* 1. pr. (CCSL 44: 7. 4)
and speaks of Simplicianus' 'fatherly affection' (*affectum . . . paternum*) and 'fatherly kindness'
(*benigne paterneque*) towards him in *ep.* 37. 1 and 3 respectively (CSEL 34: 63. 9 and 64. 9–10).
[57] *conf.* 8. 2. 3: 'So I visited Simplicianus, father to the then bishop Ambrose in the
receiving of grace. Ambrose truly loved him as one loves a father' (trans., 134–5; CCSL 27:
114. 1–2: 'Perrexi ergo ad Simplicianum, patrem in accipienda gratia tunc episcopi Ambrosii
et quem uere ut patrem diligebat'). Cf. Ambrose to Simplicianus, *ep.* 37. 2 (Maurist).

translation that he first read the 'books of the Platonists' (8. 2. 3). As we
have seen, these books played a crucial role in his intellectual conversion,[58]
liberating him from the last chains of Manichean materialism and dualism,
and from the academic scepticism to which progressive disillusionment
with Manicheism had led. But not only did they help him to break with the
past, they also built upon the foundational understanding of Christianity
that he had gained from Ambrose. Highly significant (in the light of his
Pauline commentaries) is Augustine's clear implication that his former
difficulties with Paul 'simply vanished' as a result of his Neoplatonic reading (7. 21. 23).[59] At the same time, the books of the Platonists were not
enough, and this fact helps to explain why Victorinus is named as the translator during the narrative of his conversion but not earlier during the discussion of the Platonic books: Victorinus' work as a translator was about
to be eclipsed by an even greater work, wrought by God. The crucial point
to note, however, is that in two separate but closely connected instances,
Victorinus is portrayed as God's instrument in Augustine's conversion.[60]

Victorinus in Augustine's Development as an Interpreter
of the Bible

Only one reference to Victorinus by name[61] occurs in Augustine's writings
outside Book 8 of the *Confessions*, but it is an extremely important reference.
In Book 2 of the *De doctrina christiana* Victorinus is numbered among the
past worthies who spoiled the Egyptians of their gold (Exodus 3: 22, understood as an allegory of Christianity's lawful assimilation of the best of

---

[58] Cf. O'Donnell, *Augustine: Confessions*, ii. 413: 'As long as A.'s goal was intellectual
enlightenment, the reading of the *platonicorum libri* was the decisive intellectual event that
reoriented his ways of thinking as nothing before or after would do.'

[59] trans., 130. CCSL 27: 110. 2–3: 'et perierunt illae quaestiones'. Augustine was not the
only Christian Platonist wrestling with Paul at this time: Simplicianus was as well (cf.
Ambrose, *ep.* 37 [Maurist]), opening up the intriguing possibility that Simplicianus may have
introduced Augustine to Victorinus' Pauline commentaries at this time (cf. Cipriani,
'Agostino lettore', 414–16).

[60] The translation that Augustine used for his momentous reading of Aristotle's *Categories*
(*conf.* 4. 16. 28–9) may also have been Victorinus'. Cf. Marrou, *Saint Augustin et la fin de la
culture antique*, 34, Courcelle, *Late Latin Writers*, 168, and Chadwick, trans., 69 n. 33. This
possibility is doubted, however, by O'Donnell, *Augustine: Confessions*, ii. 265, following
Hadot, *Marius Victorinus*, 187–8.

[61] It is possible that Marius Victorinus is the unnamed Platonist (*quidam Platonicus*) of *ciu.*
10. 29 who, according to Simplicianus, thought the opening of St John's Gospel 'should be
inscribed in letters of gold and set up in the most prominent place in every church' (Bettenson,
trans., 417; CCSL 47: 306. 99–104: 'aureis litteris conscribendum et per omnes ecclesias in
locis eminentissimis proponendum esse'). This possibility, though incapable of proof, is taken
very seriously by Monceaux, *Histoire littéraire*, iii. 377, Hadot, *Marius Victorinus*, 237, and
others.

classical culture and civilization).[62] This suggests that Augustine sees himself as the heir and champion of a *tradition*, a tradition replacing the ancient
alliance of paganism and classical culture by a Christian culture centred
on Scripture. The authors Augustine names are (in order): Cyprian,
Lactantius, Victorinus,[63] Optatus, and Hilary. By including Victorinus in
such a list Augustine is paying him no small tribute.

Thus twice in writings from the first years of his episcopate Augustine
saw in Victorinus a model for both the abandonment of secular ambition
and the dedication of pagan learning to the service of the heavenly Word of
God.[64] That Augustine's devotion to Christian philosophy[65] did not mean
the abandonment of secular studies is seen with exceptional clarity in the
Cassiciacum dialogues (*De Academicis, De beata uita, De ordine*) composed
in the months following his conversion, where Augustine and his companions are shown discussing philosophy and reading Cicero and Virgil.[66]
Despite Augustine's disparaging remark in the *Confessions* that these dialogues 'still breathe the spirit of the school of pride' (9. 4. 7),[67] he nevertheless affirms that they were written in the service of God.[68] For Augustine
it was a period not only of intellectual exploration but also of literary
experimentation and indeed of literary aspiration. He later speaks of himself at this period as having been 'still puffed up with the usages of secular
literature'.[69] From a literary point of view the Cassiciacum dialogues are
serious experiments in form largely modelled on the philosophical dialogues of Cicero. In addition to the Cassiciacum dialogues, Augustine
wrote two books of *Soliloquia* and even made plans to write a vast encyclopedia of the liberal arts,[70] modelled on Varro, that would be a kind of

[62] *doctr. chr.* 2. 40. 60–1. This allegorical interpretation of Exod. 3: 22 also appears in
c. Faust. 22. 91 (citing *doctr. chr.*) and *conf.* 7. 9. 15.
[63] That the reference is to Victorinus of Pettau (cf. e.g. Doignon, 'Nos bons hommes de foi',
803) is possible but not probable. In a closely related passage written not long after *doctr. chr.*
2. 40. 60–1, Augustine clearly identifies the Egyptian gold with the Platonic books translated
by Marius Victorinus (*conf.* 7. 9. 15, cf. 8. 2. 3; note too that the 'Platonists' (*platonici*) are the
only philosophers named in *doctr. chr.* 2. 40. 60–1 (at CCSL 32: 73. 2)).
[64] Victorinus had once used his eloquence in the devil's service; now God had cleansed it so
that it might be *useful to the Lord for every good work* (2 Tim. 2: 21)' (*conf.* 8. 4. 9 (trans., 139;
CCSL 27: 119. 28: ' "utilia domino ad omne opus bonum" ')).
[65] As voiced, for example, in *Acad.* 3. 20. 43 (CCSL 29: 60–1).
[66] Concerning Virgil, for example, Augustine says: 'Every evening before dinner I used to
read half a book of Virgil with them' (*ord.* 1. 8. 26 (CCSL 29: 102. 112–13: 'ante cenam cum
ipsis dimidium uolumen Vergili audire cotidie solitus eram')).
[67] trans., 159. CCSL 27: 136. 5–6: 'adhuc superbiae scholam . . . anhelantibus'.
[68] *conf.* 9. 4. 7 (CCSL 27: 136. 4–5: 'Ibi quid egerim in litteris iam quidem seruientibus
tibi').
[69] *retr.* pr. 3 (Bogan, trans., 5; CCSL 57: 6. 46–7: 'adhuc saecularium litterarum inflatus
consuetudine').   [70] *retr.* 1. 6 (CCSL 57: 17).

prolegomenon to philosophy. Of that grand but unfinished project only the
books on grammar,[71] logic,[72] and music[73] have survived. The picture of
Augustine that we have so far—exploring the intersection of Platonism and
Christianity, expounding Cicero and Virgil as a grammarian, writing books
on grammar and logic—naturally invites comparison with Victorinus.[74]

Augustine's earliest piece of biblical exegesis, like so much of his writing
after his return to Africa, is a polemical work directed against the
Manichees: the *De Genesi aduersus Manicheos*. His aim was 'to show how
everything in Genesis is to be understood first of all not in the figurative but
in the proper sense'.[75] He found it increasingly necessary,[76] however, to
turn to figurative interpretation;[77] this necessity frustrated his primary aim
and drove him finally to abandon the project before completion.

Other projects were undertaken, with mixed results. In particular, there
were many unfinished and arguably unsuccessful ventures after his ordination to the priesthood in 391, which ended forever his hopes for a tranquil
life of contemplation. O'Donnell has suggested that a 'writer's block'
seized him;[78] Lawless prefers to attribute such difficulties as Augustine
experienced to the extraordinary demands made upon him as a parish
priest.[79] What we know for certain is that in a letter of 391 written to his
bishop, Valerius, he had expressed acute anxiety particularly about his
unfitness to be a minister of God's Word and his need to have free time to
study Scripture.[80] Whether or not his request was fully granted, the

---

[71] Law, 'St Augustine's *De grammatica*', examines 'the grammatical basis of the claim to
authenticity of the two Late Latin grammars attributed to Augustine' and argues persuasively
that 'the *Ars breuiata* is very possibly a genuine work of the young Augustine's' (183).

[72] Though listed under 'Dubious Works' in Di Berardino, *Patrology*, iv. 400, the *De dia-
lectica* is given unqualified acceptance by Chadwick (*Augustine*, 34) and others (see the list of
authors cited by Law, 'St Augustine's *De grammatica*', 156 n. 8).

[73] *De musica*.

[74] In addition to translating certain Neoplatonic works and Aristotle's *Categories*,
Victorinus is widely regarded as the author of an *Ars grammatica*, commentaries on Cicero's *De
inuentione* and *Topica*, and logical treatises. There is perhaps less agreement that he wrote a lost
commentary on Virgil's *Aeneid*. On all these matters see Hadot, *Marius Victorinus*.

[75] *Gn. litt.* 8. 2. 5 (Taylor, trans., 2: 35; CSEL 28. 1: 232. 23–4: 'memor tamen quid maxime
uoluerim . . . ut non figurate sed proprie primitus cuncta intellegerentur').

[76] Cf. *Gn. adu. Man.* 2. 2. 3.

[77] Augustine's use of figurative interpretation was presumably inspired in part by
Ambrose's allegorical interpretations of the Old Testament.

[78] *Augustine: Confessions*, i. pp. xlii–iv and nn. 69–72.

[79] In pp. 222–7 of his review of O'Donnell, *Augustine: Confessions*, in *Augustinian Studies*,
25 (1994), 215–30.

[80] *ep.* 21. Cf. *s.* 355. 2 and Possidius, *Vita* 4. Augustine's anxiety becomes even more
intelligible when we consider that Valerius' insistence that he preach violated African church
tradition, which reserved the right of preaching for bishops (cf. Possidius, *Vita* 5. 3 and Peter
Brown, *Augustine of Hippo*, 139–40).

writings of Augustine's priesthood suggest a very intense study indeed of the sacred text, for they include exegesis of the Psalms, Genesis (again), and the Sermon on the Mount, as well as the letters of Paul. At the same time that his study of Scripture was deepening, he was becoming more familiar with the use of various literary genres and methods of interpretation.[81] In addition to his second attempt at a literal commentary on Genesis (393/4),[82] the following are especially noteworthy. The *quaestiones* format, which he had begun using as early as 388, was carried forward and refined in the *De diuersis quaestionibus octoginta tribus* and in the *Expositio quarundam propositionum ex epistula apostoli ad Romanos*, leading ultimately to a masterpiece in the *Ad Simplicianum*, the first work of his episcopate.[83] The *Enarrationes in Psalmos*, begun in 392, were ultimately to constitute the only complete exposition on the Psalms by any of the Fathers. The *De sermone domini in monte* represents his first New Testament commentary. Finally we may note his reflections on preaching and exegesis in the first three books of the *De doctrina christiana*.[84] Thus, drawing largely upon his training as a grammarian and rhetor, Augustine spared no pains to expound the Word of God as clearly, as accurately, and as effectively as he could in order to meet the pastoral responsibilities thrust upon him by his ordination to the priesthood.

Augustine's reconsideration and reinterpretation of Paul in the mid-390s was provoked largely by a need to counter 'the most radical and self-confident of Paul's expositors': the Manichees.[85] His pastoral responsibilities as a recently ordained priest, however, meant that the sophisticated Neoplatonic arguments he had used in earlier writings could no longer be his weapon of choice.[86] Only a scripturally based argument would be effective, and for that a thorough re-examination of Paul was necessary. As a teacher Augustine stressed the need for teachers,[87] and while he may not

[81] Simonetti, *Biblical Interpretation*, 103.

[82] *Gn. litt. inp.*

[83] On Augustine's use of this genre see G. Bardy's Introduction to *diu. qu.* in BA 10: 11–20, and Mosher, trans., *Saint Augustine: Eighty-three Different Questions*, 1–10.

[84] If these examples fail to convince, there is always the abecedarian *Psalmus contra partem Donati* (394)!   [85] Peter Brown, *Augustine of Hippo*, 151.

[86] Cf. Fredriksen, 'Beyond the Body/Soul Dichotomy', 89–92, and *Augustine on Romans*, ix–xii.

[87] Cf. e.g. *util. cred.* 7. 17: 'You need Asper, Cornutus, Donatus and innumerable others if you are to understand any poet whose poems and plays apparently win applause. Will you boldly venture without a teacher to study books, which, whatever they may be otherwise, are at least holy and full of divine teachings, and are widely famed with the assent of almost the whole human race? Will you dare to pass sentence on them without a teacher?' (Burleigh, trans., 304–5; CSEL 25. 1: 21. 26–22. 2). Peter Brown, *Augustine of Hippo*, 264, remarks that 'Augustine lived in an age oppressed by reverence for the "expert".'

always have taken his own advice,[88] we know that in studying Galatians he did, for in a letter written at this time he asks Jerome for translations of Greek commentators on the Bible, especially Origen,[89] and explicitly states that he has been reading Jerome's commentary on Galatians.[90]

Is it legitimate, however, to hypothesize that Augustine consulted Victorinus as well? Indeed, is there any evidence that Augustine even knew that Victorinus had written commentaries on Paul? Although Augustine never refers to Victorinus' Pauline commentaries, I presume that he was at least aware of the existence of the one on Galatians for the following reasons. As I have said, he states in his first letter to Jerome that he has been reading Jerome's commentary on Galatians,[91] and inasmuch as he proceeds to criticize that commentary, I presume he did not read it cursorily. If this presumption is correct, he must have read the prologue to the work as a whole. It is a remarkable prologue, entirely appropriate for such a remarkable commentary.[92] Moreover, it deals directly with one of the two main points[93] on which Augustine criticizes Jerome: his interpretation of the incident between Peter and Paul at Antioch (Gal. 2: 11–14). If Augustine did pass over what Jerome says in this prologue, it was extraordinarily imprudent of him—especially in the light of the fact that when he composed this letter prudential motives were clearly in the forefront of his mind.

Now immediately prior to mentioning the Antioch incident in his prologue, Jerome speaks memorably of Victorinus as the only person who might be thought to have produced a Latin commentary on Galatians before him.[94] He goes on to criticize Victorinus' commentary in striking terms. Regardless of whether or not Augustine read Jerome's commentary as a whole, he must surely have read the prologue with its memorable statement about Victorinus. Jerome himself presumed that Augustine had done so and used this presumption as grounds for rebutting him.[95] Thus,

---

[88] Cf. Peter Brown, *Augustine of Hippo*, 49 n. 4. Similarly O'Donnell, *Augustine: Confessions*, ii. 264: 'A. was essentially self-taught.'

[89] *ep.* 28. 2. 2.

[90] Ibid. 28. 3. 3: 'I have read certain writings, said to be yours, on the Epistles of the Apostle Paul, in which you were attempting to explain some difficulties in Galatians' (Parsons, trans., 95; CSEL 34. 1: 107. 6–7: 'Legi etiam quaedam scripta, quae tua dicerentur, in epistulas apostoli Pauli, quarum ad Galatas cum enodare uelles').   [91] Ibid.

[92] Harnack called it 'the most interesting Latin commentary that we possess' ('Der kirchengeschichtliche Ertrag', ii. 147).

[93] The other concerns the Old Testament canon.

[94] PL 26: 308A.

[95] Jerome, *ep.* 112. 4 (= Augustine, *ep.* 75. 3. 4): 'To this I answer, first, that your Prudence should have remembered the little Prologue to my commentary [sc. on Galatians] in which I said of myself: [extended quotation]' (Parsons, trans., 345 (modified); CSEL 34. 2: 285. 15–17:

leaving to one side anything Augustine may have learned earlier from Simplicianus, I maintain that Augustine must have known that Victorinus had written a commentary on Galatians.

Presuming, therefore, that Augustine knew Victorinus had written a commentary on Galatians, could he have rested content with having consulted Jerome but not Victorinus?[96] Considered in the abstract and from a modern point of view, the choice between Jerome and Victorinus is not difficult: Victorinus may be passed over with few qualms. Thus Lightfoot asserted that Jerome's was 'the most valuable of all the patristic commentaries on the Epistle to the Galatians', whereas Victorinus' was 'as an exposition almost worthless'.[97] Yet they would have appeared very differently to Augustine, for Victorinus had not only attained the very pinnacle of Augustine's own profession but had also been his God-given model of how a man at the height of cultural prestige can find the humility to relinquish all and enter the service of Christ. This Jerome could never be for Augustine.[98] A further difficulty with Jerome's commentary, apart from its alarming interpretation of the dispute between Peter and Paul at Antioch, is the sheer vastness of its erudition.[99]

The basic question that Augustine faced was this: How can one trained in grammar and rhetoric adapt his skills for the interpretation of Paul in humble service to the Church? To some extent it was only natural that he should employ the exegetical method of the schools.[100] On the other hand, the fact that the text was a text of Sacred Scripture meant that it was necessary to be cautious,[101] especially for someone who had for so long been

'ad quae primum respondeo debuisse prudentiam tuam praefatiunculae commentariorum meorum meminisse dicentis ex persona mea . . .').

[96] It is notable that both Jerome and Ambrosiaster claim to have consulted Victorinus. Jerome, *Comm. on Galatians*, Preface to Book 1 (PL 26: 308A), implies that he has read Victorinus' commentary on Galatians. Ambrosiaster, *Comm. on Romans* 5. 14 (CSEL 81. 1: 177. 24–6) implies that he has consulted Victorinus' *Comm. on Romans*. For the position that Ambrosiaster also read Victorinus' *Comm. on Galatians* see Cooper, *Understanding*.

[97] *Galatians*, 232, 231. And cf. Harnack's judgement on Jerome's *Comm. on Gal.* in n. 92 above.

[98] Nor could Ambrosiaster, even though his commentaries on Paul are widely regarded as the most penetrating written before the Renaissance (cf. Souter, *Earliest Latin Commentaries*, 44 (referring to Harnack and Jülicher) and TeSelle, *Augustine the Theologian*, 157).

[99] Cf. Marrou, *Saint Augustin et la fin de la culture antique*, 443. That Augustine recognized the inferiority of his erudition is indicated by his request to Jerome in *ep.* 28. 2. 2 for translations of Greek commentaries and by his explicit statement to Jerome in *ep.* 73. 2. 5: 'For I neither have nor can have as much knowledge of the Divine Scriptures as I see abounds in you' (Parsons, trans., 336; CSEL 34. 2: 269. 9–11: 'nam neque in me tantum scientiae scripturarum diuinarum est aut esse iam poterit, quantum inesse tibi uideo').

[100] Marrou, *Saint Augustin et la fin de la culture antique*, 424.

[101] Cf. e.g. Augustine's statement in *mor.* 1. 1. 1 that 'an explanation of the Scriptures

misled by Manicheism. One way of being cautious was to turn to prece-
dents, and the most trustworthy precedent here was Victorinus.

A prima-facie difficulty with this line of reasoning, however, is Jerome's
famous remark that Victorinus' writings are 'extremely obscure, to be
understood only by the learned'.[102] If so, what use could they have been to
Augustine? Jerome's judgement, however, can hardly refer to Victorinus'
Pauline commentaries,[103] but must refer rather to his theological treatises
against the Arians, which are marked by intricate philosophical argument
and much technical jargon (including an abundance of Greek terms).[104]
Whatever Victorinus' rhetorical strategy may have been in writing these
treatises,[105] in writing his Pauline commentaries he intended to produce
what he calls *commentatio simplex* ('simple commentary').[106] Cooper has
argued that the term *simplex* refers not to style, as Souter and others have
claimed,[107] but to procedure: it signifies 'a renunciation of lengthy philosophical elaborations concerning the matters touched upon by the biblical
text'.[108] For such elaborations the reader must turn to the theological
treatises, as Victorinus himself remarks.[109] The procedure is thus that of a
teacher methodically explicating a text for students: he adheres closely to
the text, relies heavily on paraphrase, regularly summarizes the train of
thought, and carefully unravels the syntax of the longer periods—in short,
he uses a method similar to the one he had used in his commentary on
Cicero's *De inuentione*.[110] In Victorinus' Pauline commentaries, therefore,
'although the neo-platonic scholar appears from time to time, it is above all
the grammarian who comes to the fore, the teacher accustomed to

should be sought from those who are by profession teachers of Scripture' (Gallagher and
Gallagher, trans., 3; PL 32: 1311. 1–3: 'Scripturarum expositionem ab iis petendam esse, qui
earum doctores se esse profitentur').

[102] 'valde obscuros, qui nisi ab eruditis non intelliguntur' (*De viris illustribus* 101 (BP 12:
206)).

[103] This view clashes with that of Lightfoot (*Galatians*, 231), who regards Victorinus'
Comm. on Gal. as 'obscure' and 'confused'.

[104] This inference may be drawn from Jerome's statement itself: 'Victorinus . . . scripsit
Adversus Arium libros more dialectico valde obscuros, qui nisi ab eruditis non intelliguntur, et
Commentarios in Apostolum (*De viris illustribus* 101 (BP 12: 206)).

[105] See Simonetti in Di Berardino, *Patrology*, iv. 71–2; Hadot, *Marius Victorinus*, 272–5
(and the references given there).

[106] In the preface to the second book of his *Comm. on Eph.* (CSEL 83. 2: 60. 16). Similarly
he calls it *simplex expositio* in *Comm. on Eph.* 1: 11 (CSEL 83. 2: 18. 25–6) and *expositio
uerborum simplex* in *Comm. on Gal.* 4: 18 (CSEL 83. 2: 151. 24–5).

[107] Souter, *Earliest Latin Commentaries*, 28. Others are cited in Cooper, *Understanding*.

[108] Cooper, *Understanding*.

[109] *Comm. on Gal.* 4: 18 (CSEL 83. 2: 151. 22–152. 28).

[110] Erdt, *Marius Victorinus Afer*, 93–6; Hadot, *Marius Victorinus*, 289–90, 308. For important differences, which should also be kept in mind, see Cooper, *Understanding*.

expounding Cicero and Virgil'.[111] And so, in contrast to his theological treatises, his Pauline commentaries may be said to have been written more at the level of the ordinary educated Christian.[112]

As a teacher of the Word Augustine desired just such simple commentary. From the time of his earliest surviving works Augustine had taken pains to accommodate his teaching to the capacity of his audience,[113] and this was especially the case now. His immediate audience was probably the brethren of his own monastic community and would have included some who were relatively uneducated, such as Possidius, his future biographer.[114] Beyond Augustine's own community there were those who regarded him as a spokesman for the Church, not without cause: at the Council of Hippo on 8 October 393 he had addressed the African bishops[115] on the subject of the Creed in his *De fide et symbolo*, a text marked by its author's deepening involvement in Scripture and his gift for lucid exposition. And finally there were the needs of the ordinary members of his congregation—not that they were intended readers of his *Commentary on Galatians*,[116] but rather that the straightforward interpretation to be worked out there would also be useful in his preaching.[117] So from a variety of aspects, Augustine would have been primarily concerned to meet the needs of an audience that was relatively unlearned. In addition, a simple commentary would have best suited his own grammatical background, his incomplete though growing mastery of Scripture, and his partiality for a kind of *explication de texte* (as opposed to variorum commentary) as a means of elucidating so difficult an author as Paul. In the hands of Victorinus, moreover, *commentatio simplex* had proved effective in dealing with real theological issues in a way that Jerome's method of variorum commentary

[111] Simonetti, *Biblical Interpretation*, 92.

[112] Souter, *Earliest Latin Commentaries*, 28, who adds: 'The style he here employs is what the rhetoricians themselves called the ἰσχνόν, *tenue*, the plain, unvarnished, unadorned style.'

[113] Cf. the remarks of Robert P. Russell in the Introduction to his translation of *Divine Providence and the Problem of Evil*, p. iv. For a nuanced statement by Augustine himself see *doctr. chr.* 4. 8. 22–9. 23.

[114] Augustine describes Possidius as uneducated in the liberal arts in *ep.* 101. 1. Possidius lived in the monastery at Hippo from 391 until he became bishop of Calama, perhaps as early as 397 (Mandouze, *Prosopographie*, 890).

[115] Of that audience Peter Brown has remarked, 'To judge by some of the problems treated in passing, Augustine's audience must have included some very simple bishops indeed' (*Augustine of Hippo*, 142). For the date of the Council see CCSL 149: 20.

[116] On the generally low level of education of those who heard Augustine preach see Van der Meer, *Augustine the Bishop*, 132–4.

[117] Cf. e.g. the striking similarity between the treatment of Paul's rebuke of Peter at Antioch in *exp. Gal.* and that in Mainz sermon no. 27 (dated 397), recently published by F. Dolbeau, 'Sermons inédits de saint Augustin'. (On this similarity see further Ch. 3, n. 146.)

had not,[118] and we know that at this time, perhaps more than at any other time in his career, Augustine was seeking definitive answers to real Pauline problems.

As well as offering a practical illustration of *commentatio simplex*, Victorinus' commentary on Galatians would also have offered an illustration of a commentary that was in part polemical[119] and thus precisely the kind Augustine needed in Hippo, where the Catholics were virtually a persecuted minority.[120]

Various objections may be thought to undermine this argument. First, it is not obvious why we should presume that Augustine turned to a specific model when Victorinus himself did not. Could he not have relied mainly on his skill and experience as a grammarian, as Victorinus had done? This plausible objection may be answered by considering the difference in personalities and circumstances of the two writers. Augustine, as we have seen, had only recently and unexpectedly entered upon a difficult and demanding Church office, and this radical change in his life exacerbated an already anxious nature. Victorinus, on the other hand, appears to us as a man of great self-confidence, independence, and originality.[121] When he began to comment on the letters of Paul, he held no Church office, his spectacularly distinguished career lay behind him, and, having been baptized in extreme old age,[122] he must have known his life was near its end. It is understandable that in his eagerness to offer some service to the Church in the little time he had left, he should have deliberately bypassed the work of his Greek predecessors and gone straight to the heart of the matter: the divine mystery which it was Paul's mission to proclaim.[123]

It may also be objected that if we turn to the first exposition of Paul that

[118] Simonetti, *Biblical Interpretation*, 92, believes that Victorinus' 'habit of adhering strictly to the sense of the [pagan] authors he explained' was carried over into his exegesis of Paul, enabling him 'to grasp the development of Paul's thought in each individual letter.' By contrast, that development is often obscured in Jerome's Pauline commentaries owing to his tendency to place two or more conflicting interpretations of a passage side by side without decisively judging between them.

[119] For both Victorinus and Augustine the polemical element is important but not so important as the author's desire for clarity of understanding (not only for his readers but also for himself). This point is emphasized with regard to Victorinus in Erdt, *Marius Victorinus Afer*, 197.

[120] Catholics were troubled not only by the Manichees but also and especially by the Donatists, who were predominant in Hippo. Cf. P. Brown, *Augustine of Hippo*, 139.

[121] Cf. the observation of Simonetti in Di Berardino, *Patrology*, iv. 80: 'The position of Marius Victorinus in the context of the anti-Arian polemic appears to be that of an isolated individual who is little bound to preceding tradition.'

[122] 'in extrema senectute' (Jerome, *De viris illustribus* 101 (BP 12: 206)).

[123] In the judgement of Hadot (*Marius Victorinus*, 299–301), this mystery is the underlying theme of Victorinus' Pauline commentaries.

Augustine undertook at this time—his *Propositions from Romans*—it is clear that this exposition is not indebted to Victorinus for its genre, since it is more in the genre of *quaestiones* than of continuous commentary.[124] This is true, but our argument is that this was still a time of intense literary experimentation for Augustine, so that having attained some measure of success in interpreting Romans by means of the *quaestiones* format, he decided to attempt to interpret Galatians by means of a formal commentary, and in so doing turned to Victorinus as a model. And there are good grounds for believing that Augustine regarded his Galatians commentary as a success. First, not only did he succeed in bringing the work to completion, unlike so many others that he wrote at this time, but it was also his only complete commentary on any book of the Bible, and a certain pride is still detectable in his opening sentence on this work in the *Retractations*.[125] Second, its successful completion emboldened him to undertake a vast commentary on Romans along similar lines.[126] Third, nearly three decades later he quoted the *Commentary on Galatians* at length,[127] and, fourth, when he reviewed it in the *Retractations*, while he did wish to clarify certain points, he seemed satisfied with the work as a whole. It is a reasonable inference, therefore, that at this moment in his career, Augustine produced what he judged to be a successful Pauline commentary along the lines laid down by Victorinus.

A third possible objection is that when Augustine provides Jerome with names of authorities for his view that the dispute between Peter and Paul at Antioch was not feigned, he cites Ambrose and Cyprian but not

[124] That Victorinus wrote a (lost) commentary on Romans is the clear implication of Ambrosiaster, *Comm. on Romans* 5: 14 (CSEL 81. 1: 177. 24–6). That it was in the form of a continuous commentary is an inference based on the form of the three Pauline commentaries by Victorinus that have survived.

[125] *retr.* 1. 24. (23). 1: 'After this book [sc. *exp. prop. Rm.*], I explained the same Apostle's Letter to the Galatians, not in part, that is, omitting some portions, but in a continuous fashion and in its entirety' (Bogan, trans., 101 (modified); CCSL 57: 71. 2–4: 'Post hunc librum exposui eiusdem apostoli epistulam ad Galatas non carptim, id est aliqua praetermittens, sed continuanter et totam'). On Augustine's pride in his *Commentary on Gal.* see G. Bardy, Introduction to *diu. qu.*, BA 10: 34. In calling *exp. Gal.* Augustine's only complete commentary on any book of the Bible, I am using the term 'commentary' in the same technical sense that would apply to all the other ancient Latin commentaries on Galatians discussed in this book. By contrast, Augustine's *en. Ps.*, while a complete treatment of the Book of Psalms, mainly comprises homilies and sermons and thus represents a different literary genre.

[126] Cf. *retr.* 1. 25. (24): 'I had also undertaken an explanation of the Epistle to the Romans as of that to the Galatians. If it had been finished, there would be several books of this work' (Bogan, trans., 104; CCSL 57: 73. 3–5: 'Epistulae quoque ad Romanos sicut ad Galatas expositionem susceperam. Sed huius operis si perficeretur plures libri erant futuri'). Augustine goes on to explain why he was unable to sustain the project.

[127] *exp. Gal.* 35. 8 is quoted in its entirety at *ench.* 21. 80 (CCSL 46: 94. 78–83).

Victorinus.[128] It is reasonable to suppose here, however, that Augustine, having read Jerome's *Commentary on Galatians*, was well aware of his damning remarks on Victorinus' competence as a biblical exegete and saw not only the futility of naming Victorinus as an authority but also the danger of causing Jerome further offence.

More formidable are the difficulties posed by the naming of Ambrose. Nowhere in his extant works does Ambrose refer to the incident at Antioch related by Paul. Baxter, following Goldbacher, has argued persuasively that the Ambrosian text Augustine has in mind is in fact the commentary on Galatians by Ambrosiaster.[129] But if Augustine thought 'Ambrosiaster' was Ambrose in 405 when he provided Jerome with the names of his authorities, and if he had thought this in 394–5 when he wrote his *Commentary on Galatians*,[130] then it is difficult to understand why he should have felt any need to consult Victorinus as a model. My reply to this possible objection is that if Augustine thought he had a commentary on Paul by Ambrose in the mid-390s, why did he never once refer to it? At the very least, a brief reference to it in Letter 37 to Simplicianus (if not in the *Ad Simplicianum* itself) would have been the kind of *beau geste* one would expect from Augustine. And we do find him referring to Ambrose elsewhere at this time.[131] It would appear that in the mid-390s Augustine did *not* attribute this commentary to Ambrose but, to the extent that he knew it at all, knew it as an anonymous work.[132]

While other objections may be raised, the evidence taken as a whole creates a reasonable presumption in favour of the view that Augustine knew and used Victorinus' Pauline commentaries. Moreover, a remarkable affinity of theology and spirituality may be discerned in the writings of the two men: both place a strong emphasis on predestinating grace and justification by faith, the insufficiency of good works, and the importance of humility. First proposed by Gore, this affinity was strongly endorsed by

---

[128] *ep.* 82. 3. 24 (CSEL 34. 2: 376. 13–15).

[129] Baxter, 'Ambrosiaster cited as "Ambrose" in 405', following Goldbacher, CSEL 34: 376. 13 n.

[130] That Augustine's *exp. prop. Rm.*, written immediately before *exp. Gal.*, shows traces of the use of Ambrosiaster's *Comm. on Romans* is alleged by A. J. Smith, 'Latin Sources', 202.

[131] See e.g. *epp.* 31. 8, 36. 14. 32, and 44. 4. 7.

[132] With Souter, *Earliest Latin Commentaries*, 39–40, I would argue that the Pauline commentary of 'Ambrosiaster' first circulated anonymously. Cf. the summary statement by M. G. Mara in Di Berardino, *Patrology* iv. 180: '[The commentary] must in fact have been anonymous from the beginning.' See also Baxter, 'Ambrosiaster cited as "Ambrose" in 405', 187: 'It is noteworthy that, writing much later on exactly the same point in *Ep.* 180. 5, Augustine still quotes Cyprian but omits "Ambrose" from his list of authorities; had the intervening years taught him that the earlier attribution was wrong, and did he hesitate then to refer to an authority that was anonymous?' (See further section 2. c below.)

Harnack and acknowledged by even so cautious a scholar as Hadot.[133] Yet what has been almost entirely overlooked is the even greater similarity that exists when the commentaries are viewed as literary artefacts. If, as Hadot has said,[134] Victorinus' work on the Trinity may have served, if only in some minimal sense, as a model for Augustine's own work on the Trinity, how much more would Victorinus' Pauline commentaries have served as a model for Augustine's *Commentary on Galatians*, especially at such an uncertain and tumultuous time in Augustine's career as a theologian, exegete, writer, and spokesman for the Church? In choosing the specific genre that he did, Augustine revealed far more than a mere aesthetic whim, for to choose a genre is at the same time to place oneself within one specific tradition and not others, and to align oneself with specific teachers and not others.[135]

In sum, there are reflections in Augustine's *Commentary* of Victorinus' theological agenda and the literary genre he chose to implement it. It is true that we are still in the realm of the hypothetical, but this is surely better than suppressing a mass of evidence the core of which, as we have seen, is expressly given by Augustine himself. For suppression has been the practical (though unintended) effect of acknowledging the 'antecedent probability' of literary influence but pursuing it no further. The end result has been to leave Augustine's *Commentary* like Melchizedek, 'without father, without mother, without descent'.[136] Antecedent probability should not be passed over lightly. Here Newman's observation is very apt: 'In all matters of human life, presumption verified by instances, is our ordinary instrument of proof, and, if the antecedent probability is great, it almost supersedes instances.'[137] If, then, the antecedent probability of Victorinus' influence on Augustine's *Commentary on Galatians* is given its due weight, not only may that commentary be seen to have arisen out of something more than thin air, but also seemingly minor coincidences may be viewed positively, as corroborating the thesis, rather than negatively, as failing to establish it.

---

[133] Gore,'Victorinus Afer', 1137–8; Harnack, *History of Dogma*, v. 35 n. 1; Hadot, 'L'Image', 433.

[134] In his introduction to P. Henry and P. Hadot, *Marius Victorinus: Traités théologiques sur la Trinité*, i. 86.

[135] Guitton, *Le Temps et l'éternité*, 31.

[136] Heb. 7: 3 (AV). Not only has *exp. Gal.* been left like Melchizedek, but so has Augustine's list of *uiri illustres* in *doctr. chr.* 2. 40. 61.

[137] Newman, *Essay on Development*, 83.

Direct Evidence of Augustine's Use of Victorinus'
Commentary on Galatians

We may begin by examining three such coincidences. The first involves the interpretation of the words *before whose eyes Jesus Christ was proscribed* (Gal. 3: 1).[138] Both commentators assume that to be *proscribed* means to be publicly condemned to banishment and to the confiscation of one's property. This in itself is a coincidence,[139] though not a significant one. A significant coincidence occurs in the precise way in which Victorinus and Augustine understand Christ to have suffered the confiscation of his property. Victorinus' interpretation is as follows: 'Christ, therefore, was *proscribed*, that is, his property was divided and sold—the property, of course, that existed in us, which was proscribed, sold, and lost by the persuasive power of Judaism. . . . So you are foolish, Galatians: your souls have lost Christ and his property.'[140] Augustine's interpretation is strikingly similar: 'In other words, they saw Christ Jesus lose his *inheritance* and his *possession*, specifically to those who were taking it away and banishing the Lord. They, in order to take away Christ's *possession* (meaning the people in whom he dwelt by right of grace and faith), were calling those who had believed Christ back—back from the grace of faith whereby Christ has possession of the Gentiles to works of the law' (*exp. Gal.* 18. 2). The interpretation given by Victorinus and Augustine is not really paralleled by any other Latin author in the early Church. The contrast with Ambrosiaster, for example, is telling. Even though Ambrosiaster also reads *proscribed* in Gal. 3: 1 and also makes reference to the notion of confiscated property, his reference is minimal and his chief concern is plainly elsewhere: 'Obviously, to the eyes of the foolish Christ appears *proscribed*, that is, despoiled or condemned; but to the eyes and minds of the wise not only is he not condemned, but he himself is seen to have condemned death by his cross.'[141]

A second coincidence involves the use of the phrase 'hope of salvation' (*spes salutis*). There is only one instance of this phrase in the entire Vulgate,

---

[138] This coincidence was noted by Souter, *Earliest Latin Commentaries*, 193 n. 2.

[139] By contrast, Pelagius takes *proscribed* as a reference not to banishment but to execution, and he does not discuss the idea of confiscation of property at all (Souter, *Expositions*, ii. 317. 12–18).

[140] 'Ergo proscriptus Christus est, id est bona eius distracta et vendita sunt, quae utique in nobis erant, Iudaismi persuasione proscripta sunt, vendita et perdita. . . . Stulti ergo vos, Galatae: perdidistis ex vestris animis Christum et eius bona' (CSEL 83. 2: 126. 10–13, 21–2).

[141] CSEL 81. 3: 30. 5–9. Jerome, on the other hand, prefers the reading *praescriptus* ('written about beforehand') to *proscriptus* and interprets it to mean that Christ was 'written about beforehand' in the Law and the Prophets (PL 26: 348B).

and it is not in Galatians.[142] In Victorinus' *Commentary on Galatians*, however, there are seven instances[143]—yet none in any of his other writings. In
Augustine the phrase occurs only twice[144] prior to his *Commentary on
Galatians* and then five times in that text.[145] Moreover, for both Victorinus
and Augustine it is a phrase of crucial importance and indeed a key to
understanding the letter as a whole. Thus in the Preface to the first book of
his commentary Victorinus says: 'Paul writes this letter in order to correct
the Galatians, to call them back from Judaism so they would preserve faith
in Christ alone and have from Christ the *hope of salvation*, the hope of his
promises. For no one will be saved by works of the law.'[146] Similarly for
Augustine the point at issue is where one should place one's hope. The
parallelism between the two is perhaps clearest in their comments on Gal.
5: 2. Victorinus maintains that Paul condemns the Galatians specifically for
placing their hope for salvation in carnal circumcision: 'He shows plainly
that Christ will be of no benefit if anyone places hope in circumcision, that
is, in carnal circumcision.'[147] Augustine's view is close: 'He says that Christ
will be of no benefit to them if they let themselves be circumcised, but he
means if it is done as his opponents wanted it to be done—so that they
placed their hope for salvation in circumcision of the flesh.'[148] Neither the
phrase nor the concept appears anywhere in the Galatians commentaries of
Jerome and Ambrosiaster.

For the third coincidence I am indebted to Nello Cipriani, who has
recently examined Victorinus' and Augustine's commentaries on Galatians
afresh in order to settle the question of dependence once and for all.[149]

[142] 1 Thess. 5: 8: *Nos . . . simus induti . . . galeam spem salutis.*

[143] Preface to Book 1 (CSEL 83. 2: 95. 9) ; *Comm. on Gal.* 1: 3 (CSEL 83. 2: 99. 6–7); *Comm. on Gal.* 1: 6 (CSEL 83. 2: 99. 5–6); *Comm. on Gal.* 2: 10 (CSEL 83. 2: 117. 11); *Comm. on Gal.* 3: 24 (CSEL 83. 2: 135. 7); *Comm. on Gal.* 4: 17 (CSEL 83. 2: 150. 10–11); and *Comm. on Gal.* 6: 16 (CSEL 83. 2: 172. 5).

[144] *mor.* 1. 28. 55 (PL 32: 1333. 17) and *c. Adim.* 11 (CSEL 25. 1: 136. 3).

[145] *exp. Gal.* 11. 2, 15. 2, 41. 5, 54. 5, and 63. 2.

[146] 'Paulus scribit hanc epistolam eos volens corrigere et a Iudaismo revocare, ut fidem tantum in Christum servent et a Christo spem habeant salutis et promissionum eius, scilicet quod ex operibus legis nemo salvetur' (CSEL 83. 2: 95. 7–10).

[147] 'Aperte ostendit non prodesse Christum, si aliqui in circumcisione spem ponat et in circumcisione carnali' (CSEL 83. 2: 157. 2–4). That *spes* here means 'hope of salvation' is made plain by the use of the phrase *spes salvationis* a few lines later (CSEL 83. 2: 158. 15).

[148] *exp. Gal.* 41. 5: 'Christum autem nihil eis profuturum esse dicit, si circumcidantur, sed illo modo, quo eos isti volebant circumcidi, id est ut in carnis circumcisione ponerent spem salutis.'

[149] Cipriani's 'Agostino lettore' appeared after my own conclusions had been reached. The seven parallels he finds between the two commentaries on Galatians are discussed on pp. 414–16 of his article. I have omitted six of these parallels from my discussion: one which I had already discussed myself (on Gal. 3: 1) and five which I found unpersuasive for various

With regard to the words *through the law I died to the law* (Gal. 2: 19) each commentator offers two possible ways of understanding Paul's meaning.[150] According to the first way, the Jewish law has for the Christian been superseded and replaced. Hence a great divide now separates Paul the Christian from the Jewish law: he is 'dead' to the law and the law is 'dead' to him. According to the second way, it is not a question of the old being replaced by the new, but rather of understanding the same law in a new manner— spiritually rather than carnally. Both Victorinus and Augustine present their two interpretations in the same order. In addition to this agreement in conception and in order of presentation, there is also striking verbal agreement in the expression of the second interpretation: Victorinus remarks that for Paul 'the very same law is, so to speak, twofold: it has one appearance when it is understood carnally and another when it is understood spiritually';[151] Augustine says that Paul spoke to the Galatians 'so that through the same law, understood spiritually, they might die to carnal observances of the law.'[152] Ambrosiaster, by contrast, does not offer alternatives, and the one interpretation he does offer differs widely from Augustine's.[153] Jerome's comment is similar to Victorinus' second alternative but expressed in terms of a slightly but significantly different Pauline contrast: that between the spirit and the letter, rather than between the spiritual and the carnal.[154]

It could be argued that none of the three examples of parallelism given above is as compelling as we would like, but the question is not what we would like but whether such examples as these constitute as much evidence of dependence as we may reasonably expect to find in Augustine. Surely we should not expect to find the sort of wholesale plagiarism that we find in

reasons (e.g. I consider that the interpretation of Gal. 2: 1 that appears in both Victorinus and Augustine does *not* demonstrate dependence by the latter on the former, since the same interpretation also appears in the Galatians commentaries of both Ambrosiaster and Jerome).

[150] The two ways are clearly signalled in each commentary. In Victorinus' commentary they are signalled by the words 'It can be taken in this way . . . On the other hand, it can be taken in this way' (Potest videri . . . Potest autem videri'). In Augustine's commentary they are signalled by the words 'Either . . . Or' ('Sive . . . Sive'), which, unfortunately, I was unable to use in my translation, having been forced to rely on circumlocution instead.

[151] 'eadem [sc. lex] ipsa velut duplex est: una cum carnaliter, altera cum spiritaliter intellegitur' (CSEL 83. 2: 123. 8–9).

[152] *exp. Gal.* 17. 3: 'ut per eandem legem spiritualiter intellectam morerentur carnalibus observationibus legis'.

[153] Ambrosiaster writes: 'He says this because through the law of faith he has died to the law of Moses. For the one who is liberated from it "dies" and lives to God, becoming his slave, purchased by Christ' (CSEL 81. 3: 28. 21–3: 'hoc dicit quia per legem fidei mortuus est legi Moysi. moritur enim qui liberatur ab ea, et vivit deo, cuius fit servus emptus a Christo').

[154] PL 26: 344c 15–345b 12.

Jerome.[155] Augustine's indebtedness to Pauline commentators over the course of his career has been well characterized by Thomas Martin: 'It would appear that most often these commentators served as dialogue or debate partners rather than actual foundational sources for his thought. They suggested themes and highlighted problems that returned Augustine to his own direct reading of Paul, enabling him to thus clarify his own understanding and articulate his unique Pauline synthesis.'[156] We may count ourselves fortunate, therefore, to have found as much evidence as we have found of Augustine's verbal dependence on Victorinus' *Commentary on Galatians*.[157] And since these verbal parallels with Augustine are found only in Victorinus and not in any of the other Latin commentators, I conclude, not that Augustine's dependence on Victorinus has been demonstrated beyond all doubt, but rather that such dependence is in the highest degree probable.[158]

Perhaps the most important parallel, however, is to be found in their interpretations of Paul's rebuke of Peter at Antioch as genuine, not feigned, and as fully warranted by Peter's behaviour. Moreover, their interpretations are heralded in the prefaces to their commentaries and, in Augustine's case, heralded with great fanfare. The importance of this parallel lies in the manifold and far-reaching ramifications it has for Augustine's understanding of ecclesiastical authority. To begin with the broadest application of the text, Augustine sees Gal. 2: 11–14 as a demonstration, on the one hand, that truth takes precedence over Church office, but on the other hand, that falling away from the truth is less important than accepting correction in a spirit of humility and love. For by such acceptance the integrity of the truth is restored. Thus Peter's authority is actually enhanced by the incident at Antioch and his legacy to the Church is even greater than Paul's because of the magnificence of the example he has set. In the combination of humility and love shown by Peter we come to the very heart of Augustine's notion of Christian authority.

[155] On Jerome's plagiarism see Hagendahl, *Latin Fathers*, 138–41, 147–50, and 308–9.

[156] 'Pauline Commentaries in Augustine's Time', in Fitzgerald, *Augustine*, 627.

[157] Nor will we find clearer evidence of dependence when we compare Augustine's *Commentary* with Jerome's, which Augustine explicitly claims to have consulted (*ep.* 28. 3. 3). The absence of more compelling evidence of dependence on Victorinus than we actually find is therefore no warrant for arguing against Augustine's having consulted Victorinus; rather, it is precisely what we ought to expect in the circumstances.

[158] This conclusion is hardly earth-shattering, but it does provide us with an important insight into Augustine's method of biblical interpretation: he made far greater use of other commentators than is generally realized. Indeed, even the great J. B. Lightfoot erred in judgement on this point when he said that Augustine had written *exp. Gal.* 'apparently without consulting previous commentators, of whom he shows no knowledge' (*Galatians*, 232).

There are, however, additional issues of authority involved here.[159] As we have noted, twice in his letters Augustine cites the great African bishop and martyr Cyprian in support of his interpretation of Gal. 2: 11–14.[160] Elsewhere, writing against the Donatists (*bapt.* 2. 1. 2 and 2. 4. 5), Augustine goes so far as to quote the interpretation of Gal. 2: 11–14 given in Cyprian's Letter 71 to Quintus. Now in the Donatist controversy both sides wished to claim the support of Cyprian, 'the hero of all Africans, to whom Catholic and Donatist alike looked as the doctor of the African Church'.[161] The Donatists pointed to Cyprian's advocacy of rebaptism; Augustine to Cyprian's emphasis on Peter's humble acceptance of Paul's rebuke for the sake of Church unity. Augustine drew a parallel between Peter and Cyprian by saying that just as Peter was worthy of shepherding Christ's flock despite his error, so was Cyprian despite his advocacy of rebaptism, for Cyprian had shown true humility when, speaking at the Council of Carthage, he had affirmed his belief that the right of private judgement must yield to the demands of Church unity (*bapt.* 2. 2. 3). He would therefore have accepted gladly the decision of a later plenary Council against rebaptism (*bapt.* 2. 4. 5). Thus Cyprian himself, whose private judgement in favour of rebaptism seemed more in line with Donatism, is recontextualized by Augustine and shown ultimately to be the champion not of separatism for the sake of purity, but of unity as the overriding requirement of Christian love. In this way Cyprian's authority is actually enhanced, for it is like that of Peter, who in John's Gospel endured rebuke for love of the flock he was to shepherd.[162]

From Augustine's point of view, therefore, much was at stake for the African Church in the interpretation of Gal. 2: 11–14 given by Cyprian. Cyprian's frank acknowledgement of Peter's fault is paralleled in Victorinus' interpretation,[163] although, for the reasons given above,[164] Augustine does not name Victorinus as an authority in his correspondence with Jerome. We do see the names of Cyprian and Victorinus explicitly linked as authorities elsewhere, however, in the passage from the *De doctrina christiana* cited above in which Augustine lists outstanding

---

[159] That of the authority of the Bible is dealt with in section 4. B of the Introduction. For the basic line of argument here I am indebted to R. S. Cole-Turner, 'Anti-Heretical Issues', 162–6. For detailed discussion and criticism of Cole-Turner's views see section 2. B beginning at n. 285.

[160] References are given in nn. 128 and 132 above.

[161] Bonner, *St Augustine of Hippo*, 238.

[162] Augustine's interpretation of John 21: 15–17 at *exp. Gal.* 15. 9.

[163] This is not to say that Victorinus must have been dependent upon Cyprian. See Hennings, *Briefwechsel*, 243.

[164] See pp. 25–6.

representatives of Church tradition.[165] This passage was written less than two years after Augustine wrote his *Commentary on Galatians*. If, as I have argued, Victorinus as well as Cyprian stands as an authority behind that commentary, not only is the commentary itself illuminated, but also the list of illustrious men in the *De doctrina christiana* takes on new clarity and coherence.[166] Finally, this hypothesis sheds considerable light on the great controversy between Augustine and Jerome, for the unnamed opponent whose interpretation of Gal. 2: 11–14 Jerome attempts to demolish in his commentary is none other than Victorinus.

B. JEROME

Having examined the relation between Augustine and Victorinus as commentators on Galatians, we may now examine their relations with Jerome. Jerome's *Commentary on Galatians* was the second of four Pauline commentaries that he composed at Bethlehem in 386 or shortly thereafter in response to importunities from Paula and her daughter Eustochium;[167] the others were on Philemon, Ephesians, and Titus (in that order[168]). Comprising three Books, each with its own full Preface, the *Commentary on Galatians* extends over some 130 columns in Migne.[169] From the Preface to Book 3 we learn that the work was dictated hurriedly to a stenographer rather than carefully composed, as Jerome would have liked.[170] This method gives to the work a certain garrulous and amorphous quality and accounts, at least in part, for some remarkable indiscretions. Nevertheless, the merits of the work as a whole are undeniable, and what H. F. D. Sparks says of Jerome's commentaries in general well describes his *Commentary on*

[165] *doctr. chr.* 2. 40. 61.

[166] For the influence of *all* the authors named in *doctr. chr.* 2. 40. 61 on Augustine's interpretation of Paul in the mid-390s, see Ch. 5 of the Introduction.

[167] On Paula and Eustochium's importunities see *Comm. on Philemon* 1 (PL 26: 603A) and *Comm. on Ephesians*, Preface to Book 1 (PL 26: 441A).

[168] Nautin, 'La Date des commentaires', 5.

[169] By comparison, Augustine's *Comm. on Gal.* occupies 43 columns, Victorinus' 51, Ambrosiaster's 36, and Pelagius' 19.

[170] *Comm. on Gal.*, Preface to Book 3: 'On account of the weakness of my eyes and bodily infirmity generally, I do not write with my own hand; and I cannot make up for my slowness of utterance by greater pains and diligence, as is said to have been the case with Virgil, of whom it is related that he treated his books as a bear treats her cubs, and licked them into shape. I must summon a secretary, and either say whatever comes uppermost; or, if I wish to think a little and hope to produce something superior, my helper silently reproves me, clenches his fist, wrinkles his brow, and plainly declares by his whole bearing that he has come for nothing' (Fremantle *et al.*, trans., 498; Latin in PL 26: 399D–400B).

Galatians in particular: the 'outstanding characteristic . . . is learning—sacred, secular, philological, textual, historical, exegetical, all mixed together'.[171] J. B. Lightfoot has epitomized the work with his characteristic clarity and balance: 'Though abounding in fanciful and perverse interpretations, violations of good taste and good feeling, faults of all kinds, this is nevertheless the most valuable of all the patristic commentaries on the Epistle to the Galatians: for the faults are more than redeemed by extensive learning, acute criticism, and lively and vigorous exposition.'[172] These and other aspects of Jerome's work will be explored below by means of comparison with Victorinus and Augustine.

Now if the basic model for Augustine's *Commentary on Galatians* was Marius Victorinus, the basic model for Jerome's was Origen, and by this simple formula much of the antagonism between Jerome on the one hand and Victorinus and Augustine on the other may be explained. For it is essentially a clash of traditions: the Greek tradition symbolized by Origen, and a more recent Latin tradition symbolized by Victorinus.

Jerome's dismissal of Victorinus as a commentator on Paul is notorious but more problematic than has generally been acknowledged. In the Preface to Book 1 of his *Commentary on Galatians* Jerome states:

I will approach a work unattempted by any writers in our language before me, and which scarcely any of the Greeks themselves have handled in a manner worthy of the dignity of the subject. Not that I am unaware that Caius Marius Victorinus, who taught rhetoric in Rome when I was a boy, published commentaries on the Apostle, but he was busily engaged with secular literature and knew nothing of the Scriptures. And no one, however eloquent, can discuss well what he does not know. What then? Am I so stupid or rash as to promise something which that man[173] was unable to do? Certainly not! In fact I consider that I have been all the more cautious and wary in that, being aware of the weakness of my talents, I have followed Origen's commentary.[174]

---

[171] 'Jerome as Biblical Scholar', 539.

[172] *Galatians*, 232.

[173] White, trans., 115, has 'Origen' here, but the *ille* of the Latin text clearly refers to Victorinus.

[174] *Comm. on Gal.*, Preface to Book 1 (trans. based upon material presented in Fremantle *et al.*, trans., 496–7, and White, trans., 115, with my own additions and emendations); PL 26: 308A–B: 'aggrediar opus intentatum ante me linguae nostrae scriptoribus, et a Graecis quoque ipsis vix paucis, ut rei poscebat dignitas, usurpatum. Non quod ignorem Caium Marium Victorinum, qui Romae, me puero, rhetoricam docuit, edidisse Commentarios in Apostolum; sed quod occupatus ille eruditione saecularium litterarum, Scripturas omnino sanctas ignoraverit: et nemo possit, quamvis eloquens, de eo bene disputare, quod nesciat. Quid igitur, ego stultus aut temerarius, qui id pollicear quod ille non potuit? Minime. Quin potius in eo, ut mihi videor, cautior atque timidior, quod imbecillitatem virium mearum sentiens, Origenis Commentarios sum secutus.'

Besides this passage Jerome mentions Victorinus several times, and each mention is laudatory. The earliest appears in his *Chronicle* (*c*.379–80), where, under the year 354, Jerome says that Victorinus was honoured with a statue in Trajan's Forum.[175] Later, in his *Apology against Rufinus* (401[176]), Jerome speaks of Victorinus as one of the standard commentators on Cicero read at school.[177] Of particular importance is the fact that in both passages Jerome mentions Victorinus in the same breath as his beloved teacher Donatus. A third reference, dated *c*.392–3,[178] numbers Victorinus among the famous Christian writers and includes a reference to his commentaries on Paul.[179]

Jerome and Origen

With the evidence seeming to point in different directions, how are we to interpret the remarks quoted above from Jerome's *Commentary on Galatians*? It will be helpful to consider first the standard by which Victorinus is being judged: that of Origen as understood by Jerome before the outbreak of the Origenist controversy in 393.[180] For Jerome, Origen was the greatest teacher of the Church after the Apostles.[181] Endowed with 'immortal genius',[182] Origen was a man of 'incomparable eloquence and knowledge, which, when once he opened his lips, made others seem mute',[183] and whose labours 'surpassed those of all previous writers, Latin

---

[175] *Hieronymi Chronicon*, in *Eusebius Werke*, 7 (GCS 47): 239. 12–15.

[176] The date given by Kelly, *Jerome*, 251.

[177] *Apology against Rufinus* 1. 16: 'I suppose that as a boy you read the commentaries of Asper on Virgil and Sallust, of Volcatius on the Orations of Cicero, of Victorinus on his Dialogues, and on the Comedies of Terence, as well as on Virgil, those of my teacher Donatus' (Hritzu, trans., 80 (altered to harmonize with the punctuation given in CCSL 79: 15. 26–30: 'Puto quod puer legeris Aspri in Vergilium ac Sallustium commentarios, Vulcatii in orationes Ciceronis, Victorini in dialogos eius, et in Terentii comoedias praeceptoris mei Donati, aeque in Vergilium')).

[178] Kelly, *Jerome*, 174.

[179] *De viris illustribus* 101 (BP 12: 206).

[180] Cf. Clark, *Origenist Controversy*, 122: 'A reading of Jerome's works in chronological order reveals that until 396, he made little or no effort to distance himself from Origen or Origenist opinions.' For a history of Jerome's statements on Origen before, during, and after the Origenist controversy see Cavallera, *Saint Jérôme*, ii. 115–27.

[181] Thus *Hebrew Names* (*c*.389–91), Preface (CCSL 72: 59. 26: 'post apostolos ecclesiarum magistrum'). Similarly a decade earlier (*c*.381) in the Preface to his translation of Origen's *Homilies on Jeremiah and Ezekiel* (quoting Didymus) (PL 25: 583D).

[182] 'immortale ingenium' (*De viris illustribus* 54. 8 (BP 12: 154); *Comm. on Titus* 3: 9 (PL 26: 595B)).

[183] *ep.* 33. 4 to Paula, dated *c*.384 (Fremantle *et al.*, trans., 46 (modified); = *ep.* 33. 5 in CSEL 54: 259. 10–12: 'gloriam eloquentiae eius et scientiae . . . et illo dicente omnes muti putabantur').

or Greek'.[184] It comes as no surprise, therefore, to hear Jerome say that having access to Origen's twenty-five volumes of commentaries on the minor prophets was like having access to the wealth of Croesus.[185] The sincerity of Jerome's praise is borne out by the evidence in his writings of his prodigious reading of Origen.[186] The matter is vividly summarized by Courcelle:

> The range of his reading in Origen is therefore extensive and his knowledge of this writer far exceeds our own, since the majority of Origen's works are lost. To Jerome, Origen appears as the indispensable source. If he writes a commentary on a book or merely on a verse of Scripture, Jerome searches out a corresponding homily by Origen on such a book or verse. If by chance he cannot find such a homily, for instance in commenting on a passage of Psalm 126, he apologizes, saying that Pamphilus no longer possessed the homily. But he regrets the thought that Origen did write it and that time destroyed it.[187]

Although Origen was an ecclesiastical controversialist, speculative theologian, and spiritual master as well as a biblical scholar, it was above all in the last of these roles that his appeal to Jerome lay, and when in the midst of the Origenist controversy Jerome said that he had praised 'the commentator, not the theologian',[188] he probably spoke more accurately than he intended. Even in terms of biblical scholarship Origen's appeal for Jerome was largely limited to his work as a textual critic,[189] exegete, and philologist (the only one who, like Jerome, had learned Hebrew); Origen's hermeneutics hardly interested him.[190] In short, Jerome's concern was less with Origen's theory of interpretation than with his actual practice of it.

In the first flush of his enthusiasm for Origen (*c*.381), Jerome made a pledge to his friend Vincentius to translate, if not the whole, then at least the bulk of Origen's writings.[191] In the Preface to his book on the etymology of

---

[184] Ibid.: 'Videtisne et graecos pariter et latinos unius labore superatos?' Cf. the Preface to his translation of Origen's *Two Homilies on the Song of Songs*: 'Origen, whilst in his other books he has surpassed all others, has in the Song of Songs surpassed himself' (Fremantle *et al.*, trans., 485; PL 23: 1117A: 'Origenes, cum in caeteris libris omnes vicerit, in Cantico Canticorum ipse se vicit').

[185] *De viris illustribus* 75. 2 (BP 12: 182).

[186] Cf. the detailed discussion in Courcelle, *Late Latin Writers*, 102–12.

[187] Ibid. 111. For Jerome's regret see *ep*. 34. 1.

[188] 'laudaui interpretem, non dogmatisten' (*ep*. 84. 2 (CSEL 55: 122. 5)).

[189] A fascinating instance of Jerome following, or at least consulting, Origen in regard to a text-critical problem occurs at *Comm. on Gal.* 3: 10 (PL 26: 357A–358A).

[190] Campenhausen, *Fathers of the Latin Church*, 148.

[191] 'Magnum est quidem, amice, quod postulas, ut Origenem faciam Latinum . . . Hoc tamen spondeo, quia si, orante te, Iesus reddiderit sanitatem, non dicam cuncta, sed permulta sum translaturus' (Preface to his translation of Origen's *Homilies on Jeremiah and Ezekiel* (PL 25: 583D and 586A)).

Hebrew names, Jerome states it as his wish 'to imitate Origen'.[192] Jerome was even accused of plagiarizing Origen, to which he responded: 'What [my accusers] consider a reproach, I regard as the highest praise, since I desire to imitate him who, I doubt not, is acceptable to all wise people.'[193]

Jerome acknowledged the fact, though not the extent, of his dependence upon Origen for his commentaries on Galatians and Ephesians. In the Preface to Book 1 of his *Commentary on Galatians* Jerome writes: 'Being aware of the weakness of my talents, I have followed Origen's commentary. For he wrote five volumes on the epistle of Paul to the Galatians and concluded the tenth book of his *Stromateis* with a brief exposition of his commentary on it. He also composed various treatises and excerpts which could stand in their own right.'[194]

Jerome also refers to Origen (presumably Origen's *Commentary*) when he discusses Gal. 3: 1, 4: 28, and 5: 24.[195] In commenting on Gal. 3: 10, 3: 13–14, and 6: 18 Jerome quotes in each case four parallel Greek versions of the Old Testament (the Septuagint, Aquila, Symmachus, and Theodotion) as well as the Hebrew.[196] His source must have been Origen's *Hexapla*, which he had either consulted directly or received through the medium of Origen's *Commentary*.[197] In commenting on Gal. 5: 13 Jerome tells us explicitly that he is simply translating a long passage from the tenth book of Origen's *Stromateis*.[198] Years later, when pressed by Augustine on his interpretation of Gal. 2: 11–14 as a sham fight, Jerome again says that he had been dependent upon the tenth book of the *Stromateis*.[199]

Other direct evidence of Jerome's dependence upon Origen emerges from comparison of his *Commentary on Galatians* with the few fragments of Origen's commentary preserved in Pamphilus' *Apology*, all but one of

---

[192] *Hebrew Names*, Preface (CCSL 72: 59. 25: 'imitari . . . Origenem').

[193] *Comm. on Micah* (392), Preface to Book Two (Fremantle *et al.*, trans., 501 (modified); CCSL 76: 473. 226–30: 'Nam quod dicunt, Origenem me uolumina compilare, et contaminari non decere ueterum scripta, quod illi maledictum uehemens esse existimant, eandem laudem ego maximam duco, cum illum imitari volo, quem cunctis prudentibus . . . placere non dubito').

[194] *Comm. on Gal.*, Preface to Book 1, as quoted by Jerome in *ep*. 112. 4 (= Augustine, *ep*. 75. 3. 4) (White, trans., 115 (corrected)). The Latin of the Preface is as follows: 'quod imbecillitatem virium mearum sentiens, Origenis Commentarios sum secutus. Scripsit enim ille vir in Epistolam Pauli ad Galatas quinque proprie volumina, et decimum Stromatum suorum librum commatico super explanatione ejus sermone complevit: Tractatus quoque varios, et Excerpta, quae vel sola possint sufficere, composuit' (PL 26: 308B–309A).

[195] See further Schatkin, 'Influence of Origen', 54–5.

[196] PL 26: 357B–C, 360C–363B, 438C.

[197] Jerome had access to the original manuscript of the *Hexapla*, which he describes in *Comm. on Titus* 3: 9 (PL 26: 595A–B).

[198] PL 26: 406B–408B.

[199] Jerome, *ep*. 112. 6 (= Augustine, *ep*. 75. 3. 6).

which are echoed by Jerome, though he does not mention Origen by name.[200]

In his *Commentary on Ephesians* Jerome's indebtedness to Origen can be measured more accurately. Although Jerome claimed to have followed Origen only 'in part' (*ex parte*),[201] comparison with the numerous and often lengthy fragments of Origen's original that have survived, together with further evidence brought forward in Jerome's own lifetime by Rufinus, shows that Jerome's indebtedness must have been enormous.[202] Rufinus even refers ironically to Jerome's commentaries on Paul as translations of Origen.[203] If, as seems highly probable, Jerome's debt to Origen for his *Commentary on Galatians* is comparable to that for his *Commentary on Ephesians*, then 'a very large proportion of [Jerome's *Commentary on Galatians*] is drawn directly from Origen'.[204]

Of his *Commentary on Galatians* Jerome says that he followed Origen and, to a lesser extent, Didymus, Apollinarius, Alexander, Eusebius of Emesa, and Theodore of Heraclea.[205] He also describes how he followed them:

Let me therefore frankly say that I have read all these; and storing up in my mind very many things which they contain, I have dictated to my amanuensis sometimes what was borrowed from other writers, sometimes what was my own, without distinctly remembering the method, or the words, or the opinions which belonged to each. I look now to the Lord in His mercy to grant that my want of skill and experience may not cause the things which others have well spoken to be lost, or to fail of finding among foreign readers the acceptance which they have met in the language in which they were first written.[206]

Additional insight into Jerome's method can be gained from his later defence of it against Rufinus's charges[207] that in his *Commentary on Ephesians* Jerome took over Origen's views indiscriminately and without regard to their orthodoxy or heterodoxy:

[200] See Schatkin, 'Influence of Origen', 55.

[201] *Comm. on Eph.*, Preface to Book 1 (PL 26: 442c).

[202] Thus Kelly, *Jerome*, 145–6. The data are conveniently summarized by Turner ('Greek Patristic Commentaries', 493–5), who observes that Jerome followed Origen with 'extreme fidelity' (493).

[203] In the Preface to his translation of Origen's *On First Principles* (Praefatio Rufini 2 (SC 252: 70. 32–4)).

[204] Turner, 'Greek Patristic Commentaries', 493.

[205] *Comm. on Gal.*, Preface to Book 1 (PL 26: 308b–309a). For discussion see Souter, *Earliest Latin Commentaries*, 107–25.

[206] *Comm. on Gal.*, Preface to Book 1 (PL 26: 309a–b), as quoted by Jerome in *ep.* 112. 4 (= Augustine, *ep.* 75. 3. 4; Cunningham, trans., 334–5).

[207] Rufinus, *Apology against Jerome* 1. 22–44.

In my *Commentary on Ephesians*, I followed as my models, to be sure, Origen and Didymus and Apollinaris[208] (who hold doctrines that are certainly contradictory) in such a way that I did not lose sight of the truth of my faith. What is the function of commentators? They expound the statements of someone else; they express in simple language views that have been expressed in an obscure manner; they quote the opinions of many individuals and they say: 'Some interpret this passage in this sense, others, in another sense'; they attempt to support their own understanding and interpretation with these testimonies in this fashion, so that the prudent reader, after reading the different interpretations and studying which of these many views are to be accepted and which rejected, will judge for himself which is the more correct; and, like the expert banker, will reject the falsely-minted coin.[209]

In a later passage Jerome further justifies his method by telling Rufinus that 'this procedure is adopted, not only by interpreters of Sacred Scripture, but also by the commentators on secular literature, Latin as well as Greek'.[210] There can be no doubt that Jerome's conception of the commentary as a literary genre derives mainly from his teacher, the distinguished Roman grammarian Donatus.[211] Indeed, the very way in which he describes the commentator's task, especially with its emphasis on gathering and preserving the opinions of previous commentators so as to produce a 'variorum commentary',[212] bears striking affinities to that of Donatus.[213]

But how is it possible for Jerome to have followed both Donatus and Origen at the same time and, as is being argued here, in the same *Commentary*? After all, the classical culture Donatus preserved in his writings and symbolized in his person was publicly repudiated by Origen.[214] At the risk of simplifying, we may say that Donatus provided Jerome with his model of one who hands down a literary tradition, while Origen provided him with the tradition itself.[215] For Jerome, the classic text is the Bible and the literary tradition to be handed down is the Christian

---

[208] Cf. *Comm. on Eph.*, Preface to Book 1 (particularly PL 26: 442c–d).

[209] *Apology against Rufinus* 1. 16 (Hritzu, trans., 79 (modified); CCSL 79: 14. 11–15. 23).

[210] Ibid. 3. 11 (Hritzu, trans., 176 (modified); CCSL 79: 83. 12–14).

[211] Holtz, *Donat*, 40–6. Further on in the extended passage just quoted Jerome refers to Donatus' commentaries as standards (*Apology against Rufinus* 1. 16 (CCSL 79: 15. 26–30, which is quoted above in n. 177)).

[212] Kaster (*Guardians of Language*, 161; cf. 276) speaks of Donatus's 'variorum commentary on Vergil'.

[213] Donatus describes the commentator's task in his Epistle to Munatius (Latin text in Hardie (ed.), *Vitae*, 1).

[214] 'Pagan literature was for Origen an indissoluble part of the tradition of pagan society, to which as a member of the persecuted church he felt himself to be implacably opposed' (Chadwick, *The Early Church*, 100).

[215] Holtz, *Donat*, 43, sees a parallel between Jerome's practice and Augustine's theory as articulated in *doctr. chr.* (esp. *doctr. chr.* 2. 40. 60).

tradition as seen in its full flowering in the Greek East and supremely in the writings of Origen. Jerome's multifarious works were intended to help to create a body of Christian literature that would not only rival but surpass that of the classical authors. Thus he states that one of his goals in preparing his catalogue of illustrious Christian authors is to rival the pagan catalogues of Suetonius and others. Kelly describes Jerome's *De viris illustribus* as 'propagandist history' designed 'to persuade [people] of the riches of the Church's literary inheritance'.[216] The same spirit of rivalry is evident in Jerome's description of Origen, cited earlier, as the author whose labours 'surpassed those of all previous writers, Latin or Greek',[217] including the Roman polymath Varro.[218] Much the same spirit animates Jerome's *Commentary on Galatians*. For example, when he comes to describe the Galatian people, he says that although he could draw upon Varro as a source he refuses to do so because he will not allow 'the uncircumcised to enter the Temple of God';[219] instead he will draw upon the Christian Lactantius. It must be remembered that at this time Jerome still felt bound by the oath he made in his famous dream of *c*.374.[220] In that dream Jerome saw himself accused by a heavenly Judge of being a Ciceronian rather than a Christian.[221] In response he took an oath never again to possess or read secular literature.[222] It is to this dream that Jerome is clearly alluding in the Preface to Book 3 of his *Commentary on Galatians* when he reminds Paula and Eustochium that he has not read Cicero, Virgil, or any pagan writer for more than fifteen years.[223]

Adopting a method, therefore, derived from Donatus, while trying like Origen to distance himself from the pagan classics, Jerome sought but never really achieved a delicate literary balance between the secular and the sacred. In consequence his life's work is marked by tension and inconsistency.[224] He did, however, largely achieve his more important goal of

[216] Kelly, *Jerome*, 174.

[217] See nn. 183–4 above.

[218] *ep*. 33. 1–5 (CSEL 54: 259).

[219] *Comm. on Gal.*, Preface to Book 2 (PL 26: 353C: 'quia nobis propositum est, incircumcisos homines non introducere in templum Dei'), alluding to Ezek. 44: 9 (see Hagendahl, *Latin Fathers*, 120 n. 5).

[220] Recounted by Jerome some ten years later in his celebrated letter to Eustochium (*ep*. 22. 30). For analysis see Kelly, *Jerome*, 41–4.

[221] ' "Ciceronianus es, non Christianus" ' (CSEL 54: 190. 12).

[222] ' "domine, si umquam habuero codices saeculares, si legero, te negavi" ' (CSEL 54: 191. 6–7).

[223] PL 26: 399C–D. The same attitude towards pagan culture is reflected in Jerome's *ep*. 21, composed *c*.383–4 (on which see Kelly, *Jerome*, 83–4).

[224] Cf. Hagendahl, *Latin Fathers*, 328: 'His inconsistency reflects the inner conflict of his soul. He was a Christian ascetic and felt strongly the incompatibility of this ideal and the

providing a bridge whereby the wealth of Greek Christianity could be made available to the Latin Church,[225] and he did so at a time when fewer and fewer people in the West were sufficiently skilled in Greek.[226] Campenhausen has summarized Jerome's mission and achievement thus: 'Jerome recognized what his home church lacked, when her modest literature was compared with the rich theological, and above all the exegetical, tradition of the Greek church. Jerome sensed the need for Western Christianity to catch up with the East intellectually, and he summoned all his strength to fulfil this need.'[227]

Jerome and Victorinus

Having gained some understanding of Jerome's literary enterprise and having seen how much of it was shaped by his passionate desire to make Origen available 'to Roman ears',[228] we are now in a better position to assess his judgement on Marius Victorinus' *Commentary on Galatians*. In one part of his statement Jerome says that Victorinus 'knew nothing of the Scriptures'.[229] Certainly the paucity of references to other parts of the Bible is a striking feature of Victorinus' commentaries.[230] How much more striking must it have appeared to Jerome as he compared Victorinus to Origen,[231] who 'knew the scriptures by heart'.[232] Hadot considers that Victorinus' apparent ignorance of the Old Testament is the particular focus of Jerome's criticism.[233] During this period Jerome, following Origen's lead, was becoming increasingly immersed in the study of the Old Testament, so much so that he would break off his projected series of

humanism of pagan antiquity. But he was also a rhetor brought up in the atmosphere of the old cultural legacy. He felt attracted and repelled—at the same time. For a time the one feeling prevailed over the other, but he never reached a stable equilibrium. As a Christian he felt bound to reject pagan literature. But he did not cease admiring it and reading it—apart from a short interruption caused by the dream. To this reading he owes more than his incomparable style. If any Latin Father can be called a humanist, it is certainly Jerome.'

[225] Hennings, *Briefwechsel*, 249.

[226] Sparks, 'Jerome as Biblical Scholar', 517.

[227] Campenhausen, *Fathers of the Latin Church*, 180.

[228] 'Romanis auribus' (Preface to Jerome's translation of Origen's *Homilies on Jeremiah and Ezekiel* (PL 25: 584D)).

[229] Jerome's statement is quoted at length in n. 174 above.

[230] Souter, *Earliest Latin Commentaries*, 22–3; Erdt, *Marius Victorinus Afer*, 94. But see now Cooper, *Understanding*, who argues that this paucity reflects a deliberate methodological decision on the part of Victorinus to interpret Paul by Paul.

[231] Recall that Jerome names Origen as his principal source just a few lines after his dismissal of Victorinus.

[232] 'scripturas memoriter tenuit' (Jerome, *ep.* 84. 8 (CSEL 55: 130. 22–3)).

[233] Hadot, *Marius Victorinus*, 238.

commentaries on Paul to begin work on a commentary on Ecclesiastes. Moreover, his plan to translate the Old Testament from the Hebrew was moving into the forefront of his mind, and he would soon write three works preparatory to that translation: *Hebrew Names*, *Hebrew Places*, and *Hebrew Questions*.[234] Indeed, in the Galatians commentary itself he speaks of his 'indefatigable study' of Hebrew.[235]

But how are we to interpret the other part of Jerome's remark, namely, that Victorinus was 'busily engaged in secular literature'? Is this intended as a generous concession? Certainly a prima-facie case could be made for interpreting it in this way, on the grounds that Jerome includes Victorinus in his *De viris illustribus* and elsewhere recalls the statue erected in his honour. Yet inclusion among the *viri illustres* by no means implies Jerome's wholehearted approval: Jerome was seemingly prepared to include almost anyone, even the notorius heretic Eunomius,[236] in order to make his list lengthier and more impressive.[237] As for the statue in the forum, the mere fact that it was in Rome was probably enough to vitiate its worth in Jerome's eyes, not only because he shared the popular view of Rome as 'Babylon', but also because he had in effect been exiled from Rome less than a year previously.[238] But the decisive consideration here is Jerome's general attitude towards pagan literature during this period. As we have shown, Jerome's famous dream still haunted him, and he alludes to it in the Galatians commentary itself.[239]

It is true that even during this period and even in the *Commentary on Galatians* Jerome cannot avoid classical allusions. Indeed, his inconsistency can be astonishingly blatant. Thus in his *Commentary on Galatians*, having grandiosely excluded Varro from the Temple of God, Jerome proceeds to cite him by name as an authority just a few lines later.[240] But this inconsistency in no way detracts from our thesis. In fact, it could even be interpreted as strengthening it if Jerome's criticism of Victorinus is taken as an example of projection: Victorinus is being criticized for failing to live up to an ideal that Jerome himself is finding it hard to achieve. If so, it is not the

---

[234] All written *c*.389–91 (Cavallera, *Saint Jérôme*, ii. 26–8; Kelly, *Jerome*, 153).

[235] 'infatigabile studium' (*Comm. on Gal.*, Preface to Book 3 (PL 26: 399D)).

[236] *De viris illustribus* 120.

[237] It is precisely Jerome's inclusion of heretics that Augustine criticizes in *ep*. 40. 6. 9 (CSEL 34. 2: 79. 12–80. 2).

[238] Kelly, *Jerome*, 112–14.

[239] *Comm. on Gal.*, Preface to Book 3 (PL 26: 399C–D) and cf. *Comm. on Eph.* 6: 4 (PL 26: 540A–B), where Jerome heaps scorn on bishops who educate their children in secular literature.

[240] In *Comm. on Gal.*, Preface to Book 2, Varro is excluded in PL 26: 353C and then cited by name in 354C.

only occasion in Jerome's life when he reacts to another 'with all the sharp-
ness of a man disowning a part of his own past'.[241] Jerome believed he
had undergone a profound conversion as a result of his dream. Victorinus,
too, had undergone a profound conversion involving the repudiation of
paganism—or so it seems in Augustine's *Confessions*. Yet Augustine's
account, as Robert Markus has noted, is anachronistic: 'The image of conversion in terms of crossing from one of the front lines on a battlefield to the
other belongs to the 390s rather than to the 350s.'[242] In fact, 'Victorinus'
passage from neo-Platonism to Christianity had been a smooth progress
along the route of a fourth-century intellectual.'[243] It is possible that
Jerome, unlike Augustine, thought that Victorinus had hardly undergone
any conversion at all.

No less than his move from Neoplatonism to Christianity, Victorinus'
move from interpreter of Cicero to interpreter of Paul seems to have
been a smooth progress, since his style and method are so similar.[244]
Jerome appears to have known Victorinus' commentary on Cicero's *De
inuentione*,[245] and in any case he can hardly have missed the evidence of the
pagan rhetor and grammarian in the Pauline commentaries. Jerome's attitude may be inferred from his rhetorical question of a few years earlier:
'What has Cicero to do with the Apostle?'[246] Perhaps even more revealing,
in the light of Victorinus' renown as a philosopher, is Jerome's remark in
the *Commentary on Galatians*: 'How few there are who now read Aristotle.
How many are there who know the books, or even the name of Plato? You
may find here and there a few old men, who have nothing else to do, who
study them in a corner.'[247] Or, in the light of Jerome's observation regarding Victorinus that 'no one, however eloquent, can discuss well what he
does not know',[248] perhaps the most striking remark is a statement made in
a letter:

[241] Brown, *Body and Society*, 380, on Jerome's hostile reaction to Origen. Much the same
could be said of Jerome's hostile reaction to Rufinus.

[242] 'Paganism', 7.

[243] Markus, *The End of Ancient Christianity*, 29, following Hadot, *Marius Victorinus*, 52–8
and 235–52.

[244] Cf. Hadot, *Marius Victorinus*, 308; Erdt, *Marius Victorinus Afer*, 93. For differences see
Cooper, *Understanding*.

[245] See Hadot, *Marius Victorinus*, 18, citing Jerome, *In Ezech*. 13. Cf. Jerome's reference to
Victorinus' commentaries on the dialogues of Cicero in *Apology against Rufinus* 1. 16 (quoted
above in n. 177).

[246] 'quid facit . . . cum apostolo Cicero?' (*ep.* 22. 29 (CSEL 54: 189. 2–3)).

[247] *Comm. on Gal.*, Preface to Book 3 (Fremantle *et al.*, trans., 498). PL 26: 401B:
'Quotusquisque nunc Aristotelem legit? quanti Platonis vel libros novere, vel nomen? Vix in
angulis otiosi eos senes recolunt.'

[248] Ibid., Preface to Book 1 (PL 26: 308A).

The art of interpreting the Scriptures is the only one of which all men everywhere claim to be masters. . . . The chatty old woman, the doting old man, and the wordy solecist, one and all take in hand the Scriptures, rend them in pieces and teach them before they have learned them. . . . But all this is puerile, and resembles the sleight-of-hand of a mountebank. It is idle to try to teach what you do not know . . . it is worse still to be ignorant of your ignorance.[249]

Finally, Jerome's rhetorical question in his *Commentary on Galatians*— 'Am I so stupid or rash as to promise something which that man was unable to do? Certainly not!'—should be seen as a left-handed compliment to Victorinus serving to highlight Jerome's own sagacity in relying upon Origen: 'In fact I consider that I have been all the more cautious and wary in that, being aware of the weakness of my talents, I have followed Origen's commentary.'[250] Just as Reticius of Autun was censured by Jerome two years earlier for failing to follow Origen, so Victorinus is being censured now for the very same reason.[251]

In addition to Jerome's general antipathy to Victorinus there is a specific point of disagreement that must be emphasized: their conflicting interpretations of Gal. 2: 11–14.[252] Commenting on this passage, Victorinus speaks plainly and repeatedly of Peter's 'sin'[253]—indeed of his 'great sin'[254]—in acting out of moral cowardice. To Jerome such an interpretation is intolerable. Although he does not refer directly to Victorinus when he comments on this passage, he does attack 'anyone' who thinks that 'Paul really withstood Peter'.[255] There can be little doubt that Jerome is attacking Victorinus as 'the representative of Latin exegesis'.[256]

Why does Jerome find such an interpretation intolerable? Above all, it is

[249] *ep.* 53. 7 to Paulinus of Nola (394) (Fremantle *et al.*, trans., 99 (corrected)). CSEL 54: 453. 3–7 and 454. 10–12: 'Sola scripturarum ars est, quam sibi omnes passim uindicent. . . . Hanc garrula anus, hanc delirus senex, hanc soloecista uerbosus, hanc uniuersi praesumunt, lacerant, docent, antequam discant. . . . Puerilia sunt haec et circulatorum ludo similia, docere, quod ignores, immo . . . nec hoc quidem scire, quod nescias.'

[250] *Comm. on Gal.*, Preface to Book 1 (PL 26: 308A–B), quoted at greater length in n. 174 above.

[251] On Reticius of Autun see *ep.* 37. 3 to Marcella (CSEL 54: 288. 10: 'rogo, non habuerat decem Origenis uolumina?').

[252] I am indebted here to the original analysis of Hennings, *Briefwechsel*, 255–6.

[253] 'peccatum Petri' (*Comm. on Gal.* 2: 11 (CSEL 83. 2: 118. 7)); 'ille . . . peccauit' (*Comm. on Gal.* 2: 11 (CSEL 83. 2: 119. 17)); 'peccatum . . . quid fecisset' (*Comm. on Gal.* 2: 12 (CSEL 83. 2: 119. 5)); 'peccatum . . . in Petro' (*Comm. on Gal.* 2: 12 (CSEL 83. 2: 119. 5–6)); 'peccauit' (*Comm. on Gal.* 2: 12 (CSEL 83. 2: 121. 64)); 'peccas' (*Comm. on Gal.* 2: 14 (CSEL 83. 2: 121. 15)); 'peccare' (*Comm. on Gal.* 2: 14 (CSEL 83. 2: 121. 17)).

[254] 'magnum peccatum' (*Comm. on Gal.* 2: 12 (CSEL 83. 2: 120. 35–6)).

[255] *Comm. on Gal.* 2: 11 ff. (*sic*) (PL 26: 339A: 'Quod si putat aliquis, vere Paulum Petro apostolo restitisse . . .').

[256] Hennings, *Briefwechsel*, 256.

because a similar interpretation had been used by Porphyry to discredit Christianity: 'His desire was to brand [Peter] with error and [Paul] with impudence, and to bring against us as a body the charge of erroneous notions and false doctrine, on the ground that the leaders of the Churches are at variance among themselves.'[257] How sharply Porphyry's charges stung Jerome may be gauged from his statement later in the *Commentary* that he hopes to devote a separate work to refuting them.[258] Two points should be noted. First, with reference to Peter, Jerome remarks in his exegesis of Gal. 2: 11–14 that Peter, after being bishop of Antioch, was translated to Rome.[259] This remark provides a clue to Jerome's deeper motivation for safeguarding Peter's reputation, for Peter is the rock on which the Church is built (Matt. 16: 18). As Yvon Bodin has argued, for Jerome this meant that Peter was established in the truth; to suggest that he had fallen into error would be to jeopardize the authority of the Church itself.[260] Secondly, if Gal. 2: 11–14 is taken at face value, Paul's behaviour is not merely impudence but the absolute height of impudence, since Paul himself had pretended to uphold the Jewish ceremonial law in repeated instances recorded in Acts and had even defended that behaviour in his letters.[261] Thus there was pretence (*simulatio*) on the part of both Peter and Paul, but no one should imagine that such pretence is incompatible with holiness, 'since even our Lord himself . . . assumed the likeness (*simulatio*) of sinful flesh' for the sake of our salvation.[262] Moreover, if Paul had really rebuked Peter publicly it would have been a flat contradiction of the Lord's precept, *If your brother sins against you, go and correct him privately* (Matt. 18: 15).[263]

The interpretation Jerome advocates is this:[264] Peter knew that after the

---

[257] *Comm. on Gal.*, Preface to Book 1 (Fremantle *et al.*, trans., 497). PL 26: 310c–311a: 'volens et illi maculam erroris inurere, et huic procacitatis, et in commune ficti dogmatis accusare mendacium, dum inter se Ecclesiarum principes discrepent.'

[258] Ibid. 2: 13 (PL 26: 341c: 'Sed et adversum Porphyrium, in alio, si Christus jusserit, opere pugnabimus').

[259] PL 26: 341c: 'primum episcopum Antiochenae Ecclesiae Petrum fuisse accepimus, et Romam exinde translatum'.

[260] Bodin, *Saint Jérôme et l'Église*, 143.

[261] In *Comm. on Gal.* 2: 11 ff. Jerome refers to Acts 16: 1–3, 18: 18, 21: 24–3, and 1 Cor. 9: 20, 10: 32–3 (PL 26: 339a–b).

[262] Ibid. 2: 11 ff. (PL 26: 340a), alluding to Rom. 8: 3 and 2 Cor. 5: 21. In PL 26: 340c Jerome calls the pretended dispute between Peter and Paul a 'holy dispute' (*sanctum iurgium*).

[263] Ibid. (PL 26: 340a–b).

[264] It must be admitted, however, that Jerome's comments are not entirely consistent with one another. Thus his remarks at *Comm. on Gal.* 2: 6 appear to imply that the conflict between Peter and Paul was not simulated but real: 'Et ita caute et pedetentim inter laudem et objurgationem Petri medius incedit, ut et praecessori apostolo deferat, et nihilominus audacter ei resistat in faciem, veritate compulsus' (PL 26: 335c). Wiles, *Divine Apostle*, 22 n. 1,

death and resurrection of Christ the Jewish ceremonial law was no longer
binding and so did not hesitate to join in table fellowship with Gentile
Christians at Antioch.[265] With the arrival of people *from James* (Gal. 2: 12),
however, he became concerned that his behaviour might scandalize Jewish
Christians, who were especially entrusted to his care, so for their sakes he
withdrew from table fellowship with Gentile Christians. Unfortunately,
the Gentile Christians misinterpreted Peter's policy[266] and inferred that
the ceremonial law must be binding on them. Paul saw that these Gentile
Christians (who were especially entrusted to *his* care) were now themselves
in danger of being scandalized. To prevent them from falling away from the
faith Paul decided to resolve the problem by pretending to rebuke Peter:

Paul opposed Peter and the others publicly so that their pretense (*hypocrisis*)[267] of
observing the Law, which was harming believers of Gentile background, might be
remedied by his pretense (*hypocrisi*) of rebuking, and that each of the two peoples
might be saved: those who praise circumcision following Peter and those who are
unwilling to be circumcised proclaiming the liberty of Paul.[268]

Thus when Paul states that Peter was 'in the wrong' he is expressing not his
own opinion but only that of believers of Gentile background whose
champion Paul is and from whose table fellowship Peter had separated himself.[269] In a revealing comparison, Jerome likens Peter and Paul to two
orators in a court of law whose dispute is not real but simulated for the sake
of their respective clients.[270]

   Although Jerome's statements thus far could be interpreted to mean that
both groups were given support—those of Jewish background by Peter,
those of Gentile background by Paul—what Jerome says later implies that

suggests that Jerome may have been following different sources. In addition, Jerome's remarks
on Gal. 2: 14 suggest that the incident was intended not to mollify Jewish believers but to
correct them (see n. 271 below).

[265] *Comm. on Gal.* 2: 11 ff. and 2: 14 (PL 26: 338c and 342a).

[266] 'non intelligentes dispensationem Petri' (PL 26: 338d).

[267] Jerome's use of this word seems ill considered, even if it does occur in the Greek text of
Gal. 2: 13 and even if, as Lightfoot observes, 'the idea at the root of ὑπόκρισις is not a false
motive entertained, but a false impression produced' (*Galatians*, 113). From Tertullian on,
hypocrisis in Latin could mean 'hypocrisy', and it means precisely that in Vg. Matt. 23: 28 and
Luke 12: 1. Moreover, Jerome himself uses it perjoratively in reference to 'the Jews' twice in
Comm. on Gal. (PL 26: 311c and 334a). (The term that occurs in Jerome's Latin text of Gal. 2:
13 is *simulatio* (PL 26: 338c).)

[268] 'Restitit secundum faciem publicam Petro et caeteris, ut hypocrisis observandae Legis,
quae nocebat eis qui ex gentibus crediderant, correptionis hypocrisi emendaretur, et uterque
populus salvus fieret, dum et qui circumcisionem laudant, Petrum sequuntur; et qui circumcidi nolunt, Pauli praedicant libertatem' (*Comm. on Gal.* 2: 11 ff. (PL 26: 339b–c)).

[269] *Comm. on Gal.* 2: 11 ff. (PL 26: 339c).

[270] Ibid. (PL 26: 340b–c). Augustine disapproves of this comparison in *ep*. 82. 2. 13.

the Jewish group was to be not so much confirmed by Peter as corrected by Paul.[271] If so, then Peter accepted the rebuke in order to give an example to Jewish Christians.

In his interpretation of Galatians 2: 11–14 Jerome not only supports Origen and virtually all his successors[272] but is also supported by them. His detailed listing of authorities in the Preface to Book 1 of his *Commentary* serves not only as a bibliography but also as a bulwark against anyone who might wish to attack his exegesis.[273] Yet ultimately it is not so much the tradition itself that Jerome feels bound to uphold absolutely, but the honour of Peter and Paul.[274]

Jerome and Augustine

Jerome's interpretation of Gal. 2: 11–14 in his *Commentary* was one of two key issues that provoked Augustine to write to Jerome,[275] initiating a correspondence that forms one of the most fascinating chapters in the history of the early Church. That correspondence, which extended over nearly a quarter of a century, is exceptionally complicated and cannot be discussed here.[276] Suffice it to say that Augustine regarded Jerome's interpretation of Gal. 2: 11–14 as such a dangerous piece of casuistry that he took the risk of raising the matter in his very first letter to the great man and

[271] Ibid. 2: 14: 'Unde et Paulus eadem arte qua ille simulabat, ei restitit in faciem, et loquitur coram omnibus; non tam ut Petrum arguat, quam ut hi, quorum causa Petrus simulaverat, corrigantur' (PL 26: 342A). I am indebted to John Bligh (*Galatians*, 181–2) for this point.

[272] The Greek exegetical tradition is reaffirmed contemporaneously with but independently of Jerome's *Comm. on Gal.* in John Chrysostom's *Comm. on Gal.* (PG 61: 611–82) and in his homily entitled 'In illud, in faciem ei restiti' (PG 51: 371–88). Writing in 404, Jerome (*ep.* 112. 6 = Augustine, *ep.* 75. 3. 6) claims John Chrysostom as a supporter of his interpretation of Gal. 2: 11–14.

[273] Hennings, *Briefwechsel*, 250, who adds (n. 138) that Jerome refers to his list in just this way in Augustine, *ep.* 75. 3. 4 (CSEL 34. 2: 287. 5–8).

[274] e.g. Jerome, *Comm. on Gal.* 2: 14: 'If anyone finds unacceptable the interpretation by which it is shown that Peter did not sin and Paul did not impudently reproach his elder, he has an obligation to show how Paul could reprove in someone else what he himself had done without being inconsistent' (PL 26: 342A–B: 'Quod si cui iste non placet sensus, quo nec Petrus peccasse, nec Paulus procaciter ostenditur arguisse majorem, debet exponere qua consequentia hoc Paulus in altero reprehendat, quod ipse commisit').

[275] *ep.* 28 in the Augustine corpus (= *ep.* 56 in the Jerome corpus). The other key issue was the authority of the Septuagint, which Augustine thought was imperilled by Jerome's acceptance of the Hebrew canon of the Old Testament. On this issue Augustine is in effect representing the Council of Hippo (393), which defined the canon as being that of the Septuagint and was troubled by Jerome's decision. See Hennings, *Briefwechsel*, 110–11.

[276] For the history of the correspondence in general and for the conflicting interpretations of Gal. 2: 11–14 in particular see Ralph Hennings' excellent study, *Briefwechsel*. The complete extant correspondence except Augustine's *ep.* 19* (Divjak) is translated into English with introductions and notes in White, *Correspondence*.

continued to pursue it doggedly for ten years. Since our main purpose is to explore the relations between the two commentaries, the correspondence and other writings will be drawn upon only as needed to illuminate those commentaries. For this reason our primary focus among the letters will be Augustine's Letter 28 of 394/5, setting forth his views of Jerome's *Commentary* at virtually the same time as he was composing his own. After examining those views we will proceed to consider whether and to what extent they are reflected in Augustine's *Commentary*.

Although Jerome will later deny it vigorously,[277] Augustine believes that Jerome's interpretation assumes Paul was lying both when he rebuked Peter[278] and when he wrote about the incident in his letter:[279] in the first instance it was those present at Antioch who were deliberately misled; in the second, it was the Galatians and all subsequent readers of the letter. Augustine writes his Letter 28 partly to point out to Jerome that such an assumption fatally undermines the credibility and authority of the entire Bible, which must be upheld at all costs. Thus for Augustine, as Wiles has observed, 'it is the words of the apostles recorded in Scripture rather than their lives which must be treated as wholly reliable'.[280] Augustine's reasoning is as follows:

I think it is extremely dangerous to admit that anything in the Sacred Books should be a lie; that is, that the men who have composed and written the Scriptures for us should have lied in their books. . . . If we once admit in that supreme authority even one well-intentioned lie, there will be nothing left of those books, because, whenever anyone finds something difficult to practise or hard to believe, he will follow this most dangerous precedent and explain it as the idea or practice of a lying author.[281]

---

[277] Jerome, *ep*. 112. 4–18 (= Augustine, *ep*. 75. 3. 4–4. 18, and n.b. *ep*. 75. 4. 18: 'Do not go on thinking that I am a master of lies, for I follow Christ, who says: "I am the Way and the Truth and the Life," and a lover of truth cannot bend under the yoke of falsehood' (Parsons, trans., 362 (CSEL 34. 2: 315. 3–6)).

[278] 'Si enim mentiebatur apostolus Paulus, cum apostolum Petrum obiurgans diceret' (*ep*. 28. 3. 4 (CSEL 34. 1: 108. 11–12)).

[279] 'et dixit et scripsit' (*ep*. 28. 3. 4 (CSEL 34. 1: 108. 15)).

[280] Wiles, *Divine Apostle*, 25.

[281] *ep*. 28. 3. 3 (Parsons, trans., 95–6 (modified); CSEL 34. 1: 107. 12–108. 10): 'mihi enim uidetur exitiosissime credi aliquod in libris sanctis esse mendacium, id est eos homines, per quos nobis illa scriptura ministrata est atque conscripta, aliquid in libris suis fuisse mentitos. . . . admisso enim semel in tantum auctoritatis fastigium officioso aliquo mendacio, nulla illorum librorum particula remanebit, quae non, ut cuique uidebitur uel ad mores difficilis uel ad fidem incredibilis, eadem perniciosissima regula ad mentientis auctoris consilium officiumque referatur.' Similarly two paragraphs later at *ep*. 28. 3. 5: 'the authority of the Divine Scriptures is undermined—leaving anyone to believe what he likes and to refuse to believe what he does not like—once the opinion has gained ground that the men through whose ministry the Scriptures have come down to us could be telling well-intentioned

The precedent is even more dangerous for being championed by the most distinguished biblical scholar in Christendom.

Jerome's views also appear to be on Augustine's mind as he writes his *Commentary*. From the beginning Augustine takes pains to stress Paul's truthfulness: Paul had 'preached the truth' to the Galatians (*exp. Gal.* 1. 6); Paul is 'truthful' because he has been sent by God (2. 2–3); Paul 'aims to make the truth he is urging, rather than himself, pleasing to people' (5. 2–4), for 'the truth is to be loved for its own sake, not for the sake of the person or angel proclaiming it' (4. 6). Paul claims he is 'not lying' and backs up his claim with a solemn oath (9. 1–3 (on Gal. 1: 20)). The fact that Paul stated the gospel privately to those of repute (Gal. 2: 2) was not because he had told any 'lies' (10. 3), for 'under no circumstances is it lawful to tell a lie' (10. 4). Augustine is especially concerned to clear Paul of any suspicion of hypocrisy:

> The fact that Paul observed what were regarded as the accepted practices in all circumstances—whether dealing with Gentile or Jewish churches—does not mean that he had fallen into hypocrisy (*simulatio*). Rather, his aim was to avoid detracting from any local custom whose observance did not hinder the attainment of the kingdom of God. He merely warned against placing one's hope for salvation in unessential things, even though he himself might honour a custom among them so as not to offend the weak. As he says to the Corinthians: *Was anyone already circumcised at the time of his call? Let him not remove the marks of circumcision. Was anyone uncircumcised at the time of his call? Let him not be circumcised. Circumcision is nothing, and uncircumcision is nothing; what matters is keeping God's commandments* (1 Cor. 7: 18–19). (*exp. Gal.* 15. 1–4)

Similarly in reference to Acts 16: 1–3 Augustine says: 'Paul himself circumcised Timothy when that young man was already a Christian. But he did so to avoid scandalizing his own people, not acting hypocritically (*simulans*) in any way but acting out of that indifference with which he says: *Circumcision is nothing, and uncircumcision is nothing* (1 Cor. 7: 19)' (*exp. Gal.* 41. 6). This sentiment is repeated later in the *Commentary*: '*For it is not circumcision or uncircumcision that counts* (Gal. 6: 15). He maintains his indifference to the end in case anyone thought he had acted hypocritically (*simulate*) in circumcising Timothy or was doing so in circumcising anyone else (if by chance another situation of this kind arose)' (63. 1).

The evidence of a passage written at about the same time as the

lies' (trans., 97 (modified)). CSEL 34. 1: 111. 9–13: 'fluctuare auctoritatem diuinarum scripturarum, ut in eis, quod uult quisque credat, quod non uult non credat, si semel fuerit persuasum aliqua illos uiros, per quos nobis haec ministrata sunt, in scripturis suis officiose potuisse mentiri'.

50	*Introduction*

Commentary militates against the possible objection that Augustine's opponents are not real but only hypothetical. Discussing Gal. 2: 11–14 in the treatise *Lying* (394/5) he remarks: 'For it was not, *as some people think*, out of the same hypocrisy (*simulatione*) [as Peter and Barnabas showed] that the apostle Paul circumcised Timothy or performed certain ceremonies according to the Jewish custom.'[282]

Finally one may note that Augustine takes the trouble to justify the public nature of Paul's rebuke of Peter, which Jerome thought would, if taken literally, violate the command of Jesus in Matt. 18: 15. Augustine says: 'It was necessary for him to say this to Peter *in front of everyone* so that by Peter's rebuke *everyone* might be put right. For it would not have been useful to correct in private an error which had done its harm in public' (*exp. Gal.* 15. 8–9).

That 'Divine Scripture neither deceives nor is deceived' is at the heart of Augustine's understanding of biblical inspiration.[283] Gal. 2: 11–14 must therefore be interpreted in such a way that 'Peter was truly corrected, and Paul has given a true narrative of the event, unless, by the admission of a falsehood here, the authority of the Holy Scriptures given for the faith of all coming generations is to be made wholly uncertain and wavering.'[284]

Not only is Augustine alarmed by the general principle implied in the assumption that Paul lied in the Scriptures, but also, as Cole-Turner has demonstrated, he is anxious about his own particular struggle with the Manichees over the authority of the Scriptures.[285] The Manichees are not named in Letter 28, but Augustine's use of 1 Tim. 4: 3[286] (a favourite proof-text of his for countering the Manichean denigration of marriage[287]) as an example of a biblical text whose authority would be undermined, points in their direction. This pointer is confirmed by Augustine's later restatement of his argument to Jerome in Letter 82:

The Manichees maintain that many parts of the Divine Scriptures are false, because they cannot twist them to a different meaning, but their detestable error is proved

---

[282]	*mend.* 5. 8 (my trans. of CSEL 41: 422. 15–17: 'Non enim, ut nonnulli putant, ex eadem simulatione etiam Paulus apostolus aut Timotheum circumcidit aut ipse quaedam ritu iudaeico sacramenta celebrauit').

[283]	*pat.* 26. 22 (CSEL 41: 687. 14: 'neque . . . scriptura diuina fallit aut fallitur'). Augustine's understanding of biblical inspiration is discussed in section 4. B of the Introduction.

[284]	Augustine, *ep.* 40. 4. 5 to Jerome (*c*.397–9) (= Jerome, *ep.* 67. 5) (Cunningham, trans., 273; CSEL 34. 2: 75. 4–7).

[285]	Cole-Turner, 'Anti-Heretical Issues', 157–62.

[286]	There is an allusion to this verse in *ep.* 28. 3. 4.

[287]	Augustine had used it in this way as far back as *mor.* 2. 18. 65, as Cole-Turner has noted ('Anti-Heretical Issues', 184). Augustine quotes 1 Tim. 4: 1–4 later as a clear and unmistakable condemnation of the Manichees (*c. Sec.* 2 (CSEL 25. 2: 906.11–23)).

by the perfect clarity of scriptural expressions; and even they do not attribute falsehood to the apostolic writers, but to some supposed corrupters of the texts. But, as
they could never prove their case by either more texts or older ones, or even by the
authority of an older language from which the Latin books were translated, they
come out of this argument defeated and put to shame by a truth so well known to all.
Does your holy Prudence not understand what an avenue we open to their malice if
we say, not that the apostolic writings were falsified by others, but that the Apostles
themselves wrote falsehoods?[288]

Augustine derived a further defensive strategy against the Manichees
from Gal. 2: 11–14: Peter's wrongdoing here and elsewhere shows that it is
not an individual's personal merit that causes him or her to be chosen to be
God's agent. Augustine used this argument to thwart the Manichean attack
on the Old Testament based on the immorality of its heroes. This is seen
vividly in a passage from his work against Faustus the Manichee in which,
after alluding to Peter's wrongdoing at Antioch,[289] Augustine recalls the
earlier incident in which Peter struck the high priest's servant with a sword
and cut off his ear (John 18: 10): '[The fact] that after this sin Peter should
become a pastor of the Church was no more improper than that Moses,
after smiting the Egyptian, should become the leader of the congregation.
In both cases the trespass originated not in inveterate cruelty, but in a hasty
zeal which admitted of correction.'[290] As will be shown below, there are
additional, independent grounds for seeing anti-Manichean elements in
Augustine's *Commentary on Galatians*, thus further solidifying the view
that Augustine is concerned that Jerome's arguments might play into the
hands of the Manichees.

We have already mentioned that Augustine had another polemical
reason for affirming the reality of Peter's wrongdoing.[291] In writing against
the Donatists Augustine was at pains to show that Cyprian, despite his
advocacy of rebaptism for the lapsed in his own lifetime, would surely have
yielded to the decision against rebaptism reached by a later plenary council.
For Cyprian considered the claims of church unity to be above those of
individual private judgement. Cole-Turner has shown that Augustine's
arguments in *On Baptism, against the Donatists* (400/1), and particularly his
stress on Peter's humble acceptance of correction, are also central to
Augustine's discussion of the true interpretation of Gal. 2: 11–14 in Letter
82 to Jerome. Cole-Turner is of the opinion, however, that the issue of

---

[288] *ep*. 82. 2. 6 (Parsons, trans., 394 (modified); CSEL 34. 2: 356. 8–19).
[289] *c. Faust*. 22. 68 (CSEL 25. 1: 665. 2–3).
[290] Ibid. 22. 70 (Stothert, trans., 299 (modified); CSEL 25. 1: 667. 26–668. 3).
[291] See the end of section 2. A above.

Peter's humility does not enter the debate between Augustine and Jerome until Augustine's Letter 82, that is, 404/5.[292] But Peter's humility is already the key point in Augustine's interpretation of Gal. 2: 11–14 in his *Commentary*, and that interpretation is directed in part against Jerome. That the same line of argumentation is present both in the *Commentary* and in Letter 82 may be seen from a comparision of the two texts. First the Letter:

Peter himself received, with the holy and loving humility which became him, the rebuke which Paul, in the interests of truth, and with the boldness of love, administered. Therein Peter left to those that came after him an example, that, if at any time they deviated from the right path, they should not think it beneath them to accept correction from those who were their juniors,—an example more rare, and requiring greater piety, than that which Paul's conduct on the same occasion left us. ... For ... it is a thing much more worthy of admiration and praise to receive admonition meekly, than to admonish a transgressor boldly.[293]

To this passage we may compare the *Commentary*:

Here I might add that out of steadfastness and love Peter—to whom the Lord had said three times, *Do you love me? Feed my sheep* (John 21: 15–17)—was entirely willing to endure this rebuke from a junior shepherd for the salvation of the flock. Moreover, it was in his rebuke that the one being rebuked proved the more admirable and difficult to imitate. For it is easy to see what you would correct in someone else and to proceed to do so by censure and criticism. It is not so easy to see what ought to be corrected in yourself and to be willing to be corrected even by yourself, let alone by another, and that a junior, and all this *in front of everyone*! Now this incident serves as a great example of humility, which is the most valuable Christian training, for by humility love is preserved. (*exp. Gal.* 15. 9–11)

In his *Commentary* Augustine is already clearly preoccupied with Peter's humble acceptance of correction. The intensity of his preoccupation may be gauged, first, by the fact that Peter's acceptance is the principal emphasis of his entire interpretation of Gal. 2: 11–14 and, secondly, by the fact—so obvious as to be forgotten—that Peter's acceptance is not part of the biblical text. Thus Augustine's emphatic assertion of Peter's real hypocrisy in the Preface to his *Commentary* (1. 4) should be seen in part as

---

[292] Cole-Turner, 'Anti-Heretical Issues', 165.

[293] *ep.* 82. 2. 22 (Cunningham, trans., 357; CSEL 34. 2: 374. 19–375. 8): 'ipse uero Petrus, quod a Paulo fiebat utiliter libertate caritatis, sanctae ac benignae pietate humilitatis accepit atque ita rarius et sanctius exemplum posteris praebuit, quo non dedignarentur, sicubi forte recti tramitem reliquissent, etiam a posterioribus corrigi, quam Paulus. ... Nam ... multo est ... mirabilius et laudabilius libenter accipere corrigentem quam audacter corrigere deuiantem.'

an attempt to ward off any pro-Donatist inroads that might be made by means of an interpretation such as Jerome's.

No other clear pointers to Jerome's commentary stand out.[294] Thus the relation of Augustine's *Commentary on Galatians* to Jerome's is essentially one of negative reaction. It is astonishing to consider the fact that Augustine did not draw upon any of Jerome's dazzling erudition. At the very least, one would have expected him to borrow some linguistic point or other from Jerome, particularly as we find Augustine very soon afterwards emphasizing the importance of linguistic expertise for the interpreter of the Bible,[295] painfully conscious of his own lack in this regard, and (no doubt thinking primarily of Jerome) commending the work of the Hebraists to biblical interpreters.[296] Yet where is the evidence of Augustine's having taken his own advice?[297] Augustine's essentially negative relation to Jerome's commentary throws great light on his own purpose in writing, which will be explored in Chapter 3.

C. AMBROSIASTER

'Ambrosiaster' ('Pseudo-Ambrose') is the name given by Erasmus to the author of a set of Pauline commentaries that had been traditionally regarded as the work of Ambrose of Milan. As noted earlier,[298] it is highly probable that these commentaries first circulated anonymously. Of the numerous attempts that have been made to identify the author none has found widespread favour. Indeed, it is still disputed whether he was of Jewish or pagan origin and whether his Christian theological background was or was not exclusively Latin.[299] As to the date of composition of the commentaries, the author states[300] and other internal evidence confirms that they were written during the pontificate of Damasus, i.e. between 366 and 384.[301] The place of composition was probably Rome.[302]

---

[294] Pincherle, *La formazione teologica*, 132 n. 16, sees similarities between their comments on Gal. 1: 1 and 1: 4. I regard these similarities as insignificant. See further n. 324 below.

[295] *doctr. chr.* 2. 11. 16.

[296] Ibid. 2. 16. 23.

[297] Of course we do have evidence elsewhere of his having done so. Thus La Bonnardière ('Jérôme "informateur" d'Augustin', 46) speaks of Augustine's frequent use of Jerome's *Hebrew Names* in his *en. Ps.*

[298] See n. 132 above and the literature cited there.

[299] M. G. Mara in Di Berardino, *Patrology*, iv. 180–1.

[300] *Comm. on 1 Timothy* 3: 15 (CSEL 81. 3: 270. 12–13): 'ecclesia . . . cuius hodie rector est Damasus'.

[301] Souter, *Earliest Latin Commentaries*, 42–3.   [302] Ibid. 43–4.

Ambrosiaster comments on thirteen Pauline letters in all. (Hebrews is excluded on the grounds that it does not come from Paul.[303]) He employs an exegetical method that concentrates on the historical-literal sense and avoids allegory. His approach thus has affinities with that of Marius Victorinus, whose *Commentary on Romans* he appears to have known.[304] His *Commentary on Galatians* is far superior to Victorinus' and to Augustine's in the extent of biblical knowledge displayed. Ambrosiaster's distinctive place in the history of Pauline interpretation is summarized by Wiles: 'for the first time we have to do with a complete set of commentaries on all the Pauline epistles apparently conceived and executed as a unity'.[305]

Turning specifically to Augustine's use of Ambrosiaster we may note that in 420/1 he cites Ambrosiaster's *Commentary on Romans* but attributes it to a certain 'Hilary'.[306] It has been argued that evidence of Augustine's knowledge of this work is already present in his writings on Romans from the mid-390s.[307] With regard to Ambrosiaster's *Commentary on Galatians* we have argued above[308] that when Augustine writes to Jerome in 405 and claims the support of Ambrose for his interpretation of Gal. 2: 11–14 he is unwittingly referring to Ambrosiaster. But does this mean that he was already influenced by Ambrosiaster's *Commentary on Galatians* at the time he wrote his own? Hennings considers that he was, arguing that a comparison of their comments on Gal. 2: 11–14 shows not only a general agreement in their view of the dispute at Antioch as real but also a specific agreement in their choice of the Latin term *error* to describe Peter's action.[309]

An even more striking agreement occurs in their interpretations of Paul's reference to Peter, James, and John as *pillars* (Gal. 2: 9). Both Augustine

---

[303] Ambrosiaster considered Hebrews to be anonymous (Souter, *Earliest Latin Commentaries*, 53) yet canonical (Bastiaensen, 'Augustin commentateur de saint Paul', 52 n. 33).

[304] See n. 124 above.

[305] Wiles, *The Divine Apostle*, 11.

[306] Specifically, in *c. ep. Pel.* 4. 4. 7 Augustine quotes from Ambrosiaster's *Comm. on Romans* 5: 12: 'In fact, the holy Hilary understood in that way the passage, *In whom all have sinned* (Rom. 5: 12), for he says, "*In whom*, that is, in Adam, *all have sinned*." Then he added, "It is clear that all have sinned in Adam as in a single mass, for all whom he begot, after he was corrupted by sin, were born under the power of sin." In writing these words, Hilary indicated without any ambiguity how one should understand: *in whom all have sinned*' (Teske, trans., *Answer to the Two Letters of the Pelagians*, 191 (CSEL 60: 528. 9–16)).

[307] Namely in *exp. prop. Rm.* and *Simpl.* For this and other evidence pertaining to Augustine's use of Ambrosiaster for his interpretation of Paul's letters see Bastiaensen, 'Augustin et ses prédécesseurs latins chrétiens', 27–8, and the literature cited there.

[308] See p. 26.

[309] Cf. Hennings, *Briefwechsel*, 257.

and Ambrosiaster note that these three had long enjoyed a special status among the apostles, having been present with Jesus at the Transfiguration.[310] But in making this observation both Augustine and Ambrosiaster are confusing James the brother of the Lord, who was one of the 'pillars', with James the son of Zebedee, who was a witness of the Transfiguration.[311] When we turn to Jerome's comment on Gal. 2: 6 we find that he too refers to the Transfiguration but avoids making the same mistake.[312] It may well be that Jerome is silently correcting Ambrosiaster, but if Augustine read Jerome rather than Ambrosiaster, would he have caught Jerome's subtle correction or would he simply have taken away with him the link with the Transfiguration? It is impossible to be sure. But the fact that Augustine could have derived his reference to the Transfiguration from Jerome makes it more difficult to argue that Augustine was dependent on Ambrosiaster.

Thus, although the hypothesis that Augustine drew upon Ambrosiaster's comments on Galatians while preparing his own has much to commend it, it cannot be demonstrated,[313] and since in the case of Ambrosiaster we lack the sort of mandate to explore literary influence that Augustine himself gave us in the case of Victorinus when he wrote about him at length in the *Confessions*, to pursue the question of Augustine's relationship with Ambrosiaster further would not be profitable.[314]

Even though we are not able to establish a firm connection between Augustine and Ambrosiaster, or between Ambrosiaster and Jerome, or between Jerome and Augustine, with regard to their interpretations of the *pillars*, our inability does not mean that there is no connection. Indeed, there clearly is some connection here, even if it cannot be specified and proved. And in general with regard to the ancient Latin commentators on Paul, we see undeniable signs of a surprisingly complex network of influence, even though most of the specific lines of influence cannot be traced directly from author A to author B. This total impression needs to be borne in mind when we look at the admittedly rather meagre results

---

[310] With Augustine, *exp. Gal.* 13. 4, compare Ambrosiaster, *Comm. on Galatians* 2: 9–10 (CSEL 81. 3: 24. 15–18).

[311] Bastiaensen, 'Augustin commentateur de saint Paul', 48, notes the fact that both refer to the Transfiguration but fails to note that both make the same mistake.

[312] Jerome seems deliberately to have omitted the name of James from his comment: 'Although, [Paul] says, the Lord had with him the apostles Peter and John, and they saw him transfigured on the mountain, and upon them the foundation of the Church has been laid' (PL 26: 335A 12–B 1: 'Licet, inquit, Petrum et Joannem Dominus secum apostolos habuerit, et transfiguratum eum in monte viderint, et super ipsos Ecclesiae sit positum fundamentum').

[313] *Pace* Mendoza, 'Introduzione', 479, who places far too much weight on Cipriani, 'L'autonomia', 15 n. 32.

[314] The same conclusion is reached by Souter, *Earliest Latin Commentaries*, 199.

we obtain from our attempts to establish definite links between any two commentators.

D. THE ANONYMOUS COMMENTATOR DISCOVERED BY H. J. FREDE

In 1973–4 H. J. Frede of the Vetus Latina Institut published an anonymous Latin commentary on Paul that had been partially preserved in a manuscript in the Hungarian National Museum in Budapest.[315] This commentary treats fourteen Pauline letters, including Hebrews, of which it represents the oldest commentary in the Latin West.[316] Its date of composition has been established by Frede as lying between 396 and 405.[317] It was used as a source by Pelagius in his commentary on Paul.[318] The principal question to be addressed here is whether there is any evidence that the anonymous author consulted Augustine's *Commentary on Galatians*. Comparison of the commentaries reveals only two notable parallels. The first occurs in their interpretations of the phrase *the present evil world* (Gal. 1: 4). Augustine remarks that '*the present world* is understood to be *evil* because of the evil people who live in it'.[319] This is paralleled by the following passage in the Budapest commentary: 'Not that the world is evil but rather that what is done in the world is evil, just as the Lord also says in the Gospel: *Sufficient for the day is its own evil* (Matt. 6: 34). Not that the day is evil, but rather that a day is called "good" or "evil" because of the things done within that period of time.'[320] Now since both Augustine and the Budapest commentator are attempting to ward off Manichean readings of Paul,[321] the parallel between them may be due simply to their common purpose rather than to any borrowing. If the Budapest commentator is borrowing from anyone here it is probably not Augustine but Jerome, since there is clear

---

[315] Frede, *Ein neuer Paulustext und Kommentar*. For a recent discussion of the question of authorship see T. S. de Bruyn, 'Constantius the *tractator*'.

[316] Frede, *Ein neuer Paulustext und Kommentar*, i. 242.

[317] Ibid. i. 215–17.

[318] Ibid. i. 196–205.

[319] *exp. Gal.* 3. 3.

[320] Gal 03: 'Non quod "saeculum malum" sit, sed quod "mala" sunt quae aguntur in "saeculo", sicut et dominus in evangelio dicit: *Sufficit diei malitia sua*; non quod "dies mala" sit, sed propter illa quae in eius tempore geruntur vel "bona" vel "mala" dicitur "dies"' (Frede, *Ein neuer Paulustext und Kommentar*, ii. 219).

[321] Frede, *Ein neuer Paulustext und Kommentar*, i. 219 cites three instances in which the anonymous commentator attacks the Manichees by name: Rm 017, Rm 31A, and Eph 9. On Augustine's anti-Manichean purpose see section 3. B below.

evidence of his borrowing from Jerome elsewhere in his commentary.[322] In his discussion of Gal. 1: 4 Jerome comments: 'But we say, it is not so much the world itself that is called evil as . . . the things that are done in it, as it is said that its own evil is sufficient for the day.'[323] This parallel is best explained as a direct borrowing from Jerome by the Budapest commentator.[324]

A second parallel occurs between the anonymous author's note on 1 Cor. 15: 31[325] and Augustine's reference to the same verse in his *Commentary on Galatians*.[326] Both remark that while the Latin version is ambiguous as to whether Paul swore in this instance, the Greek original leaves no doubt that he did. Is this parallel merely a coincidence? Inasmuch as the interpretation is not odd or eccentric but rather what one would expect on the basis of the Greek,[327] its value as evidence of borrowing is radically reduced. Our doubts about the anonymous commentator's having read Augustine's *Commentary on Galatians* become almost insurmountable when we consider how different the two writers are in terms of which passages and topics in Galatians capture their attention. Indeed, considered in these terms Augustine probably differs more widely from the anonymous commentator than from any of the others. In such circumstances direct dependence is extremely unlikely, and the two parallels we have noted are best viewed as mere coincidences.

E. PELAGIUS

Pelagius' *Expositions of Thirteen Epistles of St Paul* (*Expositiones xiii epistularum S. Pauli*) is his earliest and most important extant work. Composed in Rome between 406 and 409, it covers all the letters attributed to Paul in the New Testament. In it Pelagius shows a wide familiarity with

---

[322] See Frede, *Ein neuer Paulustext und Kommentar*, i. 215–17, 252.

[323] 'Nos autem dicimus, non tam saeculum ipsum . . . appellari malum, quam . . . ea quae in saeculo fiant: quomodo sufficere dicitur diei malitia sua' (PL 26: 314B).

[324] Pincherle, *La formazione teologica*, 118 and 132 n. 16, regards the similarity between Jerome's interpretation of Gal. 1: 4 and Augustine's as clear evidence of the latter's borrowing. But did Augustine really need Jerome's help to make the simple observation quoted above? Pincherle's point would be much more credible if Augustine, like the anonymous commentator, had also referred to Matt. 6: 34.

[325] At 1 Cor 079(b).

[326] At *exp. Gal.* 9. 4. This parallel is pointed out by Frede, *Ein neuer Paulustext und Kommentar*, i. 210–11. In fact, as Frede also points out, a much closer parallel with 1 Cor 079(b) occurs in Augustine's *s. dom. m.* 1. 17. 51.

[327] See the note attached to *exp. Gal.* 9. 4.

earlier Pauline exegesis in Latin, including Jerome, Ambrosiaster, Frede's anonymous commentator, and even Rufinus' translation of Origen's *Commentary on Romans.*

With regard to its relation to Augustine, Pelagius' commentary on Paul was written after the famous incident in which he reacted violently to Augustine's sentence in the *Confessions*, 'Grant what you command, and command what you will', but before the public outbreak of the Pelagian controversy. His reaction to Augustine in his commentary on Paul may be roughly summarized as approval for the early Augustine but disapproval for the change represented by the *Ad Simplicianum*, the first work written after he became a bishop. The latter text is weighed in the balance and found wanting because of its apparent minimization of human free will.[328] Yet there was much in Augustine's earlier interpretation of Paul that Pelagius approved and tacitly reproduced in this work, especially the defence of Christian freedom against Manichean determinism in Augustine's *Propositions from Romans.*

If Pelagius consulted Augustine on Romans, it is reasonable to suppose that he would have wanted to look at Augustine's *Commentary on Galatians* in the course of preparing his own. Is there any evidence that he actually did so? We note six parallel passages that suggest that Pelagius did consult Augustine.[329] Of these the most striking is that on the use of the Latin word *mulier* for 'woman' in Gal. 4: 4, a word that seems to imply Mary was not a virgin. Augustine comments: 'He says *mulier* instead of *femina* for 'woman' in accordance with Hebrew usage. Thus when it is said of Eve, *He made [the rib] into a woman* (*mulier*) (Gen. 2: 22), this does not mean that she had already had intercourse with the man, since she is not recorded as having had intercourse with him until after their expulsion from Paradise' (*exp. Gal.* 30. 2). With this we may compare Pelagius' comment: 'Here the term *mulier* does not refer to corruption (*corruptionis*), but to sex, just as Eve, from the moment she is made, is called *mulier* (Gen. 2: 23).'[330] Now while Pelagius may have consulted Augustine's *Commentary* at this point, his other commentaries suggest that he also knew Augustine's *Reply to Faustus*,[331] a text that offers an even closer parallel: 'By the term *mulier* Paul does not mean that she had been marred (*corrupta*) by intercourse or child-bearing. Instead, he uses it as it is used in the Scriptures—to refer simply to someone of the female sex. Thus it is written of Eve in the book of Genesis

---

[328] See especially Pelagius' *Comm. on Romans* 9: 16 and the note by De Bruyn *ad loc.* (*Pelagius' Commentary*, 118 n. 16).

[329] See the footnotes to *exp. Gal.* 3. 2, 6. 2, 15. 9, 17. 5, 30. 2, and 62. 3.

[330] Souter, *Expositions*, ii. 324. 8–10.

[331] See Souter, *Earliest Latin Commentaries*, 228.

that *God made [the rib] into a woman (mulier)* (Gen. 2: 22), although she had not had intercourse with the man.'[332] Yet another possibility is that Pelagius—and indeed Augustine himself—may be directly dependent upon Tertullian.[333] Of the many possible explanations for the parallel in question,[334] however, the simplest and most probable is that Pelagius consulted Augustine's *Commentary on Galatians*.[335]

While there are parallels, there is also much that Pelagius does not take over, most conspicuously Augustine's strongly anti-Manichean interpretation of Gal. 5: 17: 'People think that the Apostle is here denying that we have free choice of the will. They do not understand that this is said to them if they refuse to hold on to the grace of faith they have received.'[336] Since Pelagius was implacably opposed to the Manichean interpretation of the Pauline notion of 'the flesh' in Gal. 5: 17 and elsewhere,[337] one might have expected him to take up such a statement for his own use. Indeed, Augustine himself appears to have thought his remarks on Gal. 5: 17 in his *Commentary* too Pelagian, because he goes to some length in his *Retractationes* to correct them.[338] Yet Pelagius passes them by. This is just one of a number of instances where Pelagius does not make the sort of use of Augustine's *Commentary on Galatians* that one might have expected. Thus if we presume, as seems probable, that Pelagius did consult Augustine's *Commentary*, it does not appear that his attention was riveted by anything more than the occasional remark. Certainly he does not use Augustine in any sort of systematic or programmatic way.

[332] *c. Faust.* 11. 3 (my trans. of CSEL 25. 1: 317. 14–18).

[333] e.g. *De uirginibus uelandis* 5. 1–6. 1 (CCSL 2. 1213. 1–1215. 6).

[334] Both Jerome (*Comm. on Galatians* 4: 4 (PL 26: 372B) and the anonymous commentator (Gal 14A (Frede, *Ein neuer Paulustext und Kommentar*, ii. 227)) have the same interpretation as Augustine and Pelagius but not the same prooftext.

[335] Similarly Souter, *Earliest Latin Commentaries*, 194–5 and 228.

[336] *exp. Gal.* 46. 1.

[337] De Bruyn, *Pelagius' Commentary*, 16 n. 102 gives the following examples: *Comm. on Romans* 5: 10, 6: 19, 7: 15, 7: 17, 7: 18, 8: 3, 8: 7, and 8: 8.

[338] See the note attached to *exp. Gal.* 47. 1.

3

The Purpose of Augustine's
Commentary

A. ITS OSTENSIBLE PURPOSE

A first reading of Augustine's *Commentary* suggests that his purpose was simply to expound the meaning of the Letter to the Galatians line by line in a clear and concise manner. If so, then the central teaching of the *Commentary* should be the same as the central teaching of the Letter as Augustine understood it, and this is the natural implication of Augustine's opening sentence: 'The reason the Apostle writes to the Galatians is so they may understand what it is that God's grace accomplishes for them: they are no longer under the law' (1. 1). The relation of the law and grace will thus be the primary focus of attention. The Preface goes on explain the situation that called forth this Letter as a response: Certain 'Christians' of Jewish origin were telling the Galatians that the gospel would be of no benefit to them unless they submitted to circumcision and the other requirements of the law (1. 2). Peter himself had yielded to such people and been led into hypocrisy, for which Paul rebuked him (1. 4). Augustine proceeds to distinguish the situation reflected in the Letter to the Galatians from that reflected in Romans, where Augustine sees believers of Jewish origin and believers of Gentile origin as having been equally at fault and equally in need of Paul's correction (1. 5). In Galatians, however, it is believers of Jewish origin who are principally at fault (1. 6). Because of their propaganda, not only did Paul have to set the Galatians right about the truth of the gospel, he also had to re-establish his own apostolic authority, which the Judaizers had thrown into doubt (1. 3, 6–8).

Augustine's Preface creates in the reader's mind the expectation that the commentary to follow will be a straightforward exposition of Paul's meaning, and this expectation is largely fulfilled. Yet on closer examination Augustine's *Commentary* also contains emphases that differ from Paul's and comments that seem to diverge widely from the biblical text. How are these to be accounted for? Since Augustine wrote so much that was either implicitly or explicitly polemical in purpose, it is natural to inquire whether any of the emphases and apparent digressions in the *Commentary* should be regarded as polemical also.

B. ITS POLEMICAL PURPOSES

Maria Grazia Mara has argued that in addition to its ostensible purpose, Augustine's *Commentary* served as an implicit attack on various adversaries of the *truth of the gospel* (Gal. 2: 5) in Augustine's own time.[1] We have already noted Augustine's implicit polemic against Jerome's interpretation of Galatians 2: 11–14. We will now turn our attention to ways in which Augustine's *Commentary* may have served other polemical purposes. In particular we will consider whether and to what extent Augustine was deliberately opposing Manicheism, Donatism, Arianism, and paganism.

Augustine's *Commentary* and Manicheism

As a young man Augustine was an adherent of Manicheism for nearly a decade, and in that time he introduced many others to Manicheism. Partly to compensate for the damage he had done to the Catholic Church, partly to dispel lingering suspicions that he still held Manichean beliefs, Augustine resolved after his baptism in 387 to make the refutation of Manicheism one of his primary goals as an author. Between 387 and *c*.404 he published an immense body of work which is explicitly labelled 'anti-Manichean' (*contra Manicheos*) in the great list of his writings compiled after his death by Possidius.[2] But even if we accept these writings of Augustine as 'anti-Manichean' in a pre-eminent sense, there remain many others that deal with Manicheism in significant though secondary ways. Indeed, James J. O'Donnell has remarked that 'everything exegetical in [Augustine] down to 400 at least must be taken as having an anti-Manichean sub-text'.[3] We will now consider how far this judgement is borne out by the *Commentary on Galatians*. To define and describe Manicheism as Augustine understood

---

[1] Mara, 'Storia ed esegesi', 95–6.

[2] That list, called the *Elenchus* or *Indiculus*, classifies the following writings as anti-Manichean: *mor.*, *duab. an.*, *lib. arb.*, *c. Fort.*, *Gn. adu. Man.*, *c. ep. Man.*, *c. Adim.*, *c. Sec.*, *c. Fel.*, *nat. b.*, *c. Faust.*, *gr. t. nou.*, and sixteen of the questions in *diu. qu.* (Wilmart, *Operum*, 165–6).

[3] *Augustine: Confessions*, i. p. xlix n. 97.

it, however, would go well beyond the scope of this book.[4] For the purposes
of our discussion it will be sufficient to recall several Manichean doctrines
targeted by Augustine in his explicitly anti-Manichean works: its radical
dualism, according to which the material world is essentially evil; its moral
determinism, according to which our evil acts proceed inevitably from our
evil nature; its docetic Christology; and its utter rejection of the Old
Testament as the antithesis of the New.

   Paula Fredriksen has shown how Augustine's interpretation of Paul in
the mid-390s, and especially his interpretation of Paul's Letter to the
Romans, represents a new phase in his struggle against Manicheism.[5]
Hitherto, in such works as the Cassiciacum dialogues, the *De duabus
animabus*, and the first book of the *De libero arbitrio*, Augustine had
countered Manichean determinism by means of standard philosophical
arguments for free will. After becoming a parish priest, however, he
realized that this method of argumentation would be of little benefit to ordinary parishioners. African Manicheism was in a sense a 'Pauline' heresy,[6]
and so Augustine had to 'reclaim' Paul from the Manichees. In a superb
summary statement Fredriksen says:

The *Propositions from the Epistle to the Romans* and the *Unfinished Commentary on the
Epistle to the Romans* are the fruit of this phase of Augustine's campaign against the
Manichees, where he has to construct a synthetic, as well as polemical, reading of
the Apostle. Here he takes the issue they have set (the origin of evil and the nature
of man's will) and the hero they most used to support their claims (Paul), and
develops a hermeneutic that emphasizes man's moral autonomy while preserving
both the goodness of the Old Law and the gratuitous nature of God's grace.[7]

   [4] For such definition and description see e.g. Bonner, *St Augustine of Hippo*, 157–236, Lieu,
Manichaeism, 151–91, and the works by Decret listed in the Bibliography.
   [5] For the remainder of this paragraph I am dependent upon Fredriksen's own summary in
Augustine on Romans, p. ix.
   [6] The Manichees turned to Paul for a variety of reasons. One of them was that Paul's
tendency to express his views in terms of binary opposites (law/grace, flesh/spirit, light/
darkness) seemed to confirm their radical dualism. Another was their view that the Gospels are
highly unreliable, since '[these] writings are not the production of Christ or of His apostles,
but a compilation of rumors and beliefs, made, long after their departure, by some obscure
semi-Jews, not in harmony even with one another, and published by them under the name of
the apostles, or of those considered the followers of the apostles, so as to give the appearance of
apostolic authority to all these blunders and falsehoods' (the words of Faustus as quoted by
Augustine in *c. Faust.* 33. 3 (Stothert, trans., 342; CSEL 25. 1: 788. 17–23)). It is interesting
to note that the biography of the religion's founder, Mani, makes it clear that he understood
his vocation and mission in Pauline terms. On this point see Betz, 'Paul in the Mani
Biography', 217–22.
   [7] Fredriksen, *Augustine on Romans*, p. ix. She goes on to explain Augustine's reasoning:
'The Law . . . initiates the process of salvation by making man conscious of sin' (ibid. p. x).
Liberation from sin can come only by grace but human free will is not therefore otiose. In

When we turn to the *Commentary on Galatians*, the anti-Manichean element is clear.[8] The fact that the Manichees are nowhere named in this text should not startle us, for even in the *Propositions from Romans* the Manichees are named only once, and that parenthetically.[9] On the other hand, Augustine's failure to mention them makes it incumbent upon us to demonstrate with parallel passages from his explicitly anti-Manichean texts, including both compositions and transcripts of debates,[10] that when he appears to have the Manichees in mind in his *Commentary* he really does so. Thus when he refers in his *Commentary* to people who think that in Gal. 5: 17 Paul is 'denying that we have free choice of the will',[11] we may safely conclude that he has the Manichees in mind because the Manichee Fortunatus interpreted Gal. 5: 17 in precisely this way in his debate with Augustine in 392, and other evidence indicates that the Manichees in general interpreted it in this way.[12]

Other references are hardly less obvious. Thus in his comments on Gal. 1: 4, instead of discussing the weighty Christological formula (*who gave himself for our sins to deliver us from the present evil world*), as the reader might have expected, Augustine chooses to concentrate all his attention on explaining why Paul calls the present world *evil*: it is 'because of the evil people who live in it'.[13] This odd emphasis is best explained as a response to a fundamental tenet of Manichean dualism: that evil is 'an ineradicable force inherent in the physicality of the material world'.[14] Augustine also has

Augustine's words: 'By his free will man has a means to believe in the Liberator and to receive grace so that, with the liberating assistance of him who gives it, man might cease to sin' (*exp. prop. Rm.* 37 (44). 3). But what about God's choice of Jacob over Esau (Rom. 9: 11–13) and his hardening of Pharaoh's heart (Rom. 9: 17)? Augustine's answer (in Fredriksen's words) is that 'God justly elects those whom he foreknows will respond freely in faith to his call. . . . In this sense, then, man's free choice of faith determines his election' (*Augustine on Romans*, p. xi).

[8] Mara regards the Manichees as the principal opponents Augustine has in mind in this work. See 'Storia ed esegesi', esp. p. 100.

[9] *exp. prop. Rm.* 45 (53). 2–3: 'We should not think that [Rom. 8: 19–23] implies a sorrowing and sighing of trees and vegetables and stones and other suchlike creatures—for this is the error of the Manichees—nor should we think . . . ' (Fredriksen, trans., 23).

[10] The minutes of Augustine's debates with the Manichees Fortunatus and Felix are reproduced in *c. Fort.* and *c. Fel.* respectively.

[11] *exp. Gal.* 46. 1. Cf. 32. 13.

[12] *c. Fort.* 21 (CSEL 25. 1: 103. 13–17). That the Manichees in general did this is the clear implication of *cont.* 7. 18 (CSEL 41: 161. 6–17).

[13] *exp. Gal.* 3. 3.

[14] Chadwick, *Augustine*, 14. In Augustine's own words, in their account of the origin of the world the Manichees 'imagine that there is some evil in nature, which is derived and produced from a supposed "adverse first cause" of its own, [and] refuse to accept that the reason for the creation of the universe was God's good purpose to create good. They believe instead that God was compelled to the creation of the vast structure of this universe by the utter necessity of repelling the evil which fought against him, that he had to mingle the nature of his creating,

Manichean dualism in mind when he takes pains to point out that all things, without exception, serve divine providence.[15]

Augustine's attempts to vindicate the Old Testament[16] also need to be seen, at least in part, in the light of the Manichean critique of it that had so beguiled him in his youth. In the *Confessions* Augustine says that he had found the Manichean attack on the polygamy of the patriarchs so persuasive that to him the patriarchs, so far from being righteous, seemed to be self-evidently wicked.[17] Outside the *Confessions* he reports that Faustus specifically accused Abraham of acting out of lust in having a child by Hagar[18] and Sara of conniving at Abraham's adultery.[19] This provokes a sustained defence by Augustine in which he argues that both Abraham and Sara had in fact acted consistently with God's eternal law[20] that the wife has authority over her husband's body, as the husband has authority over hers (1 Cor. 7: 4). According to Augustine, when Sara was unable to have children of her own, she alienated her right over her husband's body to Hagar, with whom Abraham then had lawful intercourse for the sole purpose of procreation.[21] When we turn to the discussion of Abraham, Sara, and Hagar in the *Commentary on Galatians* we find Augustine following essentially the same line of argument and again using 1 Cor. 7: 4 as his hermeneutical key.[22]

The Manichees were also deeply offended at Moses for the curse he pronounced on Jesus when he said, *Cursed is everyone who hangs on a tree* (Deut. 21: 23).[23] Augustine responds by saying that Moses was speaking prophetically, knowing full well that for our sakes Christ would bear the

---

which was good, with the evil, which is to be suppressed and overcome, and that this good nature was thus so foully polluted, so savagely taken captive and oppressed, that it was only with the greatest toil that he can cleanse it and set it free. And even then he cannot rescue all of it, and the part which cannot be purified from that defilement is to serve as the prison to enclose the Enemy after his overthrow' (*ciu.* 11. 22; Bettenson, trans., 454; CCSL 48: 341. 32–43).

[15] *exp. Gal.* 32. 6–14. Cf. e.g. the following passages from the explicitly anti-Manichean writings: *mor.* 2. 7. 9–10; *nat. b.* 37.

[16] In addition to the examples given see *exp. Gal.* 22. 6 and 23. 5–7.

[17] *conf.* 3. 7. 12–13.

[18] *c. Faust.* 22. 30 (CSEL 25. 1: 624. 6–9).

[19] Ibid. 22. 31 (CSEL 25. 1: 624. 27–625. 2).

[20] 'aeterna lex' (CSEL 25. 1: 624. 3), defined earlier in the text as 'the divine order or will of God which requires the preservation of natural order and forbids the disruption of it' ('ratio diuina uel uoluntas dei ordinem naturalem conseruari iubens, perturbari uetans') (*c. Faust.* 22. 27 (Stothert, trans., 283 (modified); CSEL 25. 1: 621. 13–15)).

[21] Ibid. 22. 30–2 (CSEL 25. 1: 624–7). 1 Cor. 7: 4 is cited in *c. Faust.* 22. 31 (CSEL 25. 1: 625. 11–12).

[22] *exp. Gal.* 40. 12–18. 1 Cor. 7: 4 is cited in 40. 17.

[23] *c. Adim.* 21, *c. Faust.* 14, *c. Fel.* 2. 10–11.

curse pronounced on humanity following the sin of Adam. In other words, Moses foresaw that Christ would take upon himself our curse in order to do away with it. In addition to citing many passages from Paul, Augustine follows John 3: 14–15 in referring to Moses' prophetic action of placing the serpent on a pole, signifying that 'the real death into which the serpent by his fatal counsel cast mankind was hung on the cross of Christ's passion'.[24] When we turn to the *Commentary on Galatians* we find the same line of argument based upon the same prooftexts.[25]

The treatment of Moses, like the treatment of Abraham, Sara, and Hagar, illustrates Augustine's general tendency in his *Commentary on Galatians* and elsewhere to stress the continuity of the Old Testament with the New in order to ward off Manichean attempts to sever them. Thus Augustine insists that the two Testaments are inspired by the same Holy Spirit,[26] commend 'the same faith',[27] promulgate the same 'law of Christ',[28] bear witness to the same divine providence,[29] and reflect the same divine accommodation to human language.[30] A crucial part of Augustine's argument concerns the status of the legal requirements of the Old Testament. The Manichees scorned such requirements as circumcision and considered Catholics hypocrites for praising them without practising them.[31] In his reply to Faustus, Augustine accuses him of the grave hermeneutical error of failing to distinguish between the moral precepts of the Old Testament on the one hand and the symbolic precepts, or 'sacraments', on the other.[32] It is only the symbolic precepts, which prefigured Christ, that are no longer

[24] *c. Faust.* 14. 7 (Stothert, trans., 209; CSEL 25. 1: 409. 8–12: 'ad hoc pertinet et serpens ille in ligno suspensus, quo significaretur non falsam mortem Christum finxisse, sed illam ueram in ligno passionis suae suspendisse, in quam serpens ille hominem male suadendo deiecit').

[25] *exp. Gal.* 22. 3–17. Prooftexts: Num. 21: 9 and John 3: 14–15 are cited in *exp. Gal.* 22. 11–12, *c. Adim.* 21, *c. Faust.* 14. 7. Rom. 8: 3 is cited in *exp. Gal.* 22. 9, *c. Adim.* 21, *c. Faust.* 14. 5, 12. Rom. 6: 6 is cited in *exp. Gal.* 22. 10, *c. Adim.* 21, *c. Faust.* 14. 4, 12, *c. Fel.* 2. 11. Finally, 2 Cor. 5: 21 is cited in *exp. Gal.* 22. 9, *c. Faust.* 14. 5, 12.

[26] For Augustine's references to the activity of the Holy Spirit in the Old Testament see *exp. Gal.* 22. 6, 23. 6, 24. 15, and 40. 7.

[27] Ibid. 23. 5–24. 1 and 24. 12 (for 'the same faith' (*eadem fides*) see 24. 12 and cf. 23. 5). David is cited as an Old Testament example of Christian faith in *exp. Gal.* 43. 5–6, *c. Adim.* 17. 6, and *c. Faust.* 22. 66–7. (See also *c. Faust.* 12. 7: 'The whole contents of these Scriptures are either directly or indirectly about Christ' (Stothert, trans., 185; CSEL 25. 1: 335. 26–7: 'omnia, quae illis continentur libris, uel de ipso dicta sunt uel propter ipsum').)

[28] *exp. Gal.* 58. 1–3, 43. 2–3. Cf. *mor.* 1. 28. 57, *c. Faust.* 19. 7.

[29] *exp. Gal.* 24. 15. Cf. *c. Adim.* 9. 1.

[30] *exp. Gal.* 36. 2, 19. 7. Cf. *c. Adim.* 13. 2.

[31] *c. Faust.* 6. 1.

[32] *c. Faust.* 6. 2. On the gravity of Faustus' error in the judgement of Augustine, cf. Polman, *Word of God*, 113: 'His entire criticism of Faustus really amounted to the accusation that Faustus had failed to distinguish between moral and symbolic precepts.'

observed by Catholics, because they have been fulfilled once and for all by
the coming of Christ. Nevertheless, while Catholics do not practise them,
they continue to venerate them and to learn from them, since they were
given by God to prepare his people for the coming of Christ. Moral
precepts, however, continue to be binding. The fault of the Jews was not
their law but their inability to fulfil it owing to ignorance and sin. Thus both
moral and symbolic precepts relate to and find their fulfilment in Christ.
When we turn to the *Commentary on Galatians*, we find the same legal distinction being drawn between the moral and the sacramental.[33] The fault
lies not with the law, which is in fact spiritual, but rather with those who
interpret it in a carnal way[34] as if it referred to earthly rather than heavenly
rewards and punishments.[35] Hence their lives are driven by fear rather than
love and characterized by slavery rather than freedom.[36]

The desire to correct Manichean error is all the more intelligible when
we consider that Augustine was not the only former Manichee in his
monastic community at Hippo: Alypius was a former Manichee and
Profuturus and Fortunatus may well have been also.[41]

Augustine also defends the customs ordained in the Old Testament
against the attacks of Faustus by citing the practice of Paul, including his
circumcision of Timothy (Acts 16: 1–3).[37] Paul circumcised Timothy even
though Christ had already fulfilled what circumcision prophetically
signified.[38] The reason he did so was to avoid scandalizing the Jews among
whom he and Timothy would be working. Since Timothy's mother was
Jewish it was appropriate for him to be circumcised in order to show that
Jewish customs were honourable, unlike those of the Gentiles. Thus Paul
considered that there was nothing wrong with Jewish customs in and of
themselves. What was wrong was placing one's hope of salvation in them.[39]
The same points may be found in the *Commentary on Galatians*.[40]

The desire to correct Manichean error is all the more intelligible when
we consider that Augustine was not the only former Manichee in his
monastic community at Hippo: Alypius was a former Manichee and
Profuturus and Fortunatus may well have been also.[41]

---

[33] *exp. Gal.* 19 and 44.

[34] Ibid. 7. 2–4, 34. 5.

[35] Ibid. 43. 2, cf. 46.

[36] Ibid. 20. 7–8; 21. 1–2, 7; 22. 5–6, 18; 42. 7; 43. 3, 8.

[37] *c. Faust.* 19. 17. Cf. *exp. Gal.* 11. 1; 41. 6; 63. 1.

[38] *c. Faust.* 19. 17. Earlier Augustine had stated the significance of circumcision:
'Circumcision was the type of the removal of our fleshly nature, which was fulfilled in the
resurrection of Christ, and which the sacrament of baptism teaches us to look forward to in our
own resurrection' (*c. Faust.* 19. 9 (Stothert, trans., 242; CSEL 25. 1: 507. 9–12)).

[39] Ibid. 19. 7; *c. Adim.* 16. 2.

[40] Cf. *exp. Gal.* 11. 2; 41. 5–7; 42. 6; 54. 5; 63. 1–4.

[41] Alypius as a Manichee: *conf.* 6. 7. 12 (CCSL 27: 82. 49–54). Profuturus and Fortunatus
were charged with having been Manichees by Petilian: *un. bapt.* 16. 29 (CSEL 53: 31. 12–15).
The charge is accepted as true by Frend, *The Donatist Church*, 236, but rejected as false by
Mandouze, *Prosopographie*, 495, 928–9.

On the other hand, to read the *Commentary* as an anti-Manichean work is to be struck by the opportunities that Augustine does not take. Thus Augustine does not use Gal. 4: 4 (*God sent his Son, made of a woman*) to affirm the reality of Christ's birth in the face of the Manichees' denial of it, as he does on two separate occasions in his refutation of Faustus.[42] Instead, his polemical thrust is directed, first, against those who would deny Mary's virginity[43] and, secondly, against the Arians.[44] Again, in the *Commentary* the worship of the sun and moon is associated only with the Gentiles, whereas in the *Contra Faustum* Augustine says that the Manichean worship of the sun and moon is far worse than that of the Gentiles.[45] Finally we may consider Augustine's comment on Gal. 1: 15, where Paul speaks of *God, who separated me from my mother's womb*: 'One is separated, so to speak, from one's mother's womb by being parted from the blind custom of one's carnal parents.' Unlike our other Latin commentators, Augustine makes no mention of the idea that it is God who causes human beings to be born physically—an idea that the Manichees repudiated as unworthy of God. Not only does Augustine fail to take this opportunity to counter the Manichees, but his own interpretation is one the Manichees would have endorsed wholeheartedly. Indeed, Augustine himself records Faustus as having commented on Gal. 1: 15 in these words: 'It is plain that everywhere [Paul] speaks of the second or spiritual birth as that in which we are made by God, as distinct from the indecency of the first birth, in which we are on a level with other animals as regards dignity and purity, as we are conceived in the maternal womb, and are formed, and brought forth' (*c. Faust.* 24. 1).[46]

Such failures to apply anti-Manichean polemics consistently and thoroughly do not invalidate our earlier claims that there are anti-Manichean elements in the text. Indeed, the term 'failures' may be thought biased. Perhaps what I have termed 'failures' are mere accidental omissions in a text that deliberately aims at brevity and conciseness. Nevertheless,

[42] *c. Faust.* 11. 3 and 23. 7.

[43] *exp. Gal.* 30. 2.

[44] Ibid. 30. 3.

[45] Ibid. 32. 14; *c. Faust.* 20. 1–8.

[46] Stothert, trans., 318; CSEL 25. 1: 720. 20–4: 'uides ergo ubique eum in hac altera natiuitate nostra, spiritali dumtaxat adseuerantem nos a deo formari, non in priore illa obscaena ac propudiosa, quae nos nihilo praestantius neque mundius animalibus ceteris in utero materno et concepit et formauit et genuit.' Relevant also are Augustine's own words earlier, in *c. Faust.* 15. 7: 'The first of these commandments [i.e. the seven commandments relating to the love of neighbour] is, "Honour your father and your mother;" which Paul quotes as the first commandment with promise, and himself repeats the injunction. But you are taught by your demonic doctrine to regard your parents as your enemies, because their union brought you into the bonds of flesh, and placed impure fetters even on your god' (Stothert, trans., 216 (modified); CSEL 25. 1: 429. 16–22).

whether we regard them as failures or accidents, we must at least be hesitant
about supposing that the *Commentary on Galatians* is directed principally
or even largely against the Manichees.

Augustine's *Commentary* and Donatism

What has not, to my knowledge, been previously considered is the possibility that Augustine's *Commentary on Galatians* was shaped in part by
the Donatist controversy. There has been a long tradition of viewing
Augustine's career as a controversialist as falling into three main periods:
the anti-Manichean, the anti-Donatist, and the anti-Pelagian.[47] The anti-
Donatist period would then be roughly the years from 400 to 411, when the
Donatist controversy absorbed the bulk of his energies and when his most
important works against the Donatists were composed, beginning with his
treatise *Against the Letter of Parmenianus* in 400.[48] Now while this tripartite
schema has proved very serviceable as a way of bringing different aspects
of Augustine's work into sharper focus, it is after all merely a tool for the
scholar and hardly reflects the depth and complexity of Augustine's mind.
Even though no major works against Donatism have survived from
Augustine's presbyterate, this too was a period of vigorous engagement
with the Donatists, whom Augustine already viewed as posing a formidable
threat to the life of the Catholic Church at Hippo and beyond.[49]

It is therefore both desirable and necessary to consider whether and to
what extent Donatism may have influenced the way Augustine reads the
Letter to the Galatians. If we compare Augustine's *Commentary* with other
writings of his from this period that deal explicitly with Donatism,
especially his *Psalm against the Donatists*,[50] we find a number of significant
parallels. A notable theme is that of the Church's catholicity, defined in
terms of extension throughout the world.[51] The source of the Church's
catholicity is the Father's promise to the Son in Ps. 2: 8: *Ask of me, and I will
give you the Gentiles for your inheritance, and the ends of the earth for your
possession.*[52] This definition of the Church's catholicity and the use of Ps. 2:

[47] Cf. Bonner, *St Augustine of Hippo*, 133.

[48] Cf. Frend, *The Donatist Church*, 228.

[49] For evidence of Augustine's vigorous engagement with the Donatists during his
presbyterate and immediately following see Appendix 4.

[50] Further details on the Augustinian texts cited here and their background are given in
Appendix 4.

[51] *exp. Gal.* 24. 13; *ps. c. Don.* 203–4, 287; *agon.* 29. 31; *ep.* 23. 2, 4; *ep.* 35. 3; *s.* 273. 2; *en. Ps.*
10. 4; *en. Ps.* 21. s. 2. 1–2, 24, 26, 28–9, 31. The Donatists, by contrast, defined catholicity in
terms of the fullness of the sacraments (see *breuic.* 3. 3. 3).

[52] Either quoted or alluded to in *exp. Gal.* 18. 2; *ep.* 23. 2, 4; *agon.* 29. 31; *en. Ps.* 21. s. 2. 30.

8 to support it almost certainly derive from Optatus of Mileu,[53] who served as Augustine's sole source for the *Psalm against the Donatists*.[54]

An even more notable theme, for which Augustine is indebted to both Optatus and Cyprian, is that of the unity of the Church.[55] Disunity is caused and sustained by pride,[56] which refuses to accept correction.[57] No one should claim to be righteous, for all are sinners,[58] even Peter.[59] God shows no partiality, nor should we.[60] What matters is not the messenger but the message.[61] Love should be the primary motive of Christian action.[62]

In the *Commentary* the theme of unity is highlighted in Augustine's interpretation of the famous dispute between Peter and Paul at Antioch, where Paul rebuked Peter for behaving inconsistently and causing the Gentile Christians to believe they had to accept circumcision and the law in order to be saved. Augustine says that Peter acknowledged having done wrong and, in order to undo that wrong, humbly accepted a public rebuke at the hands of Paul. This shows that Peter regarded the preservation of Church unity to be of paramount importance. Later Augustine will make his exegesis of this passage in Galatians crucial to his argument in his treatise *On Baptism, against the Donatists*. There can be no doubt that the Donatists were already on his mind when he worked out his argument for the first time in the *Commentary*.[63]

In addition to common themes there are common biblical phrases and images, most notably that of the wheat and chaff on the threshing floor (Matt. 3: 12 // Luke 3: 17).[64] Augustine was later to say that this image was a trusty weapon in his struggle with the Donatists.[65]

[53] I am grateful to Henry Chadwick for pointing out to me that 'Milevis' as the name of the town is modern fiction: the ancient inscriptions in *Corpus Inscriptionum Latinarum* VIII. 1 have 'Mileu' or 'MILEV'.

[54] For the Church's catholicity defined in terms of extension throughout the world see Optatus 2. 1. 3–13 (SC 412: 236–42); 2. 9. 4 (SC 412: 260–2); 2. 11. 1–13. 3 (SC 412: 264–6); 3. 2. 8 (SC 413: 16–18); 4. 3. 3 (SC 413: 86); 7. 5. 1 (SC 413: 234). For Ps. 2: 8 as a prooftext see Optatus, 2. 1. 5–7 (SC 412: 238–40). On Optatus as Augustine's sole source for the *ps. c. Don.* see Monceaux, *Histoire littéraire*, vii. 82–3. A new translation of Optatus by Mark Edwards is listed below in the Bibliography.

[55] *exp. Gal.* 13. 5–7; 24. 13; 28. 1–30. 1; 31; *ps. c. Don.* 4–5, 44, 60–1, 71, 167, 187, 198, 224, 292; *en. Ps.* 10. 7; *en. Ps.* 21. s. 2. 19, 31; *en. Ps.* 54. 26.

[56] *exp. Gal.* 1. 5; 25. 1–10; 55; *ps. c. Don.* 21–3, 54–8, 99, 123, 213; *ep.* 23. 3, 5; *en. Ps.* 10. 7.

[57] *exp. Gal.* 15. 6–17; *ps. c. Don.* 120–3.   [58] *ps. c. Don.* 22, 37.

[59] *exp. Gal.* 1. 4; 12. 3; 13. 1–3; 15. 6–9; *ps. c. Don.* 28–9.

[60] *exp. Gal.* 12. 1–4; 13. 1–3; *ps. c. Don.* 2.

[61] *exp. Gal.* 4. 6; 5. 1–6 and 10; 12. 2–3; 13. 1–2; *ps. c. Don.* 207–8; *en. Ps.* 10. 6; *en. Ps.* 35. 9.

[62] *exp. Gal.* 8. 4; 15. 9, 11; 43. 5–6; 44–5; *ps. c. Don.* 103, 109, 125.

[63] Cf. section 2. B, beginning at n. 291 in the text.

[64] *exp. Gal.* 26. 3; 28. 8; *ps. c. Don.* 146, 178–9, 199, 213–14, 260; *ep.* 23. 6, *s.* 252. 5; *en. Ps.* 10. 4; *en. Ps.* 21. s. 2. 1; *en. Ps.* 25. s. 2. 6.

[65] *gest. Pel.* 12. 27: 'The objection was made to Pelagius that he said, "The Church on earth

But while Donatism is thus necessary for an understanding of the *Commentary on Galatians,* it is not sufficient. Why, for instance, didn't Augustine go to town on the passage in Galatians 3 on baptism, where Paul insists that there can be no distinction among those who have been baptized, for all are one in Christ Jesus? Clearly Donatism is not the key that will open all doors.

Augustine's *Commentary* and Arianism

Arianism, which affirmed that the Son of God was not God by nature but a created being, is often said to have emerged as a central concern for Augustine only later in his life when it became a pastoral problem, especially after his reception in 418 of an anonymous Arian sermon that was being circulated at Hippo.[66] Augustine had, however, personally encountered Arianism previously in Milan in 386, during the conflict between Ambrose and the Arian empress, Justina, who demanded that Ambrose surrender one of his churches for Arian worship. Ambrose and his congregation resisted her demands by staging a sit-in in which Augustine's own mother played a conspicuous role.[67] Augustine must also have heard Ambrose preach against Arianism at this time. When we turn to the time of Augustine's priesthood, we find a clear reference to the Arians, though they are not named, in his *Faith and the Creed* of 393, where Augustine speaks against 'those . . . who say that the Son is a creature, though not as the other creatures'.[68] Similarly in a text contemporaneous with the *Commentary on Galatians* Augustine speaks against 'those who contend that the Son of God is not equal to the Father'.[69] The references in the *Commentary* are less polemical and the Arians are again not named, but almost all of what Augustine says about the person of Christ derives from a tradition refined by controversy with Arians. On the other hand, it is difficult to say with certainty of any single statement that Augustine intended it to be anti-Arian. His intention may simply have been to affirm the Creed. For this reason such statements will be discussed below in the section entitled 'Scripture and the Rule of Faith'.[70]

is without stain or wrinkle." On this point the Donatists also had a long debate with us in a conference we held. But we pressed them hard regarding bad people being mixed with the good, like chaff with the wheat, on account of the comparison with a threshing floor' (Teske, trans., 353 (modified)).

[66] The anonymous Arian sermon is prefixed to Augustine's reply in *c. s. Arrian.* (PL 42). It should be noted, however, that the first seven books (at least) of *trin.* are deeply anti-Arian, and Augustine began writing this work in 399.   [67] *conf.* 9. 7. 15.

[68] *f. et symb.* 4. 5 (Burleigh, trans., 356).   [69] *diu. qu.* 69. 1 (Mosher, trans., 166).

[70] In section 4. B, immediately after n. 55 in the text.

Augustine's *Commentary* and Paganism

Augustine says that Christ's *being made a curse for us* (Gal. 3: 13) is a 'veil of blindness' to pagans or heretics who take it in a carnal sense (22. 3).[71] Although Augustine speaks elsewhere of Christians being taunted for their belief in a cursed and crucified Messiah, this kind of attack was not limited to Augustine's time but was perennial.

Perhaps a more specific historical reference lies behind Augustine's comment on the word *idolatry* in Gal. 5: 20: 'Now *idolatry* is the ultimate fornication—that of the soul. Because of it war marked by the most intense fury has been waged against the gospel and against those reconciled to God, and the remains of this war, though comparatively cool for a long time now, are warming up again.'[72] Here Augustine may have in mind the recrudescence of pagan–Christian conflict in North Africa during this period.

Most of what Augustine has to say against paganism, however, pertains to practices engaged in by his own parishioners, especially astrology. For this reason it will be more appropriate to consider Augustine's remarks on paganism as part of the *Commentary*'s pastoral purpose.[73]

C. THE PASTORAL PURPOSE OF AUGUSTINE'S *COMMENTARY*

Perhaps the single most important consideration to bear in mind when reading this text is that Augustine is writing as a priest and monk. This consideration is especially important because there has been a tendency in the past to minimize it, for reasons that are not hard to find. To begin with, the period of Augustine's priesthood was brief and yielded no major works, in vivid contrast to his long and astonishingly fruitful episcopate, while the period leading up to his conversion has benefited from the perennial fascination of the *Confessions*. Even more than his priesthood, however, Augustine's monastic life has suffered from scholarly neglect, prompting George Lawless to comment that 'Augustine's persevering response to the monastic calling . . . is possibly the most underrated facet of his personality.'[74] This neglect stems largely from the fact that Augustine

---

[71] Many pagans were conversant with the Scriptures. Cf. *cat. rud.* 8. 12.

[72] *exp. Gal.* 51. 5.

[73] Other references to paganism may be found at *exp. Gal.* 32. 2–14, 33. 1, 34. 2, and 41. 4.

[74] Lawless, *Monastic Rule*, 161.

wrote so little about his monastic life. After all, most of his monastic business was taken care of by speaking directly with his fellow monks. In addition, the authenticity of the most relevant document, the monastic rule associated with his name, has only recently been established on a scientific basis.[75] It is hardly surprising therefore that the image of Augustine as a monk-priest has largely been eclipsed in academic circles by images of Augustine as a speculative theologian, a 'hammer of heretics', and so on. Yet unless the image of the monk-priest is kept in mind we are liable to address the wrong questions to the text and to evaluate it by the wrong standards. This may seem obvious, but even a scholar as careful and judicious as J. B. Lightfoot failed adequately to appreciate Augustine's *Commentary on Galatians* for this reason, and the tone of his review is one of disappointment: 'Spiritual insight, though a far diviner gift than the critical faculty, will not supply its place. In this faculty Augustine was wanting, and owing to this defect, as a continuous expositor he is disappointing. With great thoughts here and there, his commentary on the Galatians is inferior as a whole to several of the patristic expositions.'[76] The dominant standard by which Lightfoot judged Augustine's *Commentary* was doubtless the Galatians commentary of Jerome, and if that is the standard then the judgement is fair. But what if Augustine failed to conform to that standard not so much from inability as from deliberate choice? This in fact will be our contention—that Augustine's purpose in commenting on Galatians was very different from Jerome's and cannot be adequately understood apart from the context of Augustine's priestly and monastic life. In order to set Augustine's *Commentary* in that context, further biographical analysis is necessary, beginning with a sketch of the development of Augustine's monastic vocation up to the time he composed the *Commentary*.

Augustine's monastic vocation may be traced back even prior to his conversion, though it was then inchoate and obscure. In Book 6 of the *Confessions* he speaks of the desire he shared with his friends to form a contemplative community.[77] Although that desire came to nothing at the time, it shows that Augustine was attracted to a philosophical ideal that was then widespread.[78] The monastic ideal became a major precipitating factor in Augustine's conversion when he was moved by the stories Ponticianus told about the Egyptian monk Antony, about the monastery on the outskirts of

---

[75] The greatest single contribution to the establishment of its authenticity was Luc Verheijen's monumental *La Règle de saint Augustin*. For a concise summary of the history of the problem see Lawless, *Monastic Rule*, 121–35.   [76] Lightfoot, *Galatians*, 233.

[77] *conf.* 6. 14. 24.

[78] Lawless, *Monastic Rule,* 5.

Milan fostered by Ambrose, and about two colleagues of Ponticianus' who had suddenly decided 'to serve God' and take up the monastic life at Trier.[79] In the aftermath of his conversion, Augustine himself chose 'to serve God'[80] and so resigned his position as professor of rhetoric in Milan. Whatever faults Augustine may have found later with the writings he produced during his long retreat at Cassiciacum,[81] his time there helped to clarify and strengthen his resolve. His monastic vocation came into still sharper focus after his baptism: 'We were together and by a holy decision resolved to live together. We looked for a place where we could be of most use in your service [*seruientes tibi*]; all of us agreed on a move back to Africa.'[82]

When, however, his return was delayed, Augustine sojourned in Rome for nine months and deliberately deepened his knowledge of monasticism through conversation, reading,[83] and visits to monastic communities.[84] His laudatory description of Pachomian[85] monasticism foreshadows many aspects of the life he will adopt in Africa.[86] He speaks of 'those who, despising and denying themselves the attractions of the world, and living together in perfect chastity and holiness, pass their time in prayer, reading, and spiritual conference. . . . None of them possesses anything of his own; no one is a burden to others.'[87]

After returning to Africa from Rome in the late summer of 388,[88] Augustine established a small monastic community in his home town of Thagaste.[89] Peter Brown offers a glimpse of what Augustine's life may have been like by his third year there:

---

[79] *conf.* 8. 6. 14–15 ('deo seruire': CCSL 27: 123. 71).

[80] Ibid. 9. 5. 13 (CCSL 27: 140. 2–3: 'quod et tibi ego seruire delegissem'). The phrase 'to serve God' carries special significance. Cf. Augustine's words in *ciu.* 22. 8 about his status at the time of his return to Africa in 388: 'For when I came with my brother Alypius from overseas, when we were not yet ordained though already servants of God . . .' (Bettenson, trans., 1035; CCSL 48: 816. 48–9: 'Venientes enim de transmarinis me et fratrem meum Alypium, nondum quidem clericos, sed iam Deo seruientes . . .'). Zumkeller, *Augustine's Ideal*, 19 n. 33, remarks that in *op. mon.*, a work written close in time to *conf.*, Augustine uses the phrase 'deo seruire' precisely to mean 'to become a monk'.

[81] He says in *conf.* 9. 4. 7 that the books he wrote there 'still breathe the spirit of the school of pride' (Chadwick, trans., 159).

[82] *conf.* 9. 8. 17 (Chadwick, trans., 166 (CCSL 27: 143. 4–6)).

[83] Coyle, *Augustine's 'De Moribus'*, 211–14, argues that Augustine had certainly read Jerome's *ep.* 22 to Eustochium. Lawless, *Monastic Rule*, 42, is sceptical.

[84] For visits, see *mor.* 1. 33. 70.

[85] See Coyle, *Augustine's 'De Moribus'*, 230 n. 888.

[86] Lawless, *Monastic Rule*, 40.

[87] *mor.* 1. 31. 67 (Gallagher and Gallagher, trans., 51).

[88] See Perler, *Les Voyages*, 147–8, 432.

[89] See Lawless, *Monastic Rule*, 45–58.

In the year before he was made a priest in Hippo, Augustine may already have tried to fill out his life—to organize his community, to found the personal relations within it upon a permanent code of behaviour, to be responsible for the spiritual well-being of many other people, and to exercise some real measure of authority over them. As a result, the group of like-minded enthusiasts that had gathered around him in his retirement, came, by slow and subtle stages, to resemble a 'monastery', with Augustine as a 'spiritual father'.[90]

Possidius speaks of Augustine as 'giving himself to God in a life of fasting, prayer and good works, and "meditating on God's Law day and night" (Ps. 1: 2). And what God revealed to his understanding as he reflected and prayed, he taught by sermons to those who were with him and by books to those who were not.'[91] At Thagaste his writings included a philosophical dialogue (*The Teacher*), a brilliant defence of the Christian faith against pagans and heretics (*On True Religion*), and his first work of scriptural exegesis (*On Genesis, against the Manichees*). During this time he also began composing answers to a variety of philosophical, theological, and exegetical questions posed 'by my brethren whenever they saw that I had the time'[92]—a further indication of Augustine's role as spiritual and intellectual leader. These answers were kept in the monastic library and later collected and published as the *Eighty-three Different Questions*. In addition to these writings, his correspondence was a kind of extension of community life to those not physically present, especially to his beloved friend Nebridius, whose ill-health prevented him from leaving Carthage and joining the community at Thagaste.[93] The same may be said even of his letters to married correspondents such as Antoninus, to whom he wrote these words:

I send kindest greetings to your little son, and I hope he will grow up in the practice of the saving precepts of the Lord. I pray earnestly for the members of your household that they may progress in the one faith and true devotion, which is found only in the Catholic religion. If you feel the need of my or any other help in this matter, in the name of the Lord and our mutual affection, do not hesitate to ask it.[94]

---

[90]   Brown, *Augustine of Hippo*, 135–6.

[91]   Possidius, *Vita* 3. 2 (Hoare, trans., 197). For the Latin *sermonibus* (here translated 'sermons') 'conversations' would be equally good.

[92]   *retr.* 1. 26 (25). 1 (Bogan, trans., 106). Mosher, in the Introduction to his translation of *diu. qu.*, argues that Questions 1–50 are probably to be dated to 388–91 (Mosher, trans., 10–20).

[93]   The extant African (as opposed to Italian) correspondence between Augustine and Nebridius comprises *epp.* 5–14. On Nebridius's illness, see *ep.* 10. 1. Like the brethren, Nebridius loved posing difficult questions (cf. e.g. *ep.* 11. 2).

[94]   *ep.* 20. 3 (Parsons, trans., 47 (CSEL 34. 1: 48. 20–5)).

The sensitivity of Augustine's letters and the range of his correspondents show that letter writing was for him a kind of ministry, as he himself would soon call it.[95]

His growing reputation, however, contributed to the sudden ending of his life as a layman, for on a visit to Hippo in 391 to establish a monastery there he was chosen by popular acclaim to become a priest and assist the ageing Bishop Valerius.[96] Ordination marked a turning point in Augustine's life nearly as great as that of his conversion. He was now a public figure at Hippo, being groomed to succeed Valerius as bishop. In 393 he was summoned to address the Catholic bishops assembled at the Council of Hippo. The significance of this event is brought out by Bonner: 'In view of the fact that Augustine was a priest of less than three years' standing and of the African tradition against priests preaching in the presence of a bishop, no more generous tribute could have been paid to his qualities by the African episcopate than this command to address an important provincial council.'[97] In one sense Augustine had deliberately and unrepentantly sought publicity and honour, not for his own sake 'but for the sake of those whom he could not help if he were to lose dignity by too great self-depreciation'.[98] In order to be able to preach and teach with authority he sought to secure his reputation by a variety of means, including seeking the patronage of eminent persons.

Despite all this he remained a monk. When he was ordained priest, he requested and was granted permission to build a monastery in the cathedral grounds at Hippo.[99] Some of the monks came over from Thagaste to join Augustine; others stayed behind to carry on the monastic life there.[100] So there was continuity as well as discontinuity when Augustine became a priest, and that is why his monasticism as well as his priesthood must be kept in mind when considering the *Commentary on Galatians*. In fact, as priest Augustine had pastoral responsibilites not only for those outside the monastery but also for those within it. As the only priest in this monastic community Augustine served as spiritual director and as disciplinarian.[101] Nevertheless, for the purposes of our analysis it will be useful to draw a distinction and to ask where Augustine has his fellow monks chiefly in mind and where he has his parishioners chiefly in mind. This will help us to see

[95] 'officium litterarum' (*ep.* 23. 1 (CSEL 34. 1: 63. 11)).
[96] *s.* 355. 2.
[97] Bonner, *St Augustine of Hippo*, 115.
[98] *ep.* 22. 2. 7 (Parsons, trans., 55 (CSEL 34. 1: 59. 22–3)).
[99] *s.* 355. 2. Possidius, *Vita* 5.
[100] Zumkeller, *Augustine's Ideal*, 36 and 60 n. 96.
[101] Cf. Lawless, *Monastic Rule*, 159.

both groups clearly and enable us to say with confidence that each group really is a focus of attention.

We may begin by examining evidence that Augustine's intended audience includes his fellow monks. We have already noted that for many years the monks had been in the habit of addressing questions to Augustine, their spiritual and intellectual leader, on various philosophical and theological topics. After Augustine became a bishop his answers were gathered together and published as the *Eighty-three Different Questions*. Questions 66–75 deal with the letters of Paul and were undoubtedly written at much the same time as Augustine's Pauline commentaries.[102] Thus it is reasonable to ask whether the *Commentary on Galatians* arose in a similar setting.[103]

In fact, in various parts of the commentary we can almost hear the questions the brethren must have posed to Augustine. Thus, with regard to Paul's statement in Galatians 1 that he went to Jerusalem to visit Peter, Augustine seems to be answering the question, 'Why did Paul visit Peter, unless he needed to learn the gospel from him?' (*exp. Gal.* 8. 4). In the same chapter Paul calls James 'the brother of the Lord'—in what sense is he the Lord's 'brother'? (8. 5). In Galatians 5 why does Paul say the love of neighbour fulfils the law, and not love of God and neighbour together? (45. 1). Isn't Paul denying free will when he says in Gal. 5: 17 that because of the opposition between the spirit and the flesh we *cannot* do what we want? (46. 1). Even more revealing than the kinds of questions Augustine addresses are the subjects on which he lavishes his greatest care and attention. His treatment of fraternal correction (*exp. Gal.* 57, on Gal. 6: 1), for example, stands out because of its pastoral sensitivity and psychological depth. Its recommendations appear to be directed not to spiritual beginners but to those who are spiritually advanced. A similar audience is presupposed in Augustine's discussion of Gal. 6: 2 in Question 71 of the *Eighty-three Different Questions*. In fact, if the discussion of Gal. 6: 2 in Question 71 is read immediately after the discussion of Gal. 6: 1 in the *Commentary*, it follows even more smoothly and naturally than the discussion of Gal. 6: 2 in the *Commentary* itself. If, as Zumkeller insists, Question 71 is addressed to

[102] Bardy, BA 10, pp. 30–6.

[103] It is interesting to compare what Augustine says about the origin of *exp. prop. Rm.*, written immediately prior to *exp. Gal.*: 'While I was still a priest, we who were together in Carthage at the time happened to read the Apostle's Letter to the Romans, and after some of the brethren asked me certain questions which I answered to the best of my ability, they wanted to have my answers set down in writing rather than merely spoken' (*retr.* 1. 23 (22). 1 (my trans., based on that of Bogan, 96; CCSL 57: 66. 3–67. 7)). Perler, however, cautions against simply assuming without question that by 'my brethren' Augustine means his fellow monks from Hippo (*Les Voyages*, 162).

the monks at Hippo,[104] it is hard to avoid the conclusion that the discussion of Gal. 6: 1 in the *Commentary* is addressed to them also.

Further light is thrown on the character and purpose of Augustine's *Commentary* by comparing it with his monastic *Rule*,[105] which he probably wrote down for the lay monastery at Hippo shortly after his ordination as bishop[106]—in other words, not long after the *Commentary*. But even if the *Rule* is thus to be dated *c*.397, the principles of communal living it enshrines must have been established long before this, inasmuch as Augustine had been living in community since his return to Africa in 388. So, in large part if not in its entirety, the *Rule* may be regarded as predating the *Commentary*. This rather obvious inference will have important ramifications as our discussion proceeds.

What I wish to concentrate on first are the great themes the two documents share. A central concern in both, not surprisingly, is how to maintain harmony within the community (*Rule* 1. 2). Though Christians come from different backgrounds, they are all equal in the unity of the faith (*exp. Gal.* 28. 1–5). Commenting on Gal. 2: 6 Augustine argues that those *who are reputed to be something* (*qui videntur esse aliquid*) are so reputed only by 'carnal people', for *God does not consider a person's standing* (*exp. Gal.* 12. 1–3, 13. 1–3). Similarly in his *Rule* Augustine reminds the monks that those 'who were reputed to be something in the world' (qui aliquid esse uidebantur in saeculo) should not pride themselves on that fact (*Rule* 1. 7)[107]; a person's former standing in the world is of no account (*Rule* 1. 6–7). Such differences as are acknowledged are acknowledged only as necessary concessions to human weakness (*Rule* 3. 3–5, cf. 1. 3–5; *exp. Gal.* 28. 1–5); they should not give rise to jealousy or envy, which threaten to destroy the harmony of the community (*Rule* 3. 3–5, 5. 1; *exp. Gal.* 12. 1, 45. 8, 52. 2–4). Honour is due not to a person but to God in that person (*Rule* 1. 8, 7. 1; *exp. Gal.* 5. 10, 12. 2, 13. 1–2), and pleasing God must always take precedence

---

[104] Zumkeller, *Augustine's Ideal*, 307.

[105] My terminology derives from Lawless, who in turn follows Verheijen (see Lawless, *Monastic Rule*, 65–9). Thus by the *Rule* I am referring specifically to what Verheijen called in Latin the *Praeceptum*. In accepting the authenticity of this text I am following Lawless, ibid. 127–35. Finally, unless indicated otherwise, the text and translation of the *Rule* are quoted from Lawless, ibid. 80–103.

[106] Verheijen, *Augustine's Monasticism*, 45–52. Verheijen finds 'quite plausible' N. Merlin's opinion as to the date of composition: 'It is at a time when, already a bishop, he was preparing to leave the first monastery at Hippo to go to the bishop's residence, that Saint Augustine must have composed the Rule, so as to make up by this written document for his personal absence' (Merlin, *Saint Augustin et la vie monastique*, 27, quoted ibid. 45–6). For a survey of opinions on the date of the *Rule* see Lawless, *Monastic Rule*, 148–52.

[107] My trans.

over pleasing human beings (*Rule* 4. 5; *exp. Gal.* 5. 3–10, 59. 5). In a Christian community the individual good should yield to the common good, the transient to the eternal (*Rule* 5. 2; *exp. Gal.* 17. 6),[108] for Christians are not under the law but under grace (*Rule* 8. 1; *exp. Gal.* 17. 4–10).

Augustine believed that true Christian fellowship could only be realized through spiritual love, the gift of the Holy Spirit. One of the most difficult yet necessary ways in which that love is expressed is by the correction of another person.[109] This theme represents the most important coincidence between the *Rule* and the *Commentary*, and is treated repeatedly and at length in both (*Rule* 4. 7–11, 6. 1–3, 7. 2–3; *exp. Gal.* 1. 4, 15. 6–14, 18. 1, 35. 1–8, 39. 1–2, 43. 6, 56. 1–57. 17, 59. 3). For Augustine, there is no test of our spirituality quite like our handling of another's sin (*exp. Gal.* 56. 1). A delicate balance must be struck between firmness and gentleness. Correction may have to be severe, as when a person must be charged publicly with an offence (*Rule* 4. 9; *exp. Gal.* 15. 8–9) or even expelled from the community (*Rule* 4. 9; *exp. Gal.* 32. 9–10). Although it may have to be harsh, correction can and should always proceed from love (*Rule* 6. 3, cf. 4. 8–10; *exp. Gal.* 57. 1–5). Augustine is aware of how difficult and unpleasant it often is to administer a harsh rebuke and likens it to performing surgery on an unwilling patient (*Rule* 4. 8; *exp. Gal.* 56. 14–17): however unpleasant it may be to surgeon and patient alike, the procedure must be carried out. Severity is not cruel but kind if it prevents another from perishing (*Rule* 4. 8–9; *exp. Gal.* 56. 16–17).

There are some, however, who engage in confrontation and correction for the wrong reasons. Augustine offers this guidance: 'We should never undertake the task of rebuking another's sin without first examining our own conscience by inner questioning and then responding—unequivocally before God—that we are acting out of love' (*exp. Gal.* 57. 1). Sometimes we might take this test and pass it only to find that once we begin correcting the sinner he or she responds with anger or abuse or in some other way hurts our feelings. But the minute we begin to feel hostility towards the sinner we should step back until we ourselves are healed. However frustrating such an experience may be, it can provide a very beneficial lesson in humility if we realize that in the very act of correcting someone else's sin we ourselves sin, 'when we find it easier to respond to the sinner's anger with our own anger than to the sinner's misery with our mercy'.[110]

---

[108] This idea was not, of course, uniquely Christian in its origin but was taken largely from the classical heritage of Late Antiquity. See Lawless, *Monastic Rule*, 156.

[109] For Augustine's vivid description of his own difficulties in this regard see *ep.* 95. 3.

[110] *exp. Gal.* 57 (quotation in 57.5).

Augustine's manner of discussing anger underscores the connection between these two texts. In *Rule* 6. 1 he alludes to Matt. 7: 3–5 when he says: 'Either have no quarrels or put an end to them as quickly as possible, lest anger grow into hatred, make a *splinter* into a *beam*, and turn your soul into the soul of a murderer. Thus you read: *Anyone who hates his brother is a murderer* (1 John 3: 15).[111] Van Bavel has noted that Augustine regularly combines allusions to Matt. 7: 3–5 and 1 John 3: 15, and that the subtle allusion to Matt. 7: 3–5 here implies that the audience is very familiar with it.[112] The same inference may be drawn from *exp. Gal.* 56. 17, where the allusions to these two biblical passages are no less subtle: 'Those who administer heavenly medicine wish either to perceive the *speck* in a brother's eye through a *beam* of hatreds, or to see the death of the one sinning rather than hear a word of indignation.' This allusiveness may be contrasted with Augustine's longer and plainer treatment of the same theme, including explicit quotations of both Matt. 7: 3 and 1 John 3: 15, in a sermon he delivered to a wide audience later in his career.[113] Once again the *Commentary* presupposes the monks as its audience. In fact we may go so far as to say that the treatment of this subject in the *Commentary* is even more suitable for monks than the treatment in the *Rule* itself.

This is not the only striking verbal coincidence between the two texts. In his discussion of sources of delight in *exp. Gal.* 49 Augustine uses 'the beauty of an attractive woman' as an example of a source of delight that is potentially sinful (49. 6). This example, which is rather unexpected in the context, becomes much less so when seen in the light of Augustine's *Rule*, where the theme of the lustful gaze features prominently.[114] If, then, his audience included monks already very familiar with this theme, the illustration is very apt. We may note further that in both texts Augustine concludes his remarks on the lustful gaze by saying that they are intended to apply to other problems as well.[115] Finally, in both texts spiritual beauty is commended as the only beauty worthy of our love (*exp. Gal.* 49. 6; *Rule* 8. 1).

To return to our examination of shared themes, that of spiritual leadership is given great emphasis. A spiritual leader must lead by example (*Rule*

---

[111] Lawless, trans., 99 (altered).

[112] Van Bavel, 'Parallèles', 56.

[113] *s.* 211. 1–2. This sermon is dated before 410 by Kunzelmann and La Bonnardière, between 412 and 415 by Fischer (see Hill, trans., 6: 132 n. 1). A wide audience is implied in *s.* 211. 4.

[114] *Rule* 4. 4–10—more than 20% of the entire document.

[115] Cf. *exp. Gal.* 49. 7 with *Rule* 4. 10: 'Diligently and faithfully, then, attend to my words about suggestive glances at women. Such advice holds also for detection, prevention, disclosure, proof, and punishment of other offences' (Lawless, trans., 93).

7. 3; *exp. Gal.* 15. 9–14, 38. 1, 42. 15).[116] Leadership brings care, distress, and danger (*Rule* 7. 4; *exp. Gal.* 38. 7–10). Leaders must live in holy fear, thinking of the account they will ultimately have to render for the pastoral care they gave. Such holy fear must also be instilled in those under their care (*Rule* 7. 3; *exp. Gal.* 42. 15 and cf. 13. 7). But while fear is necessary, the leader should seek not so much to be feared as to be loved (*Rule* 7. 3; *exp. Gal.* 37. 4, 43. 2–3 and 8).[117] The essence of spiritual authority is not the power that dominates but the love that serves (*Rule* 7. 3; *exp. Gal.* 15. 9, 43. 4–8, and 45. 1–10).

Thus we find more parallels between the two texts than we might have expected, especially considering the wide disparity in genre and contents between the two documents.[118] What do these parallels mean? Obviously in interpreting Galatians Augustine has in mind his own monastic community and the ways in which Paul's directives for Christian living can be implemented within it. Paul is not only a source of teaching but also a model of spiritual leadership and authority in the Church (*exp. Gal.* 1. 3–8; 2. 2–6; 10. 5–6; 42. 12 and 15), and Augustine is eager to learn from him how to exercise such leadership and authority himself. Peter, too, provides a model of leadership and authority, above all because he humbly accepted Paul's rebuke for the sake of his fellow Christians (15. 9–14). Together Paul and Peter model the giving and receiving of fraternal correction, without which Augustine believes no Christian community can grow in love.

As we pause to reflect on the image of Paul that is emerging from Augustine's *Commentary*, we are struck by how different it is from the one we normally associate with Augustine, particularly since the publication of Krister Stendahl's seminal essay, 'The Apostle Paul and the Introspective Conscience of the West'. Stendahl suggested that the tradition of Pauline interpretation running from Luther to modern Lutheran scholars, with its enormous emphasis on justification by faith as the solution to the universal predicament of the guilty conscience, had its origins not in Paul but in Augustine. For Paul's primary concern was not how the individual could find deliverance from the torments of conscience but how the Gentiles as a people could become part of the people of God.

Stendahl's suggestions were vigorously pursued by Paula Fredriksen in her article, 'Paul and Augustine: Conversion Narratives, Orthodox Traditions, and the Retrospective Self', which showed convincingly that from

---

[116] Cf. also *exp. Gal.* 20. 12 and 32. 3 (the example of Abraham).

[117] Cf. also *exp. Gal.* 21. 2, 22. 5–6 and 17–18.

[118] A large proportion of the *Rule* deals with everyday matters such as food, clothing, and caring for the sick.

the *Confessions* onwards Augustine misread Romans 7 as Paul speaking of his own experience as a Christian, and that the image of Paul as a soul in anguish that Augustine thought he saw was really a projection of himself. Nevertheless, that interpretation of Paul caught the imagination of Martin Luther and through his influence the mainstream of Protestant scholarship for centuries afterwards, until the work of Stendahl and others—above all, E. P. Sanders—brought about a sea change in the last two decades of the twentieth century.

I mention all this not because I want to challenge Stendahl, Fredriksen, or Sanders (I do not), but because I want to point out that Augustine was capable of viewing Paul from a quite different perspective. For the dominant images of Paul in his *Commentary* are those of Paul the founding father of Christian communities: preaching the gospel, upholding its truth against all attempts to undermine it, defending the status of Gentile believers as children of Abraham, striving to heal divisions and establish peace and unity in Christ. Such images resonate with Augustine as head of a fledgling monastic community, whose ethos he described in these words from the *Rule*: 'The chief motivation for your sharing life together is to live harmoniously in the house and to have one heart and one soul seeking God.' And at the end of the *Rule* he reminds the brethren: 'You are no longer slaves under the law, but a people living in freedom under grace.'[119] Augustine has therefore a vital interest in the corporate dimensions of Paul's teaching on grace, as will be confirmed when we consider his remarks on the spiritual life of his parishioners. In our own time Richard Hays has sought to remedy the imbalance caused by excessively individualistic interpretations of Paul by drawing attention to Paul's deep involvement in the communal life of the churches he addressed.[120] It is surprising to find that Augustine, the very man whose later writings contributed to the imbalance, anticipated and addressed so many of Hays's ecclesial concerns.

In addition to his fellow monks Augustine has in mind his parishioners, and the references in his *Commentary* to pastoral problems in Hippo give us some of our most vivid pictures of those parishioners. The problem of habitual swearing, familiar from Augustine's comments upon it elsewhere at this time,[121] makes a brief but memorable appearance in this text when Augustine observes that many swear, 'retaining an oath on their lips as if it were some great delicacy' (9. 2). Ignorance and misunderstanding of the

---

[119] *Rule* 1. 2 and 8. 1 (Lawless, trans., 81 and 103).

[120] Hays, 'Christology and Ethics', 268–71, 286–90; idem *Moral Vision*, 32–6.

[121] e.g. *s. dom. m.* 1. 17. 51, *c. Fort.* 22. The subject is brilliantly contextualized and illuminated in P. Brown, *Augustine of Hippo*, 146–50.

Bible represent another major problem among Augustine's parishioners. Thus when some of them hear Paul quote the passage from Deuteronomy, *Cursed is everyone who hangs on a tree* (Gal 3: 13), they think it cannot possibly refer to Jesus because that would be blasphemous, so they conclude the reference must be to Judas Iscariot.[122] Unfortunately, notes Augustine, they miss Paul's point entirely (22. 4).

The problem of astrology appears to be rampant among Augustine's parishioners. 'Our congregations', he laments, 'are full of people who obtain the times for their activities from astrologers' (35. 2). What is worse, they make no attempt to hide the fact: 'Countless numbers of the faithful boldly tell us to our face: "I never begin a journey on the second day of the month"' (35. 6). They even go so far as to give astrological advice to Augustine himself (35. 3). The picture of Augustine—to us one of the greatest figures in the history of Christian thought—being given astrological advice by illiterate peasants is not without its comic aspect. But did Augustine himself view it in this way? What immediately follows in the text indicates the very opposite. Augustine says that astrology is so deeply ingrained in his congregation that he is tempted simply to turn a blind eye towards it, instead of taking the risk of speaking out against it as he knows he should (35. 7–8), and as he reflects on the situation he is nearly carried away by anguish and grief (35. 8).[123]

In order to see how these and similar remarks[124] fit into Augustine's understanding of priestly ministry, it will be helpful to turn to the letters he wrote at the time, especially *epp.* 21–3 and 28–9. The earliest of these letters, *ep.* 21, was composed shortly after his ordination to the priesthood

[122] This particular misunderstanding on the part of Catholics was not confined to Hippo. See *c. Faust.* 14. 1 (CSEL 25. 1: 404. 2–5).

[123] We know from Augustine's later writings that astrology would remain for him a kind of ineradicable plague on Christianity. See further Van der Meer, *Augustine the Bishop*, 60–7, and the writings of Augustine referred to there. Of particular relevance is the passage from Augustine's *ep.* 55 cited by Van der Meer (p. 64), in which Augustine explains Paul's words in Gal. 4: 10–11 as referring to those who say: '"I will not start on my journey because it is an unlucky day," or "because the moon is in such a quarter," or "I will start because the position of the stars guarantees luck." "I will not carry on business this month because that star works against me," or "I will carry on because it favors the month," or "I will not plant a vineyard this year because it is a leap year"' (*ep.* 55. 13 (Parsons, trans., 271; CSEL 34. 2: 184. 3–7)). Similar polemic appears often in Augustine's writings; for an instance of it from nearly the same time as *exp. Gal.* see *doctr. chr.* 2. 21. 32–22. 34. It is worth noting that polemic against astrology was, at least implicitly, polemic against Manicheism as well, since Manicheism incorporated many astrological elements (see Lieu, *Manichaeism*, 177–9). For Augustine's account of his own early addiction to astrology and subsequent recovery from it see *conf.* 4. 3. 4–6 and 7. 6. 8–10.

[124] Other pastoral concerns voiced in this text include the need to balance firmness and flexibility (11. 1–5; 15. 1–8) and the need for religious language to be accommodated to the capacities of its hearers (10. 3–4; 19. 7; 41. 5–7; 42. 6–7).

and is addressed to his bishop, Valerius. In it, Augustine reflects on the meaning of ordained ministry:

> There is nothing in this life, and especially at this time, easier or more agreeable or more acceptable to men than the office of bishop or priest or deacon, if it is performed carelessly or in a manner to draw flattery; but in God's sight there is nothing more wretched, more melancholy, or more worthy of punishment. On the other hand, there is nothing in this life more difficult, more laborious, or more dangerous than the office of bishop or priest or deacon, but nothing more blessed in the sight of God, if he carries on the campaign in the way prescribed by our Commander (*ep.* 21. 1).[125]

The oratorical style should not lead us to doubt Augustine's sincerity. It is nothing less than spiritual warfare that he feels called by God to engage in. His first experiences as a priest, however, have shown him how utterly unprepared he is for his mission (*ep.* 21. 3). He pleads to Valerius for time to study the Scriptures in order to become a fit minister of God's word and sacrament (ibid.). He sees his ministry as entailing great danger, since he will have to render an account of his work to the Lord on the Day of Judgement (*ep.* 21. 5). He says that he himself wholeheartedly believes all that is necessary for his own salvation, 'but how', he asks, 'am I to make use of this for the salvation of others? *Not seeking my own good, but that of many, so that they may be saved* (1 Cor. 10: 33)' (*ep.* 21. 4).[126] Augustine will reaffirm his allegiance to this Pauline ideal throughout his career, including his *Commentary on Galatians*.[127] In sum, Augustine expresses an intense desire to gain a deeper knowledge of the Scriptures in order to be able to share that knowledge with the congregation for the sake of their salvation.

Letter 22 casts further light on Augustine's sense of mission. Written *c.*392 to Aurelius, the newly ordained bishop of Carthage,[128] Letter 22 proposes and eloquently pleads that Aurelius lead a great campaign throughout the North African church to correct the widespread abuses that have come about by 'licentious custom and false freedom' (*ep.* 22. 1. 4).[129] The abuses, he says, are the very ones condemned by Paul in Romans 13: 13–14[130]—*rioting and drunkenness . . . contention and envy*—but which now

---

[125] Parsons, trans. (and so throughout unless indicated otherwise), 47–8.
[126] Ibid. 49 (modified).
[127] *exp. Gal.* 5. 9.
[128] Augustine had known Aurelius since 388 (cf. *ciu.* 22. 8 (esp. CCSL 48: 816. 45–51 and 817. 97–103)). NB In Parsons' translation the recipient of the letter is wrongly identified as Valerius.   [129] trans., 54.
[130] Thus, as P. Brown observes, 'The text which he once read, for himself alone, in the sheltered garden of Milan, is turned outwards, and applied to the habits of the whole Church' (*Augustine of Hippo*, 206, referring to *conf.* 8. 12. 29 (CCSL 27: 131. 33–6)).

'seem to be treated with toleration' (*ep.* 22. 1. 2).[131] Deprecating the drunken celebrations[132] held at the tombs of the martyrs, Augustine says: 'It is so widespread an evil that I doubt if it can be cured by anything short of the authority of a council.'[133] In order to bring about this reform, Augustine emphasizes the need for Aurelius' authority as bishop of Carthage and primate of Africa. As to the manner in which it should be brought about, Augustine says that it must not be done harshly, but in a spirit of meekness and mildness (*ep.* 22. 1. 5, quoting Gal. 6: 1), so that the people may be 'won over by very gentle but very insistent warning' (ibid.).[134] If the clergy have to resort to threats they should not use their own words but the words of Scripture, since these carry such incomparable authority.

In the light of Augustine's recommendations, it is striking that soon afterwards Aurelius convened a plenary council of all Africa[135] whose purpose was to inaugurate a reformation of the African church.[136] Hardly less striking are the facts that Aurelius chose Hippo rather than his own primatial see of Carthage as its venue and that Augustine, while still only a priest, gave an address to the entire body of African bishops. Among the canons drawn up by the Council of Hippo was one calling for African church councils to be held annually thereafter,[137] and for the next three decades Augustine and Aurelius enjoyed a close working relationship which decisively shaped the course of African church history in their time.

In his next letter (*ep.* 23) Augustine takes the bold initiative to write to the Donatist bishop Maximinus expressing concern that Maximinus is reported to have approved the rebaptism of a man who had left the Catholic Church. Wishing to follow the recommendation of Paul to *serve one another through love* (Gal. 5: 13), Augustine approaches Maximinus as a true 'brother' (*ep.* 23. 1). Part of his argument against rebaptism involves an appeal to 'the authority of the Divine Scriptures' (*ep.* 23. 7).[138] He excuses himself for confronting Maximinus so boldly by emphasizing that he is only thinking of the account he will ultimately have to give to the Prince of all shepherds for the care of the flock that has been entrusted to him (*ep.* 23. 6).

[131] trans., 52.
[132] In *ep.* 22. 6 Augustine refers to them as 'these drinking bouts and extravagant banquets in cemeteries' (trans., 55; CSEL 34. 1: 58. 21: 'istae in cimiteriis ebrietates et luxuriosa conuiuia'). [133] *ep.* 22. 4 (trans., 54; CSEL 34. 1: 57. 22–58. 1).
[134] trans., 55.
[135] 'plenarium totius Africae concilium' (*retr.* 1. 17 (16) (CCSL 57: 52. 2)).
[136] For discussion of the Council of Hippo see Merdinger, *Rome*, 63–87.
[137] Canon 5 of the Hippo Breviary (CCSL 149: 34).
[138] trans., 65.

Letter 28 to Jerome (394/5) is discussed elsewhere in this book,[139] but here it is worth noting Augustine's expression of concern over Jerome's decision to translate the Old Testament from the Hebrew original rather than from the Greek Septuagint. As Augustine admits, his concern is not merely his own but that of the African church (*ep.* 28. 2. 2). And in this regard it is pertinent that the Council of Hippo had recently affirmed the authority of the Septuagint canon.[140]

Finally, in Letter 29 (*c.*395) we see how Augustine personally carried out his quest to end the drunken celebrations at the tombs of the martyrs that he had complained about in Letter 22. Writing to Alypius, now bishop of Thagaste, Augustine describes how, in order to shame his hearers into repentance by 'the authority of the Divine Scriptures' (*ep.* 29. 6), he used a range of passages from Paul condemning drunkenness, together with a passage from the Psalms threatening those who forsake the law (*ep.* 29. 5–7). Although such celebrations were tolerated as a concession to weakness when the pagans were first brought into the Church, the time has long since passed to abandon them (*ep.* 29. 10). Augustine wished to set before his hearers 'the common danger, both of themselves who are committed to us and of ourselves who have to give an account of them to the Prince of pastors' (*ep.* 29. 7).[141]

In all these letters it is clear that Augustine feels called to contribute to the spiritual reformation of the Catholic Church in Africa. The pagan customs still followed by the laity and tolerated by the clergy must be brought to an end. The Catholic way of life as exemplified by the Church in Rome and Milan[142] must be more firmly established on the basis of biblical preaching and teaching. The Donatist schism which had divided not only cities but even families must be healed. Catholic bishops, having grown demoralized in the presence of their more powerful Donatist counterparts, must be reminded of their responsibilities by church councils and held accountable to conciliar decrees. Thus by the authority of councils and the authority of the Bible reform could be effected.

That Augustine is inspired, at least in part, by Pauline principles is obvious from each of the letters we have cited, and it was only natural that

[139] For references see the Index of Augustine's Works under *Epistulae*.

[140] See Hennings, *Briefwechsel*, 110–11.

[141] trans., 103.

[142] Cf. *ep.* 22. 1. 4: 'If Africa should take the lead in stamping out these abuses, she ought to be worthy of imitation; but, as far as the greater part of Italy is concerned, and in all or most of the overseas churches, these practices either were never introduced, or, if they sprang up and took root, they were suppressed and destroyed by the vigilant care and censure of holy bishops' (trans., 53–4).

he should have turned to Paul for guidance on church reform. Paul's letters are deeply pastoral, and the pastoral problems with which Paul deals are often of the same kind as those faced by Augustine—relapses into paganism. The Pauline letters, especially if one includes the pastorals among them, as Augustine did, display Paul's use of authority for the sake of discipline and correction. Yet that authority is combined with personal self-abnegation—*by the grace of God I am what I am* (1 Cor. 15: 9). These aspects of Paul's letters, combined with Paul's willingness to speak the truth regardless of consequences and his eloquent testimony to the power of Christ's death and resurrection—all appealed to Augustine as worthy of imitation. And Paul himself encouraged such imitation repeatedly in his letters.[143] In Paul's rebuke of Peter at Antioch and in his rebuke of the Galatians Augustine found an example of the courage necessary to safeguard the truth of the gospel.

But the teaching of Paul's letters in general and of Galatians in particular is applicable not only to Augustine, but also to his parishioners. They too have lessons to learn from Paul. Corroboration of this comes from a recently discovered sermon of Augustine's,[144] dated 397. Augustine deliberately chose[145] as his text Gal. 2: 11–14 and emphasized many of the same points he had emphasized in the *Commentary*, such as Peter's example of humility.[146] Thus pastor and flock are fed from the same biblical source.

We have already seen evidence from the *Commentary* that Augustine was also thinking of Manicheism and Donatism as he wrote. We are now in a

[143] e.g. Gal. 4: 12; 1 Cor. 4: 16, 11: 1; Phil. 3: 17; 1 Thess. 1: 6.

[144] No. 27 in the Mainz codex. A provisional text appears in François Dolbeau's article 'Sermons inédits de saint Augustin', 52–63. The fact that this sermon was not preached at Hippo (ibid. 45–9) does not invalidate my point.

[145] Dolbeau, ibid. 46–7.

[146] A striking example is Augustine's commendation of the humility displayed by Peter in accepting Paul's rebuke. Cf. *exp. Gal.* 15. 10–11 with the following passage from Mainz sermon 27. 3: '[Peter] did not give an example, like Christ, of absolute perfection, but he did give one of total humility. He quietly accepted a rebuke from a man who did not precede him in the apostolate, but came after him. I hope the apostle Paul will excuse me, but what he did was easy; what Peter did was difficult. We live surrounded by daily experience of this in human relationships; I've often seen a person taking someone to task, I'm not sure if I've ever seen anyone quietly putting up with being taken to task. So what Paul did was frank and straightforward enough, but what Peter did was more admirable' (Hill, trans., pt. 3, vol. 11, p. 168 (where it is also listed as Sermon 162C/Dolbeau 10)). The Latin is as follows: 'exemplum non praebuit, sicut Christus, omnimodae perfectionis, sed totius praebuit exemplum humilitatis. Accepit aequo animo reprehendentem, in apostolatu non praecedentem, sed subsequentem. Det Paulus apostolus ueniam: quod fecit, facile est; quod Petrus fecit, difficile est. In rebus humanis uiuimus, cottidianis experimentis circumdamur: saepe uidi hominem reprehendentem, nescio utrum aliquando uiderim reprehensorem aequo animo sustinentem. Paulus ergo sincerius, sed Petrus mirabilius' (Dolbeau, ibid. 53–4).

position to see Manicheism and Donatism in proper perspective. They are being treated not as abstract problems in theology but as concrete threats facing the Catholic Church at Hippo and beyond. We have argued that the centre of the *Commentary* is to be found in its intense concentration on the Christlike virtues of humility and love as practised especially in the context of Christian correction. Inasmuch as both Manichees and Donatists represent for Augustine not merely error but arrogant claims to Christian élitism—the Manichees boasting of superior knowledge and the Donatists of a more pristine holiness—then humility is the one thing needful in both cases. Moreover, out of that humility they must pray for the willingness to accept correction from the Catholic Church, their true Mother. Only in this way can the bond of unity and love be restored. This is not explicitly stated in the *Commentary*, but when the *Commentary* is seen in the context of all the writings and activities Augustine was engaged in at this time, it would be reckless to disregard the possible links between the polemical and the pastoral elements in Augustine's interpretation of Galatians.

If this is an accurate reading, it illuminates Augustine's response to Jerome as well. For the humility to accept correction when offered out of love is the antidote to Jerome's vaulting ambition as an interpreter of Scripture, which led him into an error that threatened to overthrow the entire authority of Scripture. Obviously it would have been inappropriate for Augustine to state this plainly in his first letter to Jerome, yet he comes very near to doing so when, in the context of a discussion of the latter's interpretation of Gal. 2: 11–14, he writes:

We must find for our instructor in holy Scripture a person who approaches the holy books reverently and sincerely, not one willing to flatter himself by pointing out expedient falsehoods in any part of Scripture but one who would pass by what he does not understand rather than prefer his own judgement to the biblical truth. You can be sure that if someone calls anything untrue, that person wants to be believed instead and is attempting to shake our belief in the authority of holy Scripture.[147]

---

[147] *ep.* 28. 3. 4 (Leinenweber, trans., 43 (modified); CSEL 34. 1: 110. 9–16: 'agendum est igitur, ut ad cognitionem diuinarum scripturarum talis homo accedat, qui de sanctis libris tam sancte et ueraciter existimet, ut nolit aliqua eorum parte delectari per officiosa mendacia, potiusque id, quod non intellegit, transeat, quam cor suum praeferat illi ueritati. profecto enim cum hoc dicit, credi sibi expetit et id agit, ut diuinarum scripturarum auctoritatibus non credamus'). With this passage we may compare *doctr. chr.* 1. 37. 41 (Green, text and trans., 50–1): 'It often happens that by thoughtlessly asserting something that the author did not mean an interpreter runs up against other things which cannot be reconciled with that original idea. If he agrees that these things are true and certain, his original interpretation could not possibly be true, and by cherishing his own idea he comes in some strange way to be more displeased with scripture than with himself.' ('Asserendo enim temere quod ille non sensit quem legit plerumque incurrit in alia quae illi sententiae contexere nequeat. Quae si uera et certa esse

At the end of the letter Augustine asks Jerome for criticism of some of his own writings, which are being sent along with the letter:

This same brother is carrying some of my writings with him. If you will be so kind as to read them, I ask you to treat them with a frank and brotherly severity. For I understand the words of Scripture, *The just man shall correct me in mercy, and shall reprove me, but let not the oil of the sinner anoint my head*, to mean that one who rebukes me and thus heals me is a better friend than one whose flattery anoints my head.[148]

Thus Augustine graciously indicates that he is trying to be a true friend to Jerome, and by his own example tacitly offers Jerome a way of accepting correction without losing face.

Finally, the monastic and the priestly aspects of Augustine's life, which till now we have been considering separately, may be viewed together. They were in fact part of one and the same calling to serve the Church. As Augustine had learned from his own experience, no matter how desirable the contemplative aspect of the monastic life might be, it must yield precedence to the Church's call to active service whenever that call might come. This is what Augustine had done and what many of his fellow monks would do also. A number of them would eventually be ordained as clergy to serve the Church at Hippo, and no less than ten would eventually serve elsewhere as bishops and clergy.[149] And even monks who never would be ordained had a crucial role to play in the life of the Church. For the monastic life as Augustine understood it was a call to live the life epitomized by Paul in the saying *Owe one another nothing except to love one another* (Rom. 13: 10) and exemplified by the apostles in the earliest days of the Church (Acts 4: 32–5). However imperfectly the monks might realize this ideal, they nevertheless served the Church as a sign of what all its members were called to be and what all the chosen really would be in the fullness of God's Kingdom at the end of time.[150]

consentit, illud non possit verum esse quod senserat, fitque in eo nescio quo modo ut amando sententiam suam scripturae incipiat offensior esse quam sibi.')

[148] *ep*. 28. 4. 6 (based upon Parsons, trans., 98; CSEL 34. 1: 113. 3–9: 'sane idem frater aliqua scripta nostra fert secum. quibus legendis si dignationem adhibueris, etiam sinceram fraternamque seueritatem adhibeas quaeso. non enim aliter intellego, quod scriptum est: *Emendabit me iustus in misericordia et arguet me; oleum autem peccatoris non inpinguet caput meum*, nisi quia magis amat obiurgator sanans quam adulator unguens caput'). The quotation is from Ps. 140 (141): 5.

[149] Possidius, *Vita* 11. 1–3.

[150] On Augustine's conception of the monastery as 'a privileged anticipation of the Church's eschatological realisation' see Markus, *The End of Ancient Christianity*, 76–83.

4

Augustine as a Reader of Galatians

A. 'VARIANT READINGS'

Readings of Galatians have been as varied as its readers. While for Martin Luther in 1518 Galatians served as a warrant for defying the Pope,[1] for Heinrich Schlier in the mid-twentieth century it served as a warrant for submitting to the Pope and forsaking Luther.[2] Galatians has been read differently even by the same reader; indeed, this seems to have been the case with Paul himself. When he placed his 'signature' on it he clearly thought that the letter should end all dispute about his apostolic authority and the truth of his gospel.[3] Yet, as Raymond E. Brown has suggested, Paul found it necessary in his Letter to the Romans a few years later not merely to rephrase but actually to correct what he had said in Galatians.[4] Like Paul, Augustine read Galatians differently at different times, as he himself acknowledged in remarks made towards the end of his life.[5] While it would be highly instructive to trace the history of his interpretation of Galatians over a career spanning nearly half a century, our task must be limited so far as possible to one time and one text: the *Commentary on Galatians* of 394/5. Occasionally it will be necessary to draw from Augustine's other writings, but in doing so every effort will be made to select material that is close to the *Commentary* in time or substance or both.

[1] See *D. Martin Luthers Werke*, Kritische Gesamtausgabe ('Weimarer Ausgabe') (Weimar, 1883–), ii. 10. 19–25 and 37. 12–22. I would like to thank Dr. T. J. Deidun of Heythrop College in the University of London for directing me to these passages.

[2] See Betz, *Galatians*, p. xiii.

[3] For Paul's 'signature' see Gal. 6: 11. For the letter as putting an end to all dispute see Gal. 6: 17*a* and Betz's comment: 'When the Apostle presents his order in v 17a . . . he does so in hopeful anticipation that the problems have been solved and that there is no basis for further trouble' (*Galatians*, 324).

[4] R. E. Brown and J. P. Meier, *Antioch and Rome*, 111–22. Cf. Martyn, *Galatians*, 31: 'In writing to the Romans, Paul clarified, supplemented—perhaps one should even say modified—some of the things he had said to the Galatians about the Law and about Israel.' See also Wilckens, 'Entwicklung', 180–5.

[5] See *retr.* 1. 24 (23).

B. AUGUSTINE'S HERMENEUTICAL
PRESUPPOSITIONS

In the words of another vastly influential interpreter of Paul, Rudolf
Bultmann, 'There cannot be any such thing as exegesis without presuppositions.'[6] Bultmann regarded every interpreter of the Bible as
approaching the text with his or her own 'pre-understanding' (*Vor-
verständnis*), that is, his or her own set of beliefs and assumptions concerning its subject-matter.[7] Augustine would have agreed wholeheartedly. Like
Bultmann he was not only a practitioner of biblical interpretation but also a
theorist who often spoke about his hermeneutical presuppositions. Of these
presuppositions the following are particularly important for an appreciation of his *Commentary on Galatians*.

The Inspiration of the Bible

None of Augustine's presuppositions is more decisive for his interpretation
of Galatians than his view of its inspiration. For as J. B. Lightfoot pointed
out, systems of interpretation necessarily depend upon theories of inspiration.[8] Although Augustine does not directly and explicitly address the
question of inspiration in his *Commentary on Galatians*,[9] his views may be
gleaned from remarks made elsewhere during this period. In a work written
shortly before the *Commentary* he stated that everything in the Old and
New Testaments was written by one Spirit,[10] and in a statement made a few
years after the *Commentary* he claimed that 'in consequence of the distinctive peculiarity of the sacred writings, we are bound to receive as true whatever the canon shows to have been said by even one prophet, or apostle, or
evangelist.'[11] For Augustine, the truth of Scripture is grounded in Christ
himself. As he put it in the *Confessions*: 'Lord, surely your scripture is true,
for you, being truthful and Truth itself, have produced it.'[12] The truth of

---

[6] 'voraussetzungslose Exegese kann es nicht geben' (Bultmann, 'Ist voraussetzungslose
Exegese möglich?', 410 (Ogden, trans., 146)).   [7] Ibid. 414 (Ogden, trans., 149).

[8] Lightfoot, 'Unpublished Manuscript', 171, 172.

[9] For an indirect statement on inspiration see *exp. Gal.* 40. 7.

[10] *c. Adim.* 3. 3 (CSEL 25. 1: 121. 21–3): 'omnia tam in uetere quam in nouo testamento uno
sancto spiritu conscripta et commendata esse . . .'.

[11] *c. Faust.* 11. 5 (Stothert, trans. (and so elsewhere), 180). CSEL 25. 1: 321. 7–11: 'in illa
uero canonica eminentia sacrarum litterarum, etiamsi unus propheta seu apostolus aut
euangelista aliquid in suis litteris posuisse ipsa canonis confirmatione declaratur, non licet
dubitare, quod uerum sit.'

[12] *conf.* 13. 29. 44 (Chadwick, trans. (and so elsewhere), 300). CCSL 27: 268. 4–5: 'O
domine, nonne ista scriptura tua uera est, quoniam tu uerax et ueritas edidisti eam?'

Scripture is thus unimpeachable. If it were to be undermined, both faith and obedience would be imperilled[13] and so too would our salvation. For the truthfulness of the Bible is an integral part of the economy of salvation: 'in Christ your Son our Lord, and by your scriptures commended by the authority of your Catholic Church, you have provided a way of salvation whereby humanity can come to the future life after death'.[14]

Augustine's most celebrated defence of the truth of Scripture occurs in his correspondence with Jerome, especially as that concerns the interpretation of Galatians 2: 11–14. As this subject has already been examined above,[15] it will be sufficient here to recall a few of the salient points. It is clear from Augustine's Letter 28 to Jerome, written at the same time as the *Commentary*, that Augustine understands Jerome to imply that Paul lied both when he rebuked Peter and when he recorded the incident in his Letter to the Galatians. Augustine utterly rejects any such interpretation, saying that if a single lie is allowed anywhere in Sacred Scripture then 'nowhere in the Holy Books will there be the absolute authority of pure truth'.[16] In his *Commentary* Augustine clears Paul not only of any charge of speaking or writing deceitfully but also of any charge of acting deceitfully. Jerome argued that Paul cannot really have rebuked Peter for dissimulation since he himself had behaved like a Jew when with Jews and like a Gentile when with Gentiles.[17] Against this view Augustine insists that there was never any dissimulation on Paul's part. Even in the case of Timothy's circumcision Paul was merely honouring a custom so as not to offend the weak. In itself circumcision is an indifferent matter; it only threatens faith if one places one's hope for salvation in it.[18]

It is sometimes supposed on the basis of the correspondence between

[13] Cf. *doctr. chr.* 1. 37. 41 (Green, text and trans. (and so elsewhere), 50–1): 'Faith will falter if the authority of holy scripture is shaken' ('titubabit autem fides, si divinarum scripturarum vacillat auctoritas').
[14] *conf.* 7. 7. 11 (trans., 119). CCSL 27: 100. 5–8: 'in Christo, filio tuo, domino nostro, atque scripturis sanctis, quas ecclesiae tuae catholicae commendaret auctoritas, uiam te posuisse salutis humanae ad eam uitam, quae post hanc mortem futura est'.
[15] See under the subheading 'Jerome and Augustine' in 2. B.
[16] *ep.* 28. 3. 4 (Parsons, trans. (and so elsewhere for Augustine's letters), 96). CSEL 34. 1: 109. 9–10: 'nusquam certa erit in sanctis libris castae ueritatis auctoritas'. Cf. his statement to Jerome a few years later in *ep.* 40. 4. 5 (*c*.397–9) [= Jerome, *ep.* 67. 5]: 'Thus, [Peter] was himself truly corrected, and Paul told the truth. Otherwise, the Holy Scripture, which has been given to preserve the faith in generations to come, would be wholly undermined and thrown into doubt, if the validity of lying were once admitted' (trans., 175). CSEL 34. 2: 75. 4–7: 'ita et ipse uere correctus est et Paulus uera narrauit, ne sancta scriptura, quae ad fidem posteris edita est, admissa auctoritate mendacii tota dubia nutet et fluctuet'.
[17] As was noted earlier, in his *Comm. on Gal.* 2: 11 ff. Jerome refers to Acts 16: 1–3, 18: 18, 21: 24–3, and 1 Cor. 9: 20, 10: 32–3 in support of his view (PL 26: 339A–B).
[18] *exp. Gal.* 15. 1–4, 41. 5–7, 63. 1–4.

Augustine and Jerome that Augustine was simply insisting on the most straightforward reading of Gal. 2: 11–14. Unlike Jerome, it is said, Augustine could frankly admit that Peter erred at Antioch and so did not need to resort to Jerome's tortuous casuistry.[19] But a look at Augustine's treatment of Gal. 2: 11–14 in the context not of his correspondence but of his *Commentary* leads to a very different estimation of Augustine as a reader. In the *Commentary* we see a defence of Paul that is ingenious to the point of appearing disingenuous. Augustine believes that in his role as biblical author Paul must be regarded as infallible, a view to which the text itself is notoriously recalcitrant, since Paul appears to violate the express teaching of Jesus in at least three instances: he swears (Gal. 1: 20), in apparent violation of Matt. 5: 33–7; he says that he rebuked Peter publicly (Gal. 2: 14), in apparent violation of Matt. 18: 15; and he appears to curse (Gal. 5: 12), in violation of Matt. 5: 44.

Augustine's interpretation of Gal. 5: 12 (*I wish those who are troubling you would castrate themselves!*) clearly illustrates the lengths to which he will go to safeguard the authority of Paul and hence that of Scripture. The sort of interpretation one might naturally expect (at least from the later, anti-Pelagian Augustine[20]) would run something like this: 'It is not surprising that Paul spoke this way once. He was, after all, only human, still enclosed in a weak vessel, one who saw in his body another law taking him captive and leading him to the law of sin. We often see saintly men fall in this way.' Yet this interpretation is found not in Augustine's *Commentary* but in Jerome's.[21] Augustine's interpretation is quite different: 'And with very elegant ambiguity he inserted a blessing under the appearance of a curse when he said, *I wish those who are troubling you would castrate themselves!* Not merely "circumcise", he said, but *castrate* themselves. For thus they will become eunuchs for the sake of the kingdom of heaven and cease to sow carnal seed' (*exp. Gal.* 42. 19–20). The reasoning behind Augustine's interpretation is made clearer in his *Reply to Faustus*, where he argues that Gal. 5: 12 cannot really be a curse because Rom. 12: 14 explicitly forbids cursing

---

[19] Cf. e.g. Trench, *Exposition of the Sermon on the Mount*, 67–8: 'Augustine, too straightforward a lover of the truth to tolerate *economies* of this kind, protests with a righteous earnestness against this explanation, which he invites Jerome to defend or to withdraw.'

[20] Cf. e.g. *s.* 154 (esp. 154. 3), where Augustine argues that Paul was not wholly free of carnal concupiscence.

[21] What has just been presented is in fact a direct translation of Jerome's comment on Gal. 5: 12: 'Nec mirum esse si Apostolus, ut homo, et adhuc vasculo clausus infirmo, vidensque aliam legem in corpore suo captivantem se, et ducentem in lege peccati, semel fuerit hoc locutus, in quod frequenter sanctos viros cadere perspicimus' (PL 26: 405c–d). It must be admitted that this is not the only interpretation offered by Jerome or even the one that he prefers. Nevertheless, the mere fact that he offers it at all contrasts vividly with Augustine.

and that it would be wrong to suppose that the Apostle spoke out of anger.[22] This is casuistry to rival anything in Jerome's *Commentary*. In fact Jerome's comment on Gal. 5: 12, though written earlier, exposes the weakness of interpretations such as Augustine's: the very severity of Paul's language, he says, shows that Paul was speaking not out of love but out of anger.[23] But Augustine cannot allow this. Not only does Rom. 12: 14 militate against it, but so do the words of Jesus in the Sermon on the Mount: *Love your enemies and pray for those who persecute you* (Matt. 5: 44).[24] Indeed, the Sermon on the Mount repeatedly provides the standard from which the author of Galatians cannot possibly have deviated. Thus Augustine is quick to explain how Paul's swearing in Gal. 1: 20 does not diverge from the Lord's teaching in Matt. 5: 33–7 (*exp. Gal.* 9. 1–6).[25] Similarly Paul does not violate the Lord's teaching in Matt. 5: 21–2 when he calls the Galatians *foolish* (Gal. 3: 1), because he has a valid reason for speaking as he does (*exp. Gal.* 18. 1).

We must recall that during this period Augustine wrote a substantial commentary in two books on the Sermon on the Mount,[26] a text which he regarded as the 'perfect pattern of Christian life'.[27] His description of the relation between the New Law and the Old is particularly relevant here: 'It is one and the same God who through His holy Prophets and servants, by a disposition of time that was perfectly ordered, gave the lesser precepts to a people who as yet had to be controlled by fear, and through His Son the greater ones to a people for whom it was now expedient to be free in love.'[28] This also becomes a key to Augustine's interpretation of the relation between the Law and the Gospel in Galatians. In pointing out that the fault with the Law lay not in the Law itself but in the way the Jews interpreted

[22] *c. Faust.* 16. 22 (CSEL 25. 1: 465. 11–23).

[23] 'Nec possunt dicere orasse Apostolum pro inimicis Christi, qui ejus Ecclesias conturbabant. Nec ex dilectione prolatum, quod tumore et indignatione plenum, ipso verborum pondere demonstratur' (PL 26: 406B).

[24] Rom. 12: 14 and Matt. 5: 44 are already linked by Augustine in *s. dom. m.* 1. 21. 71 and 76 and, immediately preceding *exp. Gal.*, in *exp. prop. Rm.* 63 (71). 1–2.

[25] Cf. what Augustine wrote at this time concerning Matt. 5: 33–7 and Paul's oaths in *mend.* 15. 28: 'It is impious to say that Paul was guilty of violating the Lord's command, especially since his Epistles were written and circulated for the spiritual life and salvation of the people' (Muldowney, trans., 91 (modified); CSEL 41: 448. 20–2: 'praecepti uiolati reum Paulum, praesertim in epistulis conscriptis atque editis ad spiritalem uitam salutemque populorum nefas est dicere').

[26] *s. dom. m.* is dated 393/6.

[27] *s. dom. m.* 1. 1. CCSL 35: 1. 6–7: 'perfectum uitae christianae modum'.

[28] *s. dom. m.* 1. 2 (Jepson, trans., 12). CCSL 35: 2. 34–8: 'Unus . . . deus per sanctos prophetas et famulos suos secundum ordinatissimam distributionem temporum dedit minora praecepta populo quem timore adhuc alligari oportebat, et per filium suum maiora populo quem caritate iam liberari conuenerat.'

and practised it, Augustine again refers to Jesus' words in Matthew's Gospel.[29] Another Matthean saying of Jesus needs to be borne in mind when we come to Augustine's justification of the public nature of Paul's rebuke of Peter. Jerome said in his *Commentary* that if Paul's rebuke had been real rather than simulated it would have violated Jesus' command in Matt. 18: 15.[30] Augustine's comment answers this very objection: 'It was necessary for him to say this to Peter *in front of everyone* so that by Peter's rebuke *everyone* might be put right. For it would not have been useful to correct in private an error which had done its harm in public.'[31] Finally, the words of Jesus most often referred to in Augustine's *Commentary on Galatians* are also from Matthew's Gospel: *Take my yoke and learn from me, for I am gentle and humble of heart* (Matt. 11. 29).[32]

The idea of interpreting the words of Paul by means of the words of Jesus as presented in St Matthew's Gospel would be viewed sceptically by most contemporary scholars,[33] and for this reason we should pause to reflect on Augustine's probable justification for doing so. As Matthew was chosen by Christ to be an apostle and the authenticity of his testimony has been recognized by the whole Church since apostolic times,[34] so too with Paul and the authenticity of his testimony. Not only does Augustine underscore the harmony of Paul's testimony with that of the other apostles, he also emphasizes that Paul's gospel had to be authenticated: 'For it did not follow that if he was faithful and the faith he held was both true and accurate, then he should also be an apostle' (*exp. Gal.* 10. 5). It is not that Paul's gospel is lacking in any way but that the nature of the Church as an authoritative guide demands that its preachers be properly accredited.[35] Having secured such accreditation at the Jerusalem conference (Gal. 2: 1–10), Paul's authority is such 'that his words are now received in the Church, as if, to use his own appropriate words, Christ were speaking in him'.[36] Thus whether

[29] Matt. 15: 6, quoted in *exp. Gal.* 7. 4.

[30] Jerome, *Comm. on Gal.* 2: 11 ff. (PL 26: 340A–B), where the editors wrongly attribute Jesus' words to Luke 17: 3.   [31] *exp. Gal.* 15. 8–9.

[32] Augustine quotes or alludes to this passage five times in the course of his *Commentary*: *exp. Gal.* 5. 7, 15. 12–14, 38. 3, 44. 6, and 45. 9–10.

[33] Cf. Chadwick, 'The Enigma of St Paul', 6: 'In modern times, since the seventeenth century at least, the sense of a contrast between the gospels and the epistles has commonly found expression in a disparagement of Paul in comparison with the Sermon on the Mount.'

[34] Cf. *c. Faust.* 28. 2.

[35] Cf. *c. Faust.* 28. 4: 'For would the Church entirely believe the apostle Paul himself, though he was called from heaven after the Lord's ascension, had he not found apostles in the flesh with whom he could discuss and compare his gospel and so be recognized as being of the same fellowship as they?' (trans., 325–6 (much altered); CSEL 25. 1: 741. 24–742. 2).

[36] *c. Faust.* 28. 4 (trans., 326). CSEL 25. 1: 742. 6–8: 'ut uerba illius hodie sic audiantur in ecclesia, tamquam in illo Christus, sicut uerissime ipse dixit, locutus audiatur'. (The reference is to 2 Cor. 13: 3.)

the words quoted are from Matthew's Gospel or Paul's Letter to the Galatians, it is the same voice of Christ that is heard.

We are now in a better position to understand why Augustine will not allow that there is anything contrary to the teaching of Christ in the Letter to the Galatians: if there were, Scripture would be directly contradicting itself. Such is the *reductio ad absurdum* argument underlying Augustine's presentation. He is concerned, therefore, with much more than just the question of a deliberate lie in Scripture, though that is his primary concern. What is at stake is the whole notion of Scripture as the authoritative guide to Catholic faith and morals. Thus Augustine imposes a firm limit on the scope of private judgement allowed to the biblical interpreter.

Augustine's view of the authority of Scripture also helps to explain the disparity between his treatment of Peter and his treatment of Paul. The reason Augustine is able to accept that Peter truly erred is that Scripture itself points out his error and corrects it.[37] There is no danger of Peter's misleading the faithful. Paul's behaviour, on the other hand, is not corrected and therefore cannot need correction. The point is not that Paul is sinless but that he cannot be sinning in what he writes in Sacred Scripture. If he were, he would be inciting the faithful to sin by means of an example stamped with apostolic authority. Moreover, Paul is viewed by Augustine as a pattern of true discipleship (*exp. Gal.* 3. 6).[38]

One of Jerome's concerns in interpreting Gal. 2: 11–14 is to safeguard Peter's reputation. It is clear that Augustine does not share this concern to the same extent, but it would be wrong to think that he does not share it at all. Peter's hypocrisy at Antioch was real but it was more than redeemed by his humble acceptance of correction 'for the salvation of the flock' (*exp. Gal.* 15. 9). In fact, the example provided by Peter on this occasion is even greater than Paul's, because it is more difficult to accept a public rebuke than it is to give one (*exp. Gal.* 15. 10). Thus Peter's authority is not merely upheld but actually enhanced.

The Unity of the Bible

An integral part of Augustine's belief in biblical inspiration is his view that Scripture is a single whole comprising both the Old Testament and the New. Rightly understood, both Testaments bear witness to the same faith. While this point may seem platitudinous, it has a special relevance for our

[37] Cf. *mend.* 5. 8: 'For the hypocrisy of Peter and Barnabas is not only recorded but also rebuked and put right' (my trans. of CSEL 41: 422. 13–15: 'simulatio enim Petri et Barnabae non solum commemorata, uerum etiam reprehensa atque correcta est').

[38] See further *exp. Gal.* 37. 1, 9 and 38. 1–10.

assessment of Augustine as a reader of Galatians, for here we have a hermeneutical presupposition sanctioned in Galatians itself by Paul's interpretation of the Genesis story of Hagar and Sarah as a Christian allegory.[39]

More interesting is the particular way in which Augustine conceives Scripture as being centred on Christ: it is centred in such a way that Christ's teaching on the love of God and neighbour may serve as a hermeneutical key to Scripture.[40] How appropriate is this key for a 'pre-understanding' of Galatians? We may note, first, that Augustine does not introduce his unifying hermeneutical principle from outside but discovers it within Scripture.[41] Indeed, it even finds a partial echo in Galatians itself when Paul states: *For the whole law has been fulfilled in one phrase: 'You shall love your neighbour as yourself'* (Gal. 5: 14).[42] Second, neither for Paul nor for Jesus is the assertion of the primacy of love merely a remark made in passing. Rather, it is a conscious retrieval from the tradition of that which has been recognized as a hermeneutical key to the law in its entirety. Third, in one form or other the assertion of love's primacy is made repeatedly and emphatically in the New Testament.[43] Augustine has not therefore used a hermeneutical key that is alien to the New Testament in general or to Paul in particular, as Bultmann has been charged with doing in his use of Heidegger's existential analytic. Nor has he used a secondary idea as if it

[39] Gal. 4: 21–31. On the immense hermeneutical significance of this passage see Ricœur, 'Preface to Bultmann', 50–2.

[40] On the love of God and neighbour as the key to the unity of the Bible see esp. *doctr. chr.* 1. 36. 40 (Green, 48–9): 'So anyone who thinks that he has understood the divine scriptures or any part of them, but cannot by his understanding build up this double love of God and neighbour, has not yet succeeded in understanding them.' ('Quisquis igitur scripturas divinas vel quamlibet earum partem intellexisse sibi videtur, ita ut eo intellectu non aedificet istam geminam caritatem dei et proximi, nondum intellexit.') Cf. *doctr. chr.* 1. 40. 44 (Green, 52–3, with italics added to the trans.): 'So when someone has learnt that the aim of the command-ment is *love from a pure heart, and good conscience and genuine faith* [1 Tim. 1: 5], he will be ready to relate every interpretation of the holy scriptures to these three things and may approach the task of handling these books with confidence.' ('Quapropter cum quisque cognoverit finem praecepti esse caritatem *de corde puro et conscientia bona et fide non ficta*, omnem intellectum divinarum scripturarum ad ista tria relaturus, ad tractationem illorum librorum securus accedat.') See also *doctr. chr.* 1. 26. 27; 2. 7. 10; 3. 10. 14. For the love command in *exp. Gal.* see 19, 43. 2–45. 10, 49. 6, 58. 1–2.

[41] Jeanrond, *Theological Hermeneutics*, 23.

[42] Cf. Gal. 6: 2 and see also Rom. 13: 8–10. In *exp. Gal.* 44–5 Augustine presumes that Paul's summary statements in Gal. 5: 14 and Rom. 13: 8–10 are taken from the sayings of Jesus rather than being, for example, his own interpretation of Lev. 19: 18. Such a presumption receives strong backing from J. D. G. Dunn (*Galatians*, 291–2).

[43] e.g. Matt. 5: 43–4, 7: 12, 19: 19, 22: 35–40; Mark 12: 28–34; Luke 10: 25–8; John 13: 34, 15: 12; Rom. 13: 8–10; 1 Cor. 13; Gal. 5: 14; Col. 3: 14; Jas. 2: 8; 1 Pet. 1: 22; 1 John 3: 11, 23, 4: 7, 11; 2 John 5. On the religious and moral significance of Jesus' teaching on the love of God and neighbour see Schnackenburg, *Moral Teaching*, 90–109.

were primary, as Luther has been charged with doing in his foregrounding of the Pauline concept of 'justification by faith'. Rather, he has recovered a central hermeneutical principle sanctioned in Scripture itself by both Jesus and Paul. Thus despite the fact that Augustine is often dismissed out of hand as pre-critical, his adoption of this principle is consonant with one of the basic emphases of contemporary hermeneutics: that the reader must be open to 'the claim which confronts him or her in the work'.[44]

For Augustine, as for Jesus and Paul, the principle of love is closely related to the principle of humility, 'for by humility love is preserved' (*exp. Gal.* 15. 11). Once again we have a hermeneutical principle recovered from Scripture itself. As we have noted, a cardinal passage for Augustine is Matt. 11: 28–30, where Jesus summons his followers to learn from him how to be *gentle and humble of heart.* Humility is thus offered by Jesus himself as heuristic device, and in both the *Commentary on Galatians* and the *De doctrina christiana* this biblical passage is highlighted.

Augustine's view of humility as a differentia of Christianity is brought out with great clarity in the *Confessions.*[45] In the climax to Book 7 Augustine states that although the books of the 'Platonists'[46] enabled him to glimpse the truth from afar, they could not show him the way to reach it because 'no one there hears him who calls *Come to me, you who labour* (Matt. 11: 28). They disdain to learn from him, for he is *gentle and humble of heart.*'[47] Augustine believes that God wanted him to read the Scriptures after the Platonist books so that he 'would learn to discern and distinguish the difference between presumption and confession'.[48] He says he gained this insight especially from reading Paul.[49]

[44] Bultmann, 'Das Problem der Hermeneutik', 60–1: 'Echtes Verstehen wäre also *das Hören auf die im zu interpretierenden Werk gestellte Frage, auf den im Werk begegnenden Anspruch*' (trans., 251: 'Real understanding would, therefore, be *paying heed to the question posed in the work which is to be interpreted, to the claim which confronts one in the work*'). Cf. Jeanrond, *Theological Hermeneutics*, 110: 'A reader who truly aims at understanding a text must open himself or herself to it.'

[45] The theme of Christ's humility is one of the great themes in all Augustine's preaching and writing. As Harnack (*History of Dogma*, v. 131–2) observes, '*The type of humility exhibited in majesty*—this it was that overpowered Augustine: *pride was sin, and humility was the sphere and force of goodness.* From this he learned and implanted in the Church the new disposition of *reverence* for *humility.*' (Harnack illustrates his point from *Confessions* 7. 21. 24–7.)

[46] i.e. Neoplatonists, especially Plotinus.

[47] *conf.* 7. 21. 27 (trans., 131 (modified)). CCSL 27: 111. 31–3: 'Nemo ibi audit uocantem: *Venite ad me, qui laboratis.* Dedignantur ab eo discere, quoniam mitis est et humilis corde.' The same point is made and the same Matthean passage is cited in *conf.* 7. 9. 14.

[48] *conf.* 7. 20. 26 (trans., 130). CCSL 27: 110. 19–20: 'discernerem atque distinguerem, quid interesset inter praesumptionem et confessionem'.

[49] *conf.* 7. 21. 27: 'With avid intensity I seized the sacred writings of your Spirit and especially the apostle Paul' (trans., 130). CCSL 27: 110. 1–2: 'Itaque auidissime arripui uenerabilem stilum spiritus tui et prae ceteris apostolum Paulum.'

The humility of Jesus is extolled in the 'Christ-Hymn' found in Paul's Letter to the Philippians (Phil. 2: 6–11), a favourite passage of Augustine's that is quoted in the *Commentary on Galatians* (24. 7). Of particular relevance here is the way in which Paul introduces this hymn by urging that the humility it extols be imitated: *Let the same mind be in you that was in Christ Jesus* (Phil. 2: 5),[50] thus (from a hermeneutical point of view) establishing humility as an appropriate pre-understanding for his readers. If Paul himself calls for such a pre-understanding, its adoption by Augustine should not be considered arbitrary or adventitious.

The humility of Christ as seen in the Incarnation, so resonant a theme in Paul's letters, is continually in the background of Augustine's reading of Galatians. Indeed, by metonymy the term 'humility' may stand for the Incarnation (*exp. Gal.* 24. 10). We could not have known the intensity of God's love for us had not the Son humbled himself to share in our humanity. Since he has so shared, even to the point of undergoing crucifixion, God's love is not only made known to us, it also moves us very deeply (cf. *exp. Gal.* 18. 4). To appreciate what God has done for us we must follow his example of humility (*exp. Gal.* 25. 10). Failure to learn humility from the Lord was the cause of the Judaizers' misinterpretation of the gospel as 'a sort of debt paid for their righteousness' (*exp. Gal.* 15. 14, citing Matt. 11: 29).

If the humility and love commended and exemplified by Jesus underlie the whole of the New Testament and indeed the whole of Scripture, as Augustine believes they do, then not only may Gal. 5: 14 be interpreted in the light of Matt. 22: 37–40, but Galatians in general may be interpreted by Matthew in general, as we have seen. Augustine also interprets Galatians in the light of the other Pauline letters, especially Romans. Inasmuch as Galatians and Romans show considerable overlap in terms of content and method of argumentation (the citation of the Hebrew Bible against Judaism), commentators through the ages have almost invariably used one to interpret the other.[51] More problematic is Augustine's use of the two letters to Timothy. Augustine makes 1 Tim. 1: 8–10 a key to understanding Paul's thought on the law. The majority of contemporary scholars, accustomed to leaving the Pastorals off their list of seven authentic letters of Paul, would firmly resist such a procedure. Indeed, many would see 1 Tim. 1: 8 as quite missing the point of the Romans passage to which it alludes

[50] The importance of this verse is highlighted by Augustine in *diu. qu.* 71, a text we have already linked to the *Commentary on Galatians* (see 3. c above).

[51] This use is not without its dangers, however. I refer again to the discussion in R. E. Brown and J. P. Meier, *Antioch and Rome*, 111–22.

(Rom. 7: 12–16).[52] Yet if we prescind for the moment from the question of the authorship of the Pastorals and simply consider how Augustine is using this passage in his interpretation of Gal. 5, there is much to commend his view that 1 Tim. 1: 8–10 is very close in thought to Gal. 5: 18–23.[53] So we must not assume that because Augustine lacks critical insight into a question of authorship he must therefore also lack insight into Pauline theology.

Even more important for Augustine than 1 Timothy's teaching on the law is 2 Timothy's teaching on the correction of fellow Christians (2 Tim. 2: 24–5; 4: 2), for the latter subject directly impinges on the spirituality of daily life, especially in a monastic community such as Augustine's. Hence the emphatic words with which Augustine introduces this section of his *Commentary*: 'Now nothing proves that a man is spiritual like his handling of another's sin: Does he consider how he can liberate rather than insult the other person? How he can help rather than verbally abuse him? Does he undertake to do so to the best of his ability?' (*exp. Gal.* 56. 1). The great care with which Augustine treats the subject of Christian correction in *exp. Gal.* 56–7 even suggests that he identifies with Timothy, the man personally instructed by Paul on how to lead a Christian community. When we recall that Augustine, newly ordained as a priest, had asked Bishop Valerius for time to study the Scriptures and had expressed his motivation for such study by quoting Paul (*not seeking my own good but the good of the many, so that they may be saved*),[54] we may well agree that this latter-day disciple of Paul could hardly have found a more appropriate person to identify with than Timothy.[55]

Scripture and the Rule of Faith

Another hermeneutical presupposition is that Paul may be interpreted in the light of the rule of faith, or Creed.[56] The importance of the Creed for Augustine can hardly be overstated.[57] It is particularly important to recall

[52] e.g. Hanson, *The Pastoral Epistles*, 3 and 58–9.

[53] See *exp. Gal.* 47–9.

[54] 1 Cor. 10: 33, quoted in *ep.* 21. 4 (CSEL 34. 1: 52. 6–7: *non quaerens, quod mihi utile est, sed quod multis, ut salui fiant*). It is not fortuitous that the same half verse is quoted in the *Commentary on Galatians* (*exp. Gal.* 5. 9).

[55] See also Augustine's advice regarding the Pastorals in *doctr. chr.* 4. 16. 33: 'A person who has been given the position of teacher in the church should keep these three apostolic letters before his eyes' ('Quas tres apostolicas epistolas ante oculos habere debet cui est in ecclesia persona doctoris imposita' (Green, 236–7)).

[56] The rule of faith is identified with the Creed in *symb. cat.* 1. 1 (CCSL 46: 185. 1: 'Accipite regulam fidei, quod symbolum dicitur').

[57] For Augustine's expositions of the Creed see: *f. et symb.*; *agon.* 13. 14–33. 35; *ench.* 3. 9–29. 113; *symb. cat.*; *ss.* 212–15.

that not long before composing his *Commentary on Galatians* Augustine had spoken on the Creed 'in the presence and at the request of the bishops who were holding a Plenary Council of all Africa at Hippo Regius'.[58] What is the precise relation of the Creed to Scripture for Augustine? This question has received a wide variety of answers[59] and in the absence of a consensus we must limit ourselves to noting the fact of the relation and setting forth the evidence for it in this particular text. Only then will we be in a position to assess the role of the Creed in Augustine's interpretation of Galatians.

The presence of the Creed may be detected especially in Augustine's remarks concerning the person of Christ. Here it would seem that Augustine was echoing official Church teaching as formulated at the Councils of Nicaea (325) and Constantinople (381). Augustine's statements regarding the person of Christ are notably anti-Arian, but this is primarily because Nicene orthodoxy was itself fashioned against Arianism. As has been stated previously, Augustine's main purpose is not polemical. Augustine affirms the true divinity of Jesus Christ: the Word of God is 'God with God' ('deus apud deum') (24. 8); the Son 'is the Son by nature, since he is what the Father is' ('ille natura est filius, qui hoc est quod pater') (30. 6).[60] Though the Son enjoyed a 'natural equality' ('naturalis aequalitas') with the Father (24. 7), for the sake of our salvation he 'did not scorn participation in our nature' (30. 10). When Paul says that Christ was *made of a woman* (Gal. 4: 4) he does so 'on account of the Son of God's assumption of the nature of a created being' (30. 3). The status of baptized believers as children of God must be carefully distinguished from the Sonship of Christ, for 'we are sons of God by the kind regard of God's mercy, while he is the Son by nature' (30. 6). Augustine puts the finishing touch on these thoughts by affirming the doctrine of the Trinity: 'the Trinity itself is one God, with the same eternity and equality of deity remaining without change in three: Father, Son, and Holy Spirit' (24. 7).

The limited use of the Creed to explain relatively difficult points in Galatians may be compared with Augustine's advice given not long afterwards in the *De doctrina christiana*. There he recommends that the interpreter of Scripture turn to the rule of faith not at the first sign of trouble but rather after other methods to resolve the ambiguity (as for instance the

---

[58] Thus Augustine, *retr.* 1. 17. 16 (Bogan, trans., 74). The Council is dated 8 October 393 (CCSL 149: 20).

[59] See Polman, *Word of God*, 208–14, and the references given there.

[60] Cf. 27. 3: The only Son is the Son 'by nature' (*natura*).

examination of the wider context of the passage) have proved unavailing.
He offers as an example the interpretation of John 1: 1–2:

> The well-known heretical punctuation *In the beginning was the Word, and the Word
> was with God, and there was God,* giving a different sense in what follows (*this Word
> was in the beginning with God*), refuses to acknowledge that the Word was God. This
> is to be refuted by the rule of faith, which lays down for us the equality of the
> members of the Trinity, and so we should say *and the Word was God,* and then go on,
> *this was in the beginning with God.*[61]

We are reminded here of the anti-Arian thrust of the passages cited above
from the *Commentary*. From the point of view of interpretation theory we
may note that Augustine's implicit references to the Creed in his
Commentary are in harmony with what he explicitly suggests in the *De
doctrina christiana*, and the Creed serves as an auxiliary to biblical interpretation.

C. AUGUSTINE'S SENSITIVITY TO QUESTIONS OF TEXT AND TRANSLATION

Elsewhere in his writings Augustine evinces considerable concern, both in
theory and in practice, with establishing the correct text of Scripture.[62] Part
of his concern is to counter Manichean charges that the text of the New
Testament is corrupt.[63] Faustus, for example, thought that Rom. 1: 3, with
its reference to the Son of God's having been born of the seed of David
according to the flesh, was probably a Judaizing interpolation, since it
clearly contradicted Paul's more likely view as expressed in passages such as
2 Cor. 5: 16, where he insists he no longer knows Christ after the flesh.[64]
Augustine's reply to Faustus in defence of both passsages illustrates his
textual concern: 'In the case before us both quotations are from the

---

[61] *doctr. chr.* 3. 2. 3 (Green, 134–5): 'Illa haeretica distinctio, *in principio erat verbum, et
verbum erat apud deum, et deus erat,* ut alius sit sensus: *verbum hoc erat in principio apud deum,*
non vult deum verbum confiteri. Sed hoc regula fidei refellendum est qua nobis de trinitatis
aequalitate praescribitur, ut dicamus, *et deus erat verbum,* deinde subiungamus, *hoc erat in
principio apud deum.*' (Italics have been added to the trans.)

[62] e.g. in *doctr. chr.* 3. 1. 1 he underscores the importance for the student of the Bible of
'knowledge of languages' ('scientia linguarum') and of 'the assistance of reliable texts derived
from the manuscripts with careful attention to the need for emendation' ('adiuvante etiam
codicum veritate, quam sollers emendationis diligentia procuravit') (Green, 132–3). For
detailed theoretical discussion see *doctr. chr.* 2. 14. 21–15. 22.

[63] In addition to the example that follows see the charges attributed to Faustus in *c. Faust.*
32. 1–2 and 33. 3.

[64] *c. Faust.* 11. 1 and 4.

canonical, that is, the genuine epistles of Paul. We cannot say that the manuscript is faulty, for the best Latin translations substantially agree; or that the translations are wrong, for the best Greek texts have the same reading.'[65]

In the *Commentary on Galatians*, however, Augustine's attention to matters of text and translation is less than one might have expected. True, he repeatedly shows a grammarian's scrupulosity over matters of definition and usage, as when he explains the odd use of the word *mulier* ('woman') for the Virgin in the Latin text of Gal. 4: 4; yet his explanation does not make reference either to the Jewish idiom 'born of woman' or to the Greek text.[66] At another point his Latin version is not merely ambiguous but positively wrong. In his Latin version of Gal. 3: 19 (*and it was placed by angels in the hand of a mediator*) the antecedent of 'it' is 'seed', rather than 'law' as in the Greek.[67] It was only much later that Augustine consulted more accurate manuscripts, 'especially those in Greek (*maxime Grecos*)', and realized that he had been misled.[68]

Augustine's one reference to the Greek New Testament in his *Commentary* is to 1 Corinthians rather than Galatians: he states that the Greek copies prove clearly that 1 Cor. 15: 31 is an oath.[69] Although the extent to which Augustine mastered Greek over the course of his lifetime has been variously assessed, his knowledge of New Testament Greek at this particular time is likely to have been such that efforts to control his interpretation of Galatians by comparison with the Greek would have been difficult.[70] Yet Augustine was not one to spare himself pains. Why did he take so few here? His difficulty with Greek is not a sufficient answer; further investigation is necessary.

David Tracy has remarked that for Augustine 'the scriptures are not the revelation but . . . the authoritative witness to the original revelation'.[71] The

---

[65] *c. Faust.* 11. 6 (trans., 180 (modified)). CSEL 25. 1: 321. 25–9: 'proinde . . . ex apostoli Pauli canonicis, id est uere Pauli epistulis utrumque profertur et non possumus dicere aut mendosum esse codicem—omnes enim latini emendati sic habent—aut interpretem errasse—omnes enim graeci emendati sic habent'.

[66] ' "Born of woman" was a typical Jewish circumlocution for the human person' (Dunn, *Galatians*, 215). Here Augustine fails to address what Bultmann considers to be the crucial question for understanding the language of the New Testament: 'Where and to what extent is its Greek determined by a Semitic use of language' (Bultmann, 'Ist voraussetzungslose Exegese möglich?', 411 (Ogden, trans., 147)).

[67] See the explanatory note attached to *exp. Gal.* 24. 3.

[68] He corrects his error in the course of his review of *Gn. litt.* in *retr.* 2. 24. (50.) 2 (CCSL 57: 109. 13– 110. 18).

[69] *exp. Gal.* 9. 3–4 (and see the explanatory note there).

[70] See e.g. Courcelle, *Late Latin Writers*, 149–57.

[71] Tracy, 'Charity, Obscurity, Clarity', 136.

original revelation is the Word of God, of which the words of the Bible are merely external signs. Moreover, those signs are efficacious only if one hears the voice of Christ, 'the inward teacher'.[72] In a sense Jesus Christ, the Word made flesh, is both the teacher and the subject taught, the means and the end, the way and the destination, the sign (*signum*) and the reality (*res*). It follows that the trappings of biblical scholarship are less important than grasping the principle of love revealed in the Incarnation. After all, did not the great Jerome, despite his fabulous learning, quite misconstrue what Peter accomplished at Antioch when he humbly accepted Paul's rebuke? Peter showed that he had learned from the Lord how 'to be *gentle and humble* (Matt. 11: 29), a preserver of love'—abilities which are not mere signs (*signa*) of spiritual realities but 'the spiritual realities themselves' (*res ipsae spirituales*) (*exp. Gal.* 15. 12–14). For humility and love are precisely the realities signified by the supreme sign of the Incarnation. Augustine's subordination of biblical scholarship to Christian discipleship is well expressed in a passage written at about the same time and concluding with the same words of Jesus that are so often referred to in the *Commentary*—Matt. 11: 28–30. Having spoken of the value of erudition, he continues:

As students of the divine scriptures, equipped in this way, begin to approach the task of studying them in detail, they must ponder incessantly this phrase of the apostle Paul: *knowledge puffs up, but love builds up* (1 Cor. 8: 1). In this way, even if they leave Egypt well provided for, they realize that without first observing the passover they cannot be saved. Now *Christ our Passover has been sacrificed* (1 Cor. 5: 7); the sacrifice of Christ teaches us nothing more clearly than what he himself calls out, as if to those whom he sees suffering in Egypt under Pharaoh: *Come unto me, you who labour and are heavy laden, and I will refresh you. Take my yoke upon you and learn from me, for I am gentle and humble of heart, and you will find rest for your souls. My yoke is a soft one, and my burden light.*[73]

So important is Christian discipleship for the biblical interpreter that even a mistaken interpretation may be acceptable if it contributes to the love of God and neighbour:

If . . . he is misled by an idea of the kind that builds up love, which is the end of the

---

[72] 'illum intus magistrum' (*mag.* 12. 40 (CCSL 29: 198. 52)).

[73] *doctr. chr.* 2. 41. 62 (Green, 126–7 (modified)): 'Sed hoc modo instructus divinarum scripturarum studiosus cum ad eas perscrutandas accedere coeperit, illud apostolicum cogitare non cesset: *scientia inflat, caritas aedificat.* Ita enim sentit, quamvis de Aegypto dives exeat, tamen nisi Pascha egerit salvum se esse non posse. *Pascha* autem *nostrum immolatus est Christus*, nihilque magis immolatio Christi nos docet quam illud quod ipse clamat, tamquam ad eos quos in Aegypto sub Pharaone videt laborare: *venite ad me qui laboratis et onerati estis et ego vos reficiam. Tollite iugum meum super vos et discite a me, quoniam mitis sum et humilis corde, et invenietis requiem animis vestris. Iugum enim meum lene est et sarcina mea levis est.*'

commandment, he is misled in the same way as a walker who leaves his path by mistake but reaches the destination to which the path leads by going through a field. But he must be put right and shown how it is more useful not to leave the path, in case the habit of deviating should force him to go astray or even adrift.[74]

Thus, as David Tracy has noted, Augustinian hermeneutics allows 'for a remarkable flexibility of meaning to the scriptural texts and for a genuine plurality of readings'.[75] Nevertheless it does not allow for pure relativism, because the multiplicity of signs and readings all point in the same direction, thus providing a complex but unified course of spiritual training. And as Rowan Williams has acutely observed, 'A language which indefinitely postpones fulfilment or enjoyment is appropriate to the Christian discipline of spiritual homelessness, to the character of the believing life as pilgrimage.'[76]

To sum up, our brief look at Augustine's theory and practice of biblical interpretation has strengthened the conclusion we reached earlier on the basis of other evidence, namely that in reading Galatians Augustine was chiefly motivated by concerns that were pastoral and practical, rather than historical and philological. He approaches the text, in the words of the Book of Revelation, longing to hear 'what the Spirit saith unto the churches'. His goal, both for himself and for his audience, is not the knowledge that puffs up but the love that builds up.

D. AUGUSTINE'S INTERPRETATION OF GALATIANS: SUMMARY AND HIGHLIGHTS

In the analysis that follows I have concentrated on those points that seemed to me remarkable, either because Augustine emphasizes them or because he conspicuously fails to do so. I have included other material if it seemed helpful in bringing out the distinctive flavour of Augustine's *Commentary*.

---

[74] *doctr. chr.* 1. 36. 41 (Green, 50–1): 'Si ea sententia fallitur qua aedificet caritatem, quae finis praecepti est, ita fallitur ac si quisquam errore deserens viam eo tamen per agrum pergat quo etiam via illa perducit. Corrigendus est tamen, et quam sit utilius viam non deserere demonstrandum est, ne consuetudine deviandi etiam in transversum aut perversum ire cogatur.'

[75] Tracy, 'Charity, Obscurity, Clarity', 140. On the same page he remarks: 'What is hermeneutically interesting here is that Augustine does not allow the author's meaning in the scriptures to determine the meaning of the text. God, as the supreme author, can use the human author to state a meaning which even the author did not understand but which some later reader (e.g. Augustine) could then discern.'

[76] Williams, 'Language, Reality and Desire', 142–3.

It is hardly necessary to say that my analysis is subjective. I only hope it may prompt others to read the text for themselves.

The Destination and Recipients of the Letter

Unlike Jerome,[77] Augustine shows little interest in specifying the destination or the recipients of the letter. It is true that the recipients are identified as Gentile converts,[78] but this identification does not resolve all ambiguity. Thus Augustine notes that when Paul speaks of the *days and months and years and seasons* that the Galatians are observing (Gal. 4: 10), it is unclear whether he is referring to Gentile or Jewish practices.[79] Augustine evidently does not regard the precise identification of the destination or the recipients as essential for an understanding of Paul's message.

The Preface to Augustine's Commentary (*exp. Gal.* 1)

Like the other Latin commentators on Galatians, Augustine begins with a few words of introduction.[80] The first sentence of his Preface is a concise statement of Paul's purpose: 'The reason the Apostle writes to the Galatians is so they may understand what it is that God's grace accomplishes for them: they are no longer under the law.' Augustine then proceeds to sketch the situation that called forth Paul's response: certain Christians of Jewish origin did not understand that the purpose of the law was to point out sins, not take them away. Contrary to Paul's original preaching, they insisted that 'the gospel would be of no benefit to [the Galatians] unless they were circumcised and submitted to other carnal observances of Jewish custom' (*exp. Gal.* 1. 2). As a result of their insistence, doubt had been cast on Paul's apostolic authority and on the agreement of his gospel with that of the other apostles. Peter, moreover, had yielded to these troublemakers and acted hypocritically.

Augustine goes on to compare the occasion and purpose of Galatians with those of Romans (*exp. Gal.* 1. 5–6). In Romans Paul sought to settle a dispute that had arisen within the Roman community between Jewish and Gentile Christians; both sides were in the wrong and both sides needed to be corrected. In Galatians, however, only one principal error is addressed: that of Jewish Christians who insist that Gentile Christians must observe the law.

[77] Cf. *Comm. on Gal.*, Preface to Book 2 (PL 26: 353c–357a).
[78] *exp. Gal.* 1. 6, 32. 1, 33. 3, *et al.*
[79] *exp. Gal.* 34. 1–35. 1.
[80] The Preface was a standard feature of the commentary genre.

The end of the Preface (*exp. Gal.* 1. 7–9) leads directly into the commentary proper by noting how the purpose of the letter is already implied not only in the exordium but even in the salutation.

Augustine on Galatians 1 (*exp. Gal.* 2–9)

Galatians 1: 1–2 is intended, says Augustine, to remove any doubt about Paul's apostolic authority. 'The earlier apostles are those sent by Christ while he was still in part a human being, that is, mortal; the last is the apostle Paul, sent by Christ now wholly God, that is, immortal in every respect. The authority of Paul's witness should therefore be regarded as equal to theirs, since the glorification of the Lord compensated for any lack of honour attributable to the lateness of his commission' (*exp. Gal.* 2. 4–5). Augustine's Christological language here is taken from Hilary of Poitiers.

Commenting on Gal. 1: 4, Augustine passes over the weighty Christological formula *who gave himself for our sins* and focuses instead on the phrase *the present evil world*, no doubt in order to ward off Manichean dualism. The doxology in Gal. 1: 4–5 provides Augustine with an opportunity to introduce an important theme of the *Commentary*—that the Son of God sought neither to secure his own glory nor to do his own will. Paul's salutation is so worded as to show that 'in preaching the gospel he is following the example of the Lord by whom he was sent and neither seeking his own glory nor doing his own will' (*exp. Gal.* 3. 6). In a sense, then, Paul's apostolic authority depends on his self-abnegation. For Augustine, humility is at the heart of Jesus' teaching and example, and in *exp. Gal.* 5. 7 he refers to Jesus' words in Matt. 11: 29 (*Take my yoke and learn from me, for I am gentle and humble of heart*)—the first of five times that he will do so in the course of the *Commentary*.[81] In concluding our remarks on Paul's salutation (1: 1–5) and exordium (1: 6–11) we should note that Augustine does not mention Paul's omission of his customary thanksgiving.

In discussing Paul's background in Judaism (Gal. 1: 13–14), Augustine follows Jesus' teaching in Matthew's Gospel[82] that the fault lay not in the law itself but in the way the Jews interpreted and practised it. Augustine's emphasis on the law as blameless is in part an attempt to fend off Manicheism.

The reason why Paul visited Peter (Gal. 1: 18) was not to learn the gospel from him but rather to 'build up brotherly love between them'. The

---

[81] The others are *exp. Gal.* 15. 12–14, 38. 3, 44. 6, and 45. 9–10.
[82] See *exp. Gal.* 7. 4, where Augustine quotes Matt. 15: 6.

importance of building up the Christian community is a characteristic theme of Augustine's *Commentary*.

On Gal. 1: 19 two possible ways of understanding James as 'the brother of the Lord' are offered, both safeguarding the virginal conception of Jesus.[83]

Paul's oath in Gal. 1: 20 receives considerable attention (*exp. Gal.* 9. 1–6). Augustine's primary concern is to show that Paul did not violate Jesus' command in Matt. 5: 33–7.

Gal. 1: 21–4 provides an opportunity for Augustine to emphasize once again Paul's desire for God's glory rather than his own.

Augustine on Galatians 2 (*exp. Gal.* 10–17)

Augustine's comments on Galatians 2 omit any reference to the question of whether the visit to Jerusalem that Paul narrates is the same as that recorded in Acts 15, a question that has a significant bearing on the degree of culpability to be assigned to Peter's inconsistent behaviour at Antioch.[84] Given Augustine's silence, it would be unsafe to speculate on how he would have answered this question at this particular time.[85]

At Jerusalem Paul stated his gospel to those of repute *privately* (Gal. 2: 2), not because he had lied to the Gentiles previously but 'because he had been silent about some things that were more than the Gentiles could bear while they were still infants' (*exp. Gal.* 10. 3). Thus Augustine strengthens his case for Paul's veracity, partly because it is essential to Paul's argument in Galatians, partly because it is essential to Augustine's own understanding of Paul as a preacher of the gospel. Augustine adds a characteristic, Catholic emphasis: even though Paul's gospel was true, it still needed to be confirmed by the other apostles in order to demonstrate that Paul's efforts were not in vain. That demonstration was especially for the benefit of the Galatians.

Augustine says that normally Titus could have been circumcised (Gal. 2: 3–5), since Paul taught that whether or not a man was circumcised did not really matter (1 Cor. 7: 19). In the circumstances, however, Paul refused to allow it because the *false brethren* who were watching him wanted 'to preach

---

[83] Cf. what Augustine says on Gal. 4: 4 in *exp. Gal.* 30. 2.

[84] For if the incident at Antioch recorded in Gal. 2: 11–14 is subsequent to the Council of Jerusalem recorded in Acts 15, at which Peter was the leading advocate for the view that there is no distinction between Jew and Gentile, then his inconsistency is much more flagrant.

[85] Writing a decade later to Jerome, Augustine says he favours the view that the incident at Antioch took place before the Council of Jerusalem (*ep.* 82. 2. 11 (CSEL 34. 2: 361. 12: 'Si autem hoc, quod magis arbitror, ante illud Hierosolymitanum concilium Petrus fecit . . .')).

circumcision as necessary for salvation and to do so with the authority and approval of Paul himself' (*exp. Gal.* 11. 4).

Augustine's gloss on Gal. 2: 6 is characteristic of his thought. Those *reputed to be something* are such only in the minds of 'carnal people'; in themselves they are nothing. 'Even if they are good servants of God, it is Christ in them who is something, not they themselves' (*exp. Gal.* 12. 2). *What they once were* refers to their having been sinners, which God mercifully did not hold against them. Galatians 2: 6 should not be thought of as an insult to Paul's predecessors, for 'they were very pleased when people accepted that they had been taken from among sinners and justified by the Lord' (*exp. Gal.* 13. 2). Augustine acknowledges that the *pillars* were especially honoured among the apostles as witnesses of the Transfiguration, but in so doing confuses James the brother of the Lord with James the son of Zebedee. Augustine adds that they were not really *pillars* but only *reputed to be* (Gal. 2: 9) and directs attention to the more important foundations of the Church—its unity (*exp. Gal.* 13. 5) and its seven gifts of the Holy Spirit (*exp. Gal.* 13. 7).

Augustine prefaces his discussion of the clash between Peter and Paul at Antioch (Gal. 2: 11–14) by emphasizing, in tacit opposition to Jerome, that Paul's becoming all things to all people involved no hypocrisy. Paul was willing to be accommodating in order not to offend the weak, so long as no fundamental principle of the gospel was at stake (*exp. Gal.* 15. 1–2).

Augustine's interpretation of Gal. 2: 11–14 has already been analysed in some detail.[86] Here it must suffice to say just a few words. First, it is possible but not certain that Augustine is attempting to put a distance between the people *from James* and James himself, in other words, to suggest that they did not truly represent the mind of James (*exp. Gal.* 15. 6); this was and still is an important issue in the interpretation of Galatians, but Augustine does not address it directly.[87] Secondly, Augustine makes Peter's humble acceptance of Paul's rebuke (which is not actually recorded in the text but can only be inferred) an act of the utmost importance for the Christian reader, linking it with that key text from Matthew that we have repeatedly noted:

It was in his rebuke that the one being rebuked proved the more admirable and difficult to imitate. For it is easy to see what you would correct in someone else and to proceed to do so by censure and criticism. It is not so easy to see what ought to be

---

[86] See under Gal. 2: 11–14 in the Index of Biblical References.

[87] By contrast, Victorinus does not hesitate to place James at the forefront of the Judaizers. Indeed, he even denies his apostleship and calls him a blasphemer (see esp. *Comm. on Gal.* 1: 19 (CSEL 83: 110. 1–27)).

corrected in yourself and to be willing to be corrected even by yourself—let alone by another, and that a junior, and all this *in front of everyone*! Now this incident serves as a great example of humility, which is the most valuable Christian training, for by humility love is preserved. For nothing violates love more quickly than pride. And therefore the Lord did not say, 'Take my yoke and learn from me, because I raise four-day-old corpses from the tomb and cast out all demons and diseases from people's bodies', and other such things, but rather, *Take my yoke and learn from me, for I am gentle and humble of heart* (Matt. 11: 29). For the former are signs of spiritual realities, but to be *gentle and humble*, a preserver of love—these are the spiritual realities themselves (*exp. Gal.* 15. 10–13).

Together with the pastoral teaching derived from Gal. 6: 1 on the duty to correct the fellow Christian who has sinned, this passage contains the central core of Augustine's understanding of Galatians.

Paul's opponents lacked Peter's humility and thought that the gospel was 'a sort of debt' paid for the righteousness they had attained under the law (*exp. Gal.* 15. 14). In fact, the spiritual fulfilment of the law depends not on merits derived from works but on the grace of Christ, who lives in the believer through faith. Quoting what is for him a key text for understanding the purpose of the law (1 Tim. 1: 9),[88] Augustine stresses that the law is not imposed on the righteous person as an external restraint, for such a person is 'in it rather than under it. . . . In a sense the person who lives righteously with a love of righteousness . . . is living the law itself' (*exp. Gal.* 17. 6). What is perhaps most remarkable is Augustine's stress on the deep continuity of the law and the gospel.

In his comment on Gal. 2: 21 Augustine sees Paul as reducing his opponents' position to absurdity: 'Not even Paul's opponents would say that *Christ died for nothing*, since they wanted to be regarded as Christians' (*exp. Gal.* 17. 14).

Augustine on Galatians 3 (*exp. Gal.* 18–28)

Augustine is concerned to defend Paul's calling the Galatians *foolish* in Gal. 3: 1. Later in the same verse he reads *proscribed* and interprets it to mean that Christ was being deprived of his possession, that is, the Galatians themselves. His interpretation appears to be dependent on that of Marius Victorinus.[89]

Before commenting on Gal. 3: 2 with its contrast between *works of the law* and *hearing the faith*, Augustine introduces a long and careful distinction

---

[88] This text is alluded to in *exp. Gal.* 1. 2 and quoted in *exp. Gal.* 49. 4.

[89] For discussion see 2. A under the subheading 'Direct Evidence of Augustine's Use of Victorinus' *Commentary on Galatians*'.

between sacramental and moral works of the law (*exp. Gal.* 19). The former (e.g. circumcision), whose importance lies not in themselves but in what they signify, are the ones Paul is primarily thinking of when he contrasts works of the law with faith. This distinction is critical to Augustine's understanding of the relation between the Old Testament and the New.

Augustine follows Paul in arguing that the Galatians received the Holy Spirit not by *works of the law* but by *hearing the faith* (*exp. Gal.* 20). The law threatens those under it with physical punishment in the present if they fail to fulfil it, and so they are driven by fear. If they fulfil the law they attain *the righteousness that is by the law* (Phil. 3: 6) and receive as their reward immunity from the threatened physical punishment. By contrast, the life of faith is motivated by the love of God and has as its reward God himself, to be enjoyed fully not in this life but in the life to come (*exp. Gal.* 21). The antithesis of fear and love is fundamental to Augustine's interpretation of Galatians.

Jesus deliberately incurred the punishment threatened for lawbreakers in order 'to set those who believed in him free from the fear of such punishment'. This is the key to understanding Deut. 21: 23 [Gal. 3: 13] (*Cursed is everyone who hangs on a tree*), which is such a stumbling block to Jews, pagans, heretics, and even some Catholics (who think it must refer to Judas Iscariot). The curse that the Lord bore on the cross is properly the curse belonging to Adam. Augustine goes so far as to link Gal. 3: 13 with John 3: 14: the serpent Moses lifted up in the desert was a fitting symbol of what the Lord bore for our sake, 'for it was by a serpent's persuasion that humanity fell into the condemnation of death' (*exp. Gal.* 22).

Augustine's exegesis of Gal. 3: 15–18 is unremarkable except for his insistence that justifying faith is essentially the same in both Old and New Testaments: 'For we are saved by believing in something which is in part past, namely, the first coming of the Lord, in part future, namely, the second coming of the Lord. But they believed in the very same thing as entirely future' (*exp. Gal.* 23).

But if Abraham and others were justified by faith, then why did God give the law? The essential reason is that humanity needed to be humbled. By revealing transgression, the law crushed pride and forced humanity to confess its need for grace. Like the other Latin commentators, Augustine identifies the *mediator* of Gal. 3: 19–20 with Christ on the basis of 1 Tim. 2: 5 (*exp. Gal.* 24. 4). (This is Augustine's earliest quotation of what becomes for him a major Christological prooftext.) What is most striking about Augustine's interpretation is his focus on Christ's humility as displayed supremely in the Incarnation, in which he *emptied himself, taking the form of a slave* (Phil. 2: 7, quoted in *exp. Gal.* 24. 7). Indeed, by metonymy the term 'humility' may stand for the Incarnation (*exp. Gal.* 24. 10). Thanks to Christ's humbling of himself, 'anyone who was cast down with the proud mediator—the Devil—urging him to pride, is raised up with the humble mediator—Christ—urging him to humility' (*exp. Gal.* 24. 6). The love shown by Christ in his Incarnation inspires love in us and a desire to imitate Christ (*exp. Gal.* 24. 10). This characteristic Pauline theme is continually in the background of Augustine's interpretation of Galatians.[90]

Augustine notes that just as the Jews were humbled by being exposed as transgressors, so the Gentiles were humbled by being exposed as idolaters. Augustine is quick to add that this is not to say that the law was harmful to the Jews. Indeed, the behaviour of many Jews who became Christians shows that it was immensely beneficial, 'for recognition of the greater illness made them both desire the physician more urgently and love him more ardently' (*exp. Gal.* 26. 9).

Though they did not have the law as their *disciplinarian* (Gal. 3: 24), the Gentiles still enjoy full status as children of God through faith (*exp. Gal.* 27). To the extent that anyone is in Christ through baptism, there is no distinction between Jew and Greek, slave and free, male and female (Gal. 3: 28). But to the extent that we are still in this world as on a journey to our final destination these distinctions, though relativized, remain in force, as both Jesus and the apostles implied by their teachings. Yet in Christ we are one, and Augustine emphasizes that the one *seed* of Gal. 3: 16 'signifies not only the Mediator himself but also the Church, of which he is the head of the body' (*exp. Gal.* 28).

Augustine on Galatians 4 (*exp. Gal.* 29–40)

When Paul says, *We . . . were enslaved under the elements of the world* (Gal. 4: 3), Augustine interprets his statement as another pointer to the theme of Church unity: 'This is not to be taken as a reference to the Jews from whom Paul was descended, but rather to the Gentiles, at least here, since it is fitting for him to identify himself with the people whom he was sent to evangelize' (*exp. Gal.* 29. 4). Thus Paul identifies himself with both Jews and Gentiles in the course of this letter.

Augustine's interpretation of Gal. 4: 4–5 is intended to remove possible doubts arising from the Latin text about Jesus' virginal conception and his relation to the Father. Commenting later on the phrase *receive adoption as sons* Augustine sees in the word 're-ceive' an indicator that Christians do

[90] Cf. e.g. *exp. Gal.* 25. 10, 36. 5, 38. 3–5, and 46. 6.

not get sonship for the first time but rather get *back* the sonship that was lost in Adam (*exp. Gal.* 30).

In interpreting Gal. 4: 6 Augustine emphasizes Church unity once again. Paul, he says, used both *Abba* and *Father* for a reason: 'It was on account of the whole people, called from both Jews and Gentiles into the unity of faith. The Hebrew word was used for the Jews, the Greek for the Gentiles, yet in such a way that the fact that the two different words mean the same thing might point to the unity of the same faith and Spirit' (*exp. Gal.* 31. 2). Since the earthly Jesus had directed his message principally to *the lost sheep of the house of Israel* (Matt. 10: 6), it was right for Paul, both here and earlier in Gal. 3: 2 and 5, 'to use the presence and gift of the Holy Spirit to prove to the Gentiles that they belong to the promise of the inheritance' (*exp. Gal.* 31).

Augustine uses Gal. 4: 8 as an occasion to reflect on divine providence, which all creatures serve, either willingly or unwillingly (*exp. Gal.* 32. 8).

Galatians 4: 9 is problematic: whereas the rest of the letter speaks of carnal observances of the Jewish law as the danger threatening the Galatians, here it appears to be the superstitions of the Gentiles. On the other hand Gal. 4: 10–11, with its reference to the observance of times, could refer to either Gentile or Jewish superstition (*exp. Gal.* 33–4). Here Augustine pauses to reflect upon the superstitious observance of times as symptomatic of the widespread and acute pastoral problem posed by astrology. His reflections end on a note of personal lamentation (*exp. Gal.* 35).

Paul's having preached the gospel to the Galatians *through weakness of the flesh* (Gal. 4: 13) is construed by Augustine as meaning 'when he was suffering persecution'. The *test* to which the Galatians were then put was 'whether they would forsake him out of fear or embrace him out of love'. At that time love triumphed. Would it triumph now? (*exp. Gal.* 37).

When Paul addresses the Galatians as *my little children* he wants them to imitate him as they would a parent, and when he says he is *again in labour pains until Christ is formed in you*, he is speaking 'in the person of Mother Church'. Christ is formed in the believer by faith and by 'staying close to Christ through spiritual love'. Paul is deeply concerned, however, that the Galatians, having started along this path, may not reach the goal, which is the full measure of Christ's maturity (*exp. Gal.* 38). Indeed, he wishes he could be present with them and change his tone, by which Augustine understands Paul to mean that he wanted to rebuke them more severely (*exp. Gal.* 39).

Augustine's treatment of the allegory of Hagar and Sarah is chiefly remarkable for its digressions. One concerns the question (never raised by Paul) of Abraham's children by Keturah after Sarah's death. Augustine explores the possibility that they signify heresies and schisms. A second digression is a very doubtful defence, first, of Abraham against the charge of adultery with Hagar and, second, of Sarah against the charge of having condoned Abraham's adultery. Both digressions are largely inspired by Augustine's wish to counter the Manichees (*exp. Gal.* 40).

Augustine on Galatians 5 (*exp. Gal.* 41–55)

Galatians 5: 1 (*Stand firm*) shows that the Galatians have not yet fallen. Augustine specifies that it is not circumcision itself that nullifies the benefits of Christ but rather believing in circumcision as salvific; otherwise Paul would not have circumcised Timothy. To believe in circumcision as salvific entails placing oneself under obligation to fulfil the law in its entirety, which the Jews had been powerless to do (*exp. Gal.* 41). From this danger the Galatians are being called back 'by the authority of the apostle Paul' (*exp. Gal.* 42). What ultimately matters is *the faith that works through love* (Gal. 5: 6)—a key phrase for Augustine's interpretation of Galatians. By contrast, 'slavery under the law works by fear'.

The curse Paul seems to utter against his opponents in Gal. 5: 12 is interpreted by Augustine as 'a blessing under the appearance of a curse' (*exp. Gal.* 42. 19–20).

Augustine prefaces his remarks on the moral works of the law by stressing that they are the same in both the Old Testament and the New, but in the Old they were performed out of carnal fear while in the New they are performed out of spiritual love, which alone can actually fulfil them. Indeed, by symbolic foreshadowing the ceremonial works of the law also refer to this love. Spiritual love is a gift of the Holy Spirit, whom believers receive through faith. One reason why Paul mentions only the love of neighbour as being necessary for the fulfilment of the law is because the love of neighbour presupposes the love of God. Augustine sees Paul's exhortation to the Galatians to *walk in the Spirit* as a remedy for destructive disputes that were occurring among them, 'for the first and great gift of the Spirit is humility and gentleness (*exp. Gal.* 43–5).

Augustine begins his remarks on Gal. 5: 17 by correcting a (Manichean) misunderstanding: 'People think that the Apostle is here denying that we have free choice of the will and do not understand that this is said to them if they refuse to hold on to the grace of faith they have received.' In order to explain the role of grace Augustine uses a schema derived from Rom. 7–8 according to which the life of the believer is divided into four stages, corresponding to the four stages of the biblical history of salvation: 'prior to the law', 'under the law', 'under grace', and 'in . . . eternal peace' (*exp. Gal.* 46. 4–9). Augustine's attention is concentrated on the second and third stages, 'under the law' and 'under grace', since they reflect Christian existential experience in a way that the first and fourth stages do not: 'under the law' and 'under grace' represent two permanent and ineradicable potentialities of earthly life. Augustine makes it clear that to be 'under grace' does not mean to be free from sinful desires but to be free from their domination (*exp. Gal.* 46–8).

Useful though the four-stage schema is as a hermeneutical principle, its importance for Augustine is altogether eclipsed by the spiritual teachings that follow.[91] It is in these teachings that we find the parallels with his monastic rule and realize that Augustine is addressing his fellow monks as their spiritual director.

After Paul lists the works of the flesh he proceeds to list the works of the Spirit, which he calls *the fruit of the Spirit*. Those who exhibit the works of the Spirit are using the law lawfully (1 Tim. 1: 8–10). They exhibit them because they delight in them, 'for we necessarily act in accordance with what delights us more' (*exp. Gal.* 48–9).

The two lists are clearly not meant to correlate with each other at every point. Nevertheless it is interesting to reflect on possible correlations, some of which seem strong, e.g. fornication heads the list of carnal vices, while love heads the list of spiritual virtues. Paul's inclusion of both envy and jealousy in his list of carnal vices prompts Augustine to draw a careful distinction, thus displaying the grammarian's interest in synonyms (*exp. Gal.* 50–2).

The means by which Christians are said by Paul to have *crucified their flesh* (Gal. 5: 24) is fear—not carnal fear but the fear that *is pure and endures forever* (Ps. 18: 10), whereby we are careful not to offend him whom we love with all our heart, all our soul, and all our mind' (*exp. Gal.* 53).

Augustine on Galatians 6 (*exp. Gal.* 56–65)

Galatians 6: 1 engages Augustine's attention like no other verse in this letter, even Gal. 5: 17. He begins his discussion of it by observing that 'nothing proves that a man is spiritual like his handling of another's sin'. It

[91] As has been noted by Mendoza, 'Introduzione', 480–3, the four stages are but one manifestation—though a supremely important one—of the way in which Divine Providence orders all things. Thus the Gentiles, although they did not have the law as a *disciplinarian*, did have *the elements of the world* to keep them under restraint until the coming of Christ.

is a delicate undertaking, but 'whether to use more severity or more charm in speaking should be determined by what seems necessary for the salvation of the person being corrected'. Augustine likens Christian correction to a painful and difficult surgical procedure (*exp. Gal.* 56).

Great danger arises if the feelings of the one correcting are hurt by the opposition of the one being corrected, 'for when your feelings are hurt whatever you say will be an expression of violent retaliation and not of loving correction'. Augustine formulates a guiding rule—'Love, and say what you like'—and reflects on how it should be followed: 'We should never undertake the task of rebuking another's sin without first examining our own conscience by inner questioning and then responding—unequivocally before God—that we are acting out of love.' The act of trying to correct someone who resists correction can provide us with a lesson in humility, 'since in the very act of rebuking them we ourselves sin when we find it easier to respond to the sinner's anger with our own anger than to the sinner's misery with our mercy' (*exp. Gal.* 57).

Throughout his discussion of the hortatory material in Gal. 5 and 6, Augustine's emphasis on love and humility as the distinctive marks of the Christian remind us of his earlier emphasis on the love and humility displayed by Christ above all in his death for sinners.[92] Thus we see that for Augustine there is the closest possible correlation between the gospel of salvation Paul proclaims and the behaviour he expects from those who receive that gospel in faith. In other words, the hortatory material is absolutely central to the message of Galatians and in no sense peripheral.[93] Paul states that bearing one another's burdens fulfils the law of Christ, i.e. love. But the command to love one's neighbour is already present in the Old Testament, so that the law of Christ is the basic principle of both Testaments. The main difference consists in the motive with which that law is approached: either love or fear (*exp. Gal.* 58).

[92] See e.g. *exp. Gal.* 24.

[93] In relation to scholarly debate in our own time, Augustine would be close to Richard Hays in this regard and far from Hans Dieter Betz, who writes: 'Paul does not provide the Galatians with a specifically Christian ethic. The Christian is addressed as an educated and responsible person. He is expected to do no more than what would be expected of any other educated person in the Hellenistic culture of the time. In a rather conspicuous way Paul conforms to the ethical thought of his contemporaries' (*Galatians*, 292, quoted in Hays, *Moral Vision*, 17). Hays comments: 'According to Betz's account, Paul's gospel may provide motivation to do what is right, but it does not generate a singularly Christian account of "what is right"; Paul adopts his moral *norms* from the surrounding educated culture' (ibid., italics original). Hays's own view is that 'there is no meaningful distinction between theology and ethics in Paul's thought, because Paul's theology is fundamentally an account of God's work of transforming his people into the image of Christ' (ibid. 46). See further, Hays, 'Christology and Ethics'.

In commenting on Paul's admonitions about pride and boasting Augustine concentrates, as we might expect, on the danger of relying on other people's praise. This danger may be avoided by close and careful self-examination. In line with this, Augustine interprets Gal. 6: 5 as referring to 'burdens' of conscience, which are often increased when our desire to please others leads us to neglect our duty to correct them when they have sinned.

Augustine notes that Christians sow in this life but must wait until the life to come to gather the harvest, for in this life they live by faith in things unseen (*exp. Gal.* 61).

Augustine regards Gal. 6: 11–18 as an emphatic recapitulation of Paul's case. Paul's Jewish-Christian opponents are forcing the Galatians to be circumcised in order that they themselves may avoid being persecuted by the Jews. Thus they are driven by fear, just as they were before they became Christians. By contrast, Paul's fearlessness is demonstrated by the fact that he has written such a letter in his own hand. When Paul says that his opponents do not even keep the law themselves, he means that they cannot, since their motive principle is not love (*exp. Gal.* 62).

Paul reiterates that it is not circumcision that is harmful but placing one's hope for salvation in it. Thus no one should think that he acted in pretence in circumcising Timothy. *For it is not circumcision or uncircumcision that counts, but a new creation* (Gal. 6: 15), by which Paul means 'new life through faith in Jesus Christ' (*exp. Gal.* 63).

Augustine interprets *the marks of the Lord Jesus Christ* on Paul's body (Gal. 6: 17) as being wounds from the persecution he had suffered. Paul knew that this persecution was 'retribution for the offense of persecuting the churches of Christ. . . . Nevertheless, because of the forgiveness of sins, for which he was baptized, all those tribulations brought him not to destruction, but to the crown of victory' (*exp. Gal.* 64).

5

Conclusions

Augustine chooses to write a commentary on Galatians that is essentially pastoral, intended not merely to inform his audience but also to form them in the faith. This choice is consonant with his dual role as priest and monk: on the one hand he shares with Valerius responsibility for the Catholic parish at Hippo and is preparing eventually to succeed Valerius as bishop; on the other hand he is the spiritual director of his monastic community. Thus, while his later comments on Paul will undoubtedly do much to shape the 'introspective conscience of the West', here Augustine is reading Paul chiefly as a guide to building community. Unlike the broader parish community, which is referred to explicitly in the text, the monastic community can only be inferred. Nevertheless, the striking parallels between the *Commentary* and Augustine's monastic *Rule* sufficiently demonstrate that the immediate audience for the *Commentary* is Augustine's monastic community. Despite the wide differences in form and content between the *Commentary* and the *Rule*, the two texts illuminate each other brilliantly.

As a pastor, Augustine approaches Paul's Letter to the Galatians with this question in the forefront of his mind: 'How can we live in the Spirit so as to build up the body of Christ?' Although this is often not the first question raised in a modern academic commentary, it is neverthless faithful to Paul's characteristic emphases on Christian praxis (e.g. Gal. 5: 25: *If we live in the Spirit, let us also follow in the Spirit*) and spiritual formation (e.g. Gal. 4: 19: *My little children, for whom I am again in labour pains until Christ is formed in you*). Spiritual formation means imitating Christ (*exp. Gal.* 24. 10), and that in turn means becoming humble. For Christ is the supreme example of humility (*exp. Gal.* 25. 10) because he *emptied himself, taking the form of a slave*, in order that he might die on the cross for sinners. Thus in Augustine's view there is an indissoluble link between Paul's theology and his ethics, and if, as Richard Hays has argued, modern interpreters of Paul have often erred by failing to recognize that link, then Augustine may offer a helpful corrective.

Humility is 'the most valuable Christian training, for by humility love is preserved' (*exp. Gal.* 15. 11). Humility is also 'the first and great gift of the Spirit' (*exp. Gal.* 45. 9). Its primacy is explicitly affirmed by Christ himself in the words: *Take my yoke and learn from me, for I am gentle and humble of heart* (Matt. 11: 29). Augustine can use this Gospel saying to interpret Paul's Letter because of his presuppositions concerning the unity of all Scripture in Christ, but there is a further justification in this instance. Paul is adamant that the Galatians are not to take upon themselves *a yoke of slavery* (Gal. 5: 1) but instead to submit wholeheartedly to Christ. In fashioning an antithesis between this yoke of slavery and the yoke of Christ (e.g. *exp. Gal.* 44. 6), Augustine is simply drawing out the clear implication of Paul's thought and expressing it in the same antithetical form that Paul himself habitually used.[1] The emphasis on humility as necessary for Christian love is brought out most memorably in the interpretation of the encounter between Peter and Paul at Antioch. Augustine says that Peter humbly accepted Paul's rebuke in order to follow Christ's example and preserve Christian love.

If Peter represents the greater example (*exp. Gal.* 15. 10), Paul's example in administering correction to a fellow Christian is hardly less important, for correction is indispensable as an instrument of Christian formation. Indeed, Augustine regards it as the ultimate proof that a person is spiritual (*exp. Gal.* 56. 1). From Paul Christians can learn how to administer correction, not only because he corrected Peter and the Galatians, but also because he advised the Galatians on how they ought to correct one another (Gal. 6: 1). Augustine's pastoral reading of Galatians and the prominence he gives to the theme of Christian correction are therefore not alien impositions on the text but rather natural derivatives of it. At the same time they remind us of Augustine's original response to the Scriptures following his ordination to the priesthood, a response exactly summarized by Peter Brown: 'Plainly, what he absorbed at this time, were the lessons of the active life of S. Paul. He will identify himself passionately with the ideal of authority shown in the letters of Paul to his wayward communities: "insisting in season and out of season" . . .'[2]

Yet while Augustine is deeply concerned with Christian correction, his *Commentary* is not essentially polemical, and this is in line with his statement in the *De doctrina christiana* that the student of Scripture should be

---

[1] What E. P. Sanders refers to as Paul's ' "black-and-white thinking" ' (*Paul, the Law, and the Jewish People*, 153, and cf. 70, 80, 138–40).

[2] P. Brown, *Augustine of Hippo*, 206. For Brown's allusion to 2 Tim. 4: 2, cf. *exp. Gal.* 56. 9–12.

one who is 'gentle' and 'does not revel in controversy'.[3] Thus, while the *Commentary* includes polemical elements, most notably against the Manichees, these elements are radically subordinated to Augustine's pastoral purpose. For Christian humility automatically provides the solution to all disputes among Christians (cf. *exp. Gal.* 45. 8–10) and hence to all heresy and schism, which ultimately spring from pride.[4] Thus humility can cure Manichean pride in superior knowledge or Donatist pride in superior holiness or any other form that pride may take. It can even cure Jerome's pride as a biblical interpreter, which led him to champion an erroneous interpretation of Gal. 2: 11–14 that threatened to undermine the entire authority of the Bible.

Mention of Jerome leads naturally to the question of Augustine's sources. Although none are named in the *Commentary* several may be discerned with varying degrees of clarity. It is certain that Augustine consulted Jerome's *Commentary on Galatians,* yet he seems to have borrowed nothing from it and indeed his only measurable response to it is intensely negative. With regard to the other Latin commentators on Galatians we have argued that Augustine may have consulted Ambrosiaster and that it is highly probable that he consulted Marius Victorinus. Other notable influences are: Cyprian of Carthage, who is the main source of Augustine's interpretation of Gal. 2: 11–14; Hilary of Poitiers, whose Christological statements are reprised in Augustine's interpretation of Gal. 1: 1; and Optatus of Mileu, who is echoed above all in Augustine's insistence on the Church's catholicity, conceived in terms of universal extension in space. Augustine's indebtedness to these authors in the *Commentary on Galatians* sheds important light on a famous passage in the *De doctrina christiana* where Augustine praises Cyprian, Victorinus, Optatus, and Hilary (along with Lactantius[5]) for having despoiled the Egyptians of their gold, that is, for having taken the treasures of pagan learning and used them in the service of the gospel.[6] Augustine's listing of names differs from the sort of name-dropping done by Jerome in the *De viris illustribus,* which includes Victorinus, for example, even though Jerome treated him so harshly in his

---

[3] *doctr. chr.* 3. 1. 1 (Green, text and trans., 132–3): 'Et ne amet certamina, pietate mansuetus . . .'

[4] Cf. e.g. *Gn. adu. Man.* 2. 8. 11: 'Pride is the mother of all heretics' (CSEL 91: 130. 6–7: 'est mater omnium haereticorum superbia').

[5] Augustine drew upon Lactantius as a source at virtually the same time as he wrote *exp. Gal.* Although Lactantius is not named, Augustine is in fact dependent upon his *Divinae institutiones* 7. 24. 11 when he speaks of Virgil's fourth Eclogue as having been prophetic of Christ (*ep. Rm. inch.* 3. 3). See Bastiaensen, 'Augustin et ses prédécesseurs latins chrétiens', 45.

[6] *doctr. chr.* 2. 40. 60–1.

Commentary on Galatians. By contrast Augustine here praises authors whom he genuinely admires and has actually followed. These 'good and faithful Christians'[7] used their splendid learning in the service of the gospel, and Augustine in turn has reused it in his own exposition of Galatians. Thus when Augustine praises these famous men in the *De doctrina* he does so in part out of personal gratitude for the help they have given him in interpreting Paul—a gratitude that would be fresh in his mind if, as evidence suggests,[8] the *De doctrina* was begun just a few months after the completion of the *Commentary*.

The list of famous men who made such exemplary use of pagan learning is followed immediately in the *De doctrina* by an emphatic reminder that learning in itself is nothing if one has not also learned the more fundamental lesson of how to be *gentle and humble of heart* (Matt. 11: 29). This, says Augustine, is what the exegete must learn above all else if he or she is to unlock the meaning of the Scriptures. But this is the very same key we have already seen Augustine using to unlock the spiritual teaching of Galatians. Thus, in answer to the often-raised question of the relation of Augustine's theory of interpretation to his actual practice, we may say that here, at least, what appears as theory in the *De doctrina* was indeed already practised in the *Commentary on Galatians*.

When we combine these facts with other evidence of Augustine's method as seen in the *Commentary*—his concern to discriminate between literal and figurative meanings and between 'signs' and 'things',[9] his desire to avoid being misled by ambiguity,[10] his care to establish the correct punctuation,[11] and even his need to protest against astrology[12]—our view is strengthened that the *Commentary* furnishes a practical example of the theory of interpretation set forth in the *De doctrina* and indeed paves the way for that theory.

It would, of course, be too much to say that Augustine's *Commentary on Galatians* is the royal road to the *De doctrina*. But it is a major road that has been neglected for much too long. For it was in this, his only complete commentary on any book of the Bible, that Augustine's principles of interpretation were tested as never before and thus made ready for the hermeneutical reflection we find in the *De doctrina*. Paula Fredriksen has shown convincingly how Augustine's early commentaries on Romans may

---

[7] 'boni fideles nostri' (*doctr. chr.* 2. 40. 61 (Green, 126–7)).

[8] See O'Donovan, '*Usus* and *Fruitio* in Augustine', 395.

[9] e.g. *exp. Gal.* 36. 4–5 and 15. 11–13. With both cf. e.g. *doctr. chr.* 3. 5. 9.

[10] e.g. *exp. Gal.* 19. Cf. *doctr. chr.* 3. 6. 10 and 3. 8. 12–9. 13.

[11] e.g. *exp. Gal.* 24. 2–3. Cf. *doctr. chr.* 3. 2. 2–9.

[12] *exp. Gal.* 34–5. Cf. *doctr. chr.* 2. 21. 32–22. 34.

be viewed as wayside halts on his journey towards a transformed doctrine of grace in the *Ad Simplicianum* and beyond. The *Commentary on Galatians*, while it too sheds light on his developing doctrine of grace, has an even greater importance in providing a direct link to the theory of interpretation elaborated in the *De doctrina*.

Part II
Augustine's Commentary on the Letter to the Galatians

Text, Translation, and Notes

Epistulae ad Galatas Expositionis
liber unus

1. Praefatio. Causa propter quam scribit apostolus ad Galatas, haec est, ut intelligant gratiam dei id secum agere, ut sub lege iam non sint. (2) Cum enim praedicata eis esset euangelii gratia, non defuerunt quidam ex circumcisione quamuis Christiani nomine nondum tamen tenentes ipsum gratiae beneficium et adhuc uolentes esse sub oneribus legis, quae dominus deus imposuerat non iustitiae seruientibus sed peccato iustam scilicet legem iniustis hominibus dando ad demonstranda peccata eorum non auferenda; non enim aufert peccata nisi gratia fidei, quae per dilectionem operatur, sub hac ergo gratia iam Galatas constitutos illi uolebant constituere sub oneribus legis asseuerantes nihil eis prodesse euangelium, nisi circumciderentur et ceteras carnales Iudaici ritus obseruationes subirent. (3) Et ideo Paulum apostolum suspectum habere coeperant, a quo illis euangelium praedicatum erat, tamquam non tenentem disciplinam ceterorum apostolorum, qui gentes cogebant iudaizare. (4) Cesserat enim

---

[1] By 'the Apostle' Augustine and the Church Fathers in general mean St Paul. That *the least of the apostles, unfit to be called an apostle* (1 Cor. 15: 9), should have come to be viewed by later ages as 'the Apostle' *par excellence* is remarkable. The following considerations help to account for this development: much of the Acts of the Apostles focuses on Paul's call by the risen Lord and his subsequent missionary activity; the stature of the *apostle to the Gentiles* (Rom. 11: 13) naturally grew greater as the Church became overwhelmingly Gentile in the decades following his death; and finally, when the letters ascribed to him were gathered together and canonized they made up nearly one-third of the New Testament.

[2] i.e. believers of Jewish origin. The expression is biblical: cf. e.g. Gal. 2: 12, Acts 10: 45, 11: 2.

[3] Cf. 1 Tim. 1: 9. Here and elsewhere in this translation 'righteousness' renders the Latin *iustitia*, which could also be rendered as 'justice'.

[4] 'the grace of faith' (*gratia fidei*): a key phrase in this text, referring to God's gracious offer of forgiveness and salvation in Christ, which is received through faith. The quotation from Gal. 5: 6 highlights another aspect of faith—its enduring fruitfulness. Together the phrase and the quotation epitomize much of what Augustine has to say about faith in this commentary. (Note that all biblical quotations in this translation are printed in italics.)

[5] Literally, 'who were compelling Gentiles to Judaize (Latin: *iudaizare*)'—in other words, '. . . to live in accordance with Jewish customs'. In the Latin Bible the term occurs only at Gal. 2: 14, where it virtually transliterates the Greek ἰουδαΐζειν.

Commentary on the Letter to the Galatians

1. Preface. The reason the Apostle[1] writes to the Galatians is so they may understand what it is that God's grace accomplishes for them: they are no longer under the law. (2) For though the grace of the gospel had been preached to them, there were some from the circumcision[2] who still did not grasp the real benefit of grace. Despite being called Christians, they still wanted to be under the burdens of the law—burdens that the Lord God had imposed not on those serving righteousness but on those serving sin.[3] That is, he had given a righteous law to unrighteous people to point out their sins, not take them away. He takes away sins only by the grace of *faith, which works through love* (Gal. 5: 6).[4]

So then, these people wanted to put the Galatians, who were already under this grace, under the burdens of the law, claiming that the gospel would be of no benefit to them unless they were circumcised and submitted to other carnal observances of Jewish custom. (3) Because of this claim, the Galatians had begun to regard the apostle Paul, who had preached the gospel to them, as suspect on the ground that he did not hold the teaching of the other apostles, who were compelling Gentiles to live like Jews.[5] (4) To avoid scandalizing such people, the apostle Peter had yielded to them and had thus been led into hypocrisy,[6] as though he too believed that the gospel was of no benefit to Gentiles unless they fulfilled the burdens of the law. The apostle Paul calls him back from this hypocrisy, as he demonstrates in this very letter.[7]

(5) The point at issue in the Letter to the Romans is similar, but with this apparent difference: there he resolves an actual[8] conflict, settling a dispute that had arisen between believers of Jewish and of Gentile origin. The Jews

---

[6] Latin: *simulatio* (cf. Gal. 2: 13), understood by Augustine in a very unfavourable sense. By contrast Jerome, anxious to safeguard Peter's reputation, interprets Peter's *simulatio* in a favourable sense, noting that 'even our Lord himself . . . assumed the likeness (*simulatio*) of sinful flesh' (*Comm. on Gal.* 2: 11 ff. (PL 26: 340A), alluding to Rom. 8: 3).

[7] Cf. Gal. 2: 11–14.

[8] Reading *ipsam* with the Maurists and Rousselet, rather than Divjak's puzzling *ipsum*. (On the Latin text see Appendix 1.)

talium hominum scandalis apostolus Petrus et in simulationem ductus erat, tamquam et ipse hoc sentiret nihil prodesse gentibus euangelium, nisi onera legis implerent, a qua simulatione idem apostolus Paulus eum reuocat, sicut in hac ipsa epistula docet. (5) Talis quidem quaestio est et in epistula ad Romanos: uerumtamen uidetur aliquid interesse, quod ibi contentionem ipsum dirimit litemque componit, quae inter eos, qui ex Iudaeis et eos, qui ex gentibus crediderant, orta erat, cum illi tamquam ex meritis operum legis sibi redditum euangelii praemium arbitrarentur, quod praemium incircumcisis tamquam immeritis nolebant dari, illi contra Iudaeis se praeferre gestirent tamquam interfectoribus domini. (6) In hac uero epistula ad eos scribit, qui iam commoti erant auctoritate illorum, qui ex Iudaeis erant et ad obseruationes legis cogebant; coeperant enim eis credere, tamquam Paulus apostolus non uera praedicasset, quod eos circumcidi noluisset. (7) Et ideo sic coepit: *Miror, quod sic tam cito transferimini ab eo, qui uos uocauit in gloriam Christi, in aliud euangelium.* (8) Hoc ergo exordio causae quaestionem breuiter insinuauit. Quamquam et ipsa salutatione, cum dicit se apostolum *non ab hominibus neque per hominem*, quod in nulla alia epistula dixisse inuenitur, satis ostendit et illos, qui talia persuadebant, non esse a deo sed ab hominibus et ceteris apostolis, quantum ad auctoritatem testimonii euangelici pertinet, imparem se haberi non oportere, quandoquidem non ab hominibus neque per hominem, sed per Iesum Christum et deum patrem se apostolum nouerit. (9) Singula igitur ab ipso epistulae uestibulo permittente domino et adiuuante studium nostrum sic consideranda et tractanda suscepimus.

2. *Paulus apostolus non ab hominibus neque per hominem sed per Iesum Christum et deum patrem, qui suscitauit illum a mortuis, et qui mecum sunt omnes fratres, ecclesiis Galatiae.* (2) Qui ab hominibus mittitur, mendax est, qui per hominem mittitur, potest esse uerax, quia et deus uerax potest per hominem mittere, qui ergo neque ab hominibus neque per hominem sed per deum mittitur, ab illo uerax est, qui etiam per hominem missos ueraces

[9] By 'the salutation' Augustine means Gal. 1: 1–5; by 'the exordium' (i.e. introduction), Gal. 1: 6–11. A comprehensive literary analysis of Galatians according to formal ancient Graeco-Roman conventions has been proposed by Betz (*Galatians*, 14–25) as a key to Galatians, but there is little evidence that this kind of systematic literary analysis was of interest to Augustine or indeed to any of the other Latin commentators. Cooper, '*Narratio*', argues persuasively that Victorinus would not have deemed it appropriate to subject Galatians to a systematic analysis in terms of rhetorical conventions, since Paul himself clearly did not follow them in any systematic way. Much the same could be said of Augustine.
[10] Cf. 1 Cor. 15: 8.

thought that the reward of the gospel had been paid to them for merits accruing from works of the law and did not want this reward given to the uncircumcised, whom they regarded as undeserving. The Gentiles, on the other hand, desired to exalt themselves above the Jews, regarding them as murderers of the Lord.

(6) In this letter, however, he is writing to people troubled by those of Jewish origin who were driving them towards observances of the law. Indeed, they had begun to believe these people, as though the apostle Paul, by refusing to have the Galatians circumcised, had not preached the truth. (7) Hence he begins as follows: *I am amazed that you are so quickly deserting him who called you into the glory of Christ and turning to another gospel* (Gal. 1: 6). (8) With this exordium he has briefly introduced his reason for writing. But in fact, even in the salutation itself,[9] where he says he is an apostle *not from human beings nor through a human being* (an expression he uses in no other letter), he shows quite clearly that his opponents were not from God but *from human beings*, and that he should not be deemed inferior to the other apostles as far as the authority of his witness to the gospel is concerned; for he knows he is an apostle *not from human beings nor through a human being, but through Jesus Christ and God the Father* (Gal. 1: 1). (9) So then, if the Lord will give his consent and his help to our endeavour, we intend to examine and discuss each point, beginning from the very opening of the letter.

2. *Paul an apostle—not from human beings nor through a human being, but through Jesus Christ and God the Father, who raised him from the dead—and all the brethren who are with me, to the churches of Galatia* (Gal. 1: 1–2). (2) Anyone sent *from human beings* is untruthful. Someone sent *through a human being* may be truthful, because God who is truthful may send *through a human being*. Therefore someone sent neither *from human beings* nor *through a human being* but through God is truthful because of him who makes truthful even those sent *through a human being*. (3) Thus the earlier apostles, who were sent not from human beings but by God through a human being—that is, through Jesus Christ while he was still mortal— were truthful. And the last[10] apostle, who was sent by Jesus Christ now wholly God after his resurrection, is also truthful.[11] (4) The earlier apostles

---

[11] Augustine comments on this passage in *retr.* 1. 24 (23). 1: 'The expression, "now wholly God," was used because of the immortality which He began to possess after the Resurrection, not because of His divinity, ever immortal, from which He was never separated, and in which He was wholly God, even though He was still destined to die' (Bogan, trans., 102; CCSL 57: 71. 10–13). Augustine's striking language in *exp. Gal.* 2. 3–4 is clearly influenced by Hilary of Poitiers's *De trinitate* 11. 40–1 (CCSL 62A: 567–9), as Van Bavel has pointed out (*Recherches*, 16 n. 11).

facit. (3) Priores ergo apostoli ueraces, qui non ab hominibus sed a deo per hominem missi sunt per Iesum Christum scilicet adhuc mortalem. Verax etiam nouissimus apostolus, qui per Iesum Christum totum iam deum post resurrectionem eius missus est. (4) Priores sunt ceteri apostoli per Christum adhuc ex parte hominem, id est mortalem, nouissimus est apostolus Paulus per Christum iam totum deum, id est omni ex parte immortalem. (5) Sit ergo testimonii eius aequalis auctoritas, in cuius honorem implet clarificatio domini, si quid habebat ordo temporis minus. (6) Ideo enim cum dixisset: *et deum patrem*, addidit: *qui suscitauit illum a mortuis*, ut etiam ex hoc modo breuiter iam a clarificato missum se esse commemoraret.

3. *Gratia uobis et pax a deo patre et domino Iesu Christo.* (2) Gratia dei est, qua nobis donantur peccata, ut reconciliemur deo, pax autem, qua reconciliamur deo. (3) *Qui dedit semetipsum pro peccatis nostris, ut eximeret nos de praesenti saeculo maligno.* Saeculum praesens malignum propter malignos homines, qui in illo sunt, intelligendum est, sicut dicimus et malignam domum propter malignos inhabitantes in ea. (4) *Secundum uoluntatem dei et patris nostri, cui est gloria in saecula saeculorum. Amen.* (5) Quanto igitur magis homines non debent arroganter ad seipsos referre, si quid operantur boni, quando et ipse dei filius in euangelio non gloriam suam se quaerere dixit neque uoluntatem suam uenisse facere sed uoluntatem eius, qui eum misit? (6) Quam uoluntatem gloriamque patris nunc commemorauit apostolus, ut ipse quoque domini exemplo, a quo missus est, non se quaerere gloriam suam significaret nec facere uoluntatem suam in praedicatione euangelii, sicut paulo post dicit: *Si hominibus placerem, Christi seruus non essem.*

4. *Miror, quod sic tam cito transferimini ab eo, qui uos uocauit in gloriam Christi, in aliud euangelium, quod non est aliud.* (2) Euangelium enim si aliud est, praeter id quod siue per se siue per aliquem dominus dedit, iam nec euangelium recte dici potest. (3) Vigilanter autem cum dixisset: *Transferimini ab eo, qui uos uocauit,* adiunxit: *in gloriam Christi,* quam uolebant illi euacuare, quasi frustra uenerit Christus, si iam circumcisio

---

[12] In *retr.* 1. 24 (23). 2 Augustine says that this comment 'should be interpreted in such a way that, nevertheless, we realize also that both belong to the grace of God in general, just as among the people of God, one can distinguish separately Israel and Judah, and yet that both, in general, are Israel' (Bogan, trans., 102; CCSL 57: 72. 28–31). Augustine's comment on Gal. 1: 3 is paralleled by Pelagius's: 'By which [peace], with all their sins forgiven, they have been reconciled to God' (Souter, *Expositions,* ii. 307. 10–11).

are those sent by Christ while he was still in part a human being, that is, mortal; the last is the apostle Paul, sent by Christ now wholly God, that is, immortal in every respect. (5) The authority of Paul's witness should therefore be regarded as equal to theirs, since the glorification of the Lord compensated for any lack of honour attributable to the lateness of his commission. (6) For this reason when he said, *and God the Father,* he added, *who raised him from the dead,* so as to state, if only briefly, that he was sent by the Glorified One.

3. *Grace to you and peace from God the Father and the Lord Jesus Christ* (Gal. 1: 3). (2) It is by God's *grace* that our sins are forgiven so that we may be reconciled to God; it is by *peace,* however, that we *are* reconciled to God.[12] (3) *Who gave himself for our sins to deliver us from the present evil world* (Gal. 1: 4). *The present world* is understood to be *evil* because of the evil people who live in it,[13] just as we also say that a house is evil because of the evil people living in it. (4) *According to the will of our God and Father, to whom be glory forever and ever. Amen* (Gal. 1: 4–5). (5) How much more, then, should people not arrogantly attribute it to themselves if they do anything good, seeing that the Son of God himself declared in the Gospel[14] that he was not seeking his own glory and had not come to do his own will, but the will of him who sent him. (6) The Apostle has mentioned the will and glory of the Father at this point to demonstrate that in preaching the gospel he is following the example of the Lord by whom he was sent and neither seeking his own glory nor doing his own will. As he says a little later: *If I were pleasing people, I would not be a servant of Christ* (Gal. 1: 10).

4. *I am amazed that you are so quickly deserting him who called you into the glory of Christ and turning to another gospel—not that there is another gospel* ... (Gal. 1: 6–7). (2) For if a gospel is other than that which the Lord gave (whether personally or through someone else), then it cannot rightly be called a 'gospel'. (3) But after saying, *you are deserting him who called you,* he alertly added, *into the glory of Christ*—glory which his opponents were willing to nullify, as if Christ came in vain, which would indeed be the case if circumcision of the flesh and legal works of this kind had the power to save. (4) *But some are troubling you and trying to subvert the gospel of Christ* (Gal. 1: 7). They are not *subverting* the gospel of Christ in the same way as they are *troubling* the Galatians, for the gospel of Christ remains absolutely firm. Nevertheless they are *trying to subvert* it when they draw the attention of believers away from spiritual things and back to things that are carnal.

---

[13] That Augustine focuses on this phrase rather than on the weighty Christological formula that precedes it may reflect his eagerness to oppose Manichean dualism.

[14] Cf. John 8: 50 and 6: 38.

carnis atque huiusmodi opera legis tantum ualebant, ut per illam homines salui fierent. (4) *Nisi aliqui sunt conturbantes uos et uolentes conuertere euangelium Christi.* Non quemadmodum istos conturbant, ita etiam conuertunt euangelium Christi, quia manet firmissimum, sed tamen conuertere uolunt, qui ab spiritualibus ad carnalia reuocant intentionem credentium. (5) Illis enim ad ista conuersis manet euangelium non conuersum. Et ideo cum dixisset: *conturbantes uos,* non dixit: et conuertentes, sed: *uolentes,* inquit, *conuertere euangelium Christi. Sed licet si nos aut angelus de caelo uobis euangelizauerit praeterquam quod euangelizauimus uobis, anathema sit.* (6) Veritas propter seipsam diligenda est, non propter hominem aut propter angelum, per quem annuntiatur. Qui enim propter annuntiatores diligit eam, potest et mendacia diligere, si qua forte ipsi sua protulerint. *Sicut praediximus et nunc iterum dico, si quis uobis euangelizauerit, praeterquam quod accepistis, anathema sit.* (7) Aut praesens hoc praedixerat aut, quia iterauit, quod dixit, propterea uoluit dicere: *Sicut praediximus.* Tamen ipsa iteratio saluberrime intentionem mouet ad firmitatem retinendi eam, quae sic commendatur, fidem.

5. *Modo ergo hominibus suadeo an deo? aut quaero hominibus placere? Si adhuc hominibus placerem, Christi seruus non essem.* (2) Nemo deo suadet, quia manifesta sunt illi omnia, sed hominibus ille bene suadet, qui non se illis placere uult, sed ipsam, quam suadet, ueritatem. (3) Qui enim placet hominibus, non ab ipsis suam gloriam quaerens sed dei, ut salui fiant, non iam hominibus sed deo placet, aut certe iam cum et deo placet simul et hominibus, non utique hominibus placet. (4) Aliud est enim placere hominibus, aliud et deo et hominibus. Item qui hominibus propter ueritatem placet, non iam ipse illis sed ueritas placet. (5) Placere autem dixit, quantum in seipso est, id est quantum ad eius uoluntatem attinet, ac si diceret: placere uellem. Non enim si hoc eo non agente placeat alicui quasi propter seipsum et non propter deum atque euangelium, quod annuntiat, superbiae ipsius potius, quam errori eius, cui peruerse placet, tribuendum est. (6) Iste itaque sensus est: Modo ergo hominibus suadeo an deo? aut quia hominibus suadeo, quaero hominibus placere? Si adhuc hominibus quaererem placere, Christi seruus non essem. (7) Iubet enim ille seruis suis, ut discant ab ipso mites esse et humiles corde, quod nullo modo potest, qui propter seipsum, id est propter suam quasi priuatam et propriam gloriam placere hominibus quaerit. (8) Dicit autem et alibi: *Hominibus suademus deo autem manifestati sumus,* ut intelligas, quod hic ait: *Hominibus suadeo an deo?*

(5) But even if believers are subverted in this way, the gospel remains unsubverted. And therefore although he had said, *troubling you,* he did not say, *and subverting,* but 'trying' *to subvert the gospel of Christ.*

But even if we or an angel from heaven should preach to you a gospel other than that which we preached to you, let him be accursed! (Gal. 1: 8) (6) The truth is to be loved for its own sake, not for the sake of the person or angel proclaiming it. For anyone who loves it for the sake of those proclaiming it is capable of loving lies—if those proclaiming it happen to have put forward their own opinions. *As we said before, so now I say again, if anyone should preach to you a gospel other than that which you received, let him be accursed!* (Gal. 1: 9). (7) He says, *As we said before,* either because he had told them this earlier in person, or because he was repeating what he had just said. In either case, the mere repetition shifts their attention in a very helpful way to the importance of holding firmly to the faith that has been entrusted to them.

5. *Now am I striving to persuade people, or God? Or am I trying to please people? If I were still pleasing people, I would not be a servant of Christ* (Gal. 1: 10). (2) No one can persuade God, because to God all things are manifest.[15] On the other hand, someone who aims to make the truth he is urging rather than himself pleasing to people is persuading them in an excellent way. (3) Someone who pleases people in order that they may be saved, not seeking personal glory but God's glory through them, is not in that case pleasing people but God—or at least pleasing God and people at the same time, and not just people. (4) It is one thing to please people, another to please both God and people. Similarly in the case of one who pleases people for the sake of the truth: it is not the person as such who pleases them but the truth. (5) Paul said *please* in so far as it depended on him, that is, in so far as it was in his power to choose—as if he had said 'If I were still trying to please'. For if someone is pleased not because of God and the gospel being proclaimed but because of Paul himself, though Paul did not intend it, this should not be attributed to pride on the part of Paul but to error on the part of the one who is pleased by the wrong thing. (6) The meaning then is this: 'Now am I striving to persuade people, or God? And since it is people that I am striving to persuade, does that mean I am simply trying to please people? If I were still trying to please people, I would not be a servant of Christ.'

(7) Christ tells his servants to learn from him to be *gentle and humble of heart* (Matt 11: 29), a thing which is utterly impossible for anyone seeking

---

[15] Cf. 2 Cor. 5: 11.

non utique deo, sed hominibus suadendum. (9) Non ergo moueat quod alibi dixit: *Sicut et ego omnibus per omnia placeo*, addidit enim: *Non quaerens, quod mihi prodest, sed quod multis, ut salui fiant.* (10) Nulli autem prodest, ut saluus fiat, si homo ei propter seipsum placeat, qui non placet utiliter, nisi cum propter deum placet, id est ut deus placeat et glorificetur, cum dona eius attenduntur in homine aut per ministerium hominis accipiuntur, cum autem sic homo placet, non iam homo sed deus placet. (11) Utrumque ergo recte dici potest: et ego placeo et non ego placeo. Si enim adsit bonus intellector piusque pulsator, patebit utrumque et nulla inter se repugnantia repellet intrantem.

6. *Notum enim uobis facio, fratres, euangelium, quod euangelizatum est a me, quia non est secundum hominem. Neque enim ego ab homine accepi illud neque didici sed per reuelationem Iesu Christi.* (2) Euangelium, quod secundum hominem est, mendacium est. Omnis enim homo mendax, quia quicquid ueritatis inuenitur in homine non est ab homine sed a deo per hominem. (3) Ideo iam quod secundum hominem est nec euangelium dicendum est, quale illi afferebant, qui in seruitutem ex libertate attrahebant eos, quos deus ex seruitute in libertatem uocabat.

7. *Audistis enim conuersationem meam aliquando in Iudaismo, quia supra modum persequebar ecclesiam dei et uastabam illam et proficiebam in Iudaismo supra multos coetaneos meos in genere meo abundantius aemulator existens paternarum mearum traditionum.* (2) Si persequendo et uastando ecclesiam dei proficiebat in Iudaismo, apparet Iudaismum contrarium esse ecclesiae dei non per illam spiritualem legem, quam acceperunt Iudaei, sed per carnalem conuersationem seruitutis ipsorum. (3) Et si aemulator, id est imitator paternarum suarum traditionum persequebatur Paulus ecclesiam dei, paternae ipsius traditiones contrariae sunt ecclesiae dei, non autem legis illius culpa est. (4) Lex enim spiritualis est nec carnaliter se cogit intelligi, sed illorum uitium est, qui et illa, quae acceperunt, carnaliter

---

[16] Jerome quotes the same two passages from 1 and 2 Cor. in his comment on Gal. 1: 10 (PL 26: 321A 1–10).

[17] An allusion to Matt. 7: 7–8, a favourite passage of Augustine's for showing the right way to approach the Bible—prayerfully (see e.g. *conf.* 12. 1. 1 and 13. 38. 53 (significantly, the concluding sentence of the entire work)).

[18] Pelagius quotes the same verse in his comment on Gal. 1: 10 (Souter, *Expositions*, ii. 309. 2). Note that in this translation, references to the Psalms give the numbering of the Latin Bible first, followed by the numbering of the English Bible in parentheses if it differs.

[19] Cf. Augustine's famous remark: 'No one has anything of his own except lying and sin' (*Io. eu. tr.* 5. 1 (CCSL 36: 40. 6–7: 'Nemo habet de suo, nisi mendacium et peccatum')).

to please people for his own sake, that is, for his own (so to speak) private and personal glory. (8) Moreover, in another place Paul says: *We strive to persuade people, but we are manifest to God* (2 Cor. 5: 11), so that when he says here, *Am I striving to persuade people, or God?*, you can be sure that it is not God who is to be persuaded, but people. (9) What he said elsewhere should cause no difficulty: *Just as I try to please everyone in everything I do*, for he added: *not seeking my own good, but that of many, so that they may be saved* (1 Cor. 10: 33).[16] (10) If one pleases others for his own sake, it is of no benefit for their salvation. One pleases others in a useful way only when one does so for the sake of God, that is, in order that God may be found pleasing and so be glorified. Since it is God's gifts that people look for in a person or receive through a person's ministry, then if someone is pleasing in this way it is not really that person who is pleasing but God. (11) Therefore both 'I please' and 'I do not please' can rightly be said. For if the listener is capable of understanding clearly and knocks[17] devoutly, he will find both doors open, and no contradictions will prevent him from entering.

6. *I assure you, brethren: the gospel I preached is not of human origin. For I neither received it nor learned it from any human source; it came through a revelation of Jesus Christ* (Gal. 1: 11–12). (2) A gospel of human origin is a lie, for *every human being is a liar* (Ps. 115 (116): 11; Rom. 3: 4),[18] since whatever truth is found in a person comes through that person from God, not from any human source.[19] (3) And so the term 'gospel' must not be applied to what is of human origin. Such were the claims put forward by those who sought to bring from freedom into slavery a people whom God had called from slavery into freedom.

7. *You have heard about my earlier life in Judaism, how I persecuted the Church of God beyond measure and tried to destroy it. And I advanced in Judaism beyond many of my Jewish contemporaries by emulating the traditions of my fathers with greater zeal* (Gal. 1: 13–14). (2) If by *persecuting the Church of God* and *trying to destroy it* Paul *advanced in Judaism*, it is clear that Judaism is opposed to the Church of God, not because of the spiritual law that the Jews received but because of their own carnal and slavish way of life. (3) And if by *emulating* (that is, imitating) *the traditions of his fathers* Paul persecuted the Church of God, the traditions of his fathers are opposed to the Church of God. Nevertheless, the law is not to blame.[20] (4) For *the law is spiritual* (Rom. 7: 14) and does not force anyone to understand it carnally. The fault lies rather with those who view what they have received in a carnal manner and, moreover, have handed down many

---

[20] That the law *was* to blame was a contention of the Manichees. Cf. e.g. *Simpl.* 1. 1. 16 (CCSL 44: 19–20).

sentiunt et multa etiam sua tradiderunt dissoluentes, sicut dominus dicit, mandatum dei propter traditiones suas.

8. *Cum autem placuit deo, qui me segregauit de uentre matris meae et uocauit per gratiam suam, reuelare filium suum in me, ut annuntiarem eum in gentibus, continuo non acquieui carni et sanguini.* (2) Segregatur quodammodo de uentre matris, quisquis a carnalium parentum consuetudine caeca separatur, acquiescit autem carni et sanguini, quisquis carnalibus propinquis et consanguineis suis carnaliter suadentibus assentitur. (3) *Neque ueni Hierosolimam ad praecessores meos apostolos, sed abii in Arabiam et iterum reuersus sum Damascum. Deinde post annos tres ascendi Hierosolimam uidere Petrum et mansi apud illum diebus quindecim.* (4) Si cum euangelizasset Paulus in Arabia, postea uidit Petrum, non ideo ut per ipsum Petrum disceret euangelium, nam ante eum utique uidisset, sed ut fraternam caritatem etiam corporali notitia cumularet. (5) *Alium autem apostolorum non uidi nisi Iacobum fratrem domini.* Iacobus domini frater uel ex filiis Ioseph de alia uxore uel ex cognatione Mariae matris eius debet intelligi.

9. *Quae autem scribo uobis, ecce coram dei, quia non mentior.* Qui dicit: *ecce coram deo, quia non mentior,* iurat utique. Et quid sanctius hac iuratione? (2) Sed non est contra praeceptum iuratio, quae *a malo est* non iurantis sed incredulitatis eius, cui iurare cogitur. Nam hinc intelligitur ita dominum prohibuisse a iurando, ut quantum in ipso est quisque, non iuret, quod multi faciunt in ore habentes iurationem tamquam magnum aut suaue aliquid. (3) Nam utique apostolus nouerat praeceptum domini et iurauit tamen. Non enim audiendi sunt, qui has iurationes esse non putant. (4) Quid enim facient de illa: *Cotidie morior per uestram gloriam, fratres, quam habeo in Christo Iesu domino nostro?* quam graeca exemplaria manifestissimam iurationem esse conuincunt. (5) Quantum ergo in ipso est, non iurat apostolus, non enim appetit iurationem cupiditate aut delectatione

[21] The question of the Lord's 'brothers' was hotly debated in the fourth century. Of the two views mentioned here, the former is associated particularly with Epiphanius, the latter with Jerome. Both were intended to safeguard the perpetual virginity of Mary. A third view, associated with Helvidius and Jovinian but not mentioned here, held that the brothers were sons of Mary and Joseph born after Jesus. On the virginity of Mary see also *exp. Gal.* 30. 2. Elsewhere Augustine's view coincides with that of Jerome. Cf. e.g. *Io. eu. tr.* 28. 3 (CCSL 36: 278. 7–24). For a detailed discussion of the ancient evidence see Lightfoot, *Galatians*, 252–91, and Buby, *Mary of Galilee*, iii., esp. 140–203.

[22] Reading *coram deo* with the Maurists and Rousselet, rather than Divjak's *coram dei*, which is clearly a misprint since the following sentence reads *coram deo*.

[23] Cf. Matt. 5: 33–7. Augustine considers that the Lord's prohibition against swearing does not apply in cases where swearing is necessary to win someone to true belief. He treats the same subject less laconically in the contemporaneous *s. dom. m.* 1. 17. 51 (CCSL 35: 56–9).

teachings of their own, thus, as the Lord says, *nullifying the commandment of God because of their traditions* (Matt. 15: 6).

8. *But when it pleased God, who separated me from my mother's womb and called me through his grace, to reveal his Son in me that I might preach him among the Gentiles, I did not immediately trust in flesh and blood* (Gal. 1: 15–16). (2) One is *separated,* so to speak, from one's *mother's womb* by being parted from the blind custom of one's carnal parents; one *trusts in flesh and blood,* on the other hand, by assenting to carnal advice from one's carnal family and relatives. (3) *Nor did I go to Jerusalem to those who were apostles before me, but instead I went away into Arabia. And again I returned to Damascus. Then after three years I went up to Jerusalem to see Peter, and remained with him fifteen days* (Gal. 1: 17–18). (4) If Paul visited Peter after preaching the gospel in Arabia, it was not in order to learn the gospel from him; had that been the case, he would surely have seen Peter first. Rather, he visited Peter so that by meeting him in person he might build up brotherly love between them. (5) *But I did not see any of the other apostles except James the Lord's brother* (Gal. 1: 19). James is understood to be the Lord's brother because he was one of Joseph's sons by another wife or perhaps one of the relatives of the Lord's mother Mary.[21]

9. *In what I am writing to you, before God,[22] I am not lying!* (Gal. 1: 20). Anyone who says, *before God, I am not lying!,* is undoubtedly swearing. And what is more sacred than this oath? (2) But an oath is not against the Lord's command if the *evil* from which it comes is not that of the person swearing but that of the unbelief of the person to whom he is forced to swear.[23] For we see that the Lord prohibited swearing so far as it lies within a person's power—though many disregard the prohibition, keeping an oath on their lips as if it were some great delicacy. (3) There can be no doubt that the Apostle knew the Lord's command, yet he still swore. Those who do not regard these as oaths are not to be taken seriously. (4) For what will they make of this: *By your glory, brethren, which I have in Christ Jesus our Lord: I die every day!* (1 Cor. 15: 31)—which the Greek copies very clearly prove to be an oath.[24] (5) Therefore the Apostle does not swear so far as it lies within his power, for he does not resort to swearing because it gives him pleasure or enjoyment. (6) It is more than '*Yes, Yes*' or '*No, No*', and therefore *comes from evil,*[25] but the *evil* lies in the weakness or unbelief of those who are not otherwise moved to faith.

---

[24] Although the Latin version of 1 Cor. 15: 31 is ambiguous and may or may not mean '*I swear* by your glory', the word νή in the original Greek makes it clear that Paul is indeed swearing, as Augustine explains in *s. dom. m.* 1. 17. 51 (CCSL 35: 57. 1236–58. 1248) and *doctr. chr.* 3. 4. 8 (Green, text and trans., 140–1).   [25] Matt. 5: 37.

iurandi. (6) Amplius est enim quam: *est, est, non, non* et ideo: *a malo est,* sed infirmitatis aut incredulitatis eorum, qui non aliter mouentur ad fidem. (7) *Deinde ueni in partes Syriae et Ciliciae. Eram autem ignotus facie ecclesiis Iudaeae, quae in Christo sunt.* Animaduertendum non in sola Hierosolima Iudaeos in Christo credidisse nec tam paucos fuisse, ut ecclesiis gentium miscerentur, sed tam multos, ut ex illis ecclesiae fierent. (8) *Tantum autem audientes erant, quia qui aliquando nos persequebatur, nunc euangelizat fidem, quam aliquando uastabat; et in me magnificabant deum.* (9) Hoc est, quod dicebat non se placere hominibus utique per seipsum sed ut in illo magnificaretur deus, hoc est, quod etiam dominus dicit: *Luceant opera uestra coram hominibus, ut uideant bona facta uestra et glorificent patrem uestrum, qui in caelis est.*

10. *Deinde post annos quattuordecim iterum ascendi Hierosolimam cum Barnaba assumpto etiam Tito,* tamquam testimoniis pluribus agit, cum etiam istos nominat. (2) *Ascendi autem secundum reuelationem,* ne moueret eos, quare uel tunc ascenderit, quo tam diu non ascenderat. Quapropter si ex reuelatione ascendit, tunc proderat, ut ascenderet. (3) *Et exposui illis euangelium, quod praedico in gentibus, seorsum autem his, qui uidentur.* Quod seorsum exposuit euangelium eis, qui eminebant in ecclesia, cum iam illud exposuisset coram omnibus, non ideo factum est, quod aliqua falsa dixerat, ut seorsum paucioribus uera diceret, sed aliqua tacuerat, quae adhuc paruuli portare non poterant, qualibus se ad Corinthios lac dicit dedisse, non escam. (4) Falsum enim dicere nihil licet, aliquando autem aliquid ueri tacere utile est. Perfectionem ipsius opus erat, ut scirent ceteri apostoli. (5) Non enim sequebatur, ut, si fidelis esset ueramque et rectam teneret fidem, iam etiam apostolus esse deberet. (6) Illud autem quod subiungit: *Ne forte in uacuum curro aut cucurri,* non ad illos, cum quibus seorsum contulit euangelium, sed ad istos, quibus scribit, quasi per interrogationem dictum intelligendum est, ut ex eo appareret non eum in uacuum currere aut cucurrisse, quia iam etiam attestatione ceterorum nihil ab euangelii ueritate dissentire approbatur.

---

[26] Cf. Pelagius, *Comm. on Gal.* 1: 22 (Souter, *Expositions,* ii. 311. 13–14): 'Those of Jewish origin had churches apart, and did not merge with those of Gentile origin.'

[27] Not only before those in Jerusalem, but before those to whom he is writing as well. Cf. *exp. Gal.* 10. 6.   [28] 1 Cor. 3: 2.

[29] Literally, they had to know 'his perfection' (*perfectionem ipsius*), which consists essentially in his having received his gospel not *from any human source* but *through a revelation of Jesus Christ* (Gal. 1: 12), so that his gospel cannot have been lacking in any way. Cf. *exp. Gal.* 1. 8, 2. 4–5, and especially 12. 4–5.

(7) *Then I came into the regions of Syria and Cilicia. And I was not known by sight to the Judaean churches that are in Christ* (Gal. 1: 21–2). It should be noted that the Jews who had come to believe in Christ were not limited to Jerusalem. Nor were they so few in number that they had to merge with Gentile churches, but rather so numerous that they formed churches of their own.[26] (8) *They only heard it being said: 'He who once persecuted us is now preaching the faith he once tried to destroy.' And they glorified God in me* (Gal. 1: 23–4). (9) In other words, he was saying that he absolutely did not please people for his own sake but in order that God might be glorified in him, as the Lord says also: *Let your works shine before others so that they may see the good things you have done and glorify your Father who is in heaven* (Matt. 5: 16).

10. *Then after fourteen years I went up to Jerusalem again with Barnabas, taking Titus with me also* (Gal. 2: 1)—as though having additional testimonies for pleading his case,[27] since he refers to them by name. (2) *I went up in response to a revelation* (Gal. 2: 2)—so as not to make them wonder why, for example, he went up at that time after not going up for so long; if he went up by revelation then it was right for him to go up at that time. (3) *And I stated to them the gospel that I preach among the Gentiles, but I did so privately to those of repute* (Gal. 2: 2). The fact that he stated the gospel privately to those who were pre-eminent in the Church when he had already stated it openly to all was not done because he had told any lies and was now telling the truth privately to a select few, but because he had been silent about some things that were more than the Gentiles could bear while they were still infants. He tells the Corinthians that to such people he had given milk, not solid food.[28] (4) Under no circumstances is it lawful to tell a lie, but occasionally it is helpful to be silent about some aspect of the truth. As regards the other apostles, however, it was necessary for them to know that he was perfectly qualified.[29] (5) For it did not follow that if he was faithful and the faith he held was both true and accurate, then he should also be an apostle. (6) He adds: *Lest perhaps I am running or have run in vain* (Gal. 2: 2)—where he has in mind not those with whom he discussed the gospel privately but those to whom he is writing. We are to infer from this that the conference made it clear that he neither *was running nor had run in vain*, because the fact that he in no way disagrees with the truth of the gospel is now also confirmed by the witness of others.[30]

---

[30] Cf. *c. Faust.* 28. 4: 'For would the Church entirely believe the apostle Paul himself, though he was called from heaven after the Lord's ascension, if he had not found apostles in the flesh with whom he could discuss and compare his gospel and so be recognized as belonging to the same fellowship as they?' (my trans., based on Stothert, 325–6, of CSEL 25. 1: 741. 24–742. 2).

11. *Sed neque Titus, qui mecum erat*, inquit, *cum esset Graecus, compulsus est circumcidi*. Quamuis Titus Graecus esset et nulla eum consuetudo aut cognatio parentum circumcidi cogeret, sicut Timotheum, facile tamen etiam istum circumcidi permisisset apostolus. (2) Non enim tali circumcisione salutem docebat auferri, sed si in ea constitueretur spes salutis, hoc esse contra salutem ostendebat. (3) Poterat ergo ut superfluam aequo animo tolerare secundum sententiam, quam alibi dixit: *Circumcisio nihil est et praeputium nihil est, sed obseruatio mandatorum dei*. (4) Propter: *subintroductos autem falsos fratres* non est compulsus Titus circumcidi, id est, non ei potuit extorqueri, ut circumcideretur, quia illi, *qui subintroierunt*, dicit, *proscultare libertatem* eorum, uehementer obseruabant et cupiebant circumcidi Titum, ut iam circumcisionem etiam ipsius Pauli attestatione et consensione, tamquam saluti necessariam praedicarent et sic eos, ut ait, *in seruitutem redigerent*, id est sub onera legis seruilia reuocarent. (5) *Quibus se nec ad horam*, id est nec ad tempus *cessisse* dicit *subiectioni, ut ueritas euangelii permaneret ad gentes*.

12. Denotabant autem suspectumque haberi uolebant inuidi apostolum Paulum, quod aliquando persecutor ecclesiarum fuerit, et ideo dicit: *De his autem, qui uidentur esse aliquid, quales aliquando fuerint, nihil mea interest*. (2) Quia et qui uidentur esse aliquid, carnalibus hominibus uidentur esse aliquid, nam non sunt ipsi aliquid. Et si enim boni ministri dei sunt, Christus in illis est aliquid, non ipsi per se. (3) Nam si ipsi per se essent aliquid, semper fuissent aliquid. *Quales aliquando fuerint*, id est, quia et ipsi peccatores fuerunt, nihil sua dicit interesse, quia *deus hominis personam non accipit*, id est sine personarum acceptione omnes ad salutem uocauit non reputans illis delicta eorum. (4) Et ideo absentibus illis, qui priores facti

[31] Cf. Acts 16: 1–3 and Augustine's reference to these verses in the contemporaneous *mend*. 5. 8: 'Although Timothy was called without having been circumcised, nevertheless, because he had been born of a Jewish mother and was under an obligation to help her relatives by indicating that in the Christian doctrine he had not learned to despise the rites of the Old Law, he was circumcised by the Apostle' (Muldowney, trans., 64; CSEL 41: 423. 18–22).

[32] By contrast, Pelagius interprets the passage as implying that Titus *was* circumcised, although he had not been *compelled* to be (Souter, *Expositions*, ii. 312. 10–14).

[33] Neither here nor elsewhere in his writings does Augustine mention the variant reading of Gal. 2: 5 in which the negative is omitted (*we yielded submission*). This reading is in fact preferred by Victorinus (CSEL 83. 2: 113–15) and Ambrosiaster (CSEL 81. 3: 19–22), who point out that Paul did yield in the case of Timothy (Acts 16: 1–3). On the other hand, Jerome (PL 26: 333C 7–334B 9) argues that the negative is vital to the sense of the passage. Pelagius (Souter, *Expositions*, ii. 312. 17) appears to retain the negative. Amid such diversity it is remarkable that Pelagius is the only one of these commentators to conclude that Titus was in fact circumcised. On the evidence of the Latin Fathers see Lightfoot, *Galatians*, 121–2.

11. *But not even my companion Titus, although he was a Greek, was compelled to be circumcised* (Gal. 2: 3). Though Titus was a Greek and not obliged by any custom or parental relationship to be circumcised (as was the case with Timothy[31]), yet the Apostle might easily have allowed even him to be circumcised. (2) For he was not trying to teach that salvation is taken away by such circumcision but rather to show that it is contrary to salvation to place one's hope for it in circumcision. (3) Thus he could calmly tolerate it as something superfluous, as when he says elsewhere: *Circumcision is nothing, and uncircumcision is nothing; what matters is keeping God's commandments* (1 Cor. 7: 19). (4) *But on account of false brethren secretly brought in* (Gal. 2: 4) Titus was not compelled to be circumcised.[32] In other words, there was no compelling argument that could make him submit to circumcision, because, the Apostle says, those *who slipped in to examine our freedom* were watching Titus closely, eager to see him circumcised. Their goal was to preach circumcision as necessary for salvation and to do so with the authority and approval of Paul himself, and thus, he says, *bring them back into slavery,* that is, *bring them back* under the slavish burdens of the law. (5) *To them,* he says, he *did not yield submission even for an hour*—that is, even for a moment—*that the truth of the gospel might remain for the Gentiles* (Gal. 2: 5).[33]

12. Moreover, they were keeping an eye on the apostle Paul, whom they envied and wanted to be viewed with suspicion because he had once been a persecutor of the churches. That is why he says: *But from those reputed to be something—what they once were makes no difference to me* (Gal. 2: 6). (2) For they are *reputed to be something* by carnal people; they are not something in themselves. Even if they are good servants of God, it is Christ in them who is something, not they themselves. (3) If they were something in themselves, then they would always have been so. *What they once were*—the fact that they themselves had been sinners[34]—makes no difference to him, he says, because *God does not consider a person's standing.* That is, without considering their *standing,* God has called all to salvation, *not counting their trespasses against them* (2 Cor. 5: 19).

(4) Thus, despite the absence of those who had been appointed as apostles earlier, Paul was made complete by the Lord, so that when he con-

---

[34] This interpretation is typically Augustinian and indeed typically Pauline (cf. e.g. 1 Cor. 15: 8–10), but most commentators think that Paul is referring to the prestige that Peter, James, and John enjoyed because of their personal connections with the earthly Jesus. This is the view of Pelagius (Souter, *Expositions,* ii. 313. 3–5), and in the light of 13. 4 below it is surprising that Augustine himself did not adopt it. Ambrosiaster's interpretation (CSEL 81. 3: 23. 1–18) is also typical of him: Paul is contrasting his own legal expertise with the conspicuous lack of it on the part of the 'pillars'.

erant apostoli, Paulus a domino perfectus est, ut quando cum eis contulit nihil esset, quod perfectioni eius adderent, sed potius uiderent eundem dominum Iesum Christum, qui sine personarum acceptione saluos facit, hoc dedisse Paulo, ut ministraret gentibus, quod etiam Petro dederat, ut ministraret Iudaeis. (5) Non ergo inuenti sunt in aliquo dissentire ab illo, ut, cum ille se perfectum euangelium accepisse diceret, illi negarent et aliquid uellent tamquam imperfecto addere, sed e contrario pro reprehensoribus imperfectionis approbatores perfectionis fuerunt. (6) *Et dederunt dexteras societatis*, id est consenserunt in societatem et paruerunt uoluntati domini consentientes, ut Paulus et Barnabas irent *ad gentes, ipsi autem in circumcisionem*, quae praeputio, id est, gentibus contraria uidetur. (7) Nam etiam sic potest intelligi, quod ait: *e contrario*, ut ordo iste sit: Mihi enim qui uidentur, nihil apposuerunt, sed e contrario, ut nos quidem *in gentes* iremus, quae sunt contrariae circumcisioni, ipsi *autem in circumcisionem*, consenserunt mihi et Barnabae, hoc est, *dexteras societatis nobis dederunt*.

13. Neque in contumeliam praecessorum eius putet quis ab eo dictum: *Qui uidentur esse aliquid, quales aliquando fuerint, nihil mea interest*. (2) Et illi enim tamquam spirituales uiri uolebant resisti carnalibus, qui putabant aliquid ipsos esse et non potius Christum in eis, multumque gaudebant, cum persuaderetur hominibus et seipsos praecessores Pauli, sicut eundem Paulum ex peccatoribus iustificatos esse a domino, qui personam hominis non accipit, quia dei gloriam quaerebant non suam. (3) Sed quia carnales et superbi homines, si quid de uita ipsorum praeterita dicitur, irascuntur et in contumeliam accipiunt, ex animo suo coniciunt apostolos. (4) Petrus autem et Iacobus et Iohannes honoratiores in apostolis erant, quia ipsis tribus se in monte dominus ostendit in significatione regni sui, cum ante sex dies dixisset: *Sunt hic quidam de circumstantibus, qui non gustabunt mortem, donec uideant filium hominis in regno patris sui*. (5) Nec ipsi erant columnae sed uidebantur. Nouerat enim Paulus sapientiam aedificasse sibi domum et non tres columnas constituisse sed septem, qui numerus uel ad unitatem ecclesiarum refertur—(6) solet enim pro uniuerso poni, sicut in euangelio

---

[35]   The underlying Latin of Gal. 2: 6 (*Qui uidentur esse aliquid* (cf. Gal. 2: 2, 9)) is ambiguous, reflecting the ambiguity of Paul's Greek (τῶν δοκούντων εἶναί τι), and could be interpreted as an insult. On the Greek see Betz, *Galatians*, 86–7, and the literature cited there.

[36]   Matt. 17: 1–8 // Mark 9: 2–8 // Luke 9: 28–36. Augustine confuses James the brother of the Lord with James the son of Zebedee, as does Ambrosiaster *ad loc.* (CSEL 81. 3: 24. 9–18). In commenting on the same passage Jerome also refers to the Transfiguration but does not make the same error (PL 26: 335ᴀ 12–14; 337ʙ 1–7).

ferred with them they had nothing to add to his perfection but rather recognized that the same Lord Jesus Christ, who saves without *considering a person's standing*, had given Paul a commission to serve the Gentiles just as he had given Peter a commission to serve the Jews. (5) Hence they were not found to disagree with him on any point; if they had disagreed, then when he said he had received the gospel perfectly complete they would have denied it and tried to add what was lacking. *To the contrary* (Gal. 2: 7), instead of censuring his gospel for being imperfect they confirmed its perfection. (6) *And they gave us the right hand of fellowship* (Gal. 2: 9). In other words, they joined in fellowship and by so doing submitted to the Lord's will that Paul and Barnabas *should go to the Gentiles while they themselves went to the circumcised*, who were regarded as being contrary to the uncircumcised, that is, the Gentiles. (7) For what he says may also be understood in such a way that *to the contrary* refers to a class of people, thus: Those of repute added nothing, but agreed with me and Barnabas that while they went to the circumcised, we should go *to the contrary*, that is, to the Gentiles, who are in a contrary position with respect to circumcision. In token of their agreement they *gave to us the right hand of fellowship*.

13. Nor should anyone suppose that he was insulting his predecessors when he said: *Those reputed to be something*[35]—*what they once were makes no difference to me*. (2) For Paul's predecessors were spiritual men and also wanted to resist those who were carnal—who considered them, rather than Christ in them, to be something. They were very pleased when people accepted that they had been taken from among sinners and justified by the Lord, who *does not consider a person's standing*, just as Paul himself had been. For they were seeking God's glory, not their own. (3) But because people who are carnal and proud become angry and take it as an insult if anything is said about their own earlier lives, they assume that the apostles would have reacted in the same way. (4) But Peter, James, and John were particularly honoured among the apostles because it was to them that the Lord showed himself on the mountain in a prefiguration of his kingdom[36] six days after saying: *There are some standing here who will not taste death until they see the Son of Man in his Father's kingdom* (Matt. 16: 28 OL). (5) Nor were they really *pillars*, but rather they *were reputed to be* (Gal. 2: 9). For Paul knew that Wisdom had built herself a house and had set up not three pillars but seven,[37] which may refer either to the unity of the churches— (6) since the number seven usually symbolizes the whole, as in the Gospel saying: *That one will receive in this world seven times as much* (Matt. 19:

---

[37] Cf. Prov. 9: 1.

dictum est: *Accipiet in hoc saeculo septies tantum*, ac si diceret: *Quasi nihil habentes et omnia possidentes*. (7) Unde etiam Iohannes ad septem scribit ecclesias, quae utique uniuersitatis ecclesiae personam gerunt—uel certe ad septenariam operationem spiritus sancti magis refertur septenarius numerus columnarum, sapientiae et intellectus, consilii et fortitudinis, scientiae et pietatis et timoris dei, quibus operationibus domus filii dei, hoc est ecclesia continetur.

14. Quod autem ait: *Tantum ut pauperum memores essemus, quod et studui hoc ipsum facere*, communis cura erat omnibus apostolis de pauperibus sanctorum, qui erant in Iudaea, qui rerum suarum uenditarum pretia ad pedes apostolorum posuerant. (2) Sic ergo ad gentes missi sunt Paulus et Barnabas, ut ecclesiae gentium, quae hoc non fecerant, ministrarent hortatione ipsorum eis, qui hoc fecerant, sicut ad Romanos dicit: (3) *Nunc autem pergam Hierusalem ministrare sanctis; placuit enim Macedoniae et Achaiae communionem aliquam facere in pauperes sanctorum, qui sunt in Hierusalem. Placuit enim illis et debitores eorum sunt. Si enim spiritualibus eorum communicauerunt gentes, debent et in carnalibus ministrare eis.*

15. In nulla ergo simulatione Paulus lapsus erat, quia seruabat ubique, quod congruere uidebat, siue ecclesiis gentium siue Iudaeorum, ut nusquam auferret consuetudinem, quae seruata non impediebat ad obtinendum regnum dei, (2) tantum admonens, ne quis in superfluis poneret spem salutis, etiam si consuetudinem in eis propter offensionem infirmorum custodire uellet. (3) Sicut ad Corinthios dicit: *Circumcisus quis uocatus est? non adducat praeputium. In praeputio quis uocatus est? non circumcidatur.* (4) *Circumcisio nihil est et praeputium nihil est sed obseruatio*

---

[38] Rev. 1: 4.

[39] Cf. Isa. 11: 2.

[40] Cf. 1 Cor. 12.

[41] Acts 4: 34–5. Acts 4: 32–5 profoundly influenced Augustine's ideal of the monastic life. See Verheijen, *Saint Augustine's Monasticism*.

[42] Literally, 'in carnal things' (*in carnalibus*).

[43] 'into hypocrisy': following the widely attested variant *in . . . simulationem* rather than Divjak's more difficult reading, *in . . . simulatione*.

[44] Cf. 1 Cor. 9: 19–23 and *ep*. 40. 4–6 (CSEL 34. 1: 73–7).

[45] *remove the marks of circumcision*: This had been done by Jews who wished to become completely Hellenized (see e.g. 1 Macc. 1: 11–15). In such cases a man would undergo a surgical procedure to draw the foreskin forward so as to cover the scars of circumcision. Augustine's Latin version of 1 Cor. 7: 18 clearly refers to this surgical procedure (*Non adducat praeputium*—literally, 'Let him not draw the foreskin forward'), and Augustine himself alludes to the procedure in *mend*. 5. 8 (CSEL 41: 422. 26–423. 3). Nevertheless, for Augustine as for Paul, what matters most is the symbolism: 'circumcision' stands for Jewish customs generally.

29 // Mark 10: 30 // Luke 18: 30 OL), as if to say: *As having nothing and yet possessing all things* (2 Cor. 6: 10), (7) and in this regard John also writes to the seven churches,[38] which clearly represent the Church as a whole. Or perhaps it refers not so much to the number of pillars as to the sevenfold work of the Holy Spirit, which consists of imparting wisdom and under-standing, counsel and fortitude, knowledge and piety, and the fear of God[39]—by which the house of the Son of God, the Church, is held together.[40]

14. *Only we were to remember the poor, which was the very thing I had set myself to do* (Gal. 2: 10). All the apostles took part in caring for the poor among the saints in Judaea, who had sold their possessions and laid the proceeds at the feet of the apostles.[41] (2) Thus Paul and Barnabas were sent to the Gentiles to encourage the Gentile churches, which had not done this, to minister to the churches that had, as Paul tells the Romans: (3) *But now I am going to Jerusalem to minister to the saints; for Macedonia and Achaia have been pleased to make a contribution for the poor among the saints at Jerusalem. They were pleased to do this, and indeed they owe it to them, for if the Gentiles have come to share in their spiritual blessings, they should also minister to them in material things*[42] (Rom. 15: 25–7).

15. The fact that Paul observed what were regarded as the accepted practices in all circumstances—whether dealing with Gentile or Jewish churches—does not mean that he had fallen into hypocrisy.[43] Rather, his aim was to avoid detracting from any local custom whose observance did not hinder the attainment of the kingdom of God. (2) He merely warned against placing one's hope for salvation in unessential things, even though he himself might honour a custom among them so as not to offend the weak.[44] (3) As he says to the Corinthians: *Was anyone already circumcised at the time of his call? Let him not remove the marks of circumcision.*[45] *Was anyone uncircumcised at the time of his call? Let him not be circumcised.* (4) *Circumcision is nothing, and uncircumcision is nothing; what matters is keeping God's commandments. Everyone should remain in the state in which he was called* (1 Cor. 7: 18–20). (5) This refers, of course, to those customs or situations in life which do not in any way harm a person's faith or good morals. Obviously if a man was a thief when he was called he should not continue stealing![46] (6) Now when Peter came to Antioch he was rebuked by Paul not for observing the Jewish custom in which he had been born and raised (although among the Gentiles he did not observe it), but for wanting to impose it on the Gentiles. Peter did this after seeing certain people who had

---

[46] Although this remark could be taken as a faint echo of Eph. 4: 28, it is better simply to enjoy it as a bit of Augustinian humour.

mandatorum dei. Unusquisque in qua uocatione uocatus est, in ea permaneat.
(5) Hoc enim ad eas consuetudines uel conditiones uitae retulit, quae nihil
obsunt fidei bonisque moribus. Non enim si latro erat quisque, cum
uocatus est, debet in latrocinio permanere. (6) Petrus autem, cum uenisset
Antiochiam, obiurgatus est a Paulo non, quia seruabat consuetudinem
Iudaeorum, in qua natus atque educatus erat, quamquam apud gentes eam
non seruaret, sed obiurgatus est, quia gentibus eam uolebat imponere,
cum uidisset quosdam uenisse ab Iacobo, id est a Iudaea, nam ecclesiae
hierosolimitanae Iacobus praefuit. (7) Timens ergo eos, qui adhuc putabant
in illis obseruationibus salutem constitutam, segregabat se a gentibus et
simulate illis consentiebat ad imponenda gentibus illa onera seruitutis,
quod in ipsius obiurgationis uerbis satis apparet. (8) Non enim ait: *Si tu,*
cum Iudaeus sis, gentiliter et non Iudaice uiuis, quemadmodum rursus ad
consuetudinem Iudaeorum reuerteris? sed *quemadmodum,* inquit, *gentes*
cogis iudaizare? Quod autem hoc ei *coram omnibus* dixit, necessitas coegit, ut
omnes illius obiurgatione sanarentur. (9) Non enim utile erat errorem, qui
palam noceret, in secreto emendare. Huc accedit, quod firmitas et caritas
Petri, cui ter a domino dictum est: *Amas me? pasce oues meas,* obiurgationem
talem posterioris pastoris pro salute gregis libentissime sustinebat.
(10) Nam erat obiurgatore suo ipse, qui obiurgabatur, mirabilior et ad
imitandum difficilior. Facilius est enim uidere, quid in alio corrigas, atque
id uituperando uel obiurgando corrigere quam uidere, quid in te
corrigendum sit, libenterque corrigi uel per teipsum nedum per alium,
adde posteriorem, adde *coram omnibus.* (11) Valet autem hoc ad magnum
humilitatis exemplum, quae maxima est disciplina christiana, humilitate
enim conseruatur caritas, nam nihil eam citius uiolat quam superbia.
(12) Et ideo dominus non ait: Tollite iugum meum et discite a me, quoniam
quatriduana de sepulcris cadauera exsuscito atque omnia daemonia de
corporibus hominum morbosque depello et cetera huiusmodi, sed *tollite,*
inquit, *iugum meum et discite a me, quia mitis sum et humilis corde.* (13) Illa
enim signa sunt rerum spiritualium, mitem autem esse et humilem caritatis
conseruatorem res ipsae spirituales sunt, ad quas per illa ducuntur, qui

47 Gal. 2: 12.
48 Augustine may be trying to ward off the view that the Judaizers truly represented the
mind of James, a view associated with the heretical Symmachians and accepted by Victorinus
ad loc., who refers to James as their 'authority' (*auctor ad Symmachianos* (CSEL 83. 2: 119.
26–7)). Augustine mentions the Symmachians in the context of a discussion of Gal. 2: 11–14
and related matters in *c. Faust.* 19. 17 (CSEL 25. 1: 514–16).

come *from James*[47] (that is, from Judaea, since James presided over the church of Jerusalem[48]). (7) Peter feared these people who still thought that salvation was based on Jewish observances; in consequence, he separated himself from the Gentiles and pretended to agree that they should have to bear those slavish burdens which are clear enough from Paul's rebuke. (8) For he does not say, *If you, though a Jew, live like a Gentile and not like a Jew, how can you revert to the custom of the Jews?* but rather, *how can you force the Gentiles to live like Jews?* (Gal. 2: 14). It was necessary for him to say this to Peter *in front of everyone* so that by Peter's rebuke *everyone* might be put right. (9) For it would not have been useful to correct in private an error[49] that had done its harm in public.[50] Here I might add that out of steadfastness and love Peter—to whom the Lord had said three times, *Do you love me? Feed my sheep* (John 21: 15–17)—was entirely willing to endure this rebuke from a junior shepherd for the salvation of the flock. (10) Moreover, it was in his rebuke that the one being rebuked proved the more admirable and difficult to imitate. For it is easy to see what you would correct in someone else and to proceed to do so by censure and criticism. It is not so easy to see what ought to be corrected in yourself and to be willing to be corrected even by yourself, let alone by another, and that a junior, and all this *in front of everyone!* (11) Now this incident serves as a great example of humility, which is the most valuable Christian training, for by humility love is preserved. For nothing violates love more quickly than pride. (12) And therefore the Lord did not say, 'Take my yoke and learn from me, because I raise four-day-old corpses from the tomb and cast out all demons and diseases from people's bodies', and other such things, but rather, *Take my yoke and learn from me, for I am gentle and humble of heart* (Matt. 11: 29). (13) For the former are signs of spiritual realities, but to be *gentle and humble*, a preserver of love—these are the spiritual realities themselves. People who have become engrossed in bodily sights and incapable of being moved by what is ordinary and familiar are led by signs to realities when

---

[49] While Victorinus in his exegesis of Gal. 2: 11–14 speaks repeatedly and emphatically of Peter's 'sin' (*peccatum*), Augustine does not use the word 'sin' but speaks only of Peter's 'error' (*error*). How significant is his choice of words in this instance? Was he deliberately trying to limit Peter's culpability? Although the Latin term *error* typically implies that the moral lapse in question is venial (cf. *OLD*), such an implication is doubtful in the present circumstances. First, Augustine states that Peter acted from fear (rather than, e.g., from ignorance) (*exp. Gal.* 15. 7, echoing Gal. 2: 12), and for Augustine fear is the polar opposite of love, the one true motive for Christian behaviour (cf. e.g. *exp. Gal.* 43. 2–3). Second, Augustine, unlike Jerome, does not try to avoid the strong term 'hypocrisy' (*simulatio*) that Paul uses for Peter's action (Gal. 2: 13) but rather highlights it by using it twice in the Preface to his *Commentary* (*exp. Gal.* 1. 4). So while Augustine does not judge Peter's action as severely as Victorinus does, he does not trivialize it either. [50] Similarly Pelagius (Souter, *Expositions*, ii. 315. 5–6).

oculis corporis dediti fidem inuisibilium, quia iam de notis usitatisque non possunt, de nouis et repentinis uisibilibus quaerunt. (14) Si ergo et illi, qui cogebant gentes iudaizare, didicissent mites esse et humiles corde, quod a domino Petrus didicerat, saltem correcto tanto uiro ad imitandum inuitarentur nec putarent euangelium Christi iustitiae suae tamquam debitum redditum, (15) sed *scientes quoniam non iustificatur homo ex operibus legis, nisi per fidem Iesu Christi*, ut impleat opera legis adiuuante infirmitatem suam non merito suo sed gratia dei, non exigerent de gentibus carnales legis obseruationes, sed per ipsam gratiam fidei spiritualia opera legis eos implere posse cognoscerent. (16) Quoniam ex operibus legis, cum suis uiribus ea quisque tribuerit, non gratiae miserantis dei, non iustificabitur omnis caro, id est omnis homo siue omnes carnaliter sentientes. (17) Et ideo illi, qui cum iam essent sub lege Christo crediderunt, non, quia iusti erant, sed ut iustificarentur, uenerunt ad gratiam fidei.

16. Peccatorum autem nomen gentibus imposuerant Iudaei iam uetusta quadam superbia, tamquam ipsi iusti essent uidendo stipulam in oculo alieno et non trabem in suo. (2) Secundum eorum morem locutus apostolus ait: *Nos natura Iudaei et non ex gentibus peccatores*, id est, quos appellant peccatores, cum sint et ipsi peccatores. (3) *Nos ergo*, inquit, *natura Iudaei*, cum gentiles non essemus, quos ipsi peccatores appellant, *tamen et nos peccatores in Christo Iesu credimus, ut iustificemur per fidem Christi*. (4) Non autem quaererent iustificari, nisi essent peccatores. An forte quia in Christo uoluerunt iustificari, peccauerunt? quia si iam iusti erant, aliud quaerendo utique peccauerunt, sed si ita est, inquit, ergo *Christus peccati minister est*. (5) Quod utique non possunt dicere, quia et ipsi, qui nolebant nisi circumcisis gentibus tradi euangelium, in Christo crediderant. Et ideo quod dicit: *absit*, non solus sed cum ipsis dicit. (6) Destruxit autem superbiam gloriantem de operibus legis, quae destrui et deberet et posset, ne gratia fidei uideretur non necessaria, si opera legis etiam sine illa iustificare crederentur. (7) Et ideo praeuaricator est, si rursus illa aedificat dicens, quod opera legis etiam sine gratia iustificant, ut Christus peccati minister inueniatur. Posset ergo illi obici dicenti: *Si enim quae destruxi, haec eadem rursus aedifico, praeuaricatorem meipsum constituo*. (8) Quid ergo, quia fidem Christi oppugnabas antea, quam nunc aedificas, praeuaricatorem te

---

[51] i.e. miracles (cf. *trin.* 8. 7. 11 (CCSL 50: 286. 48–62)). This sentence may refer to the Neoplatonic notion of 'ascent'. On this notion see *conf.* 7. 10. 16 and 7. 17. 23 and O'Donnell's comments in *Augustine: Confessions*, ii. 434–7 and 454–5.

new and unexpected visible occurrences[51] rouse them to seek a faith in things invisible. (14) If, then, those who were trying to compel the Gentiles to live like Jews had also learned what Peter had learned from the Lord— how to be *gentle and humble of heart*—then at least they would have been drawn by the example of that great man's correction to imitate him and would not have supposed that the gospel of Christ was a sort of debt paid for their righteousness. (15) Instead, *knowing that a person is justified not by works of the law but through faith in Jesus Christ* (Gal. 2: 16)—that is, a person fulfils the works of the law when his weakness is aided not by his own merits but by the grace of God—they would not have demanded from the Gentiles carnal observances of the law but would have known that the Gentiles could fulfil spiritual works of the law through the grace of faith. (16) *For by works of the law* (that is, if people attribute them to their own power and not to the grace of the merciful God), *no flesh* (in other words, no person, or none who think in a carnal way) *will be justified*. (17) And there- fore those who believed in Christ when they were already under the law came to the grace of faith not because they were righteous but in order to become so.

16. Now the Jews called the Gentiles 'sinners' out of a certain long- standing pride, as if they themselves were righteous in seeing *the speck in someone else's eye and not the beam in their own* (Matt. 7: 3 // Luke 6: 41). (2) The Apostle is speaking according to their usage when he says: *We are Jews by birth, not Gentile sinners* (Gal. 2: 15). In other words, they call them 'sinners' even though they themselves are sinners also. (3) *We*, then, *Jews by birth*, although we were never Gentile 'sinners', yet *we too*—as sinners[52]— *believe in Christ Jesus in order to be justified by faith in Christ* (Gal. 2: 16). (4) Now they would not seek to be justified unless they were sinners. Or did they sin, perhaps, because they wanted to be justified in Christ? For if they were already righteous, then by seeking something different they sinned in any case. But if so, he says, *is Christ then an agent of sin?* (Gal. 2: 17). (5) There is no way that Paul's opponents can say this, because even they, who were unwilling to entrust the gospel to the Gentiles unless they were circumcised, believed in Christ. For this reason when he says, *Certainly not!*, he is not doing so alone but with these very people. (6) Moreover, he destroyed the pride that boasted about works of the law—pride that should and could have been destroyed, lest the grace of faith appear unnecessary (as it would appear if they believed works of the law could justify even with- out it). (7) And therefore he is a *transgressor* if he *builds those things up again*

---

[52] Unlike Divjak, who regards the word 'sinners' (*peccatores*) here as part of the biblical quotation, I prefer to regard it as an amplification made by Augustine for emphasis.

constituis? Sed illam non destruxit, quia destrui non potest. (9) Hanc autem
superbiam uere destruxerat constanterque destruebat, quia destrui poterat.
(10) Et ideo non ille praeuaricator est, qui rem ueram, cum conaretur
destruere et postea ueram esse ac destrui non posse cognosceret, tenuit
eam, ut in ea aedificetur, sed ille praeuaricator est, qui, cum destruxerit rem
falsam, quia destrui potest, eam rursus aedificat.

17. *Mortuum* autem se *legi* dicit, ut iam sub lege non esset, sed tamen *per
legem*, siue quia Iudaeus erat et tamquam paedagogum legem acceperat,
sicut postea manifestat. (2) Hoc autem agitur per paedagogum, ut non sit
necessarius paedagogus, sicut per ubera nutritur infans, ut iam uberibus
non indigeat, et per nauem peruenitur ad patriam, ut iam naui opus non sit,
siue per legem spiritualiter intellectam legi mortuus est, ne sub ea carnaliter
uiueret. (3) Nam hoc modo per legem, legi ut morerentur, uolebat, cum eis
paulo post ait: *Dicite mihi sub lege uolentes esse, legem non legistis? Scriptum est
enim, quod Abraham duos filios habuit* et cetera, ut per eandem legem
spiritualiter intellectam morerentur carnalibus obseruationibus legis.
(4) Quod autem adiungit: *ut deo uiuam*, deo uiuit, qui sub deo est, legi
autem, qui sub lege est, sub lege autem uiuit, in quantum quisque peccator
est, id est in quantum a uetere homine non est mutatus. (5) Sua enim uita
uiuit et ideo lex supra illum est, quia qui eam non implet infra illam est.
Nam *iusto lex posita non est*, id est imposita, ut supra illum sit. (6) In illa est
enim potius quam sub illa, quia non sua uita uiuit, cui coercendae lex
imponitur. Vt enim sic dicam ipsam quodammodo legem uiuit, qui cum
dilectione iustitiae iuste uiuit non proprio ac transitorio sed communi ac
stabili gaudens bono. (7) Et ideo Paulo non erat lex imponenda, qui dicit:
Viuo autem iam non ego, uiuit uero in me Christus. Quis ergo audeat Christo
legem imponere, qui uiuit in Paulo? (8) Non enim audet quis dicere
Christum non recte uiuere, ut ei coercendo lex imponenda sit. (9) *Quod
autem nunc uiuo*, inquit, *in carne*, quia non posset dicere Christum adhuc
mortaliter uiuere, uita autem in carne mortalis est, *in fide*, inquit, *uiuo filii*

[53] Presumably Paul, as addressed by an imaginary interlocutor—an example of the rhetorical figure known as *subiectio* or *responsio* in Latin, *hypophora* (ὑποφορά) in Greek. (See Lausberg, *Handbuch*, sects. 771–5.) Augustine examines Paul's use of this figure in *doctr. chr.* 4. 7. 13 and 4. 20. 39 (Green, text and trans., 212–13 and 246–7).

[54] Cf. Gal. 3: 24–5 and see the note on *disciplinarian* attached to *exp. Gal.* 27. 1.

[55] For the preceding interpretation of Gal. 2: 19 Augustine appears to be dependent on Victorinus. See Introduction, 2. A, under 'Direct Evidence'.

[56] For this expression see Rom. 6: 6, Eph. 4: 22, Col. 3: 9.

[57] Pelagius alludes to the same verse in his comment on Gal. 2: 19.

by saying that works of the law can justify even without grace, so that Christ becomes *an agent of sin*. It could then be objected against such a position: *For if I build up again the very same things that I destroyed, I make myself a transgressor* (Gal. 2: 18). (8) 'What then? Because in the past you[53] opposed the faith in Christ that you are now building up, do you *make yourself a transgressor?*' But he has not destroyed that, because it cannot be destroyed. (9) On the other hand, Paul had truly destroyed this pride and continued to destroy it, because it could be destroyed. (10) And so that person is not a transgressor who, after trying to destroy something true and then realizing that it was true and incapable of being destroyed, took hold of it in order to be built up in it. Rather, he is a transgressor who, after destroying something false (since it can be destroyed), builds *that* up again.

17. Now he says he *died to the law* (Gal. 2: 19) and so is no longer under the law, but nevertheless he did this *through the law*. Why does he say this? One explanation is that he said it because he was a Jew and had received the law as a kind of *disciplinarian*, as he shows later.[54] (2) Now a kind of death is brought about *through* the *disciplinarian*, with the intended result that the *disciplinarian* is not necessary, just as an infant is breast-fed with the result that its mother's milk is no longer necessary, and one arrives at one's homeland by ship with the result that the ship is no longer necessary. Another explanation is that *through the law* understood spiritually he *died to the law*, in order that he might not live under it carnally. (3) For it is in this way, *through the law*, that he wanted them to *die to the law*, when he says to them a little later: *Tell me, you who desire to be under the law, have you not read the law? For it is written that Abraham had two sons*, etc. (Gal. 4: 21–2), so that through the same law, understood spiritually, they might die to carnal observances of the law.[55] (4) He adds, *that I might live to God*. He *lives to God* who is under God, but he lives to the law who is under the law. Now one lives under the law in so far as one is a sinner, that is, in so far as he has not changed from the *old self*.[56] (5) For he lives by his own life and therefore the law is over him, because one who does not fulfil it is under it. For *the law is not laid down for the righteous person* (1 Tim. 1: 9),[57] that is, it is not imposed so as to be over him. (6) For he is in it rather than under it, because he does not live by his own life, which the law was imposed to restrain. I might put it this way: in a sense the person who lives righteously with a love of righteousness—who rejoices not in his own, transitory good but in the common, permanent good[58]—is living the law itself. (7) And therefore the law was not to be imposed on Paul, who says: *It is no longer I who live, but*

---

[58] Cf. *ep.* 140. 68 (CSEL 44: 215. 7–9): 'the proud . . . delight in their own private good and shrink from the common good of all, which is God, with a hollow exaltation'.

dei, ut etiam sic Christus uiuat in credente habitando in interiore homine per fidem, ut postea per speciem impleat eum, cum absorptum fuerit mortale a uita. (10) Vt autem ostenderet, quod uiuit in illo Christus, et quod in carne uiuens in fide uiuit filii dei, non meriti sui esse sed gratiae ipsius, *qui me*, inquit, *dilexit et tradidit seipsum pro me*. (11) Pro quo utique nisi pro peccatore, ut eum iustificaret? Et dicit hoc, qui Iudaeus natus et educatus erat et abundantius aemulator extiterat paternarum suarum traditionum. Ergo etsi pro talibus se tradidit Christus, etiam ipsi peccatores erant. (12) Non ergo meritis iustitiae suae datum dicant, quod non opus erat iustis dari. *Non enim ueni uocare iustos*, ait dominus, *sed peccatores*, ad hoc utique, ne sint peccatores. (13) Si ergo Christus me dilexit et tradidit seipsum pro me, *non irritam facio gratiam dei*, ut dicam per legem esse iustitiam. *Nam si per legem iustitia, ergo Christus gratis mortuus est*, id est sine causa mortuus est, quando per legem, id est per opera legis, quibus Iudaei confidebant, posset esse iustitia in hominibus. (14) Gratis autem mortuum Christum nec illi dicunt, quos refellit, quoniam Christianos se uolebant haberi. Non ergo recte per illa legis opera Christianos iustificari suadebant.

18. Quibus recte dicit: *O stulti Galatae, quis uos fascinauit?* Quod non recte diceretur de his, qui numquam profecissent, sed de his, qui ex profectu defecissent. (2) *Ante quorum oculos Christus Iesus proscriptus est, crucifixus*, hoc est, quibus uidentibus Christus Iesus hereditatem suam possessionemque suam amisit, his utique auferentibus eam dominumque inde expellentibus, qui ex gratia fidei, per quam Christus possidet gentes, ad legis opera eos, qui crediderant Christum, reuocabant auferendo illi possessionem suam, id est, eos in quibus iure gratiae fideique inhabitabat. (3) Quod in ipsis Galatis accidisse uult uideri apostolus, nam ad hoc pertinet, quod ait: *ante quorum oculos*. (4) Quid enim tam ante oculos eorum

---

[59] Cf. Eph. 3: 16–17.

[60] For the contrast between faith and sight see 2 Cor. 5: 7, a favourite verse of Augustine's.

[61] Especially in the light of Matt. 5: 22. Cf. *s. dom. m.* 1. 9. 25 (CCSL 35: 26. 563–72). For discussion see Introduction, 4. B, under 'The Inspiration of the Bible'.

[62] Two points concerning Augustine's OL version of Gal. 3: 1 should be noted. The first point is that Augustine, like Victorinus, Ambrosiaster, and Pelagius, reads *proscriptus* ('proscribed') and understands it in the technical sense of being publicly condemned to banishment (or even death) and to the confiscation of one's property. (Proscription was a means by which Roman rulers eliminated their enemies.) The second point is that although Augustine reads the Latin in the way I have translated it, the Latin itself is somewhat ambiguous.

[63] An allusion to Ps. 2: 7–8.

[64] Augustine's interpretation of this verse is remarkably similar to that of Victorinus: 'Christ, therefore, was *proscribed*, that is, his property was divided and sold—the property, of

Christ who lives in me (Gal. 2: 20). Who then would dare to impose the law on Christ who lives in Paul? (8) For no one would dare to say that Christ does not live rightly and therefore the law should be imposed to restrain him. (9) Since he could not say that Christ still lived mortally (while life *in the flesh* is mortal), he says, *The life I now live in the flesh I live in faith in the Son of God*, meaning that *Christ lives* in the believer by dwelling in the 'inner self' through faith[59] so that afterwards he may satisfy him through sight,[60] when *what is mortal* has been *swallowed up by life* (2 Cor. 5: 4). (10) Furthermore, it is not due to his own merit but Christ's grace that *Christ lives in him* and that the life he lives *in the flesh* he lives *in faith in the Son of God*. To show this Paul speaks of the one *who loved me and gave himself for me*. (11) Precisely for whom, unless for the sinner, in order to justify him? And the one saying this had been born and raised a Jew, and had *emulated the traditions of his fathers with greater zeal* (Gal. 1: 14). If, therefore, Christ gave himself for such, they were sinners. (12) And so they should not say that he gave himself on account of the merits of their own righteousness, because there was no need for him to give himself for the righteous. *For I have come not to call the righteous*, said the Lord, *but sinners* (Matt. 9: 13 // Mark 2: 17 // Luke 5:32)—surely for this reason, that they might not be sinners. (13) If, then, Christ *loved me and gave himself for me, I do not nullify the grace of God* by saying that righteousness is *through the law*. *For if righteousness were through the law, then Christ died for nothing*. In other words, Christ died for no reason, since righteousness was available among people through the law (that is, through its works, in which the Jews put their trust). (14) But not even Paul's opponents would say that *Christ died for nothing*, since they wanted to be regarded as Christians. They are wrong, therefore, to try to persuade Christians that righteousness is through works of the law.

18. He rightly says to these people: *You foolish Galatians! Who has bewitched you?* (Gal. 3: 1). It would not be right[61] to say this of people who had never made progress, but it is right to say it of people who had turned away from the progress they had made. (2) *Before whose eyes Christ Jesus was proscribed—after being crucified!*[62] In other words, they saw Christ Jesus lose his *inheritance* and his *possession*,[63] specifically to those who were taking it away and banishing the Lord. They, in order to take away Christ's *possession* (meaning the people in whom he dwelt by right of grace and faith), were calling those who had believed Christ back—back from the grace of faith whereby Christ has possession of the Gentiles to works of the law.[64] (3) The

course, that existed in us, which was proscribed, sold, and lost by the persuasive power of Judaism' (CSEL 83. 2: 126. 10–13).

contigit, quam quod in ipsis contigit? Cum autem dixisset: *Iesus Christus proscriptus est*, addidit, *crucifixus*, ut hinc eos maxime moueret, cum considerarent, quo pretio emerit possessionem, quam in eis amittebat, ut parum esset gratis eum mortuum, quod superius dixerat. (5) Illud enim ita sonat, tamquam non peruenerit ad possessionem, pro qua sanguinem dedit. Proscripto autem etiam, quae tenebat, aufertur, sed haec proscriptio non obest Christo, qui etiam sic per diuinitatem dominus est omnium, sed ipsi possessioni, quae huius gratiae cultura caret.

19. Hinc iam incipit demonstrare, quemadmodum gratia fidei sufficiat ad iustificandum sine operibus legis, ne quis diceret non se quidem operibus legis tantum totam hominis iustificationem tribuere, sed neque tantum gratiae fidei, ex utroque autem perfici salutem. (2) Sed haec quaestio, ut diligenter tractetur, ne quis fallatur ambiguo, scire prius debet opera legis bipartita esse. Nam partim in sacramentis, partim uero in moribus accipiuntur. (3) Ad sacramenta pertinent circumcisio carnis, sabbatum temporale, neomeniae, sacrificia atque omnes huius modi innumerabiles obseruationes, ad mores autem: *Non occides, non moechaberis, non falsum testimonium dices* et cetera talia. (4) Num quidnam ergo apostolus ita potest non curare, utrum christianus homicida aut moechus sit, an castus atque innocens, quemadmodum non curat, utrum circumcisus carne an praeputiatus sit? (5) Nunc ergo de his operibus maxime tractat, quae sunt in sacramentis, quamquam et illa interdum se admiscere significet. Prope finem autem epistulae de his separatim tractauit, quae sunt in moribus, et illud breuiter, hoc autem diutius. (6) Haec enim onera potius nolebat imponi gentibus, quorum utilitas in intellectu est, nam haec omnia exponuntur christianis, ut, quid ualeant, tantum intelligant, etiam facere non cogantur. (7) In obseruationibus autem, si non intelligantur, seruitus sola est, qualis erat in populo Iudaeorum et est usque adhuc. Si autem et obseruentur illa et intelligantur non modo nihil obsunt, sed etiam prosunt aliquid, si tempori congruant, sicut ab ipso Moyse prophetis quoque

[65] Cf. Rom. 3: 28.

[66] The discussion in *exp. Gal.* 19 is illuminated by and in turn illuminates the discussion of biblical ambiguity in *doctr. chr.* 3, esp. 3. 6. 10 and 3. 8. 12–9. 13 (Green, text and trans., 142–7).

[67] Such a division was widely accepted by the Fathers, both Latin and Greek. On this point see Wiles, *Divine Apostle*, 66–9. According to Augustine, the Manichees erred by failing to recognize this division. See e.g. *c. Faust.* 6. 2 (CSEL 25. 1: 285. 9–286. 14).

[68] In *ep.* 138. 1. 7 Augustine defines sacraments thus broadly: 'Signs, when they refer to divine things, are called "sacraments"' ('Signa, cum ad res divinas pertinent, sacramenta appellantur' (CSEL 44: 131. 10)).

Apostle wants the Galatians to realize that this has happened in their very midst, which is why he says: *before whose eyes*. (4) What has happened *before their eyes* so much as what has happened in their very midst? Moreover, when he said, *Jesus Christ was proscribed*, he added, *after being crucified!*, so as to move them very deeply when they considered the price Christ paid for the possession he was losing in them. And so it is not enough to say (as the Apostle said earlier) that *Christ died for nothing*. (5) For that sounds as though Christ has not attained to the possession for which he gave his blood. But when Christ is also *proscribed*, what he was holding is taken away. However, this proscription does not harm Christ (who by his divinity is Lord of all), but the possession itself, which is deprived of the care of his grace.

19. Now from this point the Apostle begins to show how the grace of faith is sufficient for justification apart from works of the law,[65] in case anyone was saying that while he does not attribute a person's entire justification to works of the law alone, neither does he attribute it to the grace of faith alone, but rather claims that salvation is accomplished by both. (2) But in order to treat this question carefully and avoid being misled by ambiguity,[66] one must first realize that the works of the law are in two divisions.[67] Some come under sacraments,[68] others under morals. (3) Under sacraments are: circumcision of the flesh, the temporal sabbath, new moons, sacrifices, and all the countless observances of this kind. Under morals are: *You shall not kill, You shall not commit adultery, You shall not bear false witness* (Exod. 20: 13–14, 16; Deut. 5: 17–18, 20), and the like. (4) Now surely, it is impossible that the Apostle does not care whether a Christian is a murderer and an adulterer or chaste and innocent, in the same way that he does not care whether a man is circumcised or uncircumcised in the flesh. (5) At present, therefore, he is dealing mainly with these latter, sacramental works (although he indicates that he sometimes includes the former as well, while near the end of the letter,[69] when dealing briefly with sacramental works, he deals separately and at greater length with morals). (6) For he preferred that these burdens, whose usefulness lies in what they signify, not be laid upon the Gentiles. For all these are explained to Christians so they may simply understand their significance without being forced to carry them out. (7) In the case of observances that are not understood, however, it is mere slavery, as it was for the Jewish people and still is. But if they are both observed and understood, not only are they in no way harmful, they even do some good if they are appropriate for the time, just as they did when Moses himself and

[69] i.e. beginning at Gal. 5: 13. See *exp. Gal.* 43. 2.

obseruata sunt, congruentibus illi populo, cui adhuc talis seruitus utilis erat, ut sub timore custodiretur. (8) Nihil enim tam pie terret animam, quam sacramentum non intellectum, intellectum autem gaudium pium parit et celebratur libere, si opus est tempori; si autem non est opus, cum suauitate spirituali tantummodo legitur et tractatur. (9) Omne autem sacramentum cum intelligitur, aut ad contemplationem ueritatis refertur aut ad bonos mores. (10) Contemplatio ueritatis in solius dei dilectione fundata est, boni mores in dilectione dei et proximi, in quibus duobus praeceptis tota lex pendet et prophetae. Nunc igitur, quemadmodum circumcisio carnis et cetera huiusmodi legis opera, ubi iam gratia fidei est, non sint necessaria, uideamus.

20. *Hoc solum*, inquit, *uolo discere a uobis: ex operibus legis spiritum accepistis an ex auditu fidei?* Respondetur: utique ex auditu fidei. (2) Ab apostolo enim praedicata est eis fides, in qua praedicatione utique aduentum et praesentiam sancti spiritus senserant, sicut illo tempore in nouitate inuitationis ad fidem etiam sensibilibus miraculis praesentia sancti spiritus apparebat, sicut in Actibus apostolorum legitur. (3) Hoc autem factum erat apud Galatas, antequam isti ad eos peruertendos et circumcidendos uenissent. Iste ergo sensus est: Si in illis operibus legis esset salus uestra, non uobis spiritus sanctus nisi circumcisis daretur. (4) Deinde intulit: *Sic stulti estis, ut cum spiritu coeperitis, nunc carne consummemini.* (5) Hoc est, quod superius in exordio dixerat: *Nisi aliqui sunt conturbantes uos et uolentes conuertere euangelium Christi.* Conturbatio enim ordini contraria est, ordo est autem a carnalibus ad spiritualia surgere, non ab spiritualibus ad carnalia cadere, sicut istis acciderat. (6) Et haec est euangelii conuersio retrorsus, quod quia bonum non est non est euangelium, cum hoc annuntiatur. (7) Quod autem dicit: *Tanta passi estis,*

---

[70] i.e. it is not actually celebrated. 'Spiritual enjoyment' comes from recognizing how Christ was foretold in the Old Testament.

[71] Cf. Matt. 22: 37–9 // Mark 12: 28–31 // Luke 10:25–8.

[72] 'by *hearing the faith*': or, more literally, 'by *the hearing of faith*' (Latin: *ex auditu fidei*). The Latin genitive *fidei* in Gal. 3: 2, like the corresponding Greek genitive πίστεως in the original, can also be taken as a subjective genitive referring to the hearing that proceeds from faith. But in 20. 2 it is clear that Augustine is taking it as an objective genitive.

[73] See Acts 2: 1–13, 3: 1–10, etc., and cf. *ciu.* 22. 5 (CCSL 48: 811. 46–63).

[74] Rom. 5: 5 is cited again in 44. 4 below and over 200 times all together in Augustine's writings. For analysis and discussion of this crucially important text see La Bonnardière, 'Le Verset paulinien *Rom.*, V. 5'.

[75] Latin: *in vobis*, here interpreted as Augustine interprets the same phrase in 38. 1–4 below. However, 'among you' is also possible here.

the prophets observed them, accommodating themselves to people for whom such slavery was still useful as a way of keeping them in fear. (8) For nothing so fills a soul with holy fear as a sacrament that is not understood. But once understood it produces holy joy and is celebrated freely if it is essential for the time. Now if it is not essential, it is simply read and interpreted with spiritual enjoyment.[70] (9) Moreover, every sacrament, when understood, refers either to the contemplation of the truth or to good morals. (10) The contemplation of the truth is founded upon the love of God alone, good morals upon the love of God and neighbour;[71] *on these two commandments, all the law and the prophets depend* (Matt. 22: 40). Now then, let us see how circumcision of the flesh and other similar works of the law are no longer necessary where the grace of faith is present.

20. *There is just one thing*, he says, *that I would like to learn from you: Did you receive the Spirit by works of the law, or by hearing the faith?* (Gal. 3: 2). Undoubtedly by *hearing the faith*.[72] (2) For the Apostle preached the faith to them, and it was undoubtedly in that preaching that they perceived the coming and presence of the Holy Spirit, just as the presence of the Holy Spirit showed itself in perceptible miracles when the invitation to the faith was new, as we read in the Acts of the Apostles.[73] (3) Moreover, this happened in the presence of the Galatians before the arrival of those who were intent on subversion and circumcision. The meaning, therefore, is this: 'If your salvation lay in those works of the law, the Holy Spirit would not be given to you unless you were circumcised.' (4) He then says: *Are you so foolish that after beginning with the Spirit you now want to be made perfect by the flesh?* (Gal. 3: 3). (5) That is, as he said earlier in the exordium: *but some are troubling you and trying to subvert the gospel of Christ* (Gal. 1: 7). For trouble is contrary to order; moreover, order consists in rising from carnal to spiritual things, not in falling from spiritual to carnal things as had happened to them. (6) The latter is tantamount to turning the gospel backwards, and when it is proclaimed it is not the gospel, because it is not good. (7) *Have you suffered so much?* (Gal. 3: 4). By then they had endured much for the faith, but not out of fear as though they were under the law. Rather, in those very sufferings they had conquered fear by love, *because God's love was poured out in their hearts through the Holy Spirit* (Rom. 5: 5),[74] whom they had received. (8) *Have you suffered so much, then, for no reason?* (Gal. 3: 4)—you who want to fall away from love, which has borne so much in you,[75] and back into fear,[76] *if indeed* you have *suffered so much for no reason*. What is said to have been done *for no reason* is superfluous. Something superfluous,

---

[76] Cf. Rom. 8: 15–17.

multa iam pro fide tolerauerant, non timore, tamquam sub lege positi, sed magis in ipsis passionibus caritate timorem uicerant, quoniam caritas dei diffusa est in cordibus eorum per spiritum sanctum, quem acceperant. (8) *Sine causa ergo*, inquit, *tanta passi estis*, qui ex caritate, quae in uobis tanta sustinuit, ad timorem relabi uultis, si tamen sine causa tanta passi estis. Quod enim sine causa factum dicitur, superfluum est, superfluum autem nec prodest nec nocet; hoc uero uidendum est, ne ad perniciem ualeat. (9) Non enim hoc est non surgere, quod est cadere, quamuis isti nondum cecidissent, sed iam inclinarentur, ut caderent. (10) Nam utique adhuc in eis spiritus sanctus operabatur, sicut consequenter dicit: *Qui ergo tribuit uobis spiritum et uirtutes operatur in uobis, ex operibus legis an ex auditu fidei?* (11) Respondetur: utique ex auditu fidei, sicut superius tractatum est. Deinde adhibet exemplum patris Abraham, de quo in epistula ad Romanos uberius apertiusque dissertum est. (12) Hoc enim maxime in eo uictoriosum est, quod, antequam circumcideretur, deputata est fides eius ad iustitiam et ad hoc rectissime refertur, quod ei dictum est: *Quia benedicentur in te omnes gentes*, imitatione utique fidei eius, qua iustificatus est, etiam ante sacramentum circumcisionis, quod ad fidei signaculum accepit, et ante omnem seruitutem legis, quae multo post data est.

21. Quod autem ait: *Quicumque enim ex operibus legis sunt, sub maledicto sunt legis*, sub timore uult intelligi non in libertate, ut scilicet corporali praesentique uindicta uindicaretur in eos, qui non permanerent in omnibus, quae scripta sunt in libro legis, ut facerent ea. Huc quoque accederet, ut in ipsa corporum poena etiam maledicti ignominiam formidarent. (2) Ille autem iustificatur apud deum, qui eum gratis colit, non scilicet cupiditate appetendi aliquid ab ipso praeter ipsum aut timore amittendi. (3) In ipso enim solo uera nostra beatitudo atque perfecta est et, quoniam inuisibilis est oculis carneis, fide colitur, quamdiu in hac carne uiuimus, sicut supra dixit: *Quod autem nunc uiuo in carne, in fide uiuo filii dei*, et ipsa est iustitia. (4) Quo pertinet quod dictum est: *Quia iustus ex fide uiuit*. Hinc enim ostendere uoluit, quia in lege nemo iustificatur, quia scriptum est iustum ex fide uiuere. (5) Quare intelligendum est in lege, quod nunc ait: *in operibus legis*, dictum esse et hoc istis, qui in circumcisione carnis et talibus obseruationibus continentur, in quibus qui uiuit ita in lege est, ut

---

[77] Gal. 3: 6–9.
[78] See Rom. 4.
[79] Cf. Gal. 3: 6 (Gen. 15: 6), Rom. 4: 3.
[80] See the note on 'sacraments' attached to *exp. Gal.* 19. 2.

however, neither helps nor harms; but in this case they must watch out lest it lead to destruction. (9) For to fall is not the same thing as not to rise; although they had not yet fallen, they were leaning that way.

(10) Now it is clear that the Holy Spirit was still working in them. As he goes on to say: *He therefore who gives the Spirit to you and works miracles among you, does he do it by works of the law, or by hearing the faith?* (Gal. 3: 5). (11) Undoubtedly by hearing the faith, as was explained previously. Then he cites the example of our father Abraham,[77] who is discussed more fully and clearly in the letter to the Romans.[78] (12) For Abraham's chief glory is that, before he was circumcised, his faith was counted as righteousness.[79] What was said to him refers to this most fittingly: *For in you shall all nations be blessed* (Gal. 3: 8 (Gen. 12: 3, 18: 18)), that is, in imitation of his faith, by which he was justified even before the sacrament[80] of circumcision, which he received as a seal of faith before all slavery to the law, which was given much later.

21. *For all who depend on works of the law are under the curse of the law* (Gal. 3: 10). Here Paul wants us to understand '*under* fear and not free', since immediate physical punishment would, of course, be inflicted on those *who did not abide by all the things written in the book of the law, and do them* (Gal. 3: 10 (Deut. 27: 26)). One might add that they also feared the infamy of the curse that went with the physical penalty. (2) But the person who is *justified before God* (Gal. 3: 11) worships God gratis, that is, neither out of a desire to obtain anything from God except God himself, nor out of fear of losing anything except God himself. (3) For our only true happiness and perfection[81] is in him, and since he is invisible to fleshly eyes, as long as we live in the flesh we worship in faith, as the Apostle said earlier: *the life I now live in the flesh I live in faith in the Son of God* (Gal. 2: 20), and this is righteousness. (4) With this in mind he says: *for the righteous live by faith* (Gal. 3: 11 (Hab. 2: 4)). What is at issue here is to show that *no one is justified by the law* (Gal. 3: 11), since it is written that *the righteous live by faith.* (5) Therefore the expression *the law* as used here means 'works of the law' and refers to those people held in check by circumcision of the flesh and observances of this kind. Whoever lives by these things is so involved in the law as to be living under it. (6) But, to repeat, he is now using the expression *the law* in place of 'the actual works of the law', as is clear from what follows. For he says: *But the law does not depend on faith, but 'Whoever does them shall live by them'* (Gal. 3: 12 (Lev. 18: 5)). (7) He does not say: 'Whoever does it shall live by it'—so you may understand that in this passage he is using *the law* in

---

[81] Reading *perfectio* with Rousselet, rather than *perfecta* with Divjak. (*Perfectio* is also the reading of the oldest extant MS of *exp. Gal.*, Vat. lat. 491.)

sub lege uiuat. (6) Sed legem, ut dictum est, pro ipsis operibus legis nunc posuit, quod de posterioribus manifestatur. Ait enim: *Lex autem non est ex fide, sed qui fecerit ea, uiuet in illis.* (7) Non ait: qui fecerit eam, uiuet in ea, ut intelligas legem in hoc loco pro ipsis operibus positam. Qui autem uiuebant in his operibus, timebant utique ne, si non ea fecissent, lapidationem uel crucem uel aliquid huiusmodi paterentur. (8) Ergo *qui fecerit ea*, inquit, *uiuet in illis*, id est, habebit praemium, ne in ista morte puniatur. Non ergo apud deum, cuius ex fide, si quis in hac uita uixerit, cum hinc excesserit, tunc eum magis habebit praesentissimum praemium. (9) Non itaque ex fide uiuit, quisquis praesentia, quae uidentur, uel cupit uel timet, quia fides dei ad inuisibilia pertinet, quae post dabuntur. Nam est ista quaedam in operibus legis iustitia, quando sine suo praemio relicta non est, ut qui fecerit ea uiuet in eis. (10) Vnde et ad Romanos dicit: *Si enim Abraham ex operibus iustificatus est, habet gloriam, sed non ad deum.* Aliud est ergo non iustificari, aliud non iustificari apud deum. (11) Qui omnino non iustificatur, nec illa seruat, quae temporale habent praemium, nec illa quae aeternum, qui autem in operibus legis iustificatur non apud deum iustificatur, quia temporalem inde expectat uisibilemque mercedem. (12) Sed tamen est etiam ista, ut dixi, quaedam, ut sic dicam, terrena carnalisque iustitia, nam et ipse apostolus eam iustitiam uocat, cum alibi dicit: *Secundum iustitiam, quae in lege est, conuersatus, qui fuerim sine querela.*

22. Propterea dominus Iesus Christus iam libertatem daturus credentibus, quaedam earum obseruationum non seruauit ad litteram. (2) Vnde etiam cum sabbato esurientes discipuli spicas euulsissent, respondit indignantibus dominum esse filium hominis etiam sabbati. Itaque illa carnaliter non obseruando carnalium conflagrauit inuidiam et suscepit quidem poenam propositam illis, qui ea non obseruassent, sed ut credentes in se talis poenae timore liberaret, quo pertinet, quod adiungit: (3) *Christus nos redemit de maledicto legis factus pro nobis maledictum, quia scriptum est: Maledictus omnis qui pendet in ligno.* Quae sententia spiritualiter intelligentibus sacramentum est libertatis, carnaliter autem sentientibus, si Iudaei sunt, iugum est seruitutis, si pagani aut haeretici, uelamentum est caecitatis. (4) Nam quod quidam nostri minus in scripturis eruditi

---

[82] Matt. 12: 1–8 // Mark 2: 23–8 // Luke 6: 1–5.

[83] Or 'envy', as in *exp. Gal.* 52. The Latin is *inuidia*.

[84] Cf. Heb. 2: 15.

[85] Deut. 21: 23 is a 'sacrament of freedom' because it is a sacred sign pointing prophetically to the means by which Christ would set humanity free.

place of 'works of the law'. Now those who were living by these works undoubtedly feared that if they did not do them, they would suffer stoning or crucifixion or something of this kind. (8) Therefore *whoever does them*, he says, *shall live by them*, that is, shall have a reward: he will not be punished by having to undergo such a death. But in that case his reward is not with God, for whoever has lived his life *by faith* in God will have God as a very present reward when he departs this life. (9) And so whoever desires or fears present, visible things does not live by faith, for faith in God refers to invisible things that will be given hereafter. For there is a kind of righteousness by works of the law that is not without its reward, such that *whoever does them shall live by them*. (10) In this regard he also says to the Romans: *For if Abraham was justified by works he has something to boast about, but not before God* (Rom. 4: 2). Thus it is one thing not to be justified, another not to be justified *before God*. (11) One who is not justified at all observes neither the things that have a temporal reward nor the things that have an eternal reward. On the other hand, one who is justified by works of the law is not justified *before God*, because he expects from them temporal and visible compensation. (12) But nevertheless, as I have said, there really is a kind of earthly and carnal righteousness (so to speak), for even the Apostle himself calls it righteousness when he says in another passage: *according to the righteousness that is by the law, I was blameless* (Phil. 3: 6).

22. Consequently, on the verge of granting freedom to believers the Lord Jesus Christ did not follow certain observances to the letter. (2) Thus, when the disciples were hungry on the sabbath and plucked heads of grain, he responded to those who objected by saying that the Son of Man is Lord even of the sabbath.[82] And so by not observing those things in a carnal way he incurred the hatred[83] of carnal people and indeed received the punishment laid down for those not observing them, but he did so to set those who believed in him free from the fear of such punishment.[84] With this in mind the Apostle continues: (3) *Christ redeemed us from the curse of the law by being made a curse for us, for it is written: 'Cursed is everyone who hangs on a tree'* (Gal. 3: 13 (Deut. 21: 23)). To those who understand it spiritually this sentence is a sacrament of freedom,[85] but to those who take it carnally it is a yoke of slavery if they are Jews, a veil of blindness[86] if they are pagans or heretics. (4) Moreover, some of our own people,[87] less learned in the

---

[86] Cf. 2 Cor. 3: 14–16. Among the heretics who misinterpreted Deut. 21: 23 the Manichees were undoubtedly in the forefront of Augustine's mind. Cf. *c. Adim.* 21, *c. Faust.* 14, *c. Fel.* 2. 10–11. (The same imagery from 2 Corinthians is applied to the Manichees in *c. Faust.* 12. 4 (CSEL 25. 1: 332–3) and elsewhere.)

[87] Not merely the Catholics in Hippo, since Faustus is also familiar with Catholics who think like this. Cf. *c. Faust.* 14. 1 (CSEL 25. 1: 404. 2–4).

sententiam istam nimis timentes et scripturas ueteres debita pietate approbantes non putant hoc de domino esse dictum sed de Iuda traditore eius, aiunt enim propterea non esse dictum: Maledictus omnis, qui figitur in ligno, sed: *qui pendet in ligno*, quia non hic dominus significatus est, sed ille, qui se laqueo suspendit, nimis errant nec attendunt se contra apostolum disputare, qui ait: *Christus nos redemit de maledicto legis factus pro nobis maledictum quia scriptum est: Maledictus omnis, qui pendet in ligno.* (5) Qui ergo pro nobis factus est maledictum, ipse utique pependit in ligno, id est, Christus, qui nos liberauit a maledicto legis, ut non iam timore iustificaremur in operibus legis, sed fide apud deum, quae non per timorem sed per dilectionem operatur. (6) Spiritus enim sanctus, qui hoc per Moysen dixit, utrumque prouidit, ut et timore uisibilis poenae custodirentur, qui nondum poterant ex inuisibilium fide uiuere, et ipse timorem istum solueret suscipiendo, quod timebatur, qui timore sublato donum dare poterat caritatis. (7) Nec in hoc, quod maledictus appellatus est, qui pendet in ligno, contumelia in dominum putanda est. Ex parte quippe mortali pependit in ligno, mortalitas autem unde sit, notum est credentibus. Ex poena quippe est et maledictione peccati primi hominis, quam dominus suscepit et peccata nostra pertulit in corpore suo super lignum. (8) Si ergo diceretur: Mors maledicta est, nemo exhorresceret, quid autem nisi mors domini pependit in ligno, ut mortem moriendo superaret? eadem igitur maledicta, quae uicta est. (9) Item si diceretur: peccatum maledictum est, nemo miraretur. Quid autem pependit in ligno nisi peccatum ueteris hominis, quod dominus pro nobis in ipsa carnis mortalitate suscepit? Vnde nec erubuit nec timuit apostolus dicere peccatum eum fecisse pro nobis addens: *Vt de peccato condemnaret peccatum.* (10) Non enim et uetus homo noster simul crucifigeretur, sicut idem apostolus alibi dicit, nisi in illa morte domini peccati nostri figura penderet, ut euacuaretur corpus peccati, ut ultra non seruiamus peccato. (11) In eius peccati et mortis figura etiam Moyses in heremo super lignum exaltauit serpentem. Persuasione quippe serpentis homo in damnationem mortis cecidit. Itaque serpens ad significationem ipsius mortis conuenienter in ligno exaltatus est, in illa enim figura mors domini pendebat in ligno. (12) Quis autem abhorreret, si diceretur: Maledictus serpens, qui pendet in ligno? Et tamen mortem carnis domini praefigurans serpens pendebat in ligno, cui sacramento ipse dominus attestatus est dicens: *Sicut exaltauit*

---

[88] Cf. Matt. 27: 3–5.   [89] Cf. Gal. 5: 6.   [90] 2 Cor. 5: 21.

Scriptures, unduly fearful about this passage and with due piety approving the ancient Scriptures, do not think that this refers to the Lord but to Judas his betrayer. They say that the reason the words are not 'Cursed is everyone who is nailed to a tree' but *who hangs on a tree*, is because it is not the Lord who is meant here but the one who hanged himself by a noose.[88] But they completely miss the point and fail to see that their view contradicts what the Apostle says: *Christ redeemed us from the curse of the law by being made a curse for us, for it is written: 'Cursed is everyone who hangs on a tree.'* (5) He, therefore, who was *made a curse for us*, certainly is the one who hung on a tree— Christ, who set us free from the curse of the law that we might no longer be justified in fear by works of the law but by faith before God, which works not through fear but through love.[89] (6) For the Holy Spirit, speaking through Moses, provided for both in such a way that those who were not yet able to live by faith in invisible things might be restrained by fear of visible punishment, and Christ himself might break down that fear by taking upon himself the thing that was feared and, once the fear was taken away, bestow the gift of love. (7) Nor is it to be thought an insult to the Lord that the one *who hangs on a tree* is called *cursed*. Indeed, in his mortal aspect he hung on a tree, but believers know the origin of our mortality—it comes from the penalty and curse for the sin of the first human being, which the Lord took upon himself and *bore our sins in his body on the tree* (1 Pet. 2: 24). (8) If, then, it should be said, 'Death is cursed', no one would be horrified, but what hung on the tree except the death of the Lord, that by dying he might overcome death? The same thing is cursed, then, as is conquered. (9) Similarly, if it should be said, 'Sin is cursed', no one would be amazed. But what hung on the tree except the sin of the old humanity, which the Lord took upon himself in the very mortality of the flesh for us. For this reason the Apostle was neither ashamed nor afraid to say that God made him to be sin for us,[90] adding: *that by sin he might condemn sin* (Rom. 8: 3). (10) For *our old humanity* would not have been *crucified together with him*, as the same apostle says elsewhere, unless in the Lord's death there had hung a figure of our sin, *so that the body of sin might be destroyed, that we might serve sin no longer* (Rom. 6: 6). (11) It was also in a figure of this sin and death that Moses in the desert lifted up the serpent on a tree.[91] For it was by a serpent's persuasion that humanity fell into the condemnation of death. And so it was fitting for a serpent to be lifted up on a tree as a sign of that death, for in that figure the death of the Lord was hanging on a tree. (12) But if it were said, 'Cursed is the serpent that hangs on a tree', who would shudder at it? And

[91] Num. 21: 9.

Moyses serpentem in heremo, ita exaltari oportet filium hominis super terram.
(13) Non enim et hoc in contumeliam domini Moysen fecisse aliquis
dixerit, cum tantam in ea cruce salutem hominum esse cognosceret, ut non
ob aliud ad eius indicium serpentem illum erigere iuberet, nisi ut eum
intuentes, qui morsi a serpentibus morituri erant, continuo sanarentur.
(14) Nec propter aliud ille serpens aeneus factus erat, nisi ut permansurae
passionis domini fidem significaret. (15) Etiam uulgo quippe dicuntur
aenea, quorum numerus manet. Si enim obliti essent homines et
obliteratum esset de memoria temporis, quod Christus pro hominibus
mortuus est, uere morerentur. Nunc autem tamquam aenea permanet
crucis fides, ut, cum alii moriantur, alii nascantur, ipsam tamen sublimem
permanere inueniant, quam intuendo sanentur. (16) Non igitur mirum, si
de maledicto uicit maledictum, qui uicit de morte mortem et de peccato
peccatum, de serpente serpentem. Maledicta autem mors, maledictum
peccatum, maledictus serpens, et haec omnia in cruce triumphata sunt.
(17) *Maledictus igitur omnis qui pendet in ligno.* Quia ergo non ex operibus
legis sed ex fide iustificat Christus credentes in se, timor maledictionis
crucis ablatus est, caritas benedictionis Abrahae propter exemplum fidei
permanet ad gentes. (18) *Vt annuntiationem,* inquit, *spiritus per fidem
accipiamus,* id est, ut non, quod timetur in carne, sed quod spiritu diligitur,
credituris annuntietur.

23. Vnde etiam testamenti humani mentionem facit, quod utique multo
est infirmius quam diuinum. *Tamen hominis confirmatum testamentum,*
inquit, *nemo irritum facit aut superordinat.* (2) Quia cum testator mutat
testamentum, non confirmatum mutat, testatoris enim morte confirmatur.
Quod autem mors testatoris ualet ad confirmandum testamentum eius,
quia consilium mutare iam non potest, hoc incommutabilitas promissionis
dei ualet ad confirmandam hereditatem Abrahae, cuius fides deputata est ad
iustitiam. (3) Et ideo semen Abraham, *cui dictae sunt promissiones,* Christum
dicit apostolus, hoc est omnes Christianos fide imitantes Abraham, quod ad
singularitatem redigit commendando, quod non dictum est: et seminibus,

---

[92] Cf. Col. 2: 15.

[93] 'will' (Latin: *testamentum*): the term may also be translated 'covenant' here and elsewhere
in 23, and in 25. 4 below 'covenant' is the preferred translation. Everywhere else in this text
testamentum has been translated 'Testament'.

[94] Augustine quotes Gal. 3: 15–22 and 4: 21–6 as examples of the 'restrained style' (*submissa
dictio*) in *doctr. chr.* 4. 20. 39 (Green, text and trans., 244–7).

[95] Cf. Heb. 9: 16–17.

yet the serpent hung on a tree to prefigure the death of the Lord's flesh—a sacrament to which the Lord himself has borne witness: *Just as Moses lifted up the serpent in the desert, so must the Son of Man be lifted up above the earth* (John 3: 14). (13) For no one can say that Moses did this, too, as an insult to the Lord, since Moses knew how great the salvation was that lay in the cross. So the only reason he had the serpent raised up as a sign was in order that those who had been bitten by serpents and were going to die might look upon it and immediately be healed. (14) Nor is there any other reason why the serpent was made of bronze except to signify faith in the enduring passion of the Lord. (15) Indeed, we commonly call things of an enduring kind 'bronze'. For if people had forgotten that Christ died for humanity and it was effaced from the history of the time, then they truly would be dying. But now, like bronze, the faith of the cross endures so that, although some die and others are born, they still find this lofty faith enduring, by whose contemplation they are healed. (16) It is not wonderful, therefore, if he who overcame death by death and sin by sin and the serpent by the serpent, overcame the curse by the curse. Not only that, but death is cursed, sin is cursed, the serpent is cursed, and all these things are triumphed over in the cross.[92] (17) *Cursed*, therefore, *is everyone who hangs on a tree.* Thus, because Christ justifies those who believe in him not by works of the law but by faith, the fear inspired by the curse of the cross is taken away, and the love inspired by the blessing of Abraham (which he received for his example of faith) remains for the Gentiles. (18) *That we might receive*, he says, *the preaching of the Spirit through faith* (Gal. 3: 14 OL), that is, so that what is loved in the Spirit, not what is feared in the flesh, may be preached to those who will believe.

23. In this regard he also mentions a human will,[93] which is necessarily much weaker than a divine will. *Yet no one*, he says, *annuls or adds to the will of an ordinary human being once it has been ratified* (Gal. 3: 15).[94] (2) The reason is that if the testator is changing his will, it cannot have been ratified, for it is ratified by the testator's death.[95] Moreover, just as the testator's death serves to ratify his will because he is no longer able to change his decision, so the unchangeableness of God's promise serves to ratify the inheritance of Abraham, whose faith was counted as righteousness.[96] (3) And therefore the Apostle says that the *seed* of Abraham *to whom the promises were made* (Gal. 3: 16) is Christ, that is, all Christians who imitate Abraham by faith. He interprets *seed* as a singular by pointing out what was not said: not *and to seeds* but *to your seed*, because the faith is one and it is not

---

[96] Cf. Gal. 3: 6 (Gen. 15: 6), Rom. 4: 3.

sed *semini tuo*, quia et una est fides et non possunt similiter iustificari, qui uiuunt ex operibus carnaliter, cum his, qui uiuunt ex fide spiritualiter. (4) Inuincibiliter autem quod infert, lex nondum data erat nec posset post tot annos ita dari, ut antiquas Abrahae promissiones irritas faceret. Si enim lex iustificat, non est iustificatus Abraham, qui multum ante legem fuit. (5) Quod quia dicere non possunt, coguntur fateri non legis operibus iustificari hominem, sed fide. Simul etiam nos cogit intelligere omnes antiquos, qui iustificati sunt, ex ipsa fide iustificatos. (6) Quod enim nos ex parte praeteritum, id est primum aduentum domini, ex parte futurum, id est secundum aduentum domini credendo salui efficimur, hoc totum illi, id est utrumque aduentum futurum credebant reuelante sibi spiritu sancto, ut salui fierent. (7) Vnde est etiam illud: *Abraham concupiuit diem meum uidere et uidit et gauisus est*.

24. Sequitur quaestio satis necessaria. Si enim fides iustificat et priores sancti, qui apud deum iustificati sunt, per ipsam iustificati sunt, quid opus erat legem dari? (2) Quam quaestionem tractandam sic intulit interrogans et dicens: *Quid ergo?* (3) Huc usque enim interrogatio est, deinde infertur responsio: *Lex transgressionis gratia proposita est, donec ueniret*, inquit, *semen cui promissum est, dispositum per angelos in manu mediatoris. Mediator autem unius non est, deus uero unus est.* (4) Mediatorem Iesum Christum secundum hominem dici ex illa eiusdem apostoli sententia fit planius, cum ait: *Vnus enim deus, unus et mediator dei et hominum homo Christus Iesus.* (5) Mediator ergo inter deum et deum esse non posset, quia unus est deus, *mediator autem unius non est*, quia inter aliquos medius est. Angeli porro, qui non lapsi sunt a conspectu dei, mediatore non opus habent, per quem reconcilientur. (6) Item angeli, qui nullo suadente spontanea praeuaricatione sic lapsi sunt, per mediatorem non reconciliantur. Restat ergo, ut qui mediatore superbo

---

[97] In other words, the fact that the faith is one means that there is only one way to be justified before God.

[98] Cf. Gal. 3: 17.

[99] Augustine later modified his view as to how this passage should be punctuated. See *retr.* 1. 24 (23). 2 (CCSL 57: 72. 32–7). (On punctuation in antiquity see the note attached to *exp. Gal.* 56. 11.)

[100] In Augustine's Latin version the antecedent of *it* is *seed*. Much later, after consulting other MSS, especially ones in Greek, he realized that his Latin version had been incorrect and that the antecedent ought to have been *the law*. See *retr.* 2. 24 (50). 2 (CCSL 57: 109. 13–110. 18). (In Augustine's Latin version, instead of *dispositum* the reading ought to have been *disposita* (thus Pelagius) or, better still, *ordinata* (Jerome and the Vulgate).)

[101] In thinking that Jesus Christ, rather than Moses, is the mediator that Paul is referring to, Augustine agrees with the vast majority of patristic commentators, including Origen, Victorinus, Ambrosiaster, Jerome, and Chrysostom.

possible for those who live carnally by works of the law to be justified in the same way as those who live spiritually by faith.[97] (4) He brings forward the irrefutable argument, moreover, that the law had not yet been given and could not be given after so many years in such a way as to annul the ancient promises made to Abraham.[98] For if the law justifies, then Abraham, who lived long before the law, was not justified. (5) Since they cannot say this, they are forced to admit that a person is justified not by works of the law but by faith. And it also forces us to realize that all those who were justified in ancient times were justified by the same faith. (6) For we are saved by believing in something which is in part past, namely, the first coming of the Lord, in part future, namely, the second coming of the Lord. But they believed in the very same thing as entirely future, namely, both comings, which the Holy Spirit revealed to them in order to save them. (7) Accordingly there is also that saying: *Abraham longed to see my day, and he saw it, and was glad* (John 8: 56).

24. There follows an unavoidable problem. For if faith justifies and the earlier saints who were justified before God were justified by faith, why did the law have to be given? (2) The Apostle introduces this problem for discussion by asking: *What then?* (Gal. 3: 19). (3) For the question extends thus far and then the answer is introduced:[99] *The law was enacted on account of transgression,* he says, *until the seed should come to whom the promise was made; and it*[100] *was placed by angels in the hand of a mediator. Now there is no mediator where there is only one; but God is one* (Gal. 3: 19–20). (4) That Jesus Christ is called *mediator*[101] according to his human nature is made clearer by the same apostle when he says: *For there is one God, and there is one mediator between God and human beings, Jesus Christ, himself a human being* (1 Tim. 2: 5).[102] (5) So there could not be a mediator between God and God because God is one, and *there is no mediator where there is only one* because an intermediary implies a number of parties. Moreover, the angels who have not fallen away from the contemplation of God have no need for a mediator by whom they may be reconciled. (6) Likewise, the angels who have fallen away by voluntary transgression, without anyone urging them on, are not reconciled by a mediator. It remains, therefore, that anyone who was cast down with the proud mediator—the Devil—urging him to pride, is raised up with the humble mediator—Christ—urging him to humility. (7) For if the Son of God had wished to remain in natural equality with the Father and had not *emptied himself, taking the form of a slave* (Phil. 2: 7), he would not be the *mediator between God and human beings*, because the Trinity itself

---

[102] This is Augustine's earliest citation of what becomes for him a central Christological text. (It is quoted again in full in 63. 10 below.)

diabolo superbiam persuadente deiectus est, mediatore humili Christo humilitatem persuadente erigatur. (7) Nam si filius dei in naturali aequalitate patris manere uellet nec se exinaniret formam serui accipiens, non esset mediator dei et hominum, quia ipsa trinitas unus deus est, eadem in tribus, patre et filio et spiritu sancto, deitatis aeternitate et aequalitate constante. (8) Sic itaque unicus filius dei, mediator dei et hominum factus est, cum uerbum dei deus apud deum et maiestatem suam usque ad humana deposuit et humilitatem humanam usque ad diuina subuexit, ut mediator esset inter deum et homines homo per deum ultra homines. (9) Ipse est enim *speciosus forma prae filiis hominum* et unctus oleo exultationis prae participibus suis. (10) Sanati sunt ergo ab impietate superbiae, ut reconciliarentur deo, quicumque homines humilitatem Christi et per reuelationem, antequam fieret, et per euangelium, posteaquam facta est, credendo dilexerunt, diligendo imitati sunt. (11) Sed haec iustitia fidei, quia non pro merito data est hominibus, sed pro misericordia et gratia dei, non erat popularis, antequam dominus homo inter homines nasceretur. (12) *Semen* autem *cui promissum est*, populum significat, non illos paucissimos, qui reuelationibus ea futura cernentes, quamuis per eandem fidem salui fierent, populum tamen saluum facere non poterant. (13) Qui populus sane, si per totum orbem consideretur—nam de toto orbe ecclesiam Hierusalem caelestem congregat—pauci sunt, quia uia angusta paucorum est, in unum tamen congregati, quotquot existere potuerunt, ex quo euangelium praedicatur, et quotquot poterunt usque in finem saeculi per omnes gentes adiunctis sibi etiam illis quamuis paucissimis, qui ex fide domini, fide prophetica ante ambos aduentus eius salutem gratiae perceperunt, implent sanctorum beatissimum ciuitatis sempiternae statum. (14) Superbienti ergo populo lex posita est, ut, quoniam gratiam caritatis nisi humiliatus accipere non posset et sine hac gratia nullo modo praecepta legis impleret, transgressione humiliaretur, ut quaereret gratiam nec se suis meritis saluum fieri, quod superbum est, opinaretur, ut esset non in sua potestate et uiribus iustus, sed in manu mediatoris iustificantis impium. (15) Per angelos autem ministrata est omnis dispensatio ueteris testamenti agente in eis spiritu sancto et ipso uerbo ueritatis nondum incarnato, sed numquam ab aliqua ueridica administratione recedente.

---

[103] Literally, 'before Christ's humility (*humilitatem Christi*) took place'. Thus by metonymy the term 'humility' may stand for the Incarnation.
[104] Cf. Matt. 7: 13–14.

is one God, with the same eternity and equality of deity remaining without change in three: Father, Son, and Holy Spirit. (8) And so God's only Son became the *mediator between God and human beings* when the Word of God, God with God, both laid down his own majesty to the level of the human and exalted human lowliness to the level of the divine, in order that he—a human being who through God was beyond human beings—might be the *mediator between God and human beings*. (9) For he is the one *beyond human beings in the beauty of his form* (Ps. 44: 3 (45: 2)) and *anointed with the oil of gladness beyond his companions* (Ps. 44: 8 (45: 7)). (10) Thus, through revelation before Christ humbled himself[103] and through the gospel afterwards, all who by believing loved and by loving imitated Christ's humility were cured of the impiety of pride in order to be reconciled to God. (11) But because this righteousness of faith was not given to human beings on account of merit but on account of God's mercy and grace, it was not generally available before the Lord was born as a human being among human beings.

(12) Now *the seed to whom the promise was made* signifies a people, not those very few who, although they were saved through the same faith when they discerned the things to come by revelations, could not save the people. (13) These people, if considered throughout the whole world—for he gathers the Church, the heavenly Jerusalem, from the whole world—are still few, because the narrow way is found by few.[104] Yet as many as have been able to come forth since the proclamation of the gospel, and as many as are able to come forth throughout all nations until the end of the world, are gathered into one. These people, together with those, though very few, who obtained the salvation of grace by faith in the Lord (that is, prophetic faith before both of his comings) fill the most blessed state of the saints of the eternal city. (14) The law was ordained, therefore, for a proud people so that they might be humbled by their transgression (since they could not receive the grace of love unless they were humbled, and without this grace they could not fulfil the precepts of the law at all), so that they might seek grace and not assume they could be saved by their own merits (which is pride), and so that they might be righteous not by their own power and strength, but by the hand of a mediator who justifies the impious.[105]

(15) Now it was through angels that the whole dispensation of the Old Testament was administered. The Holy Spirit was active in them and the Word of truth himself, though not yet incarnate, never withdrew from any true administration. (16) Because it was through angels (who, like the

---

[105] Cf. Rom. 4: 5.

(16) Quia per angelos disposita est illa dispensatio legis, cum aliquando suam, aliquando dei personam, sicut prophetarum etiam mos est, agerent, perque illam legem morbos ostendentem non auferentem etiam praeuaricationis crimine contrita superbia est. (17) *Dispositum est per angelos semen in manu mediatoris*, ut ipse liberaret a peccatis iam per transgressionem legis coactos confiteri opus sibi esse gratiam et misericordiam domini, ut sibi peccata dimitterentur et in noua uita per eum, qui pro se sanguinem fudisset, reconciliarentur deo.

25. In istis enim erat per transgressionem legis confringenda superbia, qui gloriantes de patre Abraham quasi naturalem se habere iactabant iustitiam et merita sua in circumcisione ceteris gentibus tanto perniciosius quanto arrogantius praeferebant, gentes autem facillime etiam sine huiusmodi legis transgressione humiliarentur. (2) Homines enim nullam ex parentibus originem iustitiae se trahere praeuidentes simulacrorum etiam seruos inuenit euangelica gratia. Non enim sicut istis dici poterat non fuisse illam iustitiam parentum eorum in colendis idolis, quam esse arbitrabantur, ita etiam Iudaeis dici poterat falsam fuisse iustitiam patris Abraham. (3) Itaque illis dicitur: *Facite ergo fructum dignum poenitentiae et ne dixeritis uobis: patrem habemus Abraham. Potens est enim deus de lapidibus istis suscitare filios Abraham.* (4) Istis autem dicitur: *Propter quod memores estis, quia uos aliquando gentes in carne, qui dicimini praeputium ab ea, quae dicitur circumcisio in carne manufacta, qui eratis illo tempore sine Christo, alienati a societate Israel et peregrini testamentorum et promissionis spem non habentes et sine deo in hoc mundo.* (5) Denique illic infideles de oliua sua fracti, hic autem fideles de oleastro in oliua illorum inserti esse monstrantur. (6) Illorum ergo erat de legis transgressione atterenda superbia, sicut ad Romanos, cum scripturarum uerbis peccata eorum exaggerasset: *Scitis autem*, inquit, *quoniam quaecumque lex dixit his, qui in lege sunt, loquitur, ut omne os obstruatur et reus fiat omnis mundus deo*, Iudaei scilicet de transgressione legis et gentes de impietate sine lege. (7) Vnde et iterum ait: *Conclusit enim deus omnia in incredulitatem, ut omnium misereatur.* (8) Hoc et nunc dicit refricans ipsam quaestionem: *Lex ergo aduersus*

---

[106] Cf. what Augustine writes with reference to Gal. 3: 19 in *trin*. 3. 26: 'So the Lord used to speak in those bygone days through angels, and through angels the Son of God, who would come from the seed of Abraham to mediate between God and men, was preparing his coming, arranging to find people to receive him by confessing themselves guilty, convicted of transgression by the law they had not fulfilled' (Hill, trans., 144 (CCSL 50: 157. 166–70)).

[107] Cf. *Thesaurus Linguae Latinae* under *praevideo*, II B 1.

prophets, sometimes represented themselves and sometimes represented God) that the dispensation of the law was put in place, and because the law reveals diseases without taking them away, pride was crushed in the very indictment of the transgression. (17) *The seed was placed by angels in the hand of a mediator* so that he might liberate from their sins those now forced through transgression of the law to confess that they need the grace and mercy of the Lord, so that their sins might be forgiven and they might be reconciled to God in a new life through him who had poured out his blood for them.[106]

25. For transgression of the law was the means by which pride was to be broken in this people who, bragging about their father Abraham, boasted that they had a kind of natural righteousness. And the more arrogantly they flaunted the merits they claimed from circumcision, the more harm they did to the Gentiles. Now the Gentiles could very easily be humbled even without such transgression of the law. (2) For when the grace of the gospel found them, they realized[107] that they could claim no righteousness from their parents—that indeed they were slaves to idols. While it could thus be said to the Gentiles that the righteousness they thought belonged to their idol-worshipping parents was non-existent, it could not be said to the Jews that the righteousness of their father Abraham was false. (3) Accordingly it is said to the latter: *Bear fruit, therefore, worthy of repentance and do not say to yourselves, 'We have Abraham for our father'; for God can produce children for Abraham out of these very stones* (Matt. 3: 8–9 // Luke 3: 8). (4) But to the former it is said: *You remember, therefore, that at one time you were Gentiles in the flesh, called 'the uncircumcision' by those called 'the circumcision' (which is done in the flesh by hand). You were then without Christ, alienated from the community of Israel, strangers to the covenants, having no hope of the promise, and without God in this world* (Eph. 2: 11–12). (5) To sum up: in the first case unbelievers are shown to have been broken off from their own olive tree; in the second case believers are shown to have been grafted into it from a wild olive tree.[108] (6) The pride of the former was therefore to be ground down by transgression of the law, as he said to the Romans after he had piled up their sins by quoting the words of Scripture: *Now you know that whatever the law has said is addressed to those under the law, so that every mouth may be silenced and the whole world may be held accountable to God* (Rom. 3: 19)—the Jews for their transgression of the law and the Gentiles for their impiety without the law. (7) Accordingly he says again: *For God has imprisoned all in unbelief, that he may have mercy upon all* (Rom. 11: 32). (8) This is what he is

---

[108] Cf. Rom. 11: 17–24.

promissa dei? absit. Si enim data esset lex, quae posset uiuificare, omnino ex lege esset iustitia. Sed conclusit scriptura omnia sub peccato, ut promissio ex fide Iesu Christi daretur credentibus. (9) Non ergo lex data est, ut peccatum auferret sed ut sub peccato omnia concluderet. Lex enim ostendebat esse peccatum, quod illi per consuetudinem caecati possent putare iustitiam, ut hoc modo humiliati cognoscerent non in sua manu esse salutem suam, sed in manu mediatoris. (10) Maxime quippe humilitas reuocat, unde nos deiecit superbia. Et ipsa humilitas est accommodata percipiendae gratiae Christi, qui singulare humilitatis exemplum est.

26. Nec quisquam hic tam imperite dixerit: Cur ergo non profuit Iudaeis, quod per angelos legem ministrantes in manu mediatoris dispositi sunt? Profuit enim, quantum dici non potest. (2) Quae enim gentium ecclesiae uenditarum rerum suarum pretia ad pedes apostolorum posuerunt, quod tot milia hominum tam repente fecerunt? (3) Nec turbae infidelium considerandae sunt, omnis enim area multis partibus ampliorem habet paleam quam frumentum. Vnde autem etiam illa eiusdem apostoli uerba ad Romanos nisi de sanctificatione Iudaeorum? (4) *Quid ergo? numquid reppulit deus plebem suam? absit. Nam et ego Israelita sum ex semine Abraham de tribu Beniamin. Non reppulit deus plebem suam, quam praesciuit.* (5) Cum autem laudaret prae ceteris ecclesiis gentium ecclesiam Thessalonicensium, similes eos factos ait ecclesiis Iudaeae, quia multa a contribulibus suis pro fide passi erant, quomodo et illi a Iudaeis. (6) Hinc est et illud, quod paulo ante commemoraui, quod ait ad Romanos: *Si enim spiritualibus eorum communicauerunt gentes, debent et in carnalibus ministrare eis.* (7) De ipsis ergo Iudaeis etiam consequenter dicit: *Prius autem quam ueniret fides, sub lege custodiebamur conclusi in eam fidem, quae postea reuelata est.* (8) Vt enim tam prope inuenirentur et tam de proximo ad deum uenditis suis rebus accederent, quod dominus eis praecepit, qui uellent esse perfecti, lege ipsa factum est, sub qua custodiebantur *conclusi in eam fidem*, id est in aduentum

---

[109] 'All' here renders the Latin neuter *omnia*, which reflects the Greek neuter τὰ πάντα of the original. On the use of the neuter rather than the masculine, cf. Lightfoot, *Galatians*, 148: 'The neuter is naturally used where the most comprehensive term is wanted.'

[110] Acts 4: 34–5. Referring to the same passage from Acts in *doctr. chr.* 3. 6. 10–11 (Green, text and trans., 142–5), Augustine says that the Gentile churches did not do this because they had not received the same training under the law that the Jewish churches had.

[111] Cf. Matt. 3: 12.

[112] 1 Thess. 2: 14.

[113] See *exp. Gal.* 14. 3.

[114] Cf. Eph. 2: 17.

saying now also, reopening the same issue: *Is the law then against the promises of God? Certainly not! For if a law had been given that could confer life, then righteousness would indeed be by the law. But the Scripture has imprisoned all*[109] *under sin, that what was promised by faith in Jesus Christ might be given to those who believe* (Gal. 3: 21–2). (9) The law was not given, therefore, to take away sin but to imprison all under sin. For the law showed that what the Jews, blinded by custom, could regard as righteousness was sin, so that having been humbled in this way they might recognize that their salvation does not rest in their own hands but *in the hand of a mediator*. (10) For more than anything else, it is humility that calls us back from the place to which pride cast us down. And this same humility is appropriate for receiving the grace of Christ, who is the supreme example of humility.

26. Nor would anyone be so ignorant as to say at this point: 'Why then did being placed in the hand of a mediator by angels who were administering the law not benefit the Jews?' For it did benefit them—who can say how much? (2) For which of the Gentile churches laid the proceeds from the sale of their possessions at the apostles' feet,[110] which so many thousands of people did so readily? (3) Nor are the multitudes of unbelievers to be considered, for the whole threshing floor has in many parts more chaff than wheat.[111] Moreover, why did the same apostle say the following to the Romans, unless he was referring to the sanctification of the Jews? (4) *What then? Has God rejected his people? Certainly not! For I myself am an Israelite, a descendant of Abraham, a member of the tribe of Benjamin. God has not rejected his people whom he foreknew* (Rom. 11: 1–2). (5) Moreover, when he praised the Thessalonian church above the other Gentile churches, he said that they had become like the Judaean churches because they had suffered much for the faith at the hands of their own fellow countrymen, just as the Judaean churches had suffered at the hands of the Jews.[112] (6) It is for this reason also that he makes the statement to the Romans that I mentioned a little earlier:[113] *For if the Gentiles have come to share in their spiritual blessings, they should also minister to them in material things* (Rom. 15: 27). (7) Concerning the Jews themselves, therefore, he also says accordingly: *Now before faith came, we were imprisoned and guarded under the law until faith, which was revealed afterwards* (Gal. 3: 23). (8) The fact that they were found so near and approached so very near to God[114] that they sold their possessions (as the Lord commanded those who would be perfect[115]) was accomplished by the very law under which they were *imprisoned and guarded until faith*, that is, until the coming of faith, *which was revealed afterwards*. For their

---

[115] Matt. 19: 21.

eius fidei, *quae postea reuelata est*, conclusio enim eorum erat timor unius dei. (9) Et quod praeuaricatores ipsius legis inuenti sunt, non ad perniciem sed ad utilitatem ualuit eis, qui crediderunt, cognitio enim maioris aegritudinis et desiderari medicum uehementius fecit et diligi ardentius. (10) Cui enim plurimum dimittitur, plurimum diligit.

27. *Itaque lex*, inquit, *paedagogus noster fuit in Christo*, hoc est quod ait: *Sub lege custodiebamur conclusi in ea*. (2) *Posteaquam uenit fides, iam non sumus sub paedagogo*. Eos ergo nunc reprehendit, qui faciunt irritam gratiam Christi, quasi enim nondum uenerit, qui uocaret in libertatem, sic adhuc uolunt esse sub paedagogo. (3) Quod autem filios dei dicit esse omnes per fidem, quia induerunt Christum quicumque in Christo baptizati sunt, ad hoc ualet, ne gentes de se desperarent, quia non custodiebantur sub paedagogo, et ideo se filios non putarent, sed per fidem induendo Christum omnes fiunt filii non natura, sicut unicus filius, qui etiam sapientia dei est, neque praepotentia et singularitate susceptionis ad habendam naturaliter et agendam personam sapientiae sicut ipse mediator unum cum ipsa suscipiente sapientia sine interpositione alicuius mediatoris effectus, sed filii fiunt participatione sapientiae id praeparante atque praestante mediatoris fide. (4) Quam fidei gratiam nunc indumentum uocat, ut Christum induti sint, qui in eum crediderunt et ideo filii dei fratresque eius mediatoris effecti sunt.

28. In qua fide non est distantia Iudaei neque Graeci, non serui neque

[116] Latin: *conclusio*. Cf. *s*. 161. 4 (PL 38: 879. 59–880. 1), where *conclusio* is synonymous with *carcer*. Similarly Vg. Isa. 42: 7.　　　　[117] Cf. Luke 7: 47.

[118] *Disciplinarian* renders (though not without difficulty) the Latin *paedagogus*, which in turn transliterates the Greek παιδαγωγός dictated by Paul. In antiquity these terms referred to the familiar figure of the slave who took children to school and supervised their conduct in general. When discipline was called for, he did not spare the rod. Hence in Augustine the *paedagogus* of the law is often associated with fear (see e.g. *util. cred*. 3. 9 (CSEL 25. 1: 12. 27–13. 2)). For a passing reference to Augustine's own childhood *paedagogus* see *conf*. 1. 19. 30 (CCSL 27: 16. 8).

[119] Cf. 1 Cor. 1: 24. For Augustine's reflections on the Son as the Wisdom of God see esp. *trin*. 7. 2. 3–7. 3. 5 (CCSL 50: 249–54).

[120] sc. 'of human nature'. Other examples of 'assumption' (Latin: *susceptio*) used on its own as a brachylogy for the Incarnation include *f. et symb*. 4. 8 (CSEL 41: 12. 3–6), *trin*. 1. 13. 28 (CCSL 50: 69. 6–7), and *ep*. 187. 13. 40 (CSEL 57: 117. 16–18). And cf. the reference to the Son of God's 'assumption of the nature of a created being' (*susceptionem creaturae*) in 30. 3 below.

[121] 'Role' renders the Latin *persona*, whose original meaning—an actor's mask—may still be glimpsed in the background here. At this time the term *persona* had not attained the technical precision that it was to have in later Christological formulations such as the Tome of Leo (449). For an attempt to define *persona* as it is used in Augustine's earlier writings see Van Bavel, *Recherches*, 7.

prison[116] was fear of the one God. (9) And the fact that they were found to be transgressors of this law served not to harm but to benefit those who believed, for recognition of the greater illness made them both desire the physician more urgently and love him more ardently. (10) For the one to whom much is forgiven, loves much.[117]

27. *And so the law,* he says, *was our disciplinarian*[118] *until Christ* (Gal. 3: 24), in other words, *we were imprisoned and guarded under the law until faith* (Gal. 3: 23). (2) *After the coming of faith, we are no longer under a disciplinarian* (Gal. 3: 25). Thus he is now rebuking those who are nullifying the grace of Christ, for they still want to be *under a disciplinarian,* as though the one who called them to freedom had not yet come. (3) Now his statement, *You are all sons of God through faith, since whoever has been baptized into Christ has put on Christ* (Gal. 3: 26–7) is intended to prevent the Gentiles from despairing of themselves and thinking they were not sons because they had not been guarded under a disciplinarian. On the contrary, it is by *putting on Christ* through faith that all are made sons—not by nature (as is the case with the only Son, who is indeed the Wisdom of God[119]), and not by superior power or a unique assumption,[120] accomplished in order to have and perform the role[121] of Wisdom naturally. (Such was the case with the Mediator himself, who has been made one with the very Wisdom that assumed him without the interposition of any mediator). Rather, we are made sons by participation in Wisdom, with faith in the Mediator preparing and paving the way for it. (4) He refers to this grace of faith as something 'put on', since those who have believed in Christ have *put on Christ* and have thus been made sons of God and brothers of the Mediator.

28. In this faith there is no distinction between Jew and Greek, slave and free, male and female; since all have been baptized, all are one in Christ Jesus.[122] (2) And if this is accomplished by faith, by which we walk righteously in this life, how much more perfectly and completely will it be accomplished by sight itself,[123] when we see *face to face* (1 Cor. 13: 12)? (3) For now, although we have *the first-fruits of the spirit* (Rom. 8: 23),[124]

---

[122] A conflation of Gal. 3: 27–8 and Rom. 10: 12.

[123] Cf. 2 Cor. 5: 7.

[124] By *the first-fruits of the spirit* (*primitiae spiritus*) Augustine almost certainly understands the human spirit as the first offering in a process whose goal is the offering of one's entire being—body, soul, and spirit—to God. Thus elsewhere Augustine speaks of 'the first-fruits of my spirit' (*primitiae spiritus mei*) (*conf.* 12. 16. 23 (CCSL 27: 227. 16)). Cf. *exp. prop. Rm.* 45 (53). 16–20 (CSEL 84: 28. 3–20), *f. et symb.* 10. 23 (CSEL 41: 28. 9–19), and esp. *diu. qu.* 67. 6 (CCSL 44A: 170–2). By contrast, Ambrose, Ambrosiaster, and Pelagius interpret the phrase to mean the first gift of the Holy Spirit. For further discussion with references to secondary literature see O'Donnell, *Augustine: Confessions,* iii. 131–3. On the tripartite division of human nature into body, soul, and spirit see the passage from *f. et symb.* just cited.

liberi, non masculi et feminae, in quantum enim omnes fideles sunt, omnes unum sunt in Christo Iesu. (2) Et si hoc facit fides, per quam in hac uita iuste ambulatur, quanto perfectius atque cumulatius id species ipsa factura est, cum uidebimus facie ad faciem? (3) Nam nunc quamuis primitias habentes spiritus, qui uita est, propter iustitiam fidei, tamen quia adhuc mortuum est corpus propter peccatum, differentia ista uel gentium uel conditionis uel sexus iam quidem ablata est ab unitate fidei, sed manet in conuersatione mortali eiusque ordinem in huius uitae itinere seruandum esse et apostoli praecipiunt, qui etiam regulas saluberrimas tradunt, quemadmodum secum uiuant pro differentia gentis Iudaei et Graeci et pro differentia conditionis domini et serui et pro differentia sexus uiri et uxores, uel si qua talia cetera occurrunt, et ipse prior dominus, qui ait: *Reddite Caesari, quae Caesaris sunt, et deo, quae dei sunt.* (4) Alia sunt enim, quae seruamus in unitate fidei sine ulla distantia et alia in ordine uitae huius tamquam in uia, ne nomen dei et doctrina blasphemetur. (5) Et hoc non solum propter iram ut effugiamus offensionem hominum, sed etiam propter conscientiam, ut non simulate quasi ad oculos hominum ista faciamus, sed pura dilectionis conscientia propter deum, *qui omnes homines uult saluos fieri et in agnitionem ueritatis uenire.* (6) *Omnes ergo*, inquit, *uos unum estis in Christo Iesu*, et addidit: *Si autem*, ut hic subdistinguatur et subaudiatur, *uos unum estis in Christo Iesu* ac deinde inferatur: *ergo Abrahae semen estis*, ut iste sit sensus: Omnes ergo uos unum estis in Christo Iesu, si autem uos unum estis in Christo Iesu, uos ergo Abrahae semen estis. (7) Superius enim dixerat: *Non dicit: et seminibus tamquam in multis sed tamquam in uno et semini tuo, quod est Christus.* (8) Hic ergo ostendit unum semen Christum, non tantum ipsum mediatorem intelligendum esse uerum etiam ecclesiam, cuius ille corporis caput est, ut omnes in Christo unum sint et capiant secundum promissionem hereditatem per fidem, in quam conclusus erat, id est in cuius aduentum tamquam sub paedagogo custodiebatur populus usque ad aetatis opportunitatem, qua in libertatem uocandi erant, qui in eodem populo secundum propositum uocati sunt, id est qui in illa area frumentum inuenti sunt.

---

[125] '*spirit* . . . sin': cf. Rom. 8: 10.
[126] 'the most characteristic image of the spiritual life in [Augustine's] middle age' (Brown, *Augustine*, 152). On the profound change it represented in Augustine's understanding of Paul see ibid. 151–2.

which is life, on account of the righteousness of faith, yet because the body is still dead on account of sin,[125] that difference, whether of peoples or of legal status or of sex, while indeed already removed in the unity of the faith, remains in this mortal life. That this order is to be observed on this life's journey[126] is the teaching of the apostles, who hand down very salutary rules as to how Christians should live together with regard to differences of people (Jews and Greeks), status (masters and slaves), sex (husbands and wives), and the like; and it is also the teaching of the Lord himself, who said earlier: *Give to Caesar the things that are Caesar's, and to God the things that are God's* (Matt. 22: 21 // Mark 12: 17 // Luke 20: 25). (4) For there are some things which we observe in the unity of the faith without any distinction, and other things which we observe in the order of this life as on a journey, *lest the name and teaching of God be blasphemed* (1 Tim. 6: 1). (5)[127] And this is *not only because of anger*, so that we may avoid offending human beings, *but also because of conscience* (Rom. 13: 5), so that we do not observe those things hypocritically, as though only for mortal eyes, but with a clear conscience of love on account of God,[128] *who desires all to be saved and to come to the knowledge of the truth* (1 Tim. 2: 4).

(6) *So you are all one in Christ Jesus* (Gal. 3: 28), he said, and added: *But if* (and here we should pause and supply the words 'you are one in Christ Jesus',[129] so that what follows may be inferred) *then you are Abraham's seed* (Gal. 3: 29). This then is the meaning: 'So you are all one in Christ Jesus. But if you are one in Christ Jesus, then you are Abraham's seed.' (7) For earlier he had said: *It does not say 'and to seeds', referring to many, but 'and to your seed', referring to one, namely Christ* (Gal. 3: 16). (8) So here he shows that the one seed, Christ, signifies not only the Mediator himself but also the Church, of which he is the head of the body.[130] So all are one in Christ and receive the inheritance through faith, according to the promise. Until faith they were imprisoned as if under a disciplinarian. In other words, until faith came the people were guarded until that opportuneness of age when those who were called according to God's purpose,[131] that is, who were found to be wheat on that threshing floor,[132] were to be called to freedom.

---

[127] In this section Augustine has in mind Paul's teaching in Rom 13: 1–7 on the duties of Christians towards civil authorities. He treats the same teaching more fully in *exp. prop. Rm.* 64 (72)–66 (74) (CSEL 84: 44–7).

[128] Cf. Eph. 6: 5–7; Col. 3: 22–3; 1 Tim. 1: 5.

[129] Evidently the words *you are Christ's* (*uos Christi*) were missing after *But if* (*si autem*) in Augustine's text. Cf. Souter's reconstruction in *Earliest Latin Commentaries*, 171.

[130] Cf. Col. 1: 18.

[131] Cf. Rom. 8: 28.

[132] Cf. Matt. 3: 12.

29. Ad hoc enim adiungit: *Dico autem: quanto tempore heres paruulus est, nihil differt a seruo, cum sit dominus omnium, sed sub procuratoribus et actoribus est usque ad praefinitum tempus a patre: sic et nos, cum essemus paruuli, sub elementis huius mundi eramus seruientes.* (2) Quaeri autem potest, quomodo secundum hanc similitudinem sub elementis huius mundi fuerint Iudaei, cum illis per legem, quam acceperunt, unus deus, qui fecit caelum et terram, colendus commendaretur. (3) Sed potest esse alius exitus capituli huius, ut, cum superius legem paedagogum fecerit, sub quo erat ille populus Iudaeorum, nunc procuratores et actores dicat elementa mundi, sub quibus seruiebant gentes, ut filius ille paruulus, id est populus propter unam fidem ad unum semen Abrahae pertinens, quoniam et de Iudaeis et de gentibus congregatus est, partim fuerit sub paedagogo legis tempore pueritiae suae, (4) id est ex ea parte, qua de Iudaeis congregatus est, partim sub elementis huius mundi, quibus tamquam procuratoribus et actoribus seruiebat ex ea parte, qua de gentibus congregatus est, ut quod miscet apostolus personam suam non dicens: cum essetis paruuli, sub elementis huius mundi eratis, sed dicens: *Cum essemus paruuli sub elementis huius mundi eramus seruientes,* non pertineat ad significationem Iudaeorum, ex quibus Paulus originem ducit, sed magis ad gentium, hoc dumtaxat loco, quoniam et eorum personae decenter se potest adnectere, quibus ad euangelizandum missus est.

30. Deinde iam dicit ueniente plenitudine temporis deum misisse filium suum ad liberandum paruulum heredem seruientem ex parte legi tamquam paedagogo, ex parte elementis huius mundi tamquam procuratoribus et actoribus. *Misit deus,* inquit, *filium suum factum ex muliere.* (2) Mulierem pro femina posuit more locutionis Hebraeorum. Non enim, quia de Eua dictum est: *formauit eam in mulierem,* iam passa erat concubitus uiri, quod

---

[133] The term 'elements' (*elementa*) is ambiguous. Thus it could refer to the physical elements (earth, air, fire, and water), to the bodies composed of them (especially the sun, the moon, and the stars), or to the demonic powers that controlled these bodies. Here Augustine seems to understand it mainly in terms of the last two (cf. 32. 14 below). By way of contrast, Jerome, after mentioning these three possibilities, chooses to interpret the 'elements' in yet another way, as God's elementary teachings contained in the law and the prophets (*Comm. on Galatians* 4: 3 (PL 26: 371A 6–372A 5)).

[134] Gal. 3: 24.

[135] As opposed to Gal. 2: 15, for example, where the *we* refers exclusively to Jews.

[136] Augustine means that in ordinary Latin usage *mulier* refers specifically to a woman who has had sexual intercourse, so that its occurrence in Gal. 4: 4 would imply that Mary was not a virgin. *Femina,* the more general term for woman, carries no such implication. On Mary's virginity see also the note attached to 8. 5 above. On whether Pelagius consulted Augustine on Gal. 4: 4 see Introduction, 2. E.

29. For this reason the Apostle adds: *What I mean is this: as long as the heir is a child he is no different from a slave, although he is the lord of all; but he is under guardians and trustees until the date set by his father. So we too, when we were children, were enslaved under the elements*[133] *of this world* (Gal. 4: 1–3). (2) Now one might ask: how, according to this analogy, were the Jews *under the elements of this world*, since they were directed by the law they had received to worship the one God who made heaven and earth? (3) But there may be another solution here: while earlier[134] he portrayed the law as a *disciplinarian* whom the Jewish people were under, now he speaks of *the elements of this world* as *guardians and trustees* under whom the Gentiles were virtual slaves. Thus during his childhood the son—that is, the people on account of the one faith belonging to the one seed of Abraham, since it is gathered from both the Jews and the Gentiles—was in part under the *disciplinarian* of the law (4) (namely, the part gathered from the Jews), and in part under *the elements of this world*, to which it was enslaved as if under *guardians and trustees* (namely, the part gathered from the Gentiles). Consequently the Apostle speaks of the combination in his own person, saying not 'When *you* were children, *you* were under the elements of this world', but *When* we *were children,* we *were enslaved under the elements of this world.* This is not to be taken as a reference to the Jews from whom Paul was descended, but rather to the Gentiles, at least here,[135] since it is fitting for him to identify himself with the people whom he was sent to evangelize.

30. Then he says that when the fullness of time had come, God sent his Son to liberate the child, the *heir* who was subject in part to the law as to a *disciplinarian*, in part to *the elements of this world* as to *guardians and trustees. God sent his Son,* he says, *made of a woman* (Gal. 4: 4). (2) He says *mulier* instead of *femina* for 'woman' in accordance with Hebrew usage. Thus when it is said of Eve, *He made [the rib] into a woman (mulier)* (Gen. 2: 22), this does not mean that she had already had intercourse with the man, since she is not recorded as having had intercourse with him until after their expulsion from Paradise.[136]

(3) Now the Apostle said *made*[137] on account of the Son of God's assumption of the nature of a created being,[138] because those who are born of

---

[137] On the equivalence of 'made' (*factus*) and 'born' (*natus*) see Augustine's comment on Rom. 1: 3 in *c. Faust.* 11: 4: 'Instead of "*made of the seed of David*" some Latin versions have "*born . . .*", which is not so literal a rendering of the Greek but gives the same meaning' (my trans., based on Stothert, 180, of CSEL 25. 1: 319. 25–320. 1).

[138] Here and in 30. 6, 10 below Augustine is opposing the Arian view that the Son is not of one being with the Father but belongs essentially to the created order. Augustine's anti-Arian thrust is even clearer in a parallel passage written shortly before this one in *f. et symb.* 4. 5–6 (CSEL 41: 8. 12–11. 2; and NB 8. 22–3: 'Likewise those are excluded who say that the Son is a creature, though not as the other creatures' (Burleigh, trans., 356)).

non scribitur passa, nisi cum dimissi essent de paradiso. (3) *Factum* autem dixit propter susceptionem creaturae, quia qui nascuntur ex feminis non tunc ex deo nascuntur, sed tamen deus illos facit, ut sic nasci possint ut omnem creaturam. (4) *Factum* autem *sub lege* dicit, quia et circumcisus est et hostia pro illo legitima oblata est. (5) Nec mirum, si et illa legis opera sustinuit, ex quibus liberaret, qui eis seruiliter tenebantur, qui etiam mortem sustinuit, ut ex ea liberaret eos, qui mortalitate tenebantur. (6) *Vt adoptionem*, inquit, *filiorum recipiamus.* Adoptionem propterea dicit ut distincte intelligamus unicum dei filium. Nos enim beneficio et dignatione misericordiae eius filii dei sumus, ille natura est filius, qui hoc est quod pater. (7) Nec dixit: accipiamus sed: *recipiamus*, ut significaret hoc nos amisisse in Adam, ex quo mortales sumus. (8) Hoc ergo quod ait: *ut eos, qui sub lege erant, redimeret*, et ad liberandum eum populum pertinet, qui paruulus sub paedagogo seruiebat, et refertur ad id, quod dixit: *factum sub lege*. (9) Illud autem quod ait: *ut adoptionem filiorum recipiamus*, refertur ad id quod dixit: *factum ex muliere*. (10) Hinc enim adoptionem recipimus, quod ille unicus non dedignatus est participationem naturae nostrae factus ex muliere, ut non solum unigenitus esset, ubi fratres non habet, sed etiam primogenitus in multis fratribus fieret. (11) Duo enim proposuit: *factum ex muliere, factum sub lege*, sed mutato ordine respondit.

31. Iam illum populum adiungens, qui paruulus sub procuratoribus et actoribus seruiebat, id est elementis huius mundi, ne putarent se non esse filios, quia non erant sub paedagogo, *quoniam autem filii estis,* inquit, *misit deus spiritum filii sui in corda nostra clamantem: abba, pater.* (2) Duo sunt uerba, quae posuit, ut posteriore interpretaretur primum, nam hoc est abba quod pater. Eleganter autem intelligitur non frustra duarum linguarum uerba posuisse idem significantia propter uniuersum populum, qui de Iudaeis et de gentibus in unitatem fidei uocatus est, ut hebraeum uerbum ad Iudaeos, graecum ad gentes, utriusque tamen uerbi eadem significatio ad eiusdem fidei spiritusque unitatem pertineat. (3) Nam et ad Romanos, ubi similis quaestio de pace in Christo Iudaeorum gentiumque tractatur, hoc dicit: *Non enim accepistis spiritum seruitutis iterum in timore, sed accepistis spiritum adoptionis filiorum, in quo clamamus: abba, pater.* (4) Recte autem de

[139] 'born of God': cf. John 1: 13.

[140] i.e. every creature is *made*.

[141] Cf. Luke 2: 21–4.

[142] Arianism claimed that the Son of God is not 'son' by nature, but only by the grace of adoption.

women are not at that time born of God,[139] but nevertheless it is God who makes them so that they can be born in this way, just as he makes every created being.[140] (4) He says *made under the law* both because Jesus was circumcised and because the sacrifice required by the law was offered for him.[141] (5) It is not surprising that he should have submitted to the works of the law from which he was to liberate those bound to them by a kind of slavery, since he is the one who also submitted to death to liberate those bound to it by their mortality. (6) *In order that we might receive adoption as sons* (Gal. 4: 5). He says *adoption* to distinguish our sonship from that of God's only Son. For we are sons of God by the kind regard of God's mercy, while he is the Son by nature, since he is what the Father is.[142] (7) Nor did he say 'that we might get' (as if for the first time), but *that we might receive* (in the sense of 'get back'), indicating that in Adam, because of whom we are mortal, we had also lost our status as sons. (8) Thus the clause *that he might redeem those under the law* pertains to the liberation of the people that was a child subject to a disciplinarian and refers to the phrase *made under the law*. (9) But the clause *that we might receive adoption as sons* refers to the earlier phrase *made of a woman*. (10) For we receive adoption because the only Son did not scorn participation in our nature—he was *made of a woman* so as to be not merely the only-begotten, without any brothers, but also the first-born among many brothers.[143] (11) In other words, the Apostle proposed two topics—*made of a woman, made under the law*—but dealt with them in reverse order.

31. Now he adds a comment for the people that was a child subject to *guardians and trustees* (*the elements of this world*), lest they think they are not sons because they were not *under a disciplinarian: And because you are sons,* he says, *God has sent the Spirit of his Son into our hearts, crying, 'Abba! Father!'* (Gal. 4: 6) (2) He used two words so that the first might be interpreted by the second, for 'abba' means 'father'. Now it should be noted that his use of equivalent words from two languages was not redundant but elegant: it was on account of the whole people, called from both Jews and Gentiles into the unity of faith. The Hebrew word was used for the Jews, the Greek for the Gentiles, yet in such a way that the fact that the two different words mean the same thing might point to the unity of the same faith and Spirit. (3) For he also says to the Romans when discussing a similar question regarding the peace of Jews and Gentiles in Christ: *For you did not receive the spirit of slavery so as to be again in fear, but the Spirit of adoption as sons, by which we cry, 'Abba! Father!'* (Rom. 8: 15). (4) It was

[143] Cf. Rom. 8: 29.

praesentia et de dono spiritus sancti probare uoluit gentibus, quod pertineant ad promissionem hereditatis. Non enim euangelizatum est gentibus nisi post ascensum domini et aduentum spiritus sancti. (5) Coeperant enim iam Iudaei credere, cum in terris adhuc filius dei mortalem hominem gereret sicut in euangelio scriptum est: ubi quamquam et Chananaeae mulieris fidem ipse laudauerit et illius centurionis, de quo ait non se inuenisse talem fidem in Israel, (6) tamen proprie tunc Iudaeis esse euangelizatum uerbis ipsius domini satis clarum est, cum et ipsius Chananaeae deprecatione dixit non se esse missum nisi ad oues, quae perierunt domus Israel, et discipulos cum mitteret ait: (7) *In uiam gentium ne abieritis et in ciuitates Samaritanorum ne introieritis, sed ite primum ad oues, quae perierunt domus Israel.* (8) Gentium autem aliud ouile appellauit, cum diceret: *Habeo alias oues quae non sunt de hoc ouili,* quas tamen se adducturum ait, ut esset unus grex et unus pastor, quando autem nisi post clarificationem suam? (9) Post resurrectionem autem etiam ad gentes discipulos misit, cum eos interim Hierosolimae manere iussisset, donec eis secundum promissionem suam spiritum sanctum mitteret. (10) Cum ergo dixisset apostolus: *Misit deus filium suum factum ex muliere factum sub lege, ut eos, qui sub lege erant, redimeret, ut adoptionem filiorum recipiamus,* restabat, ut etiam gentes, quae non erant sub lege, ad eandem tamen adoptionem filiorum pertinere ostenderet, quod de sancti spiritus dono, qui omnibus datus est, docet. (11) Vnde se etiam Petrus de baptizato incircumciso centurione Cornelio defendit apud Iudaeos, qui crediderant, dicens non se potuisse aquam negare illis, quos iam spiritum sanctum accepisse claruerat. (12) Nam ipso grauissimo documento etiam superius usus est Paulus, cum diceret: *Hoc solum uolo discere a uobis: ex operibus legis spiritum accepistis an ex auditu fidei?* et paulo post: *qui ergo tribuit uobis spiritum et uirtutes operatur in uobis, ex operibus legis an ex auditu fidei?* (13) Sic et hic *quoniam,* inquit, *filii dei estis, misit deus spiritum filii sui in corda nostra clamantem: abba, pater.*

32. Deinde manifestissime ostendit de his etiam se dicere, qui ex gentibus ad fidem uenerant, ad quos etiam epistulam scribit. (2) *Itaque iam,*

[144] Matt. 15: 28.
[145] Matt. 8: 10 // Luke 7: 9.
[146] Matt. 15: 24.
[147] i.e. in the same way as, before the resurrection, he had sent them to the Jews. See Matt. 28: 19; Luke 24: 47.
[148] Luke 24: 49; Acts 1: 4–5.

right for him to wish to use the presence and gift of the Holy Spirit to prove to the Gentiles that they belong to the promise of the inheritance, for the Gentiles were evangelized only after the ascension of the Lord and the coming of the Holy Spirit. (5) The Jews, on the other hand, had already begun to believe while the Son of God still bore mortal human nature on earth, as it is written in the Gospel. Even though he praised the faith of both the Canaanite woman[144] and the centurion (of whom he said he had not found such faith in Israel),[145] (6) nevertheless it is quite clear from the Lord's own words that it was specifically to the Jews that the gospel was being proclaimed at that time. For in response to the plea of the Canaanite woman he said he had been sent only to the lost sheep of the house of Israel,[146] and he told the disciples whom he was commissioning: (7) *Do not go in the direction of the Gentiles or enter the towns of the Samaritans; but go first to the lost sheep of the house of Israel* (Matt. 10: 5–6). (8) Moreover, he called the Gentiles another sheepfold when he said, *I have other sheep, that are not of this fold*—sheep, nevertheless, that he says he is going to bring in, that there might be *one flock and one shepherd* (John 10: 16). But when, unless after his glorification? (9) Now after the resurrection he sent the disciples to the Gentiles also,[147] though he had ordered them to remain for a time in Jerusalem until he sent the Holy Spirit to them according to his promise.[148] (10) So when the Apostle said, *God sent his Son, made of a woman, made under the law, in order to redeem those who were under the law, so that we might receive adoption as sons* (Gal. 4: 4–5), it remained for him to indicate that the Gentiles too, who were not under the law, were still part of the same adoption as sons. He teaches this on the basis of the gift of the Holy Spirit, who has been given to all. (11) For this reason also Peter, in the presence of the Jews who had come to believe, defended himself concerning the baptism of the uncircumcised centurion Cornelius, saying that he could not refuse the water of baptism to people who had clearly received the Holy Spirit already.[149] (12) Paul also used the same powerful proof earlier when he said: *There is just one thing that I would like to learn from you: Did you receive the Spirit by works of the law, or by hearing the faith?* (Gal. 3: 2). And a little later: *He therefore who gives the Spirit to you and works miracles among you, does he do it by works of the law, or by hearing the faith?* (Gal. 3: 5). (13) So here as well: *And because you are sons of God, God has sent the Spirit of his Son into our hearts, crying, 'Abba! Father!'*

32. Then he makes it very plain that he is speaking about believers of Gentile origin, to whom he is also writing this letter. (2) *So he is no longer a*

[149] Acts 10: 47.

Augustine's Commentary on Galatians

inquit, *non est seruus sed filius*, propter id, quod dixerat: *quamdiu heres paruulus est, nihil differt a seruo.* (3) *Si autem filius*, inquit, *et heres per deum*, id est per misericordiam dei non per promissiones patrum, de quibus carnaliter sicut Iudaei natus non est, sed tamen filius Abrahae secundum imitationem fidei, cuius fidei gratiam per misericordiam domini meruit. (4) *Sed tunc quidem*, inquit, *ignorantes deum, his qui naturaliter non sunt dii, seruistis.* (5) Nunc certe quia non Iudaeis scribit sed gentibus, nec ait: seruiuimus sed *seruistis*, satis probabile est etiam superius de gentibus dictum, quod sub elementis huius mundi erant seruientes tamquam sub procuratoribus et actoribus. (6) Nam ipsa elementa utique non sunt naturaliter dii *siue in caelo siue in terra, quemadmodum multi dii et domini multi, sed nobis unus deus pater, per quem omnia et nos in ipso, et unus dominus Iesus Christus, per quem omnia et nos per ipsum.* (7) Cum autem dicit: *his, qui naturaliter non sunt dii, seruistis,* satis demonstrat unum uerum deum natura esse deum, quo nomine trinitas fidelissimo et catholico gremio cordis accipitur. (8) Eos autem, qui natura non sunt dii, propterea superius procuratores actoresque appellat, quia nulla creatura est, siue quae in ueritate manet dans gloriam deo, siue quae in ueritate non stetit quaerens gloriam suam. Nulla inquam creatura est, quae non uelit, nolit, diuinae prouidentiae seruiat, sed uolens facit cum ea quod bonum est de illa uero, quae hoc non uult, fit, quod iustum est. (9) Nam si etiam ipsi praeuaricatores angeli cum principe suo diabolo non recte dicerentur procuratores uel actores diuinae prouidentiae, non dominus magistratum huius mundi diabolum diceret nec uteretur illo ad correptionem hominum ipsa potestas apostolica eodem Paulo alibi dicente: *quos tradidi satanae, ut discant non blasphemare*, et alio loco ad salutem. (10) Ait enim: *Ego quidem sicut absens corpore praesens autem spiritu iam iudicaui quasi praesens eum, qui sic operatus est, in nomine domini nostri Iesu Christi congregatis uobis et meo spiritu cum potentia domini nostri Iesu Christi tradere eiusmodi satanae in interitum carnis, ut spiritus saluus sit in die domini Iesu.* (11) Sed et magistratus

---

[150] At this time, Augustine held that God chooses certain people for salvation on the basis of his foreknowledge of their free decision of faith (cf. e.g. *exp. prop. Rm.* 52 (60) (CSEL 84: 33–5)). But he soon became dissatisfied with this position, viewing it as endangering the sovereignty of divine grace (cf. *retr.* 2. 1 (27). 3 (CCSL 57: 89. 16–90. 27)), and when he came to write *Simpl.* 1. 2 shortly afterwards, he argued that divine election is entirely unmerited and that faith itself is a gift of God. On the development of Augustine's thought during this period, see Burns, *Development*, esp. 17–51, and Fredriksen, 'Beyond the Body/Soul Dichotomy'.

[151] John 12: 31.

slave but a son (Gal. 4: 7), he says, referring to his earlier statement: *as long as the heir is a child, he is no different from a slave* (Gal. 4: 1). (3) *But if a son, then also an heir through God* (Gal. 4: 7), that is, through the mercy of God and not through the promises to the fathers, from whom he is not descended according to the flesh like the Jews. But he is still a son of Abraham because he imitates Abraham's faith, and he has merited the grace of this faith through the mercy of the Lord.[150] (4) *Formerly, when you did not know God, you were enslaved to beings that by nature are not gods* (Gal. 4: 8). (5) Since he is undoubtedly writing not to Jews but to Gentiles at this point and does not say 'we were enslaved' but *you were enslaved*, it is very probable that what was said above was also said of the Gentiles, because they had been enslaved under *the elements of this world* as under *guardians and trustees*. (6) For by nature those *elements* are certainly not gods, *whether in heaven or on earth, as there are many 'gods' and many 'lords', yet for us there is one God, the Father, through whom are all things and we in him, and one Lord, Jesus Christ, through whom are all things and we through him* (1 Cor. 8: 5–6). (7) Now when he says, *you were enslaved to beings that by nature are not gods*, he clearly shows that the one true God is God by nature. By this name the Trinity is understood in the depths of the most faithful Catholic heart. (8) Earlier, however, the *beings that by nature are not gods* are called *guardians and trustees* because there is no creature, whether remaining in the truth because it gives glory to God, or not standing in the truth because it seeks its own glory—there is, I say, no creature that does not, either willingly or unwillingly, serve divine providence: the willing creature together with providence accomplishes what is good; but through the creature that does not want what is good there comes about what is just. (9) For if it were not accurate to call even the fallen angels together with their prince, the Devil, *guardians or trustees* of divine providence, the Lord would not call the Devil the ruler of this world,[151] nor would apostolic authority itself use him for the sake of correction, as when Paul says elsewhere: *I have handed them over to Satan so that they may learn not to blaspheme* (1 Tim. 1: 20). And in another place he uses him for the sake of salvation (10) when he says: *For myself, though I am absent in body, I am present in spirit, and as if present, I have already pronounced judgement in the name of our Lord Jesus Christ on the man who has done this: when you are assembled and my spirit is present, with the power of our Lord Jesus Christ hand this man over to Satan for the destruction of the flesh, so that his spirit may be saved in the day of our Lord Jesus Christ* (1 Cor. 5: 3–5). (11) But the ruler[152] acts only to the extent permitted under

---

[152] Latin: *magistratus*, here a technical term denoting a civil officer charged with the administration of the law.

sub statuto imperatore non facit, nisi quantum illi permittitur, et procuratores actoresque huius mundi nihil faciunt, nisi quantum dominus sinit. (12) Non enim latet eum aliquid sicut hominem aut in aliquo est minus potens, ut procuratores atque actores, qui sunt in eius potestate aliquid ipso siue non permittente siue nesciente in subiectis sibi pro suo gradu rebus efficiant. (13) Non eis tamen rependitur, quod de ipsis iuste fit, sed quo animo ipsi faciunt, quia neque liberam uoluntatem rationali creaturae suae deus negauit et tamen potestatem, qua etiam iniustos iuste ordinat, sibi retinuit, quem locum latius et uberius in aliis libris saepe tractauimus. (14) Siue ergo solem et lunam et sidera et caelum et terram ceteraque huiusmodi gentes colebant siue daemonia, recte sub procuratoribus et actoribus fuisse intelliguntur.

33. Verumtamen ea, quae sequuntur, iam quasi explicatam quaestionem rursus implicant. Cum enim per totam epistulam non ab aliis ostendat sollicitatam fuisse Galatarum fidem, nisi ab eis, qui ex circumcisione erant et ad carnales obseruationes legis, tamquam in eis salus esset, adducere cupiebant, hoc tantum loco ad eos loqui uidetur, qui ad gentilium superstitiones redire temptarent. (2) Ait enim: *Nunc autem cognoscentes deum immo cogniti a deo quomodo reuertimini ad infirma et egena elementa, quibus rursus ut antea seruire uultis?* (3) In eo enim, quod dicit: *reuertimini*, quando non circumcisis sed gentibus loquitur, sicut in tota epistula apparet, non utique ad circumcisionem dicit eos reuerti, in qua numquam erant, sed *ad infirma*, inquit, *et egena elementa, quibus rursus ut antea seruire uultis.* (4) Quod de gentibus intelligere cogimur, his enim supra dixerat: *Sed tunc quidem ignorantes deum his, qui natura non sunt dii, seruistis*, ad quam seruitutem reuerti eos uelle significat cum ait: (5) *Quomodo reuertimini ad infirma et egena elementa, quibus rursus ut antea seruire uultis?*

34. Quod autem adiungit: *Dies obseruatis et menses et annos et tempora, timeo uos ne forte sine causa laborauerim in uobis*, magis hanc sententiam confirmare uideri potest. (2) Vulgatissimus enim est error iste gentilium, ut uel in agendis rebus uel in expectandis euentibus uitae ac negotiorum suorum ab astrologis et Chaldaeis notatos dies et menses et annos et tempora obseruent. (3) Fortasse tamen non opus est, ut hoc de gentilium errore intelligamus, ne intentionem causae, quam ab exordio susceptam ad

---

[153] Most notably in *lib. arb.*
[154] i.e. believers of Jewish origin.
[155] 'Chaldeans': experts in astrology, soothsaying, and other arts associated with Chaldea

the established Emperor, and the *guardians and trustees* of the world act only to the extent allowed by the Lord. (12) For nothing is hidden from him as if he were merely human, and he is all-powerful, so that the *guardians and trustees* in his power can do nothing to the things that are (relatively speaking) subject to them without his permitting or knowing it. (13) Yet they are repaid not because what is just comes about through them but because of the spirit in which they act. For God has not denied free will to his rational creature, and yet he has retained for himself the power by which he governs even the unjust justly. (We have discussed this topic more fully and more extensively in other books.[153]) (14) So whether it was the sun, the moon, and the stars, heaven and earth, and other things of this kind that the Gentiles worshipped, or whether it was demons, it is right to understand them as having been subject to *guardians and trustees*.

33. While at this point the matter has been virtually settled, it is complicated once again by what follows. Throughout the entire letter the Apostle shows that the faith of the Galatians has been undermined solely by people from the circumcision[154] who wanted to lure them to carnal observances of the law, as though salvation lay in them. In this one place, however, he appears to be speaking to those who were trying to return to the superstitions of the Gentiles. (2) For he says: *But now that you have come to know God, or rather to be known by God, how can you turn back to the weak and needy elements, to which you want to be enslaved again as you were before?* (Gal. 4: 9). (3) Since he is speaking not to the circumcised but to Gentiles (as is clear in the entire letter), when he says *turn back* he is certainly not saying that they are turning back to circumcision—they had never been circumcised—but *to the weak and needy elements, to which you want to be enslaved again as you were before*. (4) We are forced to understand this verse as referring to the Gentiles because he had said to them earlier: *Formerly, when you did not know God, you were enslaved to beings that by nature are not gods* (Gal. 4: 8). He indicates that they would like to turn back to this slavery when he says: (5) *how can you turn back to the weak and needy elements, to which you want to be enslaved again as you were before?* (Gal. 4: 9).

34. Moreover, what follows can be seen to confirm this view: *You are observing days and months and years and times. I fear I may have laboured over you in vain* (Gal. 4: 10–11). (2) For this error of the Gentiles is very widespread: in wondering about which course of action to take or how something in their lives or businesses will turn out, they observe days, months, years, and times as designated by astrologers and Chaldeans.[155] (3) But

(Babylonia). Biblical references to 'Chaldeans' in this sense may be found in Dan. 5: 1–11. Outside the Bible see e.g. Aulus Gellius, *Noctes Atticae* 14. 1. 1–36 (Marshall (ed.), ii. 425–32).

finem usque perducit, subito in aliud temere detorquere uelle uideamur, sed de his potius, de quibus cauendis eum agere per totam epistulam apparet. (4) Nam et Iudaei seruiliter obseruant dies et menses et annos et tempora in carnali obseruatione sabbati et neomeniae et mense nouorum et septimo quoque anno, quem uocant sabbatum sabbatorum. (5) Quae quoniam erant umbrae futurorum, iam adueniente Christo in superstitione remanserunt, cum tamquam salutaria obseruarentur a nescientibus, quo referenda sint, ut tamquam hoc dixerit apostolus gentibus: Quid prodest uos euasisse seruitutem, qua tenebamini, cum seruiretis elementis mundi, quando rursus ad talia reditis seducti ab eis, qui nondum agnoscentes libertatis suae tempus inter cetera opera legis, quae carnaliter sapiunt, etiam temporibus seruiunt, quibus et uos rursus ut antea seruire uultis et obseruare cum eis dies et menses et annos et tempora, quibus seruiebatis et antequam Christo crederetis? (6) Manifestum est enim uolumina temporum per elementa huius mundi, hoc est caelum et terram et motus atque ordinem siderum administrari. (7) Quae infirma appellat ex eo, quod infirma et instabili specie uariantur, egena uero ex eo, quod egent summa et stabili specie creatoris, ut quomodo sunt esse possint.

35. Ergo eligat lector utram uolet sententiam, dummodo intelligat ad tantum periculum animae pertinere superstitiosas temporum obseruationes, ut huic loco subiecerit apostolus: *Timeo uos, ne forte sine causa laborauerim in uobis.* (2) Quod cum tanta celebritate atque auctoritate per orbem terrarum in ecclesiis legatur, plena sunt conuenticula nostra hominibus, qui tempora rerum agendarum a mathematicis accipiunt. (3) Iam uero ne aliquid inchoetur aut aedificiorum aut huiusmodi quorumlibet operum, diebus quos aegyptiacos uocant saepe etiam nos monere non dubitant nescientes, ut dicitur, ubi ambulant. (4) Quod si locus iste de Iudaeorum superstitiosa obseruatione intelligendus est, quam spem

[156] For the 'exordium' see the note attached to *exp. Gal.* 1. 8.

[157] During this, the first month of the ancient Hebrew calendar (Hebrew: *Abib*), the Exodus from Egypt was commemorated (Exod. 13: 4, 23: 15, 34: 18; Deut. 16: 1). It corresponds roughly to March–April.

[158] The seventh year was a sabbatical year (cf. Lev. 25: 4). Augustine appears to be confusing this sabbatical year with the 'sabbath of sabbaths' spoken of in Lev. 16: 31 (LXX), which was in fact the annual Day of Atonement. There is no such confusion in his later (419) discussion of these passages in *qu.* 3. 55, 89 (CCSL 33: 213–14, 230–1).

[159] Cf. Col. 2: 16–17; Heb. 10: 1.

[160] The time of liberty was also announced in the Old Testament. Cf. Jesus' reading of Isaiah in Luke 4: 16–21.

[161] The term 'form' (*species*) derives from Plato. For discussion see O'Donnell, *Augustine: Confessions*, ii. 46–51 and the literature cited there.

perhaps there is no need for us to understand this passage in relation to the error of the Gentiles. We don't want to appear to be suddenly and rashly trying to twist Paul's cause for writing into something else—a cause which he takes up from the exordium[156] and carries through to the end. Instead, let us understand it in relation to the things he is clearly urging them to guard against throughout the entire letter. (4) For the Jews also slavishly observe days, months, years, and times in their carnal observance of the sabbath and new moon, the month of new corn,[157] and the seventh year (which they call the 'sabbath of sabbaths'[158]). (5) These things were shadows of things to come,[159] and so now that Christ has come they have remained as superstitions because people who don't know what they refer to have observed them as if they were salvific. So it is as if the Apostle had said to the Gentiles: 'What good is it for you to have escaped your former slavery to the elements of the world when you are turning to such things again? You have been led astray by those who do not yet recognize the time of their liberty along with the rest of the works of the law,[160] which they understand carnally. They, too, are enslaved to times, to which you also desire to be enslaved again and to join them in observing days, months, years, and times—things to which you were enslaved even before you came to believe in Christ.' (6) For it is evident that the cycle of the seasons is governed by the *elements of this world*, that is, heaven and earth, and the movement and configuration of the stars. (7) He calls them *weak* because they fluctuate owing to their weak and unstable form,[161] and *needy* because they need the highest and stable form of the Creator to be as they are.

35. So readers may choose whichever of the two opinions seems preferable, as long as they understand that the superstitious observance of times poses so great a danger to the soul that the Apostle has added at this point: *I fear I may have laboured over you in vain* (Gal. 4: 11). (2) Although this passage is read so publicly and authoritatively in churches throughout the world, our congregations are full of people who obtain the times for their activities from astrologers.[162] (3) Moreover, these people often do not hesitate to warn *us* as well against starting work on a building or other structure on one of the days they call 'Egyptian'.[163] As the saying goes, 'They don't know where they're going.' (4) But if this passage is to be understood as referring to the superstitious observance of the Jews, what hope is there

---

[162] The discussion from this point to the end of sect. 35 vividly illustrates Augustine's pastoral concerns. See further Introduction, 3. c.

[163] These days were thought to be unlucky. They are listed in Souter, *Earliest Latin Commentaries*, 196 n. 1, as: 2, 6, 16 Jan.; 7, 25 Feb.; 3, 24 Mar.; 21 May; 7, 20 June; 6, 18 July; 6, 21 Aug.; 2 Sept.; 20 Oct.; 2, 24 Nov.; 4, 14 Dec. *Thesaurus Linguae Latinae*, i. 963 also gives a much shorter list: 3, 21 Apr.; 3 May; 19 Sept.; 3 Oct.

habent, cum christianos se dici uelint, ex ephemeridis uitam naufragam
gubernantes, quando de diuinis libris, quos deus adhuc carnali populo
dedit, si more Iudaeorum tempora obseruarent, diceret eis apostolus:
Timeo uos, ne forte sine causa laborauerim in uobis. (5) Et tamen si
deprehendatur quisquam uel catechumenus Iudaico ritu sabbatum
obseruans tumultuatur ecclesia. (6) Nunc autem innumerabiles de numero
fidelium cum magna confidentia in faciem nobis dicunt: die post Kalendas
non proficiscor. (7) Et uix lente ista prohibemus arridentes, ne irascantur,
et timentes, ne quasi nouum aliquid mirentur. (8) Vae peccatis hominum,
quae sola inusitata exhorrescimus, usitata uero, pro quibus abluendis filii
dei sanguis effusus est, quamlibet magna sint et omnino claudi contra se
faciant regnum dei saepe uidendo omnia tolerare, saepe tolerando nonnulla
etiam facere cogimur! atque utinam, o domine, non omnia, quae non
potuerimus prohibere, faciamus!

36. Sed iam uideamus, quae sequuntur. Sane praeterieramus, quod
dictum est: *nunc autem cognoscentes deum immo cogniti a deo*. (2) Videtur
enim certe hoc loco etiam apostolica locutio congruere uelle infirmitati
hominum, ne tantummodo in ueteris testamenti libris usque ad terrenas
hominum cogitationes modus diuini eloquii descendisse uideatur. (3) Nam
quoniam correxit, quod dixerat: *cognoscentes deum*, nihil nos mouere debet.
Manifestum est enim, quamdiu per fidem ambulamus, non per speciem,
nondum nos cognouisse deum sed ea fide purgari, ut oportuno tempore
cognoscere ualeamus. (4) Sed quod in ipsa correctione ait: *immo cogniti
a deo*, si proprie accipitur, putabitur deus quasi ex tempore aliquid
cognoscere, quod ante non nouerat. (5) Translate ergo dictum est, ut oculos
dei accipiamus ipsam dilectionem eius, quam commendauit mittendo pro
impiis occidendum unicum filium, sic enim de his qui diliguntur, dicere
solemus, quod ante oculos habeantur. (6) Hoc est ergo: *cognoscentes deum
immo cogniti a deo*, quod et Iohannes dixit: *Non quod nos dilexerimus deum,
sed quoniam ipse dilexit nos*.

[164] i.e. those who have been baptized (Latin: *fidelium*).
[165] Literally, 'on the day after the Calends' (*die post Kalendas*).
[166] More than a quarter of a century later Augustine quoted *exp. Gal.* 35. 8 in full in *ench.*
21. 80 (CCSL 46: 94. 78–83) and then added: 'Some day I shall know whether immoderate
grief did not get the best of me and make me speak rashly' (Arand, trans., 80).
[167] Isa. 1: 4.
[168] Cf. Luke 13: 22–30.
[169] 'Correction' (*correctio*) is here a technical term in ancient rhetoric for a figure of speech
in which what has been said is retracted and replaced by what seems more appropriate. See
Rhetorica ad Herennium 4. 36.

for them if, while wanting to be called Christians, they steer lives of ship-wreck by means of calendars? For if they were to follow the Jewish custom and observe times taken from the divine books that God gave to a people still carnal, the Apostle would say to them: *I fear I may have laboured over you in vain.* (5) And yet if anyone, even a catechumen, is caught observing the sabbath according to the Jewish practice, the church is in an uproar. (6) But now countless numbers of the faithful[164] boldly tell us to our face: 'I never begin a journey on the second day of the month.'[165] (7) Although it isn't easy we try to put a stop to such things calmly, with a smile, so that they don't become angry, but also with fear in case they react with astonishment at such outlandish advice (as they see it).(8)[166] Alas for the sins of humanity![167] We shudder at them only when they are unfamiliar. When they are familiar, though they may be very great and cause the kingdom of God to be shut tight[168] against those who commit them, and even though the Son of God shed his blood to wash them away, by seeing them repeatedly we are led to tolerate them, and by tolerating them repeatedly we are even led to commit some of them. O Lord, may we not commit all the things we have been unable to put a stop to!

36. However, let us now see what follows. Admittedly we passed over the words *But now that you have come to know God, or rather to be known by God* (Gal. 4: 9). (2) In case divine speech should appear to have descended to the earthly thoughts of human beings only in the books of the Old Testament, it certainly appears here that the Apostle wanted his manner of expression to be suited to human weakness also. (3) For the fact that he corrected what he had said, *you have come to know God*, should not disturb us in any way. For it is clear that as long as *we walk by faith and not by sight* (2 Cor. 5: 7) we have not yet come to know God. Yet this faith is purifying us so that at the right time we may be able to know him. (4) But if what he says by way of correction,[169] *or rather to be known by God*, were taken literally, it would seem as though God comes to know something at a certain time that he did not know before. (5) Hence it is said figuratively, just as we should under-stand that 'the eyes of God' are really his love, which he has commended by sending his only Son to be put to death for the unrighteous.[170] For we ordinarily say of those we love that they are held before our eyes.[171] (6) So what Paul says—*you have come to know God, or rather to be known by God*—is what John says also: *Not that we loved God but that he loved us* (1 John 4: 10).

---

[170] Cf. Rom. 5: 6–8.
[171] Cf. e.g. *en. Ps.* 100. 5 (CCSL 39: 1410. 1–8).

37. Dicit autem: *estote sicut et ego*, qui utique, cum Iudaeus natus sim, iam ista carnalia spirituali diiudicatione contemno. (2) *Quoniam et ego sicut uos*, id est homo sum. Deinde oportune ac decenter facit eos recolere caritatem suam, ne tamquam inimicum illum deputent. (3) Dicit enim: *Fratres, precor uos, nihil me laesistis*, tamquam si diceret: Ne ergo putetis, quod ego laedere uos cupiam. *Scitis quia per infirmitatem carnis iam pridem euangelizaui uobis*, id est cum persecutionem paterer. (4) *Et temptationem uestram in carne mea non spreuistis neque respuistis*. Temptati sunt enim, cum persecutionem pateretur apostolus, utrum timore desererent eum an caritate amplecterentur. (5) *Et neque spreuistis*, inquit, tamquam utilem istam temptationem, *neque respuistis*, ut non susciperetis communionem periculi mei. *Sed sicut angelum dei excepistis me sicut Christum Iesum.* (6) Deinde admirans opus eorum spirituale commendat, ut hoc intuentes in carnalem timorem non decidant. *Quae ergo fuit*, inquit, *beatitudo uestra? Testimonium enim uobis perhibeo, quoniam, si fieri posset, oculos uestros eruissetis et dedissetis mihi.* (7) *Ergo inimicus factus sum uobis uerum praedicans?* Respondetur utique: non. Sed quid uerum praedicans, nisi ut non circumcidantur? Et ideo uide, quid adiungit: *aemulantur uos non bene*, id est, inuident uobis, qui uos carnales de spiritualibus uolunt facere, hoc est: *aemulantur non bene*. (8) Sed *excludere*, inquit, *uos uolunt, ut illos aemulemini*, hoc est imitemini, quomodo, nisi ut seruitutis iugo attineamini, sicut ipsi attinentur? (9) *Bonum est autem*, ait, *aemulari in bono semper*. Vult enim, ut seipsum imitentur. Propter hoc addidit: *et non solum cum praesens sum apud uos*. Cum enim praesenti oculos suos dare uellent, utique ipsum conabantur imitari, quem ita diligebant.

38. Ad hoc dicit etiam: *filioli mei*, ut tamquam parentem utique imitentur. *Quos iterum*, inquit, *parturio, donec Christus formetur in uobis*. (2) Magis hoc ex persona matris ecclesiae locutus est, nam et alibi dicit: *Factus sum paruulus in medio uestrum, tamquam si nutrix foueat filios suos*. (3) Formatur autem Christus in credente per fidem in interiore homine

---

[172] Jerome also offers an interpretation of *weakness of the flesh* that links it to persecutions suffered by Paul, but he includes three other possible interpretations as well: the first is that *weakness of the flesh* refers to the weakness of the Galatians, which required Paul to preach the gospel in a weakened form as if to infants; the second is that the phrase refers to Paul's physical appearance, which was unimpressive and even contemptible; the third is that it refers to a physical illness that afflicted Paul, sometimes said to be frequent severe headaches (PL 26: 380A–381C). Most modern commentators consider that it must refer to some physical illness, although there is no consensus as to what that illness might have been.

[173] Cf. Gal. 5: 1.

37. He then says: *Be as I am* (Gal. 4: 12)—I who, although born a Jew, absolutely despise those carnal things now that I have spiritual discernment. (2) *For I also am as you are*: I am human. Then in a timely and graceful fashion he makes them recall their love lest they regard him as their enemy. (3) *Brethren, I beg you*, he says, *you have done me no wrong*, as if to say, 'So do not think that I want to do you any wrong.' *You know it was through weakness of the flesh that I proclaimed the gospel to you long ago* (Gal. 4: 13), in other words, 'when I was suffering persecution'.[172] (4) *And though the circumstances put you to the test, you did not scorn or reject me* (Gal. 4: 13–14). For when the Apostle was suffering persecution, they were tested whether they would forsake him out of fear or embrace him out of love. (5) *You neither scorned*, he says, as if to say the test was useful, *nor rejected*, so as not to accept the risks of sharing in my danger. *But you welcomed me as an angel of God, as Christ Jesus*. (6) Then, admiring their spiritual work, he recommends that they look upon it as a model and not lapse into carnal fear. He says: *What has become of the blessedness that was yours? For I bear you witness that, had it been possible, you would have torn out your very eyes and given them to me*. (7) *Have I now become your enemy by preaching the truth to you?* (Gal. 4: 15–16). Certainly not! But what truth was he preaching, except that they must not be circumcised? Look, then, at what he goes on to say: *They are jealous over you, but not in a good sense* (Gal. 4: 17). In other words, those who are jealous want to make you carnal after you have become spiritual. This is what is meant by *not in a good sense*. (8) *They want to exclude you*, he says, *so that you may become jealous of them*, in other words, imitate them. But how, unless you submit to a yoke of slavery[173] as they themselves have done? (9) *It is always a good thing*, he says, *to be jealous of something good* (Gal. 4: 18). For he wants them to imitate him, and so he has added: *and not only when I am present with you*. For when he was present with them and they were willing to give him their eyes, they were undoubtedly trying to imitate this man whom they so loved.

38. For this reason he also says: *My little children* (undoubtedly so they would imitate him as they would a parent), *for whom I am again in labour pains until Christ is formed in you* (Gal. 4: 19). (2) This is spoken more in the person of Mother Church, for he also says elsewhere: *I became a little one among you, like a wet-nurse fondling her children* (1 Thess. 2: 7). (3) Now Christ is *formed* in the inner self of the believer through faith.[174] Such a person is called into the liberty of grace, is gentle and humble of heart,[175] does not boast about the merits of works (which are nothing) but by means

[174] Cf. Eph. 3: 16–17.   [175] Cf. Matt. 11: 29.

uocato in libertatem gratiae miti et humili corde, non se iactante de operum meritis, quae nulla sunt, sed ab ipsa gratia meritum aliquod inchoante, quem possit dicere minimum suum, id est seipsum, ille qui ait: *Cum enim fecistis uni ex minimis meis, mihi fecistis.* (4) Formatur enim Christus in eo, qui formam accipit Christi, formam autem accipit Christi, qui adhaeret Christo dilectione spirituali. (5) Ex hoc enim fit, ut huius imitatione sit, quod ille, quantum gradu suo sinitur: *Qui enim dicit se in Christo manere*, ait Iohannes, *debet, quomodo ille ambulauit, et ipse ambulare.* (6) Sed cum homines a matribus concipiantur, ut formentur, iam formati autem parturiantur, ut nascantur, potest mouere, quod dictum est: *quos iterum parturio, donec Christus formetur in uobis.* (7) Nisi parturitionem hanc pro curarum angoribus positam intelligamur, quibus eos parturiuit, ut nascerentur in Christo, et iterum parturit propter pericula seductionis, quibus eos conturbari uidet. (8) Sollicitudo autem talium de illis curarum, qua se quodammodo parturire dicit, tamdiu esse poterit, donec peruéniant in mensuram aetatis plenitudinis Christi, ut iam non moueantur omni uento doctrinae. (9) Non ergo propter initium fidei, quo iam nati erant, sed propter robur et perfectionem dictum est: *Quos iterum parturio, donec Christus formetur in uobis.* (10) Hanc parturitionem aliis uerbis etiam alibi commendat, ubi dicit: *Incursus in me cotidianus, sollicitudo omnium ecclesiarum. Quis infirmatur et ego non infirmor? Quis scandalizatur, et ego non uror?*

39. Quod uero subiecit: *Vellem autem nunc adesse apud uos et mutare uocem meam, quia confundor in uobis*, quid aliud intelligatur, nisi quia filios suos esse dixerat parcens eis fortasse per litteras, ne seueriore obiurgatione commoti facile in eius odium traducerentur a deceptoribus illis, quibus absens non posset resistere. (2) *Vellem* ergo, inquit, *nunc adesse apud uos et mutare uocem meam*, id est negare uos filios, *quia confundor in uobis.* Malos enim filios ne de his erubescant, etiam parentes abdicare solent.

40. Deinde subiungit: *Dicite mihi sub lege uolentes esse legem non audistis?* Et de duobus quidem filiis Abrahae quod dicit, facile intelligitur, nam ipse interpretatur hanc allegoriam. (2) Hos enim duos filios habebat Abraham,

---

[176] The stage (*gradus*) to which Augustine is referring is 'this third stage, under grace' (*exp. Gal.* 61. 8, and see esp. 46. 4–9).

[177] i.e. the Apostle's words may be troubling because they seem to disrupt the natural sequence that the reader would expect: conception, formation of the foetus, and birth of the child.

[178] Cf. Eph. 4: 13–14.

of that very grace begins to have some merit. Such a person can be called his 'least'—that is, himself—by the one who says, *For when you did it for one of the least of my brethren, you did it for me* (Matt. 25: 40). (4) For Christ is *formed* in the one who receives Christ's form, but the one who receives Christ's form is the one who stays close to Christ through spiritual love. (5) And thus it comes about that by imitation he becomes what Christ is, to the extent that it is granted to him in his present stage:[176] *For one who claims to abide in Christ*, says John, *should walk as he walked* (1 John 2: 6). (6) But since people must be conceived by their mothers in order to be formed and then, having been formed, must be involved in the process of labour in order to be born, the Apostle's words, *for whom I am again in labour pains until Christ is formed in you*, may be troubling,[177] (7) unless we understand *labour pains* to refer to the distressing cares which caused him to be 'in labour pains' in order that the Galatians might be born in Christ. And he is 'in labour pains' again on account of the dangers of seduction that he sees agitating them. (8) Now the anxiety arising from such cares for them, on account of which he says he is in a sense *in labour pains*, will last until they attain to the measure of Christ's maturity in all its fullness and so are no longer moved by every wind of doctrine.[178] (9) Thus when he says, *for whom I am again in labour pains until Christ is formed in you*, he is not referring to the beginnings of faith, because they had been born already, but rather to its strengthening and perfection. (10) He also speaks of these labour pains elsewhere in different words: *There is the daily onslaught upon me of my anxiety for all the churches. Who is weak, and I am not weak? Who is scandalized, and I am not burning?* (2 Cor. 11: 28–9).

39. He immediately adds, however: *But I wish I were present with you now and could change my tone, for I am ashamed of you* (Gal. 4: 20). How is this to be understood, unless perhaps when he called them *sons* he was sparing them in a letter out of concern that if they were upset by a more severe rebuke, they might be induced to hate him by those deceivers whom he cannot withstand because he is absent. (2) *But I wish*, he says, *I were present with you now and could change my tone*—that is, could deny that you are *sons*—*for I am ashamed of you.* For even now parents are accustomed to disown evil sons in order to avoid being put to shame by them.

40. Next he adds: *Tell me, you who desire to be under the law, have you not listened to the law?* (Gal. 4: 21). And what the law says about Abraham's two sons, at any rate, is easily understood, for he interprets this allegory himself.[179] (2) For when the two testaments were signified, Abraham had

---

[179] According to Augustine, the Manichees twisted this allegory to suit their own purposes. Cf. *util. cred.* 3. 8 (CSEL 25. 1: 11. 23–12. 8) and *c. Faust.* 22. 30–2 (CSEL 25. 1: 624–7).

cum duo testamenta significata sunt. Post mortem autem Sarae, quos de alia uxore genuit, non pertinent ad hanc significationem. (3) Et ideo multi legentes apostolum, librum autem Geneseos ignorantes, putant solos duos filios habuisse Abraham. (4) Hos ergo solos commemorat apostolus, quia solos adhuc habebat, cum haec significarentur, quae consequenter exponit, quod ille de ancilla, quae Agar uocabatur, uetus testamentum significat, id est populum ueteris testamenti propter iugum seruile carnalium obseruationum et promissa terrena, quibus irretiti et quae tantummodo sperantes de deo non admittuntur ad hereditatem spiritualem caelestis patrimonii. (5) Non autem sufficit, quod de libera uxore natus est Isaac ad significandum populum heredem noui testamenti, sed plus hic ualet, quod secundum promissionem natus est. (6) Ille autem et de ancilla secundum carnem et de libera nasci potuit secundum carnem, sicut de Cethura, quam postea duxit Abraham, non secundum promissionem sed secundum carnem suscepit filios. (7) Isaac enim mirabiliter natus est per repromissionem, cum ambo parentes senuissent. Quod si data per apostolum fiducia, qua duos illos allegorice accipiendos apertissime ostendit, uoluerit aliquis etiam Cethurae filios in aliqua rerum figura futurarum inspicere—non enim frustra de talibus personis administratione spiritus sancti haec gesta conscripta sunt—inueniet fortasse haereses et scismata significari. (8) Qui filii de libera quidem sicut isti de ecclesia, sed tamen secundum carnem nati sunt non spiritualiter per repromissionem. (9) Quod si ita est, nec ipsi ad hereditatem inueniuntur pertinere, id est ad caelestem Hierusalem, quam sterilem uocat scriptura, quia diu filios in terra non genuit. (10) Quae deserta etiam dicta est caelestem iustitiam deserentibus hominibus terrena sectantibus tamquam uirum habente illa terrena Hierusalem, quia legem acceperat. (11) Et ideo caelestem Hierusalem Sara significat, quae diu deserta est a concubitu uiri propter

---

[180] Gen. 25: 1–2.

[181] This is not to deny their historical existence. Cf. *mend.* 15. 26 (CSEL 41: 446. 21–447. 4), *ciu.* 13. 21 (CCSL 48: 404. 8–11), and *Gn. litt.* 8. 4 (CSEL 28. 1: 235. 19–20).

[182] Augustine's introduction of Keturah's sons into his discussion of Gal. 4: 21–31 is without parallel in any of the other Latin commentaries on Galatians and reflects his personal concern with the threat posed to the Catholic Church in Africa by the Manichees and the Donatists. See Mara, 'Storia ed esegesi', 96–7, and 'Note', 541–5.

[183] Cf. Gal. 4: 27 (Isa. 54: 1).

[184] Readers experiencing a pang of doubt at this point may be helped by recalling Augustine's later remark that 'the good and correct use of lust is not lust' (*libido non est bonus et rectus usus libidinis*) (*retr.* 2. 22 (48). 2 (CCSL 57: 108. 27–8)). I owe this suggestion to R. Teske, trans., WSA, pt. 1, vol. 18, p. 446 n. 119 (on *c. adu. leg.* 2. 9. 32).

these two sons. (Those he fathered by another wife after Sarah's death are irrelevant to what is being signified here.) (3) And so many who read the Apostle but are ignorant of the Book of Genesis think that Abraham had only two sons. (4) The reason the Apostle mentions only these two is that when these things were signified he had only these two. He goes on to explain that the son of the slave woman Hagar signifies the Old Testament, that is, the people of the Old Testament, on account of the slavish yoke of carnal observances and the earthly promises. Ensnared by these and hoping for nothing more from God, they are not admitted to the spiritual inheritance of the heavenly patrimony. (5) Now in order for Isaac to signify the people of the New Testament as the heir it is not enough that he was born of a free woman—what is more relevant here is the fact that he was born according to the promise. (6) For Isaac could have been born according to the flesh of either a slave woman or a free woman, just as Abraham had sons not according to the promise but according to the flesh by Keturah, whom he married afterwards.[180] (7) For Isaac was born miraculously through the promise, since both his parents had grown old. Now if someone has gained confidence from the Apostle's very clear demonstration that these two sons are to be understood allegorically[181] and also wishes to see in Keturah's sons some figure of things to come—for these events involving such persons were not recorded under the guidance of the Holy Spirit for nothing—he will perhaps find that they signify heresies and schisms.[182] (8) They are indeed sons of a free woman, as are the sons of the Church, yet they were born according to the flesh, not spiritually through the promise. (9) But if so, they are also found not to belong to the inheritance, that is, to the heavenly Jerusalem, which Scripture calls *barren*[183] because for a long time she did not bear sons on earth. (10) She is also called *deserted* because men desert heavenly righteousness when they follow earthly things, just as that earthly Jerusalem *has the husband* because it had received the law. (11) And therefore Sarah—who was long *deserted* with respect to intercourse with her husband because he knew she was barren—signifies the heavenly Jerusalem. (12) For men such as Abraham do not use women in order to satisfy their lust but in order to have descendants.[184] (13) Now in his old age Abraham had also approached[185] sterility, so that the divine promise might bestow great merit upon those believing in the face of utter despair.[186]

---

[185] 'Approached' but not 'reached'. Cf. *ciu.* 16. 28 (CCSL 48: 533. 19–40).

[186] Human merit is God's gift. Note, however, that Augustine is here referring to those who already believe. At this stage in the development of his thought on grace Augustine was not clear that the very act of faith is essentially God's gift. He later acknowledged that he had been in error. Cf. *praed. sanct.* 3. 7 (PL 44: 964–5). (See also 32. 3 above and the note on 'faith' there.)

cognitam sterilitatem. (12) Non enim tales homines, qualis erat Abraham, ad explendam libidinem utebantur feminis, sed ad successionem prolis. (13) Accesserat autem sterilitati etiam senectus, ut ex omni desperatione diuina promissio magnum meritum credentibus daret. (14) Certus ergo de promissione dei officio gignendi accessit ad aetatem iam grauem, quam in annis uigentioribus corporali copulatione deseruerat. (15) Non enim ob aliud apostolus adiuncta earum mulierum figura interpretatur, quod per prophetam dictum est: *Quoniam multi filii desertae magis quam eius, quae habet uirum*, cum et marito prior Sara sit mortua neque inter eos ullum extitisset diuortium. (16) Vnde ergo illa deserta aut illa habens uirum, nisi quod Abraham propagandae prolis operam ad Agar ancillae fecunditatem ab uxoris Sarae sterilitate transtulerat? (17) Ipsa tamen permittente et ultro offerente, ut maritus eius de ancilla susciperet filios. Antiqua enim iustitiae regula est, quam commendat ad Corinthios idem apostolus: *Mulier sui corporis potestatem non habet sed uir, similiter autem et uir sui corporis potestatem non habet sed mulier*. (18) Et huiusmodi enim debita sicut cetera in eorum, quibus debentur, potestate consistunt. Cui potestati qui fraudem non facit, ille castitatis coniugalis iura custodit. (19) Senectus autem parentum Isaac ad eam significationem ualet, quoniam noui testamenti populus, quamuis sit nouus, praedestinatio tamen eius apud deum et ipsa Hierusalem caelestis antiqua est. (20) Vnde et Iohannes ad Parthos dicit: *Scribo uobis, patres, quoniam cognouistis, quod erat ab initio*. (21) Carnales autem qui sunt in ecclesia, ex quibus haereses et scismata fiunt, ex euangelio quidem occasionem nascendi acceperunt, sed carnalis error, quo concepti sunt et quem secum trahunt, non refertur ad antiquitatem ueritatis et ideo de matre adolescentula et de patre sene sine repromissione nati sunt. (22) Quia et dominus non nisi ob antiquitatem ueritatis in Apocalypsi albo capite apparuit. (23) Nati sunt ergo tales ex occasione antiquae ueritatis in nouicio temporalique mendacio. (24) Dicit ergo nos apostolus secundum Isaac promissionis filios esse et sic persecutionem passum Isaac ab Ismaele, quemadmodum hi, qui spiritualiter uiuere coeperant, a carnalibus Iudaeis persecutionem patiebantur, frustra tamen, cum secundum scripturam

---

[187] Cf. Rom. 4: 19.   [188] Cf. Gen. 16: 1–3.   [189] Cf. 1 Cor. 7: 3.

[190] Bligh, *Galatians*, 394 n. 42, criticizes Augustine's logic here: 'The fallacy in this way of thinking is the supposition that the wife may alienate her right over the husband's body. If Sarah cannot transfer her marital right to [Hagar], Abraham has no duty or right to approach her.' Augustine was driven to this extremity in large part by his need to answer Manichean charges that the patriarchs and matriarchs of the Old Testament were immoral.

(14) Convinced therefore of God's promise in the duty of procreation, Abraham, at an age now oppressive, approached the one whom in his more vigorous years he had *deserted* with respect to sexual intercourse. (15) For there is no other reason why the Apostle introduces the figure of these women to interpret the prophecy: *For the deserted one has more children than she who has the husband* (Gal. 4: 27 (Isa. 54: 1)), since earlier with regard to her husband Sarah was also 'dead'[187] and they had not been divorced. (16) How did it come about, then, that the one woman is *deserted* and the other *has the husband*, except that Abraham had transferred the task of producing a descendant from his wife Sarah, who was barren, to the slave woman Hagar, who was fertile? (17) Yet Sarah herself voluntarily granted permission and gave the slave woman to her husband so that he might have sons by her.[188] For the rule of righteousness that the same Apostle commends to the Corinthians is ancient: *For the wife does not have authority over her own body, but the husband does; likewise the husband does not have authority over his own body, but the wife does* (1 Cor. 7: 4). (18) For even debts[189] of this kind, like others, fall under the authority of those to whom they are owed. The person who does not cheat against this authority is the one who keeps the laws of marital fidelity.[190]

(19) Now the old age of Isaac's parents signifies that although the people of the New Testament are a new people, their predestination with God and the heavenly Jerusalem itself are ancient. (20) It is for this reason also that John says to the Parthians:[191] *I am writing to you, fathers, because you have known that which was from the beginning* (1 John 2: 13). (21) Now the carnal ones in the Church—the source of heresies and schisms—did indeed receive from the gospel the opportunity to be born, but the carnal error in which they were conceived and which they carry with them does not go back to the ancient truth, and therefore they were born of a very young mother and an aged father without the promise. (22) For it was only on account of the antiquity of the truth that the Lord appeared in the Apocalypse with white hair.[192] (23) Such ones were born, therefore, from the opportunity of the ancient truth in a new and temporal lie. (24) Thus the Apostle says that *we, like Isaac, are sons of the promise* (Gal. 4: 28), and just as Isaac had been persecuted by Ishmael, so those who had begun to live spiritually were being persecuted by carnal Jews. Yet this persecution is in vain, since according to the Scripture the slave woman is cast out

---

[191] This is the earliest extant witness to the tradition that 1 John was addressed to the Parthians. Although the tradition is also reflected in many MSS of the Vulgate, it is no longer credited by scholars. On its possible origins see R. E. Brown, *The Epistles of John*, 772–4.

[192] Cf. Rev. 1: 14.

eiciatur ancilla et filius eius nec heres esse possit cum filio liberae. (25) *Nos autem,* inquit, *fratres, non sumus ancillae filii sed liberae.* Ea enim libertas nunc maxime opponenda est seruitutis iugo, quo in operibus legis tenebantur, qui ad circumcisionem istos trahebant.

41. Cum autem dicit: *state ergo,* significat eos nondum cecidisse, accommodatius enim diceret: surgite. (2) Sed quod addidit: *et ne iterum seruitutis iugo attineamini,* quandoquidem hic nullum aliud iugum potest intelligi, quo eos attineri nolit nisi circumcisionis taliumque obseruationum Iudaicarum, ita enim et sequitur: *ecce ego Paulus dico uobis, quia, si circumcidamini, Christus uobis nihil proderit,* quomodo accepturi sumus, quod ait: *ne iterum seruitutis iugo attineamini,* cum ad eos scribat, qui Iudaei numquam fuerant? (3) Nam hoc agit utique, ne circumcidantur. Sed nimirum hic declaratur et confirmatur illa sententia, de qua superius disputauimus. (4) Quid enim aliud hoc loco gentibus dicat, non inuenio nisi ut prosit illis, quod a seruitute superstitionis suae per fidem Christi liberati sunt, ne iterum serui esse uelint sub iugo obseruationum carnalium quamuis sub lege dei tamen carnalem populum seruiliter alligantium. (5) Christum autem nihil eis profuturum esse dicit, si circumcidantur, sed illo modo, quo eos isti uolebant circumcidi, id est ut in carnis circumcisione ponerent spem salutis. (6) Non enim Timotheo non profuit Christus, quia Paulus ipse illum iam christianum iuuenem circumcidit, fecit autem hoc propter scandalum suorum nihil simulans omnino, sed ex illa indifferentia, qua dicit: *Circumcisio nihil est et praeputium nihil est.* (7) Nihil enim obest ista circumcisio ei, qui salutem in illa esse non credit. Secundum hanc sententiam etiam illud addidit: *testificor autem omni homini circumcidenti se,* id est, tamquam salutarem istam circumcisionem appetenti, *quia debitor est uniuersae legis faciendae.* (8) Quod ideo ait, ut uel terrore tam innumerabilium obseruationum, quae in legis operibus scriptae sunt, ne omnes implere cogerentur, quod nec ipsi Iudaei nec parentes eorum implere potuerunt, sicut Petrus in Actibus apostolorum dicit, abstinerent se ab his, quibus eos isti subiugare cupiebant.

42. *Euacuati,* inquit, *estis a Christo, qui in lege iustificamini.* (2) Haec est illa proscriptio, qua Christum proscriptum superius dixerat, ut cum isti

---

[193] Cf. Gal. 4: 29–30 (Gen. 21: 9–10).
[194] Cf. Acts 16: 3 and the note attached to *exp. Gal.* 11. 1.
[195] Acts 15: 10.
[196] According to Augustine, the Manichees used this verse as a central prooftext in their rejection of the law. Cf. *util. cred.* 3. 9 (CSEL 25. 1: 12. 9–13).

and her son cannot be an heir alongside the free woman's son.[193] (25) *But we, brethren*, he says, *are sons not of the slave woman, but of the free* (Gal. 4: 31). For freedom must now strongly oppose the yoke of slavery by which those luring the Galatians to circumcision were held fast in works of the law.

41. Now when he says, *Stand firm, therefore* (Gal. 5: 1), he indicates that they have not yet fallen, for in that case he would more appropriately have said, 'Arise.' (2) He goes on to say: *And do not submit again to a yoke of slavery*, where the yoke to which he does not want them to submit must be that of circumcision and Jewish observances of this kind, for there follows: *Listen! I, Paul, am telling you that if you let yourselves be circumcised, Christ will be of no benefit to you* (Gal. 5: 2). Now how are we to understand the words: *Do not submit again to a yoke of slavery*, since he is writing to those who had never been Jews? (3) For he explicitly urges them not to be circumcised. But here, no doubt, the view for which we argued earlier is expressed and confirmed. (4) For what else is he saying to the Gentiles in this passage if not that it is to their benefit, having been set free through faith in Christ from the slavery of their superstition, not to agree to be slaves again under a yoke of carnal observances? For although it is the law of God, its observances were meant to bind a carnal people like slaves. (5) He says that Christ will be of no benefit to them if they let themselves be circumcised, but he means if it is done as his opponents wanted it to be done—so that they placed their hope for salvation in circumcision of the flesh. (6) For it is not the case that Christ was of no benefit to Timothy, seeing that Paul himself circumcised Timothy when that young man was already a Christian. But he did so to avoid scandalizing his own people,[194] not acting hypocritically in any way but acting out of that indifference with which he says: *Circumcision is nothing, and uncircumcision is nothing* (1 Cor. 7: 19). (7) For circumcision is not at all harmful to the man who does not believe that salvation lies in it. In conformity with this view Paul has also added: *I testify to every man who lets himself be circumcised*—that is, who seeks circumcision as if it were salvific—*that he is under obligation to fulfil the entire law* (Gal. 5: 3). (8) He says this so that at least from the terror of such countless observances as are recorded among the works of the law, the Galatians might avoid being forced to fulfil them all and be kept away from the things his opponents wanted to use to subjugate them. For as Peter says in the Acts of the Apostles,[195] neither the Jews themselves nor their ancestors were able to fulfil them all.

42. *You who are justified by the law*, he says, *are removed from Christ* (Gal. 5: 4).[196] (2) This is the proscription he was referring to earlier when he said

euacuarentur a Christo, id est, Christus ab eis tamquam a possessione, quam tenebat, abscedit, opera legis in eam possessionem tamquam in uacuam inducantur. (3) Quod quia non Christo sed illis obest, addidit: *a gratia excidistis.* Cum enim hoc agat gratia Christi, ut illi, qui debitores erant operum legis, liberentur hoc debito, isti ingrati tantae gratiae debitores esse uolunt uniuersae legis faciendae. (4) Nondum autem erat factum, sed, quia uoluntas moueri coeperat, ita plerisque locis loquitur, quasi factum sit. *Nos enim*, inquit, *spiritu ex fide spem iustitiae expectamus.* (5) In quo demonstrat ea pertinere ad fidem Christi, quae spiritualiter expectantur, non quae carnaliter desiderantur, qualibus promissionibus seruitus illa tenebatur, sicut alio loco dicit: *Non respicientibus nobis, quae uidentur, sed quae non uidentur. Quae enim uidentur, temporalia sunt, quae autem non uidentur, aeterna sunt.* (6) Deinde subiunxit: *In Christo enim Iesu neque circumcisio quicquam ualet neque praeputium*, ut illam indifferentiam declararet nihilque perniciosum esse in hac circumcisione ostenderet nisi ex illa salutem sperare. (7) Nihil ergo ualere dicit in Christo circumcisionem aut praeputium *sed fidem quae per dilectionem operatur.* Et hic illud tetigit, quia sub lege seruitus per timorem operatur. *Currebatis bene*, inquit, *quis uos impediuit ueritati non oboedire?* (8) Hoc est, quod superius ait: *Quis uos fascinauit? Suasio uestra*, inquit, *non ex eo est, qui uocauit uos.* Haec enim suasio carnalis est, ille autem in libertatem uocauit. (9) Suasionem autem eorum dixit, quod eis suadebatur. Eos autem paucos, qui ad illos ueniebant, ut ista suaderent, quia in comparatione multitudinis credentium Galatarum exigui numero erant, fermentum appellat. (10) Recipient autem isti fermentum et tota massa, id est, tota eorum ecclesia in corruptione carnalis seruitutis quodammodo fermentabitur, si tales suasores tamquam iustos et fideles recipientes honorauerint. *Ego*, inquit, *confido in uobis in domino, quod nihil aliud sapietis.* (11) Hinc utique manifestum est nondum illos fuisse possessos a talibus. *Qui autem conturbat uos*, inquit, *portabit iudicium, quicumque ille fuerit.* (12) Haec est illa conturbatio contraria ordini, ut de spiritualibus carnales fiant. Et quoniam intelligendum est fuisse quosdam, qui cum uellent eis istam seruitutem persuadere et uiderent eos

---

[197] See *exp. Gal.* 18. On the precise meaning of 'proscribed' as Augustine understands it see the note attached to *exp. Gal.* 18. 2.

[198] 'As into unoccupied land' (*tamquam in uacuam*): i.e. the land is no longer occupied because its owner has been 'proscribed'. (*Vacuus* was a technical term in Roman law.)

[199] Or *Spirit*.

that Christ was *proscribed* (Gal. 3: 1).[197] Since the result of this proscription is that they were *removed from Christ*—that is, Christ withdraws from them as from the possession he was holding on to—works of the law are brought into the possession as into unoccupied land.[198] (3) And because this injures them rather than Christ he has added: *You have fallen away from grace.* For since the grace of Christ has as its consequence that those who were under obligation to fulfil the works of the law are freed from this obligation, those ungrateful for such grace want to be *under obligation to fulfil the entire law.* (4) This had not actually happened yet, but because their will had begun to be moved he speaks in many places as if it had happened. *For in the spirit,*[199] he says, *by faith, we wait for the hope of righteousness* (Gal. 5: 5). (5) Thus he shows that it is the things we wait for spiritually rather than those we long for carnally that belong to faith in Christ. It was for the sake of such promises that that slavery[200] was retained, as he says elsewhere: *because we look not to the things that are seen but to the things that are unseen; for what is seen is transient, but what is unseen is eternal* (2 Cor. 4: 18). (6) Next he has added: *For in Christ Jesus neither circumcision nor uncircumcision matters at all* (Gal. 5: 6), in order to declare that indifference and show that there is nothing harmful in circumcision except to hope for salvation from it. (7) So he says that in Christ neither circumcision nor uncircumcision matters in any way, *but the faith that works through love.* And he has mentioned this because slavery under the law works through fear.

You were running well, he says. *Who hindered you from obeying the truth?* (Gal. 5: 7). (8) In other words, as he said earlier: *Who has bewitched you?* (Gal. 3: 1). *Your persuasion,* he says, *is not from him who called you* (Gal. 5: 8). For this *persuasion* is carnal, whereas the one who called them, called them to freedom.[201] (9) Now by their *persuasion* the Apostle was referring to that which they were being persuaded of, while he calls the few who were coming to persuade them *leaven* (Gal. 5: 9) because they were small in number compared with the multitude of believing Galatians. (10) Now if the Galatians receive and honour such persuaders as though they were righteous and faithful, they will receive the *leaven,* and *the entire batch* (that is, their entire church) will be 'leavened' by the corruption[202] of carnal slavery. *I am confident about you in the Lord that you will not think otherwise* (Gal. 5: 10). (11) From this statement it is quite clear that such persuaders have not yet gained control over the Galatians. *But he who is troubling you,*

---

[200] Cf. Gal. 5: 1.   [201] Cf. Gal. 5: 13.

[202] In Augustine's Latin version the word in Gal. 5: 9 usually rendered in English as *leavens* (*corrumpit*) implies corruption.

Pauli apostoli auctoritate reuocari, dicerent etiam ipsum Paulum id sentire sed non eis facile aperire uoluisse sententiam suam, oportunissime subiecit: *Ego autem fratres, si circumcisionem adhuc praedico, quid adhuc persecutionem patior?* (13) Etiam ab ipsis enim patiebatur persecutionem qui talia persuadere moliebantur, cum iam euangelium suscepisse uiderentur. (14) Quos tangit alio loco ubi ait: *Periculis in falsis fratribus,* et hic in capite epistulae ubi dicit: *Propter subintroductos autem falsos fratres, qui subintroierunt proscultare libertatem nostram, quam habemus in Christo Iesu, ut nos in seruitutem redigerent.* (15) Ergo si circumcisionem praedicabat, desinerent eum persequi. Qui tamen ne timerentur ab eis, quibus christiana libertas annuntiabatur aut ne ab ipso apostolo timeri putarentur, propterea superius libera plenus fiducia nomen suum etiam professus est dicens: *Ecce ego Paulus dico uobis, quia si circumcidamini, Christus uobis nihil proderit,* tamquam si diceret: ecce me imitamini, ut non timeatis, aut in me causam refundite, si timetis. (16) Quod autem dicit: *Ergo euacuatum est scandalum crucis,* sententiam illam repetit: *Si ex lege iustitia ergo Christus gratis mortuus est.* (17) Sed hic quoniam scandalum nominat, in memoriam reuocat propterea maxime in Christo passos esse scandalum Iudaeos, quia istas carnales obseruationes quas pro ipsa salute se habere arbitrabantur, eum saepe animaduertebant praeterire atque contemnere. (18) Hoc ergo ita dixit, ac si diceret: Sine causa ergo Christum, cum ista contemneret, scandalizati Iudaei crucifixerunt, si adhuc eis, pro quibus crucifixus est, talia persuadentur. (19) Et adiecit elegantissima ambiguitate quasi sub specie maledictionis benedictionem dicens: *Vtinam et abscidantur, qui uos conturbant.* (20) Non tantum, inquit, circumcidantur, sed et *abscidantur.* Sic enim fient spadones propter regnum caelorum et carnalia seminare cessabunt.

43. *Vos enim,* inquit, *in libertatem uocati estis, fratres,* quia illa conturbatio a spiritualibus ad carnalia reuocans in seruitutem trahebat. (2) Sed iam hinc opera illa legis tractare incipit, de quibus eum supra dixeram in fine epistulae tractaturum, quae ad nouum quoque testamentum pertinere nemo ambigit, sed alio fine, quo liberos ea facere decet, id est caritatis aeterna sperantis hinc praemia et ex fide expectantis. (3) Non sicut Iudaei,

---

[203] Cf. *exp. Gal.* 20. 5.

[204] In *c. Faust.* 16. 22 (CSEL 25. 1: 465. 11–23) Augustine argues that Gal. 5: 12 cannot really be a curse because Rom. 12: 14 forbids cursing. On Augustine's interpretation of Gal. 5: 12 and similar problem passages see Introduction, 4. B, under 'The Inspiration of the Bible'.

he says, *will bear his judgement, whoever he is.* (12) This is the trouble where-by spiritual people become carnal, contrary to order.[203] We must realize that there were certain people who wanted to persuade the Galatians to accept slavery but saw them being called back by the authority of the apostle Paul, and so they said that Paul himself shared their view but was reluctant to acknowledge it openly to the Galatians. For this reason Paul strategically added: *As for me, brethren, if I am still preaching circumcision, why am I still being persecuted?* (Gal. 5: 11). (13) For he was still being persecuted by the very ones who were striving to persuade the Galatians, even though by that time the persuaders seemed to have taken up the gospel. (14) He mentions these people in another place when he speaks of *danger from false brethren* (2 Cor. 11: 26) and in the section of this letter where he says: *But on account of false brethren secretly brought in, who slipped in to examine our freedom which we have in Christ Jesus, to bring us back into slavery* (Gal. 2: 4). (15) If in fact he was preaching circumcision, they would have stopped persecuting him. Now the Apostle did not want anyone to whom Christian freedom was being proclaimed to fear these people or to think that he himself feared them and therefore earlier, filled with bold confidence, he even stated his own name openly, saying: *Listen! I, Paul, am telling you that if you let yourselves be circumcised, Christ will be of no benefit to you* (Gal. 5: 2), as if to say: 'Listen! Imitate me and do not fear, or, if you do fear, let the cause of it be me!' (16) Now his statement, *In that case the scandal of the cross is removed* (Gal. 5: 11), repeats what he said earlier: *If righteousness were through the law, then Christ died for nothing* (Gal. 2: 21). (17) But here, since he says *scandal*, we are particularly reminded of the Jews, who were scandalized by Christ because they often witnessed him neglecting or even rejecting those carnal observances that they imagined they were keeping for the sake of their salvation. (18) Paul expressed himself thus, as if to say: 'There was no reason for the Jews who were scandalized to crucify Christ for rejecting their carnal observances if the people for whom he was crucified can still be persuaded to keep them.' (19) And with very elegant ambiguity he inserted a blessing under the appearance of a curse[204] when he said, *I wish those who are troubling you would castrate themselves!* (Gal. 5: 12). (20) Not merely 'circumcise', he said, but *castrate* themselves. For thus they will become eunuchs for the sake of the kingdom of heaven[205] and cease to sow carnal seed.

43. *For you were called to freedom, brethren* (Gal. 5: 13). He says this because the trouble calling them back from spiritual to carnal things was luring them into slavery. (2) But now he begins to discuss the works of the

---

[205] Cf. Matt. 19: 12.

qui timore ista implere cogebantur non illo casto permanente in saeculum saeculi, sed quo timebant praesenti uitae suae, et ideo quaedam opera legis implebant, quae in sacramentis sunt, illa uero, quae ad bonos mores pertinent, omnino non poterant. Non enim implet ea nisi caritas. (4) Quia et hominem si propterea non occidit aliquis, ne et ipse occidatur, non implet praeceptum iustitiae, sed si ideo non occidit, quia iniustum est, etiam si id possit facere impune, non solum apud homines, sed etiam apud deum. (5) Sicut Dauid cum diuinitus accepisset in potestatem regem Saul, impune utique occideret nec hominibus in se uindicaturis, quia multum ab eis diligebatur idem Dauid, nec deo, qui hanc ipsam potestatem dedisse se dixerat, ut omnino ei faceret, quod uellet. (6) Pepercit ergo diligens proximum tamquam seipsum non solum persecutum sed etiam persecuturum, qui eum corrigi quam interfici malebat, homo in ueteri testamento sed non homo de ueteri testamento, quem fides futurae hereditatis Christi reuelata et reddita saluum faciebat et ad imitandum uocabat. (7) Ideo nunc dicit apostolus: *In libertatem uocati estis, fratres, tantum ne libertatem in occasionem carnis detis*, id est, ne audito nomine libertatis impune uobis peccandum esse arbitremini. (8) *Sed per caritatem*, inquit, *seruite inuicem*. Qui enim per caritatem seruit, libere seruit et sine miseria obtemperans deo cum amore faciendo, quod docetur, non cum timore, quod cogitur.

44. *Omnis enim lex*, inquit, *in uno sermone impleta est in eo, quod diliges proximum tuum tamquam teipsum*. (2) Omnem ergo legem nunc dicit ex his operibus, quae ad bonos mores pertinent, quia et illa, quae sunt in sacramentis, cum bene a liberis intelliguntur nec carnaliter obseruantur a seruis, ad illa duo praecepta referantur necesse est, dilectionis dei et proximi. (3) Recte itaque accipitur ad hoc pertinere, quod etiam dominus

[206] See *exp. Gal.* 19. 5.

[207] Cf. 1 Tim. 1: 5, a favourite verse of Augustine's.

[208] i.e. the fear of the Lord. Cf. Ps. 18: 10 (19: 9).

[209] Cf. 1 Sam. 24 and 26.

[210] Augustine gives further illustrations of David's exemplary faith in *c. Faust.* 22. 66–7 (CSEL 25. 1: 661–4).

[211] Generally in this translation (the sole exception is 51. 3) and most notably in sects. 44–5 and 57–8 the noun 'love' renders both *caritas* and *dilectio*. These two terms appeared as synonyms in Augustine's version of Rom. 13: 10 (cf. 45. 1 below). Elsewhere Augustine defines both *caritas* and *dilectio* as 'the love of the things that ought to be loved' (*amor . . . rerum amandarum*) (*diu. qu.* 35. 2 (CCSL 44A: 52. 61–2)) and later as 'the love of the good' (*amor boni*) (*trin.* 8. 10. 14 (CCSL 50: 290. 1–2)). See further the article on 'Love' by T. J. van Bavel in Fitzgerald, *Augustine*, 509–16.

law that I said he would discuss at the end of his letter.[206] Undoubtedly these works belong to the New Testament as well as to the Old, but in the New Testament they are directed towards a different end,[207] appropriate for people who are free. These are the works of the love that hopes for eternal rewards and waits in faith. (3) Such was not the case with the Jews, who were driven to fulfil them by fear—not the fear that *is pure and endures forever*,[208] but that which made them fear for their own present lives. It was for this reason that they fulfilled certain works of the law that are counted among the sacraments. They absolutely could not, however, fulfil the works having to do with good morals, for these can be fulfilled only by love. (4) Not to kill another human being in order not to be killed oneself, does not fulfil the command of righteousness; what does fulfil it is not to kill another human being because it is unrighteous, even if one could get away with it not only with other people but even with God. (5) Thus when David providentially received King Saul into his power he could no doubt have killed him with impunity. For the people would not have exacted vengeance upon him, since their love for him was great, nor would God have done so, since it was God who said he had given David this very power to do with Saul as he pleased.[209] (6) And so it was because he loved his neighbour as himself that David spared the man who not only had persecuted him but was going to persecute him again. He preferred to see Saul corrected rather than slain. For David was a man in the Old Testament but not of the Old Testament, saved by faith in the future inheritance of Christ—a faith revealed and given, and which called for imitation.[210] (7) And so now the Apostle says: *You were called to freedom, brethren; only do not use your freedom as an opportunity for the flesh*, that is, do not think you may sin with impunity because you heard the word *freedom*. (8) *But serve one another through love*, he says. For one who serves another through love does so freely and without misery, obeying God by acting with love, since it is taught, and not fear, since it is forced.

44.[211] *For the whole law*, he says, *has been fulfilled in one phrase: 'You shall love your neighbour as yourself'* (Gal. 5: 14). (2) He says *the whole law* now, after the works having to do with good morals, because the works that are counted among the sacraments, when correctly understood by free people and not carnally observed by slaves, necessarily refer to the two commands of love of God and neighbour also.[212] (3) And thus the Lord's saying, *I have come not to abolish the law but to fulfil it* (Matt. 5: 17), ought to be understood as pertaining to this as well, because he was going to take away carnal fear

---

[212] Matt. 22: 37–40. Cf. Mark 12: 28–31 // Luke 10: 25–8.

ait: *Non ueni legem soluere sed implere*, quia erat ablaturus timorem carnalem, spiritualem autem caritatem daturus, qua sola lex impleri potest. (4) Plenitudo enim legis caritas, et, quoniam fides impetrat spiritum sanctum, per quem caritas dei diffusa est in cordibus operantium iustitiam, nullo modo quisquam ante gratiam fidei de bonis operibus glorietur. (5) Quapropter istos iactantes se de operibus legis ita refellit apostolus, dum ostendit opera uetusta sacramentorum umbras futurorum fuisse, quas iam aduentu domini libero heredi necessarias non esse monstrauit, opera uero ad bonos mores pertinentia non impleri nisi dilectione, per quam fides operatur. (6) Vnde si opera legis quaedam post fidem superflua quaedam ante fidem nulla sunt, uiuat iustus ex fide, ut et onus graue seruitutis abiciat leui sarcina Christi uegetatus et iustitiae metas non transgrediatur leni iugo caritatis obtemperans.

45. Quaeri autem potest, cur apostolus et hic solam commemorauit proximi dilectionem, qua legem dixit impleri, et ad Romanos, cum in eadem quaestione uersaretur, *qui enim diligit alterum*, inquit, *legem impleuit, nam: Non adulterabis, non homicidium facies, non furaberis, non concupisces et si quod est aliud mandatum, in hoc sermone recapitulatur: Diliges proximum tuum tamquam teipsum, dilectio proximi malum non operatur. Plenitudo autem legis caritas.* (2) Cum ergo nonnisi in duobus praeceptis dilectionis dei et proximi perfecta sit caritas, cur apostolus et in hac et in illa epistula solam proximi dilectionem commemorat, nisi quia de dilectione dei possunt mentiri homines, quia rariores temptationes eam probant, in dilectione autem proximi facilius conuincuntur eam non habere, dum inique cum hominibus agunt? (3) Consequens est autem, ut, qui ex toto corde, ex tota anima, ex tota mente deum diligit, diligat et proximum tamquam seipsum, quia hoc iubet ille, quem ex toto corde, ex tota anima, ex tota mente diligit. (4) Item diligere proximum, id est omnem hominem tamquam seipsum, quis potest, nisi deum diligat, cuius praecepto et dono dilectionem proximi possit implere? (5) Cum ergo utrumque praeceptum ita sit, ut neutrum sine

---

[213] 'Obtains': i.e. through seeking and asking (as the verb *impetrare* implies), not through earning by 'works'. Cf. 24. 14. What Augustine says should probably be read in the light of Luke 11: 13, which is in fact referred to in an illuminating parallel passage in *en. Ps.* 118 serm. 22. 1 (CCSL 40: 1736. 13–22).

[214] Cf. Col. 2: 17; Heb. 10: 1.

[215] Cf. Gal. 5: 6.

[216] Cf. Gal. 3: 11 (Hab. 2: 4); Rom. 1: 17.

[217] Cf. Matt. 11: 30.

[218] Cf. Matt. 22: 37–9 // Mark 12: 28–31 // Luke 10: 25–8.

but give spiritual love, which alone can fulfil the law. (4) For *love is the fulfilment of the law* (Rom. 13: 10). And since faith obtains the Holy Spirit,[213] through whom *the love of God has been poured out in the hearts* (Rom. 5: 5) of those who work righteousness, no one should take any pride whatsoever in good works prior to the grace of faith. (5) In this way the Apostle has refuted those boasting about works of the law, while showing that the ancient sacramental works were shadows of things to come.[214] He has demonstrated that the latter are no longer necessary for the free heir now that the Lord has come, but the works having to do with good morals are fulfilled only by love, through which faith works.[215] (6) Accordingly if certain works of the law are superfluous after faith and certain others are nothing before faith, the righteous person should live by faith,[216] so that having been invigorated by the light burden of Christ[217] he may throw away the heavy burden of slavery, and by submitting to the easy yoke of love he may not transgress the bounds of righteousness.

45. But why, one might ask, has the Apostle mentioned only the love of neighbour here when speaking of the fulfilment of the law? Likewise when dealing with the same issue in the letter to the Romans he says: *For one who loves another has fulfilled the law. The commandments, 'You shall not commit adultery; You shall not commit murder; You shall not steal; You shall not covet'; and any other commandment, are summed up in this phrase: 'You shall love your neighbour as yourself.' Love does no wrong to a neighbour; therefore love is the fulfilment of the law* (Rom. 13: 8–10). (2) Since in fact love is only made perfect through the two commands of love of God and neighbour, why is it that in both letters the Apostle mentions only the love of neighbour, unless it is because people can lie about their love of God, since it is put to the test less often, but they are more easily found guilty of not loving their neighbour when they behave wickedly towards others? (3) Moreover, it follows that a person who loves God with all his heart, all his soul, and all his mind, also loves his neighbour as himself, because the one whom he loves with all his heart, all his soul, and all his mind told him to do so.[218] (4) Similarly, who can love his neighbour—that is, everyone—as himself, if he does not love God, by whose command and gift[219] he is able to fulfil the love of neighbour? (5) Since therefore neither command can be kept without the other, in a question of works of righteousness it is usually enough to mention just one of them, but it is more appropriate to mention the one on the basis of which a person is more easily found guilty. (6) For this reason

[219] God's 'command' reveals to us what ought to be done; God's 'gift' empowers us to do it. Cf. the celebrated phrase from the *Confessions*: 'Give what you command, and command what you will' (*Da quod iubes et iube quod uis*) (*conf.* 10. 29. 40 (CCSL 27: 176. 2, 9) *et al.*).

altero possit teneri, etiam unum horum commemorare plerumque sufficit, cum agitur de operibus iustitiae, sed oportunius illud, de quo quisque facilius conuincitur. (6) Vnde et Iohannes dicit: *Qui enim non diligit fratrem suum, quem uidet, deum, quem non uidet, quomodo potest diligere?* (7) Mentiebantur enim quidam dilectionem se dei habere et de odio fraterno eam non habere conuincebantur, de quo iudicare in cotidiana uita et moribus facile est. (8) *Si autem mordetis*, inquit, *et comeditis inuicem, uidete, ne ab inuicem consumamini,* hoc enim maxime uitio contentionis et inuidentiae perniciosae disputationes inter eos nutriebantur male de inuicem loquendo et quaerendo quisque gloriam suam uanamque uictoriam, quibus studiis consumitur societas populi dum in partes discinditur. (9) Quomodo autem ista uitare possunt, nisi spiritu ambulent et concupiscentias carnis non perficiant? Primum enim et magnum munus est spiritus humilitas et mansuetudo. (10) Vnde illud, quod iam commemoraui, dominus clamat: *Discite a me, quia mitis sum et humilis corde*, et illud prophetae: *Super quem requiescit spiritus meus nisi super humilem et quietum et trementem uerba mea?*

46. Quod autem ait: *Caro enim concupiscit aduersus spiritum, spiritus autem aduersus carnem, haec enim inuicem aduersantur, ut non ea, quae uultis, faciatis,* putant hic homines liberum uoluntatis arbitrium negare apostolum nos habere nec intelligunt hoc eis dictum, si gratiam fidei susceptam tenere nolunt, per quam solam possunt spiritu ambulare et concupiscentias carnis non perficere, si ergo nolunt eam tenere, non poterunt ea, quae uolunt, facere. (2) Volunt enim operari opera iustitiae, quae sunt in lege, sed uincuntur concupiscentia carnis, quam sequendo deserunt gratiam fidei. Vnde et ad Romanos dicit: *Prudentia carnis inimica in deum, legi enim dei non est subiecta neque enim potest.* (3) Cum enim caritas legem impleat, prudentia uero carnis commoda temporalia consectando spirituali caritati aduersetur,

---

[220] Or *spirit*.

[221] *exp. Gal.* 15. 12.

[222] Augustine's version differs from both the Vg. and the LXX.

[223] By *the spirit* Augustine here understands the human spirit rather than the Holy Spirit, as is shown by 47. 1 below ('those . . . whose *spirit*') and confirmed by *diu. qu.* 70 (CCSL 44A: 197. 12–17) and *cont.* 7. 18 (CSEL 41: 161. 17–19). Augustine typically identifies the *spirit* of Gal. 5: 17 with the *mind* (*mens*) of Rom. 7: 23–5 (cf. e.g. *an. et or.* 4. 22. 36 (CSEL 60: 414. 7–12)) and implicitly does so here (cf. 46. 7, 47. 1). Most modern interpreters of Gal. 5: 17, however, think that Paul is speaking of the Holy Spirit.

[224] Most notably the Manichees. Cf. *c. Fort.* 21 (CSEL 25. 1: 103. 13–17) and *cont.* 7. 18 (CSEL 41: 161. 6–17). On Augustine's use of the Pauline notion of 'lusts of the flesh' in anti-Manichean contexts, see Babcock, 'Spirituality of Desire'.

John also says: *He has seen his brother, and has no love for him; what love can he have for the God he has never seen?* (1 John 4: 20). (7) For certain people were lying when they said they had love for God, but they were found guilty of not having it by their hatred of fellow Christians, a hatred easily judged on the basis of daily life and morality. (8) *If, however, you bite and devour one another*, he says, *take care that you are not consumed by one another* (Gal. 5: 15), for above all it was this vice of rivalry and envy that was fuelling destructive disputes among them, when they spoke evilly of one another and each sought his own glory and empty victory. Such partisan feelings consume a people's fellowship by tearing it to pieces. (9) But how can they avoid such consequences unless they *walk in the Spirit*[220] *and do not fulfil the lusts of the flesh* (Gal. 5: 16)? For the first and great gift of the Spirit is humility and gentleness. (10) Hence the saying of the Lord that I quoted earlier:[221] *learn from me, for I am gentle and humble of heart* (Matt. 11: 29), and that of the prophet: *On whom does my Spirit rest? On one who is humble and quiet and trembles at my words* (Isa. 66: 2).[222]

46. *For the flesh lusts against the spirit*[223] *and the spirit against the flesh; for these are opposed to each other, so that you cannot do what you want* (Gal. 5: 17). People[224] think that the Apostle is here denying that we have free choice of the will. They do not understand that this is said to them if they refuse to hold on to the grace of faith they have received, which alone enables them to *walk in the Spirit and not fulfil the lusts of the flesh*. So if they refuse to hold on to it, then they will not be able to do what they want. (2) For they want to perform the works of righteousness in the law but are defeated by the lust of the flesh, and in following this lust they desert the grace of faith. For this reason also Paul says to the Romans: *The wisdom of the flesh is hostile to God, for it is not subject to God's law, nor can it be* (Rom. 8: 7). (3) For since love fulfils the law but *the wisdom of the flesh*, by seeking temporal comforts, is opposed to spiritual love, how can *the wisdom of the flesh* be *subject to God's law*, that is, how can it freely and obediently fulfil righteousness and not be opposed to it? For even when it tries to do so it is necessarily defeated because it finds that it can get more temporal comfort by means of injustice than by maintaining justice. (4) The first stage[225] of human life is prior to the law, when no wickedness or malice is prohibited

---

[225] In 46. 4–9 Augustine is referring to a schema derived from Paul according to which the life of the believer is divided into four stages, corresponding to the four stages of the history of salvation: 'prior to the law' (46.4); 'under the law' (46.4); 'under grace' (46.6); and 'in ... peace' (46. 9). This schema emerges prominently in Augustine's early interpretation of Paul. Cf. esp. *exp. prop. Rm*. 12 (13–18). 1–13 (CSEL 84: 6–9) and *diu. qu*. 66. 3–7 (CCSL 44A: 154–63). For this and other schemata used by Augustine and his predecessors see A. Luneau, *L'Histoire du salut*.

quomodo potest legi dei esse subiecta, id est libenter atque obsequenter implere iustitiam eique non aduersari, quando etiam dum conatur, uincatur necesse est, ubi inuenerit maius commodum temporale de iniquitate se posse assequi quam si custodiat aequitatem? (4) Sicut enim prima hominis uita est ante legem, cum nulla nequitia et malitia prohibetur neque ulla ex parte prauis cupiditatibus resistit, quia non est, qui prohibeat, sic secunda est sub lege ante gratiam, quando prohibetur quidem et conatur a peccato abstinere se sed uincitur, quia nondum iustitiam propter deum et propter ipsam iustitiam diligit, sed eam sibi uult ad conquirendum terrena seruire. (5) Itaque ubi uiderit ex alia parte ipsam, ex alia commodum temporale, trahitur pondere temporalis cupiditatis sicque relinquit iustitiam, quam propterea tenere conabatur, ut haberet illud, quod se nunc uidet amittere, si illam tenuerit. (6) Tertia est uita sub gratia, quando nihil temporalis commodi iustitiae praeponitur, quod nisi caritate spirituali, quam dominus exemplo suo docuit et gratia donauit, fieri non potest. In hac enim uita etiamsi existant desideria carnis de mortalitate corporis, tamen mentem ad consensionem peccati non subiugant. (7) Ita iam non regnat peccatum in nostro mortali corpore, quamuis non possit nisi inhabitare in eo, quamdiu mortale corpus est. Primo enim non regnat, cum mente seruimus legi dei quamuis carne legi peccati, id est poenali consuetudini, cum ex illa existunt desideria, quibus tamen non oboedimus. (8) Postea uero ex omni parte extinguitur. Quoniam si spiritus Iesu habitat in nobis, qui suscitauit Iesum Christum a mortuis, uiuificabit et mortalia corpora nostra propter spiritum, qui habitat in nobis. (9) Nunc ergo implendus est gradus sub gratia, ut faciamus quod uolumus spiritu, etiamsi carne non possumus, id est non oboediamus desideriis peccati ad praebenda illi membra nostra arma iniquitatis, etiamsi non ualemus efficere, ut eadem desideria non existant, ut quamuis nondum simus in pace illa aeterna ex omni hominis parte perfecta, iam tamen desinamus esse sub lege, ubi praeuaricationis rea mens tenetur, dum eam concupiscentia carnis in consensionem peccati captiuam ducit, simus autem sub gratia, ubi nulla est condemnatio in his, qui sunt in Christo Iesu, quia non certantem sed uictum poena consequitur.

47. Ordinatissime itaque subiungit: *Quod si spiritu ducimini, non adhuc*

---

[226] In other words, temporal longing is experienced as a kind of gravitational force. Cf. *conf.* 13. 9. 10 (CCSL 27: 246. 16): 'My weight is my love' (*Pondus meum amor meus*). On this important Augustinian trope see O'Donnell, *Augustine: Confessions*, iii. 356–9 and the references given there.

and a person does not resist corrupt longings in any respect because there is no one to prohibit them. The second stage is under the law prior to grace, when he is indeed prohibited and tries not to sin but is defeated because he does not yet love righteousness for the sake of God and for the sake of righteousness itself, but wants it to serve him in procuring earthly things. (5) And so when he sees righteousness on the one hand and temporal comfort on the other, he is drawn by the weight of temporal longing[226] and thus abandons righteousness, which he was trying to hold on to only in order to have the comfort he now sees that he will lose if he holds on to righteousness. (6) The third stage of life is under grace, when no temporal comfort is preferred to righteousness. This is possible only through spiritual love, which the Lord taught by his example and gave by his grace. For even if desires of the flesh exist in this stage of life on account of the body's mortality, still they do not force the mind to consent to sin. (7) Thus sin no longer *reigns in our mortal body* (cf. Rom. 6: 12), although as long as the body is mortal it is impossible for sin not to dwell in us. To begin with, sin does not reign when we *serve the law of God with the mind*, even though *with the flesh we serve the law of sin* (Rom. 7: 25), that is, penal habit,[227] when desires arise from it (which, however, we do not obey). (8) But afterwards sin is extinguished in every respect, for *if the Spirit of Jesus dwells in us, the one who raised Jesus Christ from the dead will also give life to our mortal bodies on account of the Spirit dwelling in us* (cf. Rom. 8: 11). (9) At present, therefore, the stage under grace must be fulfilled so that we do what we want in the spirit (even though we cannot in the flesh), that is, we do not obey the desires of sin so as to *offer our members to it as weapons of injustice* (Rom. 6: 13), even though we cannot destroy the desires themselves. Thus, although we are not yet in that eternal peace made perfect in every part of us, nevertheless we now cease to be *under the law*, where the mind is held guilty of transgression since the lust of the flesh leads it captive into consenting to sin. But we are *under grace*,[228] where *there is no condemnation for those who are in Christ Jesus* (Rom. 8: 1) because the penalty is visited not on the one engaged in battle but on the one defeated in battle.

47. And so he adds most appropriately, *But if you are led by the Spirit,*[229] *you are no longer under the law* (Gal. 5: 18), so we may understand that they are *under the law* whose *spirit so lusts against the flesh that they cannot do what*

---

[227] 'Penal habit' (*poenalis consuetudo*) may be defined in the language of *Simpl.* 1. 1. 10 (CCSL 44: 15. 171–8) as the 'addiction to pleasure' (*adsiduitas uoluptatis*) that comes about as 'the penalty . . . of repeated sinning' (*poena frequentati peccati*) (Burleigh, trans., 380). Cf. 48. 4 below and see further Prendiville, 'Habit in St. Augustine', esp. 74–83.

[228] *under the law . . . under grace*: cf. Rom. 6: 14.

[229] Or *spirit* (but cf. 54. 4 below, where the Holy Spirit is called the 'leader').

estis sub lege, ut intelligamus eos esse sub lege, quorum spiritus ita concupiscit aduersus carnem, ut non ea, quae uolunt, faciant, id est non se teneant inuictos in caritate iustitiae, sed a concupiscente aduersum se carne uincantur, non solum ea repugnante legi mentis eorum, sed etiam captiuante illos sub lege peccati, quae est in membris mortalibus. (2) Qui enim non ducuntur spiritu, sequitur, ut carne ducantur. Non autem pati aduersitatem carnis, sed duci a carne damnatio est. (3) Et ideo *quod si spiritu*, inquit, *ducimini, non adhuc estis sub lege*. (4) Nam et superius non ait: *spiritu ambulate*, et concupiscentias carnis non habueritis, sed: *ne perfeceritis*. Quippe non eas omnino habere non iam certamen sed certaminis praemium est, si obtinuerimus uictoriam perseuerando sub gratia. (5) Commutatio enim corporis in immortalem statum sola carnis concupiscentias non habebit.

48. Deinde incipit opera carnis enumerare, ut intelligant se, si ad operandum ista desideriis carnalibus consenserint, tunc duci carne non spiritu. (2) *Manifesta autem sunt*, inquit, *opera carnis, quae sunt fornicationes, immunditiae, idolorum seruitus, ueneficia, inimicitiae, contentiones, animositates, aemulationes, dissensiones, haereses, inuidiae, ebrietates, commessationes et his similia, quae praedico uobis, sicut praedixi, quoniam qui talia agunt regnum dei non possidebunt.* (3) Agunt autem haec, qui cupiditatibus carnalibus consentientes facienda esse decernunt, etiam si ad implendum facultas non datur, ceterum qui tanguntur huiusmodi motibus et immobiles in maiore caritate consistunt, non solum non eis exhibentes membra corporis ad male operandum, sed neque nutu consensionis ad exhibendum consentientes, non haec agunt et ideo regnum dei possidebunt. (4) Non enim iam regnat peccatum in eorum mortali corpore ad oboediendum desideriis eius, quamuis habitet in eodem mortali corpore peccatum nondum extincto impetu consuetudinis naturalis, quia mortaliter nati sumus, et propriae uitae nostrae, cum et nos ipsi peccando auximus, quod ab origine peccati humani damnationisque trahebamus.

---

[230] The material in 47. 1 up to this point is reviewed and corrected by Augustine in *retr.* 1. 24 (23). 2 (CCSL 57: 72. 38–73. 52): 'My statement . . . was made according to the sense in which I understood [Gal. 5: 17 as being] applicable to those who are "under the law" not yet "under grace." For, up to this time, I had not yet realized that these words are also applicable to those who are 'under grace' not 'under the law' because they, too, lust after the lusts of the flesh against which they lust in spirit; even though they do not yield to them, yet they would not wish to have them if possible. Accordingly, they do not do whatsoever they wish, because they wish to be rid of them and cannot. For they will not have these lusts when they no longer have corruptible flesh' (Bogan, trans., 103).

they want (cf. Gal. 5: 17). In other words, they do not keep themselves undefeated in the love of righteousness but are defeated by the flesh lusting against them,[230] since it not only *fights against the law of their mind* but also *leads them captive under the law of sin that is in their mortal members* (cf. Rom. 7: 23). (2) For it follows that those who are not *led by the Spirit* are led by the flesh. Now being opposed by the flesh is not the cause of a person's condemnation, but rather being led by the flesh. (3) And so *if you are led by the Spirit*, he says, *you are no longer under the law.* (4) For earlier as well he did not say, '*Walk in the Spirit* and you will not have lusts of the flesh', but '... *and do not fulfil the lusts of the flesh*' (Gal. 5: 16). Indeed, not having them at all is no longer the battle but the reward of battle if we are victorious by persevering *under grace.* (5) For only when the body is transformed into an immortal state will there be no lusts of the flesh.

48. Next he begins to list the works of the flesh so the Galatians may understand that if they consent to carnal desires to do these things then they are being led by the flesh, not by the Spirit. (2) *Now it is obvious*, he says, *what the works of the flesh are: fornication, impurity, idolatry, witchcraft, enmity, strife, outbursts of anger, jealousy, dissension, heresies, envy, drunkenness, revelry, and the like. I warn you, as I warned you before: those who do such things will not inherit the kingdom of God* (Gal. 5: 19–21).[231] (3) Now the ones who do these works are those who consent to carnal longings and resolve to act on them, even if the opportunity to satisfy them is unavailable. But those who are moved by such emotions and yet remain unmoved in a greater love, not only not presenting their bodily members to their emotions for working evil,[232] but not even giving so much as a nod of consent to this, do not do these works and will therefore *inherit the kingdom of God.* (4) For sin no longer *reigns in their mortal bodies such that they obey its desires* (cf. Rom. 6: 12), even though sin does dwell in these same mortal bodies inasmuch as the combined force of natural habit and our own lives is not yet extinct; for by nature we were born mortal[233] and by sinning we ourselves have increased what we derived from the origin of human sin and condemnation.[234] (5) It is one thing not to sin, another not to have sin. For the person in whom sin

---

[231] Augustine's list differs from that given in the Vg. For variant readings see Sabatier, *Bibliorum*, 3: 781.

[232] Cf. Rom. 6: 13, 19.

[233] Augustine is referring to fallen human nature as distinct from human nature as originally created: mortality is a consequence of the Fall. Cf. *lib. arb.* 3. 19. 54 (CCSL 29: 307. 34–9); *Simpl.* 1. 1. 11 (CCSL 44: 15. 192–16. 195); *Gn. litt.* 6. 22. 33 (BA 48: 496, 498). Mortality is intrinsically related to sin in that it gives rise to anxiety over bodily needs and thence to earthly desires. Cf. *exp. prop. Rm.* 38 (45–6). 7, 42 (50) (CSEL 84: 20, 23), *diu. qu.* 66. 6 (CCSL 44A: 161. 236–162. 242), and *exp. Gal.* 61. 6 below.

[234] On 'the origin of human sin and condemnation' cf. Rom. 5: 12–21.

(5) Aliud est enim non peccare, aliud non habere peccatum. Nam in quo peccatum non regnat, non peccat, id est qui non oboedit desideriis eius, in quo autem non existunt omnino ista desideria, non solum non peccat, sed etiam non habet peccatum. (6) Quod etiam si ex multis partibus in ista uita possit effici, ex omni tamen parte nonnisi in resurrectione carnis atque commutatione sperandum est. (7) Potest autem mouere, quod ait: *Quae praedico uobis, sicut praedixi, quoniam qui talia agunt regnum dei non possidebunt*, si quaeratur, ubi ista praedixerit, nam in hac epistula non inuenitur. (8) Ergo aut praesens cum esset, hoc praedixerat aut cognouerat peruenisse ad illos epistulam, quae missa est ad Corinthios. (9) Ibi enim sic ait: *Nolite errare, neque fornicatores neque idolis seruientes neque adulteri neque molles neque masculorum concubitores neque fures neque auari neque ebriosi neque maledici neque rapaces regnum dei possidebunt.*

49. Hic ergo cum enumerasset opera carnis, quibus clausum est regnum dei, subiecit etiam opera spiritus, quos spiritus fructus uocat. (2) *Fructus autem spiritus est*, inquit, *caritas, gaudium, pax, longanimitas, benignitas, bonitas, fides, mansuetudo, continentia* et addidit: *aduersus huiusmodi non est lex*, ut intelligamus illos sub lege positos, in quibus ista non regnant. (3) Nam in quibus haec regnant, ipsi lege legitime utuntur, quia non est illis lex ad coercendum posita, maior enim et praepollentior delectatio eorum iustitia est. (4) Sic etiam ad Timotheum dicit: *Scimus enim, quia bona est lex, si quis ea legitime utatur, sciens hoc, quia lex iusto posita non est, iniustis autem et non subditis et impiis et peccatoribus scelestis et contaminatis, patricidis et matricidis, homicidis, fornicatoribus, masculorum concubitoribus, plagiariis, mendacibus, periuris et si quid aliud sanae doctrinae aduersatur*, subauditur: his lex posita est. (5) Regnant ergo spirituales isti fructus in homine, in quo peccata non regnant. Regnant autem ista bona, si tantum delectant, ut ipsa teneant animum in temptationibus, ne in peccati consensionem ruat. (6) Quod enim amplius nos delectat, secundum id operemur necesse est, ut uerbi gratia occurrit forma speciosae feminae et mouet ad delectationem

[235] Cf. Luke 13: 22–30.

[236] Or 'spirit'. This ambiguity, which is largely attributable to Paul himself, should not be overemphasized: our ability to grasp Augustine's basic meaning does not depend on our resolving it, since for Augustine spiritual works are accomplished 'when the human spirit co-operates with the activity of the Spirit of God' ('Quando cum Spiritu Dei operante spiritus hominis cooperatur' (*en. Ps.* 77. 8; CCSL 39: 1073. 36–7)).

[237] According to Augustine's psychological analysis, every sin consists of three elements: the suggestion, delight in the suggestion, and consent to the suggestion. The presence of these three elements makes every sin a symbolic re-enactment of the Fall. See *s. dom. m.* 1. 12. 34 (CCSL 35: 36–8).

does not *reign* (in other words, who does not *obey its desires*) does not sin. But the person in whom such desires do not exist at all, not only does not sin, but does not even have sin. (6) While in many respects this may be possible in this life, we must not hope for it in every respect until the resurrection and transformation of the flesh.

(7) Now when the Apostle says, *I warn you, as I warned you before: those who do such things will not inherit the kingdom of God*, his words may puzzle someone who asks when he warned them before, since there is no such warning earlier in this letter. (8) So either he warned them before when actually present, or he knew that the letter to the Corinthians had reached them. (9) For there he says: *Make no mistake: fornicators, idolaters, adulterers, the effeminate, sodomites, thieves, the greedy, drunkards, revilers, robbers—none of these will inherit the kingdom of God* (1 Cor. 6: 9–10).

49. Now then, when he had listed the works of the flesh, to which the kingdom of God is shut,[235] he proceeded to list also the works of the Spirit,[236] which he calls the fruits of the Spirit: (2) *But the fruit of the Spirit is love, joy, peace, patience, kindness, goodness, faith, gentleness, continence* (Gal. 5: 22–3), adding, *Against such things there is no law*, so we may understand that the people in whom these things do not reign are *under the law*. (3) Now the people in whom they do reign *use the law lawfully*, since *the law is not laid down* to restrain them, for their greater and more powerful delight is righteousness. (4) Thus he also says to Timothy: *For we know that the law is good, if one uses it lawfully, understanding this, that the law is not laid down for the righteous but for the unrighteous and disobedient, for the ungodly and sinners, for the unholy and profane, for those who kill their father or mother, for murderers, fornicators, sodomites, kidnappers, liars, perjurers, and whatever else is contrary to sound teaching* (1 Tim. 1: 8–10). We are to understand that it is for these latter that the law is laid down. (5) Therefore the spiritual fruits listed above reign in the person in whom sins do not reign. Now these good things reign if they so delight us that in the midst of temptations they keep the mind from rashly consenting to sin.[237] (6) For we necessarily act in accordance with what delights us more,[238] as for example when the beauty of an attractive woman meets our eyes and moves us towards a delight in

---

[238] Étienne Gilson comments: 'But it would be a mistake to think that the predominant delight abolishes free choice; it is, on the contrary, but a manifestation of it. The sinful delight which tempts me is not something added to my will to draw it towards something base; it is my mind's spontaneity itself finding expression in the movement which draws it to evil; nor is the delight in the good which grace substitutes for delight in evil a force which does violence to the will from within; it is the spontaneous movement of a will which has been changed and liberated, a will which henceforth tends wholly towards God. Man is truly free when he sees to it that the object of his delight is precisely liberty' (Gilson, *Christian Philosophy*, 162).

fornicationis, sed si plus delectat pulchritudo illa intima et sincera species castitatis per gratiam, quae est in fide Christi, secundum hanc uiuimus et secundum hanc operamur, ut non regnante in nobis peccato ad oboediendum desideriis eius, sed regnante iustitia per caritatem cum magna delectatione faciamus, quicquid in ea deo placere cognoscimus. (7) Quod autem de castitate et de fornicatione dixi, hoc de ceteris intelligi uolui.

50. Neque moueat uel quod non omnino ad eundem numerum et ordinem opera carnis in hac epistula enumerauit atque in illa ad Corinthios uel quod spiritualia bona pauciora pluribus carnalibus uitiis opposuit, neque ita e contrario, ut fornicationibus castitas, immunditiis munditia atque ita ceteris cetera occurrerent. (2) Non enim hoc suscepit, ut doceret, quot sint, sed in quo genere illa uitanda illa uero expetenda sint, cum carnis et spiritus nominibus a poena peccati atque peccato ad gratiam domini atque iustitiam nos conuerti oportere praediceret, ne deserendo gratiam temporalem, qua pro nobis dominus mortuus est, non perueniamus ad aeternam quietem, in qua pro nobis dominus uiuit, neque intelligendo poenam temporalem, in qua nos dominus mortalitate carnis edomare dignatus est, in poenam sempiternam incidamus, quae perseueranti aduersus dominum superbiae praeparata est. (3) Cum enim commemoratis multis operibus carnis addidit: *et his similia*, satis ostendit non se ista examinatiore numero collocasse sed liberiore sermone posuisse. (4) Hoc etiam de spiritualibus fructibus fecit. Non enim ait: aduersus haec non est lex, sed: *aduersus huiusmodi*, hoc est siue ista siue etiam cetera huiusmodi.

51. Sed tamen diligenter considerantibus non hic omni modo carnalium spiritualiumque operum oppositio inordinata atque confusa est. Ob hoc autem latet, quia pauciora uel singula quibusdam pluribus opponuntur. (2) Nam ex eo, quod carnalium uitiorum in capite posuit fornicationes, in capite autem uirtutum spiritualium caritatem, quem non diuinarum litterarum studiosum faciat intentum ad perscrutanda cetera? (3) Si enim fornicatio est amor a legitimo connubio solutus et uagus explendae libidinis consectando licentiam, quid tam legitime ad spiritualem fecunditatem coniungitur quam anima deo? (4) Cui quanto fixius inhaeserit, tanto est

---

[239] Cf. the personification of continence in *conf.* 8. 11. 27 (CCSL 27: 130).

[240] Cf. Rom. 6: 12.

[241] That Augustine should choose sexual desire as his example is interesting not merely because of his personal history as presented in the *Confessions* but also because of the paradigmatic status accorded to sexual desire in his later writings. See P. Brown, *The Body and Society*, 387–427, and the references given there.

[242] 1 Cor. 6: 9–10, quoted above in 48. 9.

fornication. But if, through the grace that is in faith in Christ, that inmost loveliness—the pure beauty of chastity[239]—delights us more, we will live and act in accordance with that, not behaving with sin reigning in us so that we obey its desires,[240] but with righteousness reigning through love with great delight. And we know that whatever we do in love is pleasing to God. (7) Now what I have said about purity and fornication I want to be understood of the other things as well.[241]

50. The fact that the Apostle has not listed the works of the flesh in exactly the same order and number in both this letter and the letter to the Corinthians,[242] or that he has opposed a smaller number of spiritual goods to many carnal vices, or that he has not arranged them antithetically so that chastity is set against *fornication*, purity against *impurity*, and so on, should not trouble us. (2) For when he used the terms *flesh* and *spirit* to warn that we must turn from sin and the penalties of sin to the grace and righteousness of the Lord (lest by deserting the temporal grace in which the Lord died for us we should not arrive at the eternal rest in which the Lord lives for us, and lest by not understanding the temporal punishment in which the Lord thought fit to subdue us—the mortality of the flesh—we should fall into everlasting punishment), he was not attempting to teach how many there are, but what kind of things are to be avoided and what kind are to be aimed at. (3) For after recording many works of the flesh he added, *and the like*, and thus showed sufficiently that he was not concerned with the number but was speaking in a general way. (4) He did this also with regard to spiritual fruits. For he did not say, 'Against these things there is no law', but, *Against such things . . .* , that is, either these or others of this kind.

51. Nevertheless, to those considering the matter carefully, the opposition here of carnal to spiritual works is not entirely disordered and confused. This fact goes unnoticed, however, because relatively few or even single items are set in opposition to many. (2) For example, since he has placed *fornication* at the head of the carnal vices and *love*[243] at the head of the spiritual virtues, what student of the divine Scriptures would not be fascinated to examine the rest? (3) For if *fornication* is sexual love[244] unconnected to a lawful marriage and wandering in search of an opportunity to gratify lust, what is so lawfully married for the sake of spiritual fruitfulness as the soul to God? (4) And the more steadfastly one adheres to God, the more chaste that person will be. Now one adheres by love. It is

---

[243] Or 'charity' (Latin: *caritas*). And so elsewhere in this section except 51. 3.

[244] *amor*. Occurring only here in *exp. Gal.*, *amor* is being contrasted with *caritas* as a neutral term to a positive. Cf. the note at the very beginning of *exp. Gal.* 44.

incorruptior. Inhaeret autem caritate. Recte igitur fornicationi opponitur caritas, in qua sola est custodia castitatis. (5) Immunditiae autem sunt omnes perturbationes de illa fornicatione conceptae, quibus gaudium tranquillitatis opponitur. Idolorum autem seruitus ultima fornicatio est animae, propter quam etiam bellum aduersus euangelium cum reconciliatis deo furiosissimum gestum est, cuius reliquiae quamuis tepidae diu adhuc tamen recalent. (6) Huic itaque pax contraria est, qua reconciliamur deo, eademque pace etiam cum hominibus custodita ueneficiorum, inimicitiarum, contentionum, aemulationum, animositatum dissensionumque uitia sanantur in nobis, ut autem in aliis, inter quos uiuimus, iusta moderatione tractentur et ad sustinendum longanimitas et ad curandum benignitas et ad ignoscendum bonitas militat. (7) Iam uero haeresibus fides, inuidiae mansuetudo, ebrietatibus et comessationibus continentia reluctatur.

52. Ne quis sane arbitretur hoc esse inuidiam, quod est aemulatio, uicina enim sunt et propter ipsam uicinitatem plerumque utrumlibet horum pro altero uel aemulatio pro inuidia uel inuidia pro aemulatione ponitur. (2) Sed quia utrumque hic locis suis dictum est, utique distinctionem de nobis flagitant. Nam aemulatio est dolor animi, cum alius peruenit ad rem, quam duo pluresue appetebant, et nisi ab uno haberi non potest. (3) Istam sanat pax, qua id appetimus, quod omnes, qui appetunt, si assequantur, unum in eo fiunt. Inuidia uero dolor animi est, cum indignus uidetur aliquid assequi etiam, quod tu non appetebas. (4) Hanc sanat mansuetudo, cum quisque ad iudicium dei reuocans non resistit uoluntati eius et magis ei credit recte factum esse quam sibi quod putabat indignum.

53. *Crucifixerunt autem carnem suam cum passionibus et concupiscentiis*, sicut consequenter dicit: *qui sunt in Christo Iesu*. (2) Vnde autem crucifixerunt nisi timore illo casto permanente in saeculum saeculi, quo cauemus offendere illum, quem toto corde, tota anima, tota mente diligimus. (3) Non enim hoc timore timet adultera, ne custodiatur a uiro, quo timet casta, ne deseratur; illi enim tristis est praesentia uiri, huic absentia. (4) Et ideo timor ille corruptus est et transire non uult hoc saeculum, iste autem castus permanet in saeculum saeculi. (5) De quo

---

[245] Idolatry is often compared to fornication in Jeremiah, Ezekiel, and Hosea. Augustine discusses divination as one kind of fornication of the soul in *doctr. chr.* 2. 23. 35.

[246] Possibly an allusion to the recrudescence of pagan–Christian conflict in North Africa during this period, on which see Markus, *The End of Ancient Christianity*, 107–23.

[247] Cf. *exp. Gal.* 3. 2.

right, then, for *love* to be opposed to *fornication*, for chastity is preserved only by love. (5) *Impurity*, on the other hand, is all the passion stirred up by that fornication; the *joy* of serenity is opposed to it. Now *idolatry* is the ultimate fornication—that of the soul.[245] Because of it war marked by the most intense fury has been waged against the gospel and against those reconciled to God, and the remains of this war, though comparatively cool for a long time now, are warming up again.[246] (6) So *peace* is contrary to this, by which we are reconciled to God[247] and by which, when it is preserved among people, the vices of *witchcraft, enmity, strife, jealousy, outbursts of anger*, and *dissension* are healed among us. And in order for us to treat these vices with due restraint when we see them in those we live among, *patience* helps us to be tolerant, *kindness* to be caring, and *goodness* to be forgiving. (7) Furthermore, *faith* resists *heresies*, *gentleness* resists *envy*, and *continence* resists *drunkenness* and *revelry*.[248]

52. One should not think that *envy* and *jealousy* are identical, even though they are synonyms and hence often substituted for one another, either jealousy for envy or envy for jealousy. (2) But because both are mentioned here, each in its own place, we must surely draw a distinction.[249] *Jealousy*, then, is the mental pain experienced when another attains something that two or more were seeking but only one could attain. (3) *Peace* heals this, by which we seek that which makes all who seek and attain it one. *Envy*, on the other hand, is the mental pain experienced when an unworthy person appears to attain something that you were not even seeking. (4) *Gentleness* heals this, when each person, appealing to God's judgement, does not resist his will but instead believes that what happened was right, rather than believing that the other person was unworthy.

53. *Those who are in Christ Jesus*, he goes on to say, *have crucified their flesh with its passions and lusts* (Gal. 5: 24). (2) Now by what have they *crucified* it, unless by that *fear* which *is pure and endures forever* (Ps. 18: 10 (19: 9)), whereby we are careful not to offend him whom we love with all our heart, with all our soul, and with all our mind?[250] (3) For the adulteress's fear of being watched by her husband is not the same as the pure woman's fear of being left by hers; for the adulteress finds the presence of her husband depressing, while for the pure woman it is his absence. (4) And therefore

---

[248] In the contemporaneous *ep.* 29 Augustine discusses the problem of drunkenness and revelry at a church festival in Hippo. With regard to the Latin text of 51. 7, the punctuation given in CSEL destroys the obvious meaning of the sentence and appears to be a printer's error, so I have changed it.

[249] Cf. Cicero, *Tusculanae Disputationes* 3. 9. 20–10. 21, 4. 7. 16–8. 17 (Pohlenz (ed.), 327. 8–328. 7, 368. 27–369. 23).

[250] Cf. Matt. 22: 37 // Mark 12: 30 // Luke 10: 27.

timore crucifigi optat propheta, cum dicit: *Confige clauis a timore tuo carnes meas.* (6) Ista crux est, de qua dominus dicit: *Tolle crucem tuam et sequere me.*

54. *Si spiritu*, inquit, *uiuimus, spiritu et sectemur.* Manifestum est certe secundum id nos uiuere, quod sectati fuerimus, sectabimur autem, quod dilexerimus. (2) Itaque si ex aduerso existant duo, praeceptum iustitiae et consuetudo carnalis, et utrumque diligitur, id sectabimur, quod amplius dilexerimus, si tantundem utrumque diligitur, nihil eorum sectabimur, sed aut timore aut inuiti trahemur in alterutram partem aut, si utrumque aequaliter etiam timemus in periculo, sine dubio remanebimus fluctu delectationis et timoris alternante quassati. (3) Sed pax Christi uincat in cordibus nostris. Tunc enim orationes et gemitus et in auxilium inuocata dextera misericordiae dei sacrificium contribulati cordis non despicit caritatemque sui ampliorem commendatione periculi, de quo liberauit, exsuscitat. (4) In eo autem illi fallebantur, quod negare quidem non poterant sectandum sibi esse spiritum sanctum assertorem ac ducem libertatis suae sed ad opera seruilia carnaliter conuersi retrorsum se conari non intelligebant. (5) Propterea non ait: si spiritu uiuimus, spiritum sectemur, sed: *spiritu sectemur*, inquit. Fatebantur enim spiritui sancto seruire oportere et eum non spiritu suo sed carne uolebant sectari non spiritualiter obtinentes gratiam dei sed in circumcisione carnali et ceteris huiusmodi spem constituentes salutis.

55. *Non efficiamur*, inquit, *inanis gloriae cupidi inuicem inuidentes et inuicem prouocantes.* (2) Prorsus magnifice et omnino diuino ordine, posteaquam eos instruxit aduersus illos, a quibus in seruitutem legis seducebantur, hoc in eis cauet, ne instructiores facti et uolentes iam calumniis carnalium respondere contentionibus studeant et appetitu inanis gloriae legis oneribus non seruientes uanis cupiditatibus seruiant.

56. Nihil autem sic probat spiritualem uirum quam peccati alieni tractatio, cum liberationem eius potius quam insultationem potiusque auxilia quam conuicia meditatur et, quantum facultas tribuitur, suscipit. (2) Et ideo dicit: *Fratres, etsi praeoccupatus fuerit homo in aliquo delicto, uos, qui spirituales estis, instruite huiusmodi.* (3) Deinde ne sibi quisque uideatur

---

[251] Cf. *exp. Gal.* 49. 6.

[252] Reading Divjak's variant, *dilectionis*, instead of his preferred *delectationis* ('delight'). *Dilectionis* appears in several important MSS and in the Maurist edition, and it gives to the paragraph as a whole greater consistency of thought and expression. For detailed discussion, see Rousselet, 'A propos d'un édition critique', 245–6.

[253] Cf. Col. 3: 15.

one fear is corrupt and does not want this world to pass away, while the other, which is pure, endures forever. (5) It is the latter fear that the prophet chooses to be crucified by when he says: *Pierce my flesh with nails from fear of you* (Ps. 118: 120 LXX). (6) This is the cross of which the Lord says, *Take up your cross and follow me* (Matt. 16: 24 // Mark 8:34 // Luke 9:23).

54. *If we live in the Spirit*, he says, *let us also follow in the spirit* (Gal. 5: 25). Surely it is clear that we live according to what we have followed, while we will follow what we have loved. (2) And so if the two—the commandment of righteousness and carnal habit—prove to be in opposition and each one is loved, we will follow the one we have loved more.[251] If each is loved to the same extent, we will follow neither but be drawn, either by fear or unwillingly, towards one or the other; or, if we also fear both equally as dangers, we will no doubt remain tossed by alternate waves of love[252] and fear. (3) But may the peace of Christ prevail in our hearts.[253] For then he does not spurn the sacrifice of a contrite heart[254]—the prayers and groans we utter when calling upon the right hand[255] of God's mercy for help—and he kindles greater love for himself in appreciation of the danger from which he has set us free. (4) But the Galatians erred because they certainly could not deny that they had to follow the Holy Spirit, the champion and leader of their freedom, yet they did not understand that they were trying to turn back in a carnal way to slavish works. (5) Therefore he does not say, '*If you live in the Spirit*, follow the Spirit', but '. . . *follow in the spirit*'. For they acknowledged that they had to serve the Holy Spirit and yet they wanted to follow not *in the spirit* but in the flesh, not obtaining God's grace in a spiritual way but placing their hope for salvation in circumcision of the flesh and other things of this kind.

55. *Let us not*, he says, *become desirous of vainglory, envying one another and provoking one another* (Gal. 5: 26). (2) What he does now is simply superb, and the order in which he does it is nothing less than divine. After instructing the Galatians against those who were luring them into the slavery of the law, he cautions them—now that they are better instructed and keen to respond to the calumnies of the carnal—lest they become eager for strife and, though not enslaved to the burdens of the law, they become instead enslaved to empty desires arising from an appetite for vainglory.

56. Now nothing proves that a man is spiritual like his handling of another's sin: Does he consider how he can liberate rather than insult the other person? How he can help rather than verbally abuse him? Does he undertake to do so to the best of his ability? (2) That is why the Apostle

---

[254] Cf. Ps. 50: 19 (51: 17).   [255] i.e. Christ. Cf. Rom. 8: 34.

instruere, etiam cum proterue exagitat irridetque peccantem aut superbe tamquam insanabilem detestatur, *in spiritu*, inquit, *mansuetudinis intendens teipsum, ne et tu tempteris*. (4) Nihil enim ad misericordiam sic inclinat quam proprii periculi cogitatio. Ita eos nec deesse uoluit fratrum correptioni nec studere certamini. (5) Multi enim homines, cum a somno excitantur, litigare uolunt aut rursus dormire, cum litigare prohibentur. Pax igitur et dilectio communis periculi cogitatione in corde seruentur, modus autem sermonis siue acrius siue blandius proferatur sicut salus eius, quem corrigis, uidetur postulare, moderandus est. (6) Nam et alio loco dicit: *Seruum autem domini litigare non oportet sed mitem esse ad omnes, docibilem, patientem.* (7) Et ne quisquam ex eo putet cessandum sibi esse a correptione erroris alterius, uide, quid adiungat: *In modestia*, inquit, *corripientem diuersa sentientes.* (8) Quomodo in modestia, quomodo corripientem, nisi cum lenitatem corde retinemus et aliquam medicamenti acrimoniam uerbo correptionis aspergimus? (9) Nec aliter accipiendum uideo, quod in eadem epistula positum est: *Praedica uerbum, insta oportune, importune, argue, hortare, increpa in omni longanimitate et doctrina.* (10) Importunitas enim oportunitati utique contraria est neque omnino ullum medicamentum sanat, nisi quod oportune adhibueris. (11) Quamquam ergo et sic possit distingui: *insta oportune*, ut alius sit sensus: *importune argue*, deinde cetera contexantur: *hortare, increpa cum omni longanimitate et doctrina*, ut tunc oportunus sentiaris, cum instas aedificando, cum autem destruis arguendo non cures, etiam si importunus uidearis, si hoc est talibus importunum: (12) ita duo quae sequuntur ad duo superiora possunt singillatim referri: *hortare, cum oportune* instas, *increpa*, cum *importune* arguis, deinde cetera duo similiter sed conuerso ordine referuntur: *cum omni longanimitate* ad sustinendas indignationes eorum, quos destruis, et: *doctrina* ad instruenda eorum studia, quos aedificas, tamen etiamsi illo usitatiore modo distinguatur: *insta oportune*, quod si hoc modo non proficis: *importune*, ita intelligendum est, ut tu oportunitatem omnino non deseras et sic accipias, quod dictum est: *importune*, ut illi uidearis importunus, qui non libenter audit, quae dicuntur in eum, tu tamen scias hoc illi esse oportunum et dilectionem curamque sanitatis eius animo teneas mansueto et modesto et fraterno. (13) Multi enim postea cogitantes, quae audierint et quam iuste audierint, ipsi se grauius et seuerius arguerunt et, quamuis perturbatiores a medico uiderentur abscedere, paulatim uerbi uigore in medullas penetrante sanati sunt. (14) Quod non fieret, si semper expectaremus

says: *Brethren, even if someone is caught doing something wrong, you who are spiritual should instruct that person* (Gal. 6: 1). (3) Then, lest they imagine they are instructing when in fact they are insolently berating and ridiculing the one sinning, or even arrogantly scorning him as incurable, the Apostle says: *in a spirit of gentleness, looking to yourself, lest you too be tempted.* (4) For nothing makes people more inclined to be merciful than the thought of their own danger. So while he did not want them to be neglectful of fraternal correction, neither did he want them to be eager for a fight. (5) For many people want to quarrel when they are woken up, and if they are prevented from quarrelling, they would rather go back to sleep. Let peace and love, then, be preserved in our hearts by the thought of the common danger.

Now whether to use more severity or more charm in speaking should be determined by what seems necessary for the salvation of the person being corrected. (6) For the Apostle also says in another passage: *A servant of the Lord should not be quarrelsome but gentle towards everyone, a good teacher, patient* (2 Tim. 2: 24). (7) And in case anyone concludes from this that he should refrain from correcting another's error, look at what the Apostle adds: *mildly correcting those who think differently* (2 Tim. 2: 25). (8) How can it be *mildly*, how can it be *correcting*, unless we both remain kind-hearted and add a dash of bitter medicine to our word of correction?

(9) Nor do I see how else to interpret what he says in the same letter: *Preach the word, be persistent in season and out of season, criticize, exhort, and reprove with all patience and teaching* (2 Tim. 4: 2). (10) *Out of season* is necessarily opposed to *in season*, and unless you administer medicine *in season* it does no good at all. (11) The verse could, therefore, also be punctuated so as to make two independent clauses,[256] thus: *be persistent in season, and out of season, criticize,* to which the rest is then added: *exhort and reprove with all patience and teaching.* In that case, you are regarded as acting *in season* when you are *persistent* in building up, but you should not worry if by *criticizing* and pulling down you appear to be acting *out of season*, so long as it is *out of season* from the point of view of those being criticized. (12) The two words that follow can then be seen to correspond to the two previous phrases, thus: *exhort*, by persisting *in season*; *reprove*, by criticizing *out of season*. Then the next two phrases are also seen to correspond, but with the order

[256] In Antiquity texts were generally without punctuation, which had to be supplied by the reader. Thus in *doctr. chr.* 3. 2. 2–5 we find Augustine explaining how to punctuate ambiguous passages of Scripture. For a fascinating introduction to the history of punctuation in the West see M. Parkes, *Pause and Effect*. Among the many plates included in this book are a fifth-century MS of Augustine's *ciu.* (plate 64) and the earliest surviving copy of the Vg. Gospels (plate 1), with annotations that may well be from the hand of Jerome himself.

periclitantem putrescentibus membris, quando eum liberet aut uri aut secari. (15) Quod nec ipsi corporis medici attendunt, qui terrenae mercedis intuitu curant. Quotus enim quisque repperitur, qui ferrum eorum aut ignem non ligatus expertus sit, cum et illi rariores sint, qui uolentes ligati fuerint. (16) Plures enim resistentes et mori se malle clamantes quam illo curari modo uix lingua ipsa eorum relicta libera omnibus membris constrinxerunt neque ad suum neque ad reluctantis sed ad ipsius artis arbitrium, quorum tamen uocibus conuiciisque dolentium nec commouetur curantis animus nec quiescit manus. (17) Medicinae autem caelestis ministri aut per odiorum trabem cernere stipulam in oculo fratris uolunt aut tolerabilius mortem uidere peccantis quam uerbum indignantis audire, quod non ita accidisset, si tam sanum animum curando alterius animo adhiberemus, quam sanis manibus illi medici aliena membra pertractant.

57. Numquam itaque alieni peccati obiurgandi suscipiendum est negotium, nisi cum internis interrogationibus examinantes nostram conscientiam liquido nobis coram deo responderimus dilectione nos facere. (2) Quod si conuicium uel minae uel etiam persecutiones eius, quem argueris, lacerauerint animum, si adhuc ille per te sanari posse uidebitur, nihil respondeas, donec saneris prior, ne forte carnalibus motibus tuis ad nocendum consentias et exhibeas linguam tuam arma iniquitatis peccato ad reddendum malum pro malo aut maledictum pro maledicto. (3) Quicquid enim lacerato animo dixeris, punientis est impetus, non caritas corrigentis. (4) Dilige et dic, quod uoles, nullo modo maledictum erit, quod specie maledicti sonuerit, si memineris senserisque te in gladio uerbi dei liberatorem hominis esse uelle ab obsidione uitiorum. (5) Quod si forte, ut plerumque accidit, dilectione quidem talem suscipis actionem et ad eam corde dilectionis accedis, sed inter agendum subrepserit aliquid, dum tibi resistitur, quod te auferat ab hominis uitio percutiendo et ipsi homini faciat infestum, postea te lacrimis lauantem huius modi puluerem multo salubrius meminisse oportebit, quam non debeamus super aliorum

---

[257] Vivid descriptions of ancient surgical practice are given by Augustine in *ciu.* 22. 8 (the story of Innocentius, which Augustine recounts as an eyewitness) and by John Chrysostom in his 'Homily on the Paralytic Let Down through the Roof' (NPNF, 1st ser., 9: 215).

[258] Cf. Matt. 7: 3–5 // Luke 6: 41–2.

[259] Augustine is talking about two different but equally unhealthy ways of dealing with a sinner: one marked by hatred, the other by cowardice.

[260] Perhaps a faint echo of Matt. 5: 11.

reversed: *with all patience*, in order to endure the indignation of those you are pulling down; *and teaching*, in order to guide the efforts of those you are building up. Yet even if it is punctuated in the more familiar way (*be persistent in season*, but if you are not successful, then persist even *out of season*), understand that you absolutely must not fail to act *in season*, and understand the phrase *out of season* to mean that you appear to be acting *out of season* from the point of view of the person who does not want to hear what is being said to him. Even so, you should realize that this is actually *in season* for him and preserve love and care for his well-being in a mind that is gentle and mild and brotherly.

(13) For many, reflecting afterwards on what they were told and how they deserved it, have in fact criticized themselves even more sternly and severely, and though they appeared to go away from the 'physician' quite upset, they were gradually healed as the force of the word penetrated their hearts. (14) This would not happen if we always waited for the patient with gangrene to ask for treatment, when cautery or surgery would save him. (15) Not even physicians of the body, who treat patients for an earthly reward, wait for that to happen. How rare is the patient who has undergone the knife or fire without being bound, while the patient bound willingly is rarer still! (16) In many cases the patient's entire body is tied down, so that even his tongue is barely left free, while he resists and screams that he would rather die than be cured in this way. This is not what those who tie the patient down want or what the patient who is struggling wants, but what the art itself requires. Yet the mind of the healer is not troubled by the uproar patients make as they feel the pain, nor is his hand still.[257] (17) Those, on the other hand, who administer heavenly medicine wish either to perceive the *speck* in their brother's eye through a *beam* of hatreds,[258] or to see the death of the one sinning rather than hear a word of indignation from him.[259] Such things would not happen if the mind we used in treating the mind of another were as healthy as the hands those physicians use in dealing with another's body.

57. So we should never undertake the task of rebuking another's sin without first examining our own conscience by inner questioning and then responding—unequivocally before God—that we are acting out of love. (2) But if the one you are criticizing hurts your feelings by verbally abusing you or threatening you or even persecuting you,[260] yet still seems capable of being healed by you, you should not respond in any way until you are healed first, lest perhaps your carnal emotions lead you to consent to doing harm and you present your tongue to sin as a weapon of injustice[261] for repaying

[261] For 'present . . . injustice', cf. Rom. 6: 13.

superbire peccata, quando in ipsa eorum obiurgatione peccamus, cum facilius nos ira peccantis iratos quam miseria misericordes facit.

58. *Alter alterius onera portate et sic adimplebitis legem Christi*, legem utique caritatis. (2) Si autem implet legem, qui diligit proximum, dilectioque proximi etiam in ueteribus scripturis maxime commendatur, in qua dilectione dicit alio loco idem apostolus recapitulari omnia mandata legis: manifestum est etiam illam scripturam, quae priori populo data est, legem Christi esse, quam uenit implere caritate, quae non implebatur timore. (3) Eadem igitur scriptura et idem mandatum, cum bonis terrenis inhiantes premit seruos, testamentum uetus, cum in bona aeterna flagrantes erigit liberos, testamentum nouum uocatur.

59. *Si enim aliquis*, inquit, *uidetur esse aliquid, cum nihil sit, seipsum seducit.* Non enim eum seducunt laudatores eius, sed ipse potius, quia, cum sibi sit ipse praesentior quam illi, mauult se in illis quaerere quam in seipso. Sed quid dicit apostolus? (2) *Opus autem suum probet unusquisque et tunc in seipso tantum gloriam habebit et non in altero*, id est intus in conscientia sua et non in altero, id est cum eum alter laudat. (3) *Unusquisque enim*, inquit, *proprium onus portabit.* Non ergo laudatores nostri minuunt onera conscientiae nostrae; atque utinam non etiam accumulent, cum plerumque ne illis offensis laus nostra minuatur, aut obiurgatione illos curare negligimus aut iactanter eis aliquid nostrum ostentamus potius quam constanter ostendimus. (4) Omitto ea, quae fingunt et mentiuntur de se homines propter hominum laudes. Quid enim ista caecitate tenebrosius ad obtinendam inanissimam gloriam errorem hominis aucupari et deum testem in corde contemnere? (5) Quasi uero ullo modo comparandus sit error illius, qui te bonum putat, errori tuo, qui homini de falso bono placere studes, de uero malo displices deo.

60. Iam cetera planissima esse existimo. Nam et illud usitatum

262 For 'repaying . . .', cf. 1 Pet. 3: 9.

263 This is the earliest form of the Augustinian maxim that attained such notoriety later when it was used (in the form 'Love, and do what you like' (*Dilige, et quod vis fac*)) to justify the coercion of the Donatists. For the later version see e.g. *ep. Io. tr.* 7. 8 (PL 35: 2033).

264 Cf. Eph. 6: 17, Heb. 4: 12.

265 Augustine reflects on this verse at length and with great pastoral insight in *diu. qu.* 71, written at about the same time as *exp. Gal.*

266 Cf. Lev. 19: 18. According to Augustine (*mor.* 1. 28. 57), the Manichees denied that such teaching occurred in the Old Testament.

267 Cf. Rom. 13: 8–10. (PL, CSEL, and now NBA mistakenly direct the reader to Matt. 5: 17.)

evil for evil or insult for insult.[262] (3) For when your feelings are hurt whatever you say will be an expression of violent retaliation and not of loving correction. (4) Love, and say what you like:[263] in no way will what sounds like an insult really be an insult if you keep clearly in mind that your intention in using the sword of God's word[264] is to liberate the person from the siege of vices. (5) But if by chance (as so often happens) you undertake such an action out of love and approach it with a loving heart but because you encounter resistance something insinuates itself, distracting your attention from the vice to be struck down and making you hostile to the person himself, then afterwards, as you wash away this kind of dust with tears, it will be necessary and really very helpful for you to remember that we should not proudly scorn the sins of others, since in the very act of rebuking them we ourselves sin when we find it easier to respond to the sinner's anger with our own anger than to the sinner's misery with our mercy.

58. *Bear one another's burdens, and in this way you will fulfil the law of Christ* (Gal. 6: 2),[265] specifically the law of love. (2) But if loving one's neighbour fulfils the law and the love of one's neighbour is especially urged in the Old Testament also[266] (in which love, the same apostle says elsewhere, all the commandments of the law are summed up[267]), then it is clear that the Scripture given to the earlier people is also the law of Christ, which he came to fulfil by love when it was not being fulfilled by fear. (3) The same Scripture and the same commandment, then, is called the Old Testament when it weighs down slaves panting for earthly goods, and the New Testament when it lifts up free people ardent for eternal goods.[268]

59. *For if anyone*, he says, *thinks he is something, when he is nothing, he is deceiving himself* (Gal. 6: 3). It is not the people praising him who are deceiving him; rather, it is he himself, because even though he is more present to himself than they are, he prefers to find out who he is from them rather than from himself. But what does the Apostle say? (2) *Let each one test his own work, and then his reason to boast will be in himself alone and not in another* (Gal. 6: 4), that is, inwardly in his own conscience and not *in another*, that is, when another praises him. (3) *For everyone*, he says, *must bear his own burden* (Gal. 6: 5). Those who praise us do not, therefore, lessen the *burdens* of our conscience. Indeed, I wish they did not actually add to them, since we often either fail to give a salutary rebuke or ostentatiously show off to them rather than showing firmness, for fear that by giving offence we may receive less praise. (4) I pass over the pretences and fabrications people make about themselves in order to obtain human praise. For

---

[268] This statement is strongly anti-Manichean in its affirmation of the essential unity of the Old and New Testaments.

praeceptum est, ut praedicatori uerbi dei praebeat necessaria, cui praedicatur. (2) Ad bona enim opera hortandi erant, ut etiam egenti Christo ministrarent staturi ad dexteram cum agnis, ut plus in eis operaretur dilectio fidei, quam legis posset timor. (3) Neque hoc quisquam maiore fiducia debet praecipere quam hic apostolus, qui manibus suis uictum transigens haec in se nolebat fieri, ut maiore pondere propter eorum magis utilitatem, qui haec exhiberent, quam propter eorum, quibus exhiberent ea, se monere omnibus demonstraret.

61. Quod autem deinde subiungit: *Nolite errare, deus non subsannatur, quod enim seminauerit homo, hoc et metet*, nouit, inter quae uerba perditorum hominum laborent, qui constituuntur in fide rerum earum, quas non uident. (2) Vident enim seminationem operum suorum, sed messem non uident. (3) Nec talis eis messis promittitur, qualis hic reddi solet, *quia iustus ex fide uiuit*. (4) *Quia qui seminauerit*, inquit, *in carne sua ex carne metet corruptionem*. (5) Hoc dicit de amatoribus uoluptatum magis quam dei. In carne enim sua seminat, qui omnia, quae facit, etiamsi bona uideantur, propterea tamen facit, ut carnaliter ei bene sit. (6) *Qui autem seminauerit in spiritu, de spiritu metet uitam aeternam.* Seminatio in spiritu est ex fide cum caritate seruire iustitiae et non obaudire desideriis peccati, quamuis de mortali carne existentibus. (7) Messis autem uitae aeternae, cum inimica nouissima destruetur mors et absorbebitur mortale a uita et corruptibile hoc induet incorruptionem. (8) In hoc ergo tertio gradu, quo sub gratia sumus, seminamus in lacrimis, cum existunt desideria de animali corpore, quibus non consentiendo renitimur, ut in gaudio metamus, cum etiam reformatio corporis ex nulla parte hominis ulla nos sollicitabit molestia ullumue temptationis periculum. (9) Nam etiam ipsum animale corpus deputatur in semine. *Seminatur* enim *corpus animale*, ait alio loco ut ad messem pertineat, quod adiunxit: *surget corpus spirituale*. (10) Huic ergo sententiae propheta concinit dicens: *Qui seminat in lacrimis, in gaudio metet*.

---

[269] On the dangers of praise see further *s. dom. m.* 2. 1. 1–2. 9 and *conf.* 10. 36. 59–38. 63.

[270] Gal. 6: 6, and cf. e.g. Matt. 10: 10, Luke 10: 7, 1 Cor. 9: 4, and 2 Thess. 3: 9.

[271] Cf. Matt. 25: 31–46. Augustine has 'lambs' (*agni*) here instead of the more familiar 'sheep' (*oves*, as in the Vg.). In referring to this passage elsewhere Augustine sometimes uses *agni* (e.g. *en. Ps.* 9. 9 (CCSL 38: 63. 12)), sometimes *oves* (e.g. *en. Ps.* 59. 8 (CCSL 39: 760. 32)).

[272] Souter (*Glossary*, 426) gives several instances of Augustine's use of *transigo* in this sense.

[273] Cf. 1 Cor. 4: 12.

[274] Cf. 1 Thess. 2: 9; 1 Cor. 9: 1–18.

[275] See *exp. Gal.* 46. 4–9.

what could be darker than the blindness that grabs at a person's error in order to obtain sheer vainglory and yet spurns God, the witness in the heart? (5) As if the error of the person who thinks you are good is really to be compared in any way with your own error when you try to please a person by means of a false good (but are really displeasing God by means of a true evil!).[269]

60. Now I think the rest is quite clear. For it is customary for the one to whom the word of God is preached to supply the needs of the preacher.[270] (2) Indeed, they had to be encouraged to do good works—to minister even now to Christ in need—so that they might stand at the right hand with the lambs,[271] and thus the love that comes from faith might accomplish greater works in them than the fear that comes from the law ever could. (3) Nor does anyone have more of a right to urge this with confidence than this apostle, who made[272] a living with his own hands[273] and refused to have these things done for him,[274] in order to be able to point to himself with greater authority as an example for all, more for the benefit of those who supplied these things than those who received them.

61. Next he adds: *Do not be deceived; God is not mocked, for whatever a person sows, that he will also reap* (Gal. 6: 7). The Apostle knew how people whose faith is in things they cannot see work amidst the taunts of the lost. (2) For these people can see the sowing of their works but not the harvest. (3) And the harvest they are promised is not like the harvests usually produced here, *for the righteous live by faith* (Gal. 3: 11 (Hab. 2: 4)). (4) *For he who sows in his own flesh will reap corruption from the flesh* (Gal. 6: 8). (5) The Apostle is referring to those who love pleasures more than they love God. For a person *sows in his own flesh* when he does everything, even what appears to be good, for the sake of his own carnal prosperity. (6) *But he who sows in the spirit will reap eternal life from the spirit.* Sowing in the spirit means serving righteousness out of faith and with love and not obeying sinful desires, even though they continue to arise from our mortal flesh. (7) Now the harvest of eternal life is when *death, the last enemy, will be destroyed* (1 Cor. 15: 26), when *what is mortal* will be *swallowed up by life* (2 Cor. 5: 4), and when *what is corruptible* will *put on incorruption* (1 Cor. 15: 53). (8) So while we are in this third stage,[275] under grace, we *sow in tears* as we resist the desires arising from our natural bodies, in order that we may *reap in joy* when our bodies are transformed.[276] When that happens, there will not be any distress or danger of temptation arising from any aspect of

---

[276] 'when our bodies are transformed': following the variant reading *reformato corpore*, which is both well attested in the MSS and the preferred reading of the Maurists and Rousselet. Divjak's preferred reading, *reformatio corporis*, destroys the Latin syntax.

(11) Bene autem seminare, id est bene operari, facilius est quam in eo perseuerare. Fructus enim solet laborem consolari, messis autem nostra in fine promittitur et ideo perseuerantia opus est. (12) *Qui enim perseuerauerit usque in finem, hic saluus erit.* (13) Et propheta clamat: *Sustine dominum, uiriliter age et confortetur cor tuum et sustine dominum.* (14) Quod nunc apostolus ait: *bonum autem facientes*, inquit, *non infirmemur: proprio enim tempore metemus infatigabiles. Itaque dum tempus habemus, operemur bonum ad omnes, maxime autem ad domesticos fidei.* (15) Quos eum credendum est nisi christianos significare? Omnibus enim pari dilectione uita aeterna optanda est, sed non omnibus eadem possunt exhiberi dilectionis officia.

62. Deinde cum docuisset opera ipsa legis, quae sunt salubria et ad bonos mores pertinent, dilectione fidei posse tantummodo impleri non timore seruili, redit ad illud, unde tota causa agitur. (2) *Vidistis*, inquit, *qualibus litteris uobis scripsi mea manu.* Cauet ne quisquam sub nomine epistulae eius fallat incautos. (3) *Qui uolunt*, inquit, *placere in carne, hi cogunt uos circumcidi, tantum ut in cruce Christi persecutionem non patiantur.* Multum enim persequebantur Iudaei eos, qui uidebantur deserere traditas huiusmodi obseruationes, quos ipse quam non timeat, satis ostendit, cum tales litteras etiam sua manu scribere uoluit. (4) Docet ergo timorem adhuc in istis operari tamquam sub lege constitutis, qui ad circumcisionem gentes cogerent. *Neque enim qui circumcisi sunt*, hi legem custodiunt. (5) Illam enim dicit custoditionem legis non occidere, non moechari, non falsum testimonium dicere et si qua huiusmodi ad bonos mores pertinere manifestum est, quae nisi caritate et spe bonorum aeternorum, quae per fidem accipiuntur, impleri non posse iam dictum est. (6) *Sed uolunt uos circumcidi*, inquit, *ut in uestra glorientur carne*, id est ut non solum non patiantur persecutionem a Iudaeis, qui nullo modo ferebant incircumcisis legem prodi, sed etiam glorientur apud eos, quod tam multos proselitos

---

[277] The Latin phrase *qualibus litteris* is ambiguous and can also mean 'with what letters', in which case Paul would be referring to his extraordinary handwriting. Had Augustine read it in this way, however, it is hard to see how he could have let it pass without a comment. As to Paul's original Greek (πηλίκοις . . . γράμμασιν), it clearly refers to handwriting and is best rendered 'with what large letters'. For the nuances of the Greek see Lightfoot, *Galatians*, 220–1, and Betz, *Galatians*, 313–14.

[278] Cf. 2 Thess. 2: 2, 3: 17.

[279] Similarly Pelagius, *Comm. on Galatians* 6: 11 (Souter, *Expositions*, ii. 341. 12–13).

[280] I presume the antecedent is 'love and hope' rather than 'eternal goods', although either is grammatically possible on the basis of the Latin. That love and hope are received through faith is implied elsewhere, e.g. *s.* 144. 2: 'So when you believe in Christ, by your believing in Christ, Christ comes into you, and you are somehow or other united to him and made into a

our being to trouble us. (9) For the natural body itself may be regarded as seed also. For he says in another passage: *it is sown a natural body*, so that what follows must pertain to the harvest: *it will rise a spiritual body* (1 Cor. 15: 44). (10) The prophet expresses the same sentiment when he says: *The one who sows in tears will reap in joy* (Ps. 125 (126): 5). (11) Now to sow well, that is, to work well, is easier than to persevere in it. For in most cases people find a reward for their labour in the fruit of that labour, but in our case the harvest is promised at the end and so we need to have perseverance. (12) *For the one who perseveres to the end will be saved* (Matt. 10: 22). (13) And the prophet cries out: *Wait for the Lord; be strong, and let your heart take courage; wait for the Lord!* (Ps. 26 (27): 14). (14) The Apostle goes on to say: *But let us not weaken in doing good, for we will reap at harvest-time if we are tireless. Therefore while we have time let us do good to everyone, but especially to those of the family of faith* (Gal. 6: 9–10). (15) To whom do you suppose he is referring, if not to Christians? For eternal life ought to be desired with equal love for everyone, but the same duties of love cannot be fulfilled for everyone.

62. Then, having shown that the very works of the law that are salutary and have to do with good morals can be fulfilled only by the love that comes from faith, not by slavish fear, he returns to his reason for pleading the entire case. (2) *You have seen*, he says, *what kind of letter*[277] *I have written to you in my own hand* (Gal. 6: 11). He is guarding against anyone deceiving the unwary by means of a letter forged in his name.[278] (3) *It is those who want to be pleasing in the flesh who are forcing you to be circumcised, only to avoid suffering persecution for the cross of Christ* (Gal. 6: 12). For the Jews were fiercely persecuting people who seemed to be abandoning traditional observances of this kind. The Apostle clearly demonstrates how little he fears their persecution by writing *this kind of letter in his very own hand*.[279] (4) Thus he shows that fear is still at work in those who would force the Gentiles towards circumcision, just as it was when they were under the law. *For not even those who are circumcised keep the law* (Gal. 6: 13). (5) By *keeping the law* he means: not killing, not committing adultery, not bearing false witness, and anything else of this sort that obviously has to do with good morals. As has already been said, these things cannot be fulfilled except by the love and hope that[280] are received through faith and directed towards

member of his body. And this cannot happen unless both hope and love come along too' (Hill, trans., 4: 431 (modified)). Discussing the interrelation of faith, hope, and love at the beginning of his handbook on that subject, Augustine assigns logical priority to faith: 'Faith believes, and hope and love pray. But without faith the other two cannot exist' (Arand, trans., 14–15 (modified); *ench.* 2. 7: 'Fides credit, spes et caritas orant. Sed sine fide esse non possunt' (CCSL 46: 51. 10–11)).

faciunt. (7) Vt enim unum proselitum facerent Iudaei, mare et terram eos circuire solere dominus dixit. (8) *Mihi autem absit gloriari nisi in cruce domini nostri Iesu Christi, per quem mihi mundus crucifixus est et ego mundo. Mundus mihi crucifixus est*, ait, ut me non teneat et: *ego mundo*, ut eum non teneam, id est ut neque mundus mihi nocere possit neque ego de mundo aliquid cupiam. (9) Qui autem in cruce Christi gloriatur, non uult placere in carne, quia persecutiones carnalium non timet, quas prior, ut crucifigeretur, ille sustinuit, ut uestigia sua sectantibus praeberet exemplum.

63. *Neque enim circumcisio aliquid est neque praeputium.* Seruat usque in finem illam indifferentiam ne quis eum putaret uel in Timothei circumcisione simulate aliquid egisse uel in cuiusquam agere, si forte aliqua talis causa extitisset. (2) Ostendit enim non ipsam circumcisionem obesse aliquid credentibus sed spem salutis in talibus obseruationibus constitutam. (3) Nam et in Actibus apostolorum hoc modo inueniuntur illi circumcisionem persuadere, ut aliter eos, qui ex gentibus crediderant, saluos fieri negent posse. (4) Non ergo ipsius operis sed huius erroris perniciem refellit apostolus. *Neque circumcisio ergo aliquid est neque praeputium, sed noua*, inquit, *creatura.* (5) Nouam creaturam dicit uitam nouam per fidem Iesu Christi et notandum uerbum est. Difficile enim inueneris creaturam uocari etiam eos, qui iam credendo in adoptionem filiorum uenerunt. (6) Dicit tamen et alio loco: *Si qua igitur in Christo noua creatura, uetera transierunt, ecce facta sunt omnia noua, omnia autem ex deo.* (7) Vbi autem dicit: *Et ipsa creatura liberabitur a seruitute interitus* et postea dicit: *non solum autem sed et nos ipsi primitias spiritus habentes*, discernit eos, qui crediderunt ab appellatione creaturae, quomodo eosdem aliquando homines aliquando non homines dicit. (8) Nam exprobrans obiecit Corinthiis quodam loco, quod adhuc homines essent, ubi ait: *Nonne homines estis et secundum hominem ambulatis?* (9) Quomodo eundem dominum etiam post resurrectionem alicubi non hominem appellat sicut in principio huius epistulae, cum ait: *non ab hominibus neque per hominem, sed per Iesum Christum*, alicubi autem hominem, sicut illo loco ubi ait: (10) *Vnus enim deus, unus et mediator dei et hominum homo Christus Iesus.* (11) *Et quicumque*, inquit, *hanc regulam sectantur, pax super illos et misericordia et*

---

281 Matt. 23: 15.
282 Cf. 1 Pet. 2: 21.
283 Acts 16: 1–3.
284 Cf. Acts 15: 1.
285 i.e. of circumcision. The Latin term *opus* may also be translated as 'work'.

eternal goods. (6) *But they want you to be circumcised so that they may boast about your flesh* (Gal. 6: 13), that is, so that not only may they *avoid suffering persecution* from the Jews, who would never allow the law to be handed over to the uncircumcised, but also that they may boast to them that they are making so many proselytes. (7) For the Lord said the Jews would cross sea and land to make a single proselyte.[281] (8) *But far be it from me to boast except in the cross of our Lord Jesus Christ, through whom the world has been crucified to me and I to the world* (Gal. 6: 14). When he says *the world has been crucified to me* he means 'it does not hold me', and when he says *I to the world* he means 'I do not hold it'—in other words, 'the world is not able to harm me, nor do I desire anything from the world'. (9) But the one who *boasts in the cross of Christ* does not *want to be pleasing in the flesh*, since he is not afraid of *persecutions* from carnal people such as Christ endured earlier in order to be crucified and thus offer an example to those following in his footsteps.[282]

63. *For it is not circumcision or uncircumcision that counts* (Gal. 6: 15). He maintains his indifference to the end in case anyone thought he had acted hypocritically in circumcising Timothy[283] or was doing so in circumcising anyone else (if by chance another situation of this kind arose). (2) For he is showing that it is not circumcision itself that is harmful to believers, but placing one's hope for salvation in such observances. (3) For we also find people in the Acts of the Apostles who urge circumcision so as to deny that believers of Gentile origin can be saved in any other way.[284] (4) The Apostle is therefore refuting not the act[285] itself but this fatal error. Thus *it is not circumcision or uncircumcision that counts*, he says, *but a new creation*. (5) The term *new creation* refers to the new life through faith in Jesus Christ and should be noted. For it is not easy to find examples of the term *creation* being applied to people who have attained adoptive sonship by believing. (6) Nevertheless, he does say in another place: *So if anyone is in Christ, there is a new creation: the old has passed away, behold all things have become new. But all things are from God* (2 Cor. 5: 17–18). (7) But when he says, *And creation itself will be set free from its bondage to decay* (Rom. 8: 21) and afterwards, *And not only [creation], but also we ourselves, who have the first-fruits of the spirit* (Rom. 8: 23),[286] he distinguishes believers from 'creation', just as he sometimes calls the same people 'human beings', sometimes not. (8) For elsewhere when upbraiding the Corinthians he charges that they are still human beings: *Are you not mere human beings*, he says, *living on a purely human level?* (1 Cor. 3: 3). (9) Similarly at one time he speaks of the Lord after his resurrection as not being human (as at the beginning of this letter:

---

[286] On *the first-fruits of the spirit* as interpreted by Augustine see the first note attached to 28. 3 above.

super Israel dei, id est eos, qui uere ad uisionem dei praeparantur non qui uocantur hoc nomine et carnali caecitate uidere dominum nolunt, quando gratiam eius respuentes serui esse temporum cupiunt.

64. *De cetero*, inquit, *laborem nemo mihi praestet*. Non uult per turbulentas contentiones taedium sibi fieri de re, quantum satis erat, exposita et in epistula, quam ad Romanos scripsit et hac ipsa. (2) *Ego enim stigmata domini Iesu Christi in corpore meo porto*, id est: habeo alios conflictus et certamina cum carne mea, quae in persecutionibus quas patior mecum dimicant. (3) Stigmata enim dicuntur notae quaedam poenarum seruilium, ut si quis uerbi gratia seruus in compedibus fuerit propter noxam, id est propter culpam, uel huiusmodi aliquid passus fuerit, stigmata habere dicatur, et ideo in iure manumissionis inferioris est ordinis. (4) Nunc ergo apostolus stigmata uoluit appellare quasi notas poenarum de persecutionibus, quas patiebatur. (5) Propter culpam enim persecutionis, qua persecutus erat ecclesias Christi, haec sibi retribui cognouerat, sicut ab ipso domino dictum est Ananiae, cum idem illum Ananias tamquam persecutorem christianorum formidaret. (6) *Ego illi ostendam*, inquit, *quae oporteat eum pati pro nomine meo*. Verumtamen propter remissionem peccatorum, in qua baptizatus erat, omnes illae tribulationes non ei ualebant ad perniciem sed ad coronam uictoriae proficiebant.

65. Conclusio epistulae tamquam subscriptio manifesta est, nam et in nonnullis aliis epistulis ea utitur: *Gratia domini nostri Iesu Christi cum spiritu uestro, fratres, Amen*.

---

[287] For 'time-servers' (*servi temporum*) cf. Augustine's comments on Gal. 4: 10 in 34. 4–5 above.

[288] i.e. than a slave without the marks.

not from human beings nor through a human being, but through Jesus Christ
(Gal. 1: 1)), but at another time as being human (as when he says: (10) *For
there is one God, and there is one mediator between God and human beings, Jesus
Christ, himself a human being* (1 Tim. 2: 5)). (11) *As for those who follow this
rule*, he says, *may peace and mercy be upon them, upon the Israel of God* (Gal.
6: 16), that is, upon those who are truly being prepared for the vision of
God, not those who are called by this name and yet because of their carnal
blindness refuse to see the Lord, whose grace they spurn in their desire to
be time-servers.[287]

64. *From now on*, he says, *let no one trouble me* (Gal. 6: 17). He has no desire
to be worn down by turbulent conflicts over a matter sufficiently explained
both in his Letter to the Romans and in this letter. (2) *For I bear the marks of
the Lord Jesus Christ in my body*. That is, 'I have other battles and contests to
fight with my flesh in the persecutions I suffer.' (3) For by *marks* are meant
the kind associated with the punishments of slaves, so that if a slave, for
instance, were in fetters on account of wrongdoing, that is, an offence, or
had suffered something of this kind, he might be said to have *marks*, and for
this reason he is of a lower rank[288] in the right to manumission. (4) The
Apostle thus wanted to apply the term *marks* to the marks of punishment,
so to speak, coming from the persecutions that he suffered. (5) For he knew
that this was retribution for the offence of persecuting the churches of
Christ. As the Lord himself told Ananias when Ananias feared Paul as a
persecutor of Christians: (6) *I will show him how much suffering he must
undergo for my name's sake* (Acts 9: 16). Nevertheless, because of the
forgiveness of sins for which he was baptized, all those tribulations brought
him not to destruction, but to the crown of victory.

65. The conclusion of the letter is clearly a kind of epistolary formula,
since he uses it in a number of other letters also:[289] *May the grace of our Lord
Jesus Christ be with your spirit, brethren. Amen* (Gal. 6: 18).

[289] Cf. especially Phil. 4: 23 and Philem. 25.

Appendix 1

THE LATIN TEXT OF AUGUSTINE'S
COMMENTARY ON GALATIANS

The most notable printed editions of the Latin text of Augustine's *Commentary on Galatians* are as follows. In the sixteenth century it appeared in three great collected editions of Augustine's works: that of Johannes Amerbach[1] (Basle, 1506), that of Erasmus (Basle, 1528–9), and that of the theologians of Louvain (Antwerp, 1576–7). In the following century an even greater edition of Augustine's collected works was produced by the French Benedictines of St Maur (Paris, 1679–1700). Augustine's *Commentary* appeared in vol. iii, pt. 2 of the Maurist edition in 1680. More than a century and a half later the collected edition of the Maurists was reproduced with few changes in J.-P. Migne's Patrologia Latina (Paris, 1841–2), with Augustine's *Commentary* appearing in vol. 35 in 1841. In the twentieth century Johannes Divjak edited Augustine's *Commentary* for Corpus Scriptorum Ecclesiasticorum Latinorum, 84 (Vienna, 1971), and more recently an edition was printed with facing Italian translation in Nuova Biblioteca Agostiniana, X/2 (Rome, 1997). The Rome edition is not, however, an independent critical edition based upon a fresh collation of the manuscripts, but rather a conflation of the CSEL and Maurist printed editions.[2]

The text produced by Divjak for CSEL is the most authoritative Latin text of Augustine's *Commentary* currently available and has therefore been used as the basis for the translation presented here.[3] In comparison with the Maurists, who examined fourteen manuscripts of Augustine's *Commentary*,[4] Divjak examined sixty-three, of which he chose twenty-eight for inclusion in his apparatus criticus. The thirty-five excluded were either exact copies of ones already included or they were 'contaminated'.[5] Divjak divided the twenty-eight manuscripts chosen for

---

[1] Augustine's *Commentary on Galatians* was not among the works of Augustine published by Amerbach prior to his collected edition of 1506 (see Halporn, *Johann Amerbach's Collected Editions*, 142–4), and in fact I have not been able to find any printed edition of the *Commentary* earlier than the one included in Amerbach's collected edition.

[2] Explicitly acknowledged on p. 459.

[3] Except where indicated otherwise by a footnote, my comments below on Divjak's CSEL edition are derived from his *Praefatio* to that edition (CSEL 84: vii–xxxi), supplemented by his communication to the 1971 Oxford Patristics Conference, 'Zur Textüberlieferung'.

[4] The list of MSS may be found in the first edition (Paris, 1680), vol. iii, pt. 2, cols. 983–4.

[5] That is, they were each copied from more than one source and hence reflect a mixture of traditions rather than a single tradition.

inclusion into three families, of which the first is superior to the other two and is therefore used as the primary basis for the text.[6] The first family comprises four principal manuscripts together with seven manuscripts of secondary importance. In Divjak's judgement the best of the principal manuscripts is one copied in a monastery in Angers in the eleventh century and housed today in the Bibliothèque Nationale in Paris, where it is catalogued as Codex Parisinus Latinus 2700. The other three principal manuscripts are: Codex Andegavensis 159 (eleventh century); Codex Bruxellensis 1058 (fifteenth century); and Codex Parisinus Latinus 12225 (twelfth century).[7] The oldest manuscript containing Augustine's *Commentary* is an eighth-century parchment manuscript from northern Italy (Codex Vaticanus Latinus 491) which Divjak assigns to his third family.[8]

In a major review of CSEL 84,[9] Jean Rousselet proposed an alternative stemma based on his own collation of manuscripts (including one that Divjak had omitted[10]) and on his examination of quotations of Augustine's commentaries in later authors, most notably the important ninth-century figures Rabanus Maurus and Claudius of Turin. With regard to Rousselet's corrections of particular readings for the *Commentary on Galatians* in CSEL 84, I have examined each correction and where I have thought Rousselet's proposal made better sense of the text I have adopted it and alerted the reader to it in a footnote. In all I have adopted five of Rousselet's corrections, to which I have added three of my own.[11] In each case I have attempted to ensure that the alternative reading is both well attested in the manuscripts and faithful to Augustine's thought as expressed elsewhere in the text or in other works from this period of his life. In addition to incorporating various corrections of the Latin text into my translation, I have often presented as biblical quotations passages and phrases that Divjak has not so presented. Here it must be admitted that judging what Augustine intended to be taken as a quotation is often highly subjective, since he was not normally worried about whether he was quoting verbatim.

The cataloguing of all extant manuscripts of Augustine is one of the great

[6] Divjak does not give his reasons for judging the first family to be superior to the other two.

[7] Divjak gives further information about these and other MSS in both the *Praefatio* to CSEL 84 and in his Oxford communication.

[8] There is a facsimile of one section of Codex Vaticanus Latinus 491, showing the concluding paragraph of *exp. prop. Rm.*, in E. A. Lowe, *Codices Latini Antiquiores*, pt. I, facing p. 3. Divjak considers that the value this codex might have had owing to its antiquity is offset by the fact that it was corrected, altered, and added to by a number of different scribes in the eighth and ninth centuries, so that it is often difficult to determine what is original and what is the work of later hands. In view of the more sophisticated methods of analysis available today, however, it is doubtful whether Divjak's judgement of thirty years ago can still stand.

[9] 'A propos d'un édition critique: pour mieux lire les Commentaires d' Augustin sur les Epîtres aux Romains et aux Galates', *Revue des Études Augustiniennes*, 18 (1972), 233–47.

[10] Berlin Görres 97 (*ii*) (tenth century).

[11] For Rousselet's corrections see the footnotes at *exp. Gal.* 1. 5, 9. 1, 21. 3, 54. 2, and 61. 8. For my own corrections see the footnotes at 15. 1, 16. 3, and 51. 7.

ongoing projects of the Vienna Academy.[12] There is no doubt that additional manuscripts and other witnesses to Augustine's *Commentary*, together with more sophisticated methods of analysis such as those made possible by computer technology, will eventually enable scholars to produce a text superior to that produced by Divjak for CSEL 84. In the meantime it is interesting to note that since editing that volume Divjak has continued to play an important role in this project. Indeed, it was in the course of cataloguing all the Augustinian manuscripts in France that he discovered a collection of previously unknown letters of Augustine,[13] a momentous discovery which has put all students of Augustine in his debt.

[12] For the results of the Academy's work to date see the volumes that have appeared in *Die handschriftliche Überlieferung der Werke des heiligen Augustinus* (Sitzungsberichte der Österreichischen Akademie der Wissenschaften; Vienna, 1969–).

[13] Edited by Divjak and published in CSEL 88 (Vienna, 1981), the collection includes twenty-seven new letters by Augustine. There is an English translation by Robert Eno in FC 81.

Appendix 2

AUGUSTINE'S LATIN VERSION OF THE BIBLE

The version of the Bible that Augustine used in writing his *Commentary* is one of the Old Latin versions, whose origins antedate those of the Vulgate by more than two hundred years. For the letters of Paul, for example, the existence of a Latin translation in North Africa is attested as far back as the *Acts of the Scillitan Martyrs,* dated 180.[1] So numerous had the Latin versions become by Augustine's time that he once complained that the situation had arisen because 'in the early days of the faith any person who got hold of a Greek manuscript and fancied that he had some ability in the two languages [sc. Latin and Greek] went ahead and translated it'.[2] Similarly Jerome once remarked that there were as many Latin versions as there were manuscripts.[3] It was in order to rectify this chaotic situation that Jerome undertook a revision of the Latin Bible at the request of Pope Damasus in 382. Although he began his revision of the Old Testament using the Greek Septuagint as his standard, within a few years he had become convinced that the Latin Old Testament must be translated directly from the original Hebrew. This conviction and the translations that were based upon it alarmed Augustine, who wrote to Jerome (*ep.* 28) requesting that he reconsider his project. Jerome, however, persisted in his epoch-making work, which was supplemented *c.*400–5 by the work of another translator, now thought to be Jerome's disciple Rufinus of Syria,[4] who concentrated on the letters of Paul and other books of the New Testament. Thus the 'Vulgate' came into being and gradually gained predominance over all other Latin versions. For Augustine and the Catholic Church in North Africa, however, the Old Latin version of the Old Testament remained the 'authorized version', as successive councils made plain.[5]

But what can be said specifically about the version of Paul's letters that

[1] Metzger, *Early Versions,* 289.

[2] *doctr. chr.* 2. 11. 16 (Green, text and trans., 72–3: 'Ut enim cuique primis fidei temporibus in manus venit codex graecus et aliquantum facultatis sibi utriusque linguae habere videbatur, ausus est interpretari').

[3] In the Preface to his translation of the Book of Joshua (PL 28: 463A: 'cum apud Latinos tot sint exemplaria, quot codices'). Some idea of the variety of Latin versions may be obtained by examining the evidence presented in the volumes of the *Vetus Latina* that have been published thus far by the Vetus Latina Institute.

[4] See De Bruyn, *Pelagius's Commentary,* 7.

[5] See e.g. Canon 36 of the Hippo Breviary (CCSL 149: 43), drafted at the Council of Hippo in 393 and ratified at the Council of Carthage in 397.

Augustine used in his *Commentary*? There is considerable scholarly agreement that Augustine's Old Latin version of Paul's letters was close to that reflected in the extant fragments of the Freising manuscript, so called for having once been in the possession of the monastery of Freising in Bavaria. This manuscript is in fact thought to have been originally copied in Spain, quite possibly as early as the sixth century, but the underlying tradition it reflects is North African. There is a critical edition of the Freising manuscript with detailed introduction in French by Donatien de Bruyne.[6] There is also a convenient three-column synopsis by Alexander Souter which sets out the Latin texts of Romans and Galatians as they appear in the Freising manuscript, in Augustine's commentaries on Paul from the mid-390s, and in the Vulgate respectively.[7] There it can be clearly seen that Augustine's readings are much closer to the Freising manuscript than they are to the Vulgate. The study of Augustine's Latin text of Galatians will be greatly facilitated when the critical edition of the Old Latin version of Galatians is published by the Vetus Latina Institute in Beuron, but that, unfortunately, will probably not be for some time.[8]

In the translation of Augustine's *Commentary*, wherever the abbreviation LXX appears after an Old Testament quotation, it means that the reading is peculiar to the Septuagint and differs significantly from the reading of the Vulgate. Where the abbreviation OL appears, it means that the reading is peculiar to the Old Latin Bible and has no exact parallel in either the Septuagint or the Vulgate.

---

[6] De Bruyne, *Les Fragments de Freising*, is listed in the Bibliography under 'Other Latin Texts'.

[7] Souter, *Earliest Latin Commentaries*, 149–80.

[8] We do, however, already have critical editions from Beuron for Ephesians, Philippians, Colossians, 1 and 2 Thessalonians, 1 and 2 Timothy, Titus, Philemon, and Hebrews. Ephesians–Colossians appear in *Vetus Latina* 24/1–2, ed. H. J. Frede (1962–71); 1 Thessalonians–Hebrews appear in *Vetus Latina* 25, pts. 1 and 2, ed. H. J. Frede (1975–91). Fascicles for the volumes on Romans and 1 Corinthians began to appear in the mid-1990s.

Appendix 3

THE HISTORICITY OF THE *CONFESSIONS*

Although I have already cited and endorsed J. J. O'Donnell's judicious remarks on the historicity of the *Confessions*,[1] it is only fair that I should offer my own views on this difficult and complex subject. To what extent is it legitimate to address what are essentially questions of historical fact to the *Confessions*? Certainly historical interrogation of the text is not easy: Augustine deliberately omits many names and dates that we would like to have, presents incidents out of chronological order and with a dramatic heightening of emotion, and generally appears more interested in symbolism and typology than in historical event as we understand it. Moreover, such past events as are included in the *Confessions* are narrated from the present perspective of Augustine the bishop, who is deliberately attempting to view them from the standpoint of the eternal. For reasons such as these a vast debate over the historical value of this text, focused principally on the scene in the garden at Milan, has persisted for more than a century, without attaining any definitive resolution.[2] But to impugn the historicity of the garden scene, the climax of the narrative of Books 1–8, is by implication to impugn the historicity of every other scene. Although the debate obviously cannot fully be entered into here, it must be engaged in to some extent in order to justify the use made above of the story of Victorinus' conversion as a historical source.[3]

On the one hand, it would be wildly anachronistic to suppose that Augustine set out to write Rankean scientific history *wie es eigentlich gewesen*, 'exactly as it happened'.[4] Yet the *Confessions* deviate not only from modern notions of historical narrative but from ancient ones as well. Indeed, because of their originality and complexity they resist classification of any kind.[5] Attempts have been made to illuminate the genre of the *Confessions* by interpreting its language and thought in exclusively Neoplatonic or Ciceronian or biblical categories, but the fact remains that in the text itself these categories have been fused into a profoundly unified whole, rendering the search for exact literary parallels highly problematic.

[1] See n. 22 in Ch. 2 of the Introduction.

[2] For a summary of the issues see Bonner, *St Augustine of Hippo*, 42–51, and A. Solignac, *Les Confessions*, BA 13: 55–84.

[3] See Introduction, 2. A, under 'Victorinus in Augustine's *Confessions*'. I would agree with O'Donnell's nuanced comments on the historicity of the garden scene in *Augustine: Confessions*, iii. 59–69, and much of what I have to say presupposes those comments.

[4] For this particular rendering of Ranke's famous phrase I am indebted to Tilley, *Bible*, 1.

[5] Cf. Conte, *Latin Literature*, 688–90.

Augustine himself described the work thus in his *Retractations*: 'The thirteen
books of my *Confessions* praise the just and good God for my evil and good acts, and
lift up the understanding and affection of men to Him.'[6] The first point to note is
the title itself, which (unusually in Augustine's works[7]) is deeply significant.
Moreover, Augustine's description suggests that the work contains elements
which are epideictic ('praise'), autobiographical ('my evil and good acts'), and
protreptic ('lift up etc.'). An additional element not explicitly referred to in his
statement is the form in which the work as a whole is cast: that of a long prayer,
modelled largely on the Psalms. No interpretation that ignores any one of these
elements can avoid being reductionistic, but provided this caution is borne in
mind, then the historical, autobiographical element—which is, after all, presented
as the basis for Augustine's praise of God and the grounds for others to praise God
also—ought to be amenable to critical examination.

We may begin by considering the title. For Augustine the term *confessio* has at
least two basic and interrelated meanings: confession of praise and confession of
sin.[8] As the quotation above suggests, it is the first of these meanings that
Augustine especially wishes to emphasize. But inasmuch as praise is subsumed
under the category of epideictic rhetoric in ancient theory, and as in practice
epideictic rhetoric condoned the fabrication of facts,[9] it has been argued that the
Confessions may be fictional.[10] Now on the one hand it must be admitted that as a
professional rhetor Augustine was guilty of such fabrication, and refers to a specific
instance of it in the *Confessions*.[11] On the other hand, as the author of the
Confessions he is acutely aware of the dangers of rhetoric and sharply critical of his
own rhetorical past.[12] But more to the point, he is conscious of the inherent danger
and difficulty of all religious language[13] and judges himself harshly for having
misrepresented God in the past, accusing himself of nothing less than idolatry.[14]
What Augustine says elsewhere points in the same direction: in a passage in *On
Lying*, written about two years before the *Confessions*, he absolutely condemns the

---

[6] *retr.* 2. 6 (32). 1 (Bogan, trans., 130 (CCSL 57: 94. 2–4: 'Confessionum mearum libri
tredecim et de malis et de bonis meis deum laudant iustum et bonum atque in eum excitant
humanum intellectum et affectum')).

[7] Cf. P. Brown, *Augustine of Hippo*, 175.

[8] A third is confession of faith. See O'Donnell, *Augustine: Confessions*, ii. 3–5, and
Bonner, *St Augustine of Hippo*, 48–51.

[9] See Burgess, *Epideictic Literature*, 116.

[10] Thus Boyle, 'A Likely Story', 24–8.

[11] *conf.* 6. 6. 9: 'How unhappy I was, and how conscious you made me of my misery, on
that day when I was preparing to deliver a panegyric on the emperor! In the course of it I
would tell numerous lies and for my mendacity would win the good opinion of people who
knew it to be untrue' (Chadwick, trans. (and so throughout), 97; CCSL 27: 79. 9–11:
'Quam ergo miser eram et quomodo egisti, ut sentirem miseriam meam die illo, quo, cum
pararem recitare imperatori laudes, quibus plura mentirer, et mentienti faueretur ab
scientibus').

[12] See *conf.* 1. 16. 25–18. 29, 3. 3. 6–4. 7, 4. 2. 2, and 6. 6. 9.

[13] That consciousness is eloquently expressed in the proem (*conf.* 1. 1. 1–5. 6).

[14] *conf.* 7. 14. 20. The same accusation is brought against others in 5. 3. 5 and 7. 9. 15.

idea that an untruth could be justified on the grounds that it had been told in order to praise God.[15]

With regard to the second meaning of *confessio*, 'confession of sin', it is notable that penance was essentially linked to baptism and the Eucharist and deemed necessary for salvation.[16] In offering his own story as an exhortation to penitence and confession,[17] therefore, Augustine the bishop is consciously involving himself in the salvation of others. Moreover, penance was the subject of ecclesiastical debate and legislation in Africa at this time,[18] and few can have taken such things more seriously and scrupulously than Augustine. Such considerations militate strongly against the interpretation of Augustine's *Confessions* as a fictional as opposed to a stylized but trustworthy representation, at least in so far as they recount past and present sins.

So from the outset Augustine is concerned to be truthful. Precisely because 'confession' has been sanctioned by God in both liturgy and Scripture, it offers Augustine hope of being able to speak to God and to others about God with some measure of authenticity. In particular the voice of the Psalmist provides him with a model of authenticity. The ability to speak to God and of God is an inestimable gift and at the same time an immense responsibility. As Augustine says elsewhere of the Psalms: when we sing the Psalms, the words are indeed ours, but they are even more the words of God.[19] Confession is in fact a grace that empowers faith to self-expression and thereby to self-understanding.

The grace of God is entirely unmerited,[20] as Augustine had understood from St Paul's saying, *What have you that you did not receive?* (1 Cor. 4: 7);[21] in fact, insight into the meaning of this verse *c*.397 had revolutionized his understanding of grace.[22] But if the theology is such, then the idea that the incidents recorded are purely and deliberately the product of Augustine's unfettered imagination is seriously undermined. Augustine insists that it is God who took the gracious initiative in his life; all the initiatives he himself had ever taken were abortive until

[15] *mend.* 12. 20–13. 21 (CSEL 41: 439–40), arguing from Exod. 20: 16 and 1 Cor. 15: 15. (A similar argument is used at *ep.* 28. 3. 4.) At *mend.* 21. 42 (CSEL 41: 463–5) he condemns the idea of lying even for the sake of another's eternal salvation.

[16] Cf. *ench.* 17. 65: 'For outside the Church there is no remission of sins. She received as her very own the pledge of the Holy Spirit, without whom no sin whatever is remitted, so that those to whom sins are remitted receive life everlasting' (Arand, trans., 66; CCSL 46: 84. 38–41: 'Extra [ecclesiam] quippe [peccata] non remittuntur: ipsa namque proprie spiritum sanctum pignus accepit, sine quo non remittuntur ulla peccata ita ut quibus remittuntur uitam consequantur aeternam').

[17] Cf. e.g. *conf.* 10. 3. 4, 11. 1. 1. Augustine also asks for prayers for his parents and himself on the basis of what he has narrated (9. 13. 37, 10. 4. 5).

[18] See e.g. Canon 30 of the Hippo Breviary (CCSL 149: 41. 170–42. 177). Augustine would have been present when that canon was originally drafted at the Council of Hippo in 393 and again when it was formally ratified at the Council of Carthage in 397.

[19] *en. Ps.* 26. en. 2. 1 (CCSL 38: 154. 4–7).

[20] It was, of course, a variation on this theme that so angered Pelagius. Cf. *perseu.* 20. 53.

[21] Echoed at *conf.* 1. 4. 4, 7. 21. 27, and 13. 14. 15.

[22] Commenting on *Simpl.* at *retr.* 2. 1. 1. (Quoted at *praed. sanct.* 4. 8.)

God's transforming grace intervened and redeemed them.[23] Augustine's conception of his writing must therefore be sharply distinguished from any Romantic notion of the artist as godlike creator.

Moreover, God's grace is portrayed as surprising, improbable, paradoxical, so that Augustine's conversion appears less a direct, linear progression than a long, circuitous odyssey.[24] In the words of another of his favourite texts from Paul: *How unsearchable are his judgements and how inscrutable his ways!* (Rom. 11: 33).[25] God's ways are not our ways; in fact, they subvert our ways. Such a view of divine providence undermines the notion that the historical element of the *Confessions* is a deliberate, fictional construct, a view further undermined by the very tone of the text, especially the wonder and awe at God's mysterious providence, and the gratitude and love for the deliverance it has accomplished. The fact that Augustine finds profound symbolic meaning in incidents, some of which seem trivial to the reader, is in harmony with this view, for the things that Augustine initially misinterpreted or failed even to notice must take on new meaning once Augustine has accepted that his life has all along been directed—even predestined—by an overarching providence.

But what if Augustine's conception of truth is transhistorical? What if he is thinking not of 'what Alcibiades did and suffered', but rather of Jesus Christ, 'the Way, the Truth, and the Life' (John 14: 6)?[26] Such an objection is accurate but misleading, for Augustine is at pains to emphasize that the eternal Truth was revealed and embodied in a historical Person, sent by God the Father 'so that from his example [humanity] should learn humility'.[27] Moreover, the confession of this sending in terms of John 1: 14 (*the Word was made flesh*) occurs at one of the great climaxes of the work: Augustine's confession that although Neoplatonism knew the Truth, it did not and indeed could not know the Truth Incarnate.[28]

---

[23] Cf. e.g. *conf.* 4. 1. 1: 'Without you, what am I to myself but a guide to my own self-destruction?' (trans., 52; CCSL 27: 40. 17: 'Quid enim sum ego mihi sine te nisi dux in praeceps?'). Cf. also his reflection on the *conf.* in *ep.* 231. 6: 'For *He made us, and not we ourselves* (Ps. 99 (100): 3); indeed, we had destroyed ourselves, but He who made us has made us anew' (Cunningham, trans., 584 (modified); CSEL 57: 509. 4–6: 'Quoniam *ipse fecit nos et non ipsi nos*; nos autem perdideramus nos, sed, qui fecit, refecit').

[24] With allusions to Virgil, Plotinus, and above all the parable of the Prodigal Son. Cf. 1. 18. 28. (Note also the use of the word *circuitus* in *conf.* 4. 1. 1, 6. 6. 9, and 8. 2. 3.)

[25] Echoed in *conf.* 4. 4. 8 (CCSL 27: 43. 19).

[26] Thus Ferrari, 'Truth and Augustine's Conversion Scene', 12, infers from various passages in the *conf.* that Augustine was thinking in terms of 'an interiorized mystical mode of truth far removed from the empirically verifiable kind called for by the debate about the conversion scene'.

[27] *conf.* 10. 43. 68 (trans., 219; CCSL 27: 192. 2–3: 'ut eius exemplo etiam ipsam discerent humilitatem'). Cf. 10. 4. 6: 'You have commanded me to serve them if I wish to live with you and in dependence on you. This your word would have meant little to me if it had been only a spoken precept and had not first been acted out' [i.e. 'by Jesus Christ'] (trans., 182 and n. 3; CCSL 27: 157. 27–9): '. . . quibus iussisti ut seruiam, si uolo tecum de te uiuere. Et hoc mihi uerbum tuum parum erat si loquendo praeciperet, nisi et faciendo praeiret').

[28] *conf.* 7. 9. 13–14; cf. 7. 18. 24–19. 25.

This incarnational theology permeates Augustine's understanding of Sacred Scripture, for the Word made flesh is the logical antecedent and archetype of the scriptural Word.[29] Now to the extent that the *Confessions* are cast in a biblical form, it suggests that Augustine intended them to be read analogously, that is, as both history and symbolism.[30] If so, his comments on biblical interpretation may provide a key to the interpretation of the *Confessions*:

But first and above all, brothers, I must in the name of the Lord to the best of my ability both urge upon you and insist upon one thing: when you hear the hidden meaning explained of a story in scripture that tells of things that happened, you must first believe that what has been read to you actually happened as read, or else the foundation of an actual event will be removed, and you will be trying to build castles in the air.[31]

The concreteness of Augustine's understanding of God's self-revelation in history is paralleled by a similar concreteness in his understanding of moral experience. Characteristic is his emphasis upon the force of habit (*consuetudo*) leading to slavery to sin.[32] According to his analysis, the pleasure associated with specific, sinful acts is recalled and enhanced by memory, provoking repetition; repetition in turn strengthens the memory, accentuates its provocative power, and leads the sinner to experience increasing difficulty in resisting temptation. Those who fail to conquer temptation are eventually conquered by it. Such an analysis gives extraordinary depth and seriousness to Augustine's view of his own and others' past. As Peter Brown has noted, for Augustine individuals 'were different from each other precisely because their wills were made different by the sum total of unique, past experiences'.[33]

This consideration in turn helps to explain the extreme care with which Augustine searches his memory in selecting incidents for inclusion in his

---

[29] Cf. e.g. *cons. eu.* 1. 35. 54, *c. Faust.* 12. 7. See further Polman, *The Word of God According to St. Augustine (passim)*.

[30] Cf. Chadwick, 'History and Symbolism in the Garden at Milan', 44–5, and Mohrmann, 'The *Confessions* as a Literary Work of Art', 378. The latter writes: 'This idea of a two-fold significance which Augustine always seeks in the Scriptures, now influences too the account of his own spiritual development, which he consciously clothed in Biblical form. Here too he takes the literal meaning as his point of departure, i.e. he describes the facts as he remembers them after so many years. But he always sees in and behind these facts a spiritual significance, a symbol. For us it is difficult to understand such a mentality, hovering between reality and symbol, but for Augustine and his contemporaries, accustomed to the methods of the Alexandrian exegetists, this attitude towards the facts was by no means uncommon. The "factum" contains one might say, the "mysterium", but—and here I tend to disagree with Courcelle—the "factum" is primary in its concrete sobriety.'

[31] *s.* 2. 7 (Hill, trans., i. 179; CCSL 41: 14. 169–74: 'Ante omnia tamen, fratres, hoc in nomine domini et admonemus quantum possumus, et praecipimus, ut quando auditis exponi sacramentum scripturae narrantis quae gesta sunt, prius illud quod lectum est credatis sic gestum, quomodo lectum est, ne subtracto fundamento rei gestae, quasi in aere quaeratis aedificare'). Cited by Mohrmann, 'The *Confessions* as a Literary Work of Art', 378. Cf. Marrou, *Saint Augustin et la fin de la culture antique*, 493.

[32] Famously described at *conf.* 8. 5. 10–12.

[33] *Augustine of Hippo*, 173–4, with a further reference to *diu. qu.* 40.

narrative.[34] Acknowledging that he is being selective,[35] he distinguishes between the occurrence and his attitude towards it—occasionally even between his present attitude and his attitude at the time.[36] He searches his memory arduously and even when he has found something that seems suitable the possibility remains that it may be false, and he implies that such falseness is sin.[37] His anxiety thus goes beyond that of a writer seeking the fittest artistic expression.[38] That is not to say that Augustine is incapable of self-deception. On the contrary, he is capable and acknowledges it.[39] But he is also extremely attentive to the possibility and prays to be delivered from it.[40] It is important to recall that the *Confessions* express not self-assurance, but the very opposite: the awareness that the self is wholly unreliable except in so far as it is truly grounded in God, and that this grounding can never be taken for granted.[41]

One stimulus to writing at least part of the *Confessions* was probably Paulinus of Nola's request for facts concerning the life of Alypius.[42] This would help to explain the 'biography of Alypius' in Book 6.[43] It is notable that here Augustine appears to have combined factual content with striking literary form,[44] suggesting that he may have done so elsewhere as well. Moreover, while the passage concerning Alypius at the gladiatorial spectacles clearly serves didactic purposes, it can hardly have been fabricated out of whole cloth, since it must have imperilled Alypius' current reputation as a bishop and judge.[45] The story's inclusion makes sense only if Alypius and Augustine shared the same understanding of confession as a divinely ordained

[34] On this topic see O'Meara, *The Young Augustine*, 5–7.

[35] e.g. *conf.* 10. 8. 12, 10. 40. 65.

[36] e.g. ibid. 3. 5. 9, 3. 12. 21.

[37] e.g. ibid. 11. 2. 3.

[38] Some of that anxiety still lingers in his remarks on *conf.* 4. 6. 11 in *retr.* 2. 6 (32). 2, where he accuses himself of having used hollow rhetoric at one point. Although the *retr.* are by no means free from *Tendenzen* and hence must be approached cautiously, it is nevertheless remarkable that Augustine does not criticize any other passage in the *conf.* in this way. That the *conf.* as a whole are not hollow rhetoric is also implied at *ep.* 231. 6 (and cf. Possidius, *Vita*, pr.). On *Tendenzen* in the *retr.* see J. Burnaby, 'The *Retractationes* of St. Augustine', and R. J. O'Connell, *The Origin of the Soul*, 321–35.

[39] e.g. *conf.* 10. 32. 48: 'That is how I see myself, but perhaps I am deceived' (trans., 207; CCSL 27: 181. 2: 'Ita mihi uideor; forsitan fallar'). See also 1. 5. 6, 10. 5. 7, 10. 41. 66.

[40] e.g. *conf.* 11. 2. 3.

[41] Cf. *conf.* 10. 40. 65: 'But in all these investigations which I pursue while consulting you, I can find no safe place for my soul except in you' (trans., 218; CCSL 27: 191. 18–20: 'Neque in his omnibus, quae percurro consulens te, inuenio tutum locum animae meae nisi in te'). The temptations associated with episcopal authority and prestige have only added to his peril (cf. 10. 36. 59).

[42] *ep.* 24. 4 and 27. 5 (CSEL 34: 76 and 100–1). The term used by Paulinus and repeated by Augustine is *historia*.

[43] *conf.* 6. 7. 11–10. 16.

[44] On the artistry of *conf.* 6. 8. 13 in particular, see Auerbach, *Mimesis*, 66–72.

[45] Certainly a similar story of youthful addiction, that of Monica to wine (*conf.* 9. 8. 18), was later used by Julian of Eclanum in a way that Augustine found deeply offensive. See *c. Iul. imp.* 1. 68 (specifically, CSEL 85. 1: 73. 7–9 (Julian's insult) and 74. 39–45 (Augustine's response)).

remedy for pride. This understanding is also necessary to account for Augustine's inclusion of so much damning evidence about his own life as a Manichee, which could be turned against him by malevolent adversaries.[46]

To try to anticipate the hermeneutics of suspicion any further would be possible but not, I think, profitable. Ultimately each reader must decide for himself or herself what degree of historical reliability to place in the *Confessions*.[47] My own conclusions are: none of the reasons I have given is compelling in and of itself. In combination, however, they carry considerable weight, for most of them are not isolated and exceptional points on the periphery of the author's interests, but ones central to his theological agenda. Moreover, their interconnections are reinforcing, so that their cumulative effect is multiplied. The combination thus establishes a high degree of probability that the *Confessions* may be approached as a source of historical facts concerning Augustine's life and shifts the burden of proof onto anyone who would wish to propose that the *Confessions* are essentially a fictional construct.[48]

[46] Cf. e.g. *c. litt. Pet.* 3. 16. 19; *Cresc.* 3. 80. 92; *c. Iul. imp.* 1. 25. Not to mention that Augustine knew some of his confessions left him open to mockery (see e.g. *conf.* 4. 1. 1; 5. 10. 20), a thing to which he was always keenly sensitive.

[47] Augustine was well aware of this and asks for love, which alone, he says, can recognize the sincerity of his voice. Cf. *conf.* 10. 3. 4–4. 5: 'The love which makes them good people tells them that I am not lying in confessing about myself, and the love in them believes me. . . . To such sympathetic readers I will indeed reveal myself' (trans., 181; CCSL 27: 157. 34–5, 3–4: 'Dicit enim eis caritas, qua boni sunt, non mentiri me de me confitentem, et ipsa in eis credit mihi. . . . Indicabo me talibus'). See also his response to Secundinus, an early reader of the *Confessions* who called in question his motives for leaving the Manichees: 'You are passing judgement on things hidden in my mind, which I obviously cannot place before your eyes and show you. . . . I can say nothing more about my mind unless you believe me; if you are unwilling, I don't know what I can do' (*c. Sec.* 1–2; CSEL 25. 2: 906. 7–8 and 907. 17–18: 'Latebras animi mei arguis, quas utique promere ad oculos tuos et demonstrare non possum. . . . De animo meo nihil amplius possum dicere, nisi ut credas mihi; quod si nolueris, non inuenio, quod faciam' (quoted by Courcelle, *Recherches*, 238 n. 7)).

[48] Of course, this is not to say that critical caution is unnecessary or that external corroboration of the narrative is unimportant.

Appendix 4

AUGUSTINE'S CONCERN WITH DONATISM IN THE
YEARS IMMEDIATELY PRECEDING AND FOLLOWING
THE *COMMENTARY ON GALATIANS*

The documentary evidence of Augustine's concern with Donatism in the years immediately preceding and following the composition of the *Commentary on Galatians*, that is, during his presbyterate and shortly thereafter,[1] is considerable, even though it is not nearly so well known as the evidence of his concern with Manicheism. In 392 he wrote a long, earnest letter (*ep.* 23) in his most diplomatic style to Maximinus, Donatist bishop of Sinitum in the diocese of Hippo, on the subject of rebaptism. The seriousness of his concern with the schism is evident from the way he speaks of what it would mean for Maximinus to help heal it:

If by your moderation, and prudence, and the love which we owe to Him who shed His blood for us, this great scandal, this great triumph of the Devil, this great destruction of souls were removed from our midst in these regions, who could describe in words the palm prepared for you by the Lord, because you originated a remedy worthy of imitation for the healing of all the members which lie wretchedly wasted with disease throughout all Africa?[2]

In the year following we find Augustine's concern over the schism shown in another way in his address on *Faith and the Creed* to the Catholic bishops assembled at the Council of Hippo.[3] In his discussion of the credal article on the Holy Church he did not fail to attack the schismatics.[4] A similar attack appears in

---

[1] His priesthood extended from 391 to 395/6. I have included writings from 396 in assessing the extent to which Donatism was a preoccupation for Augustine at the time *exp. Gal.* was composed. What Frend (*The Donatist Church*, 237 n. 1) has called 'the first sure reference to Donatism' in Augustine's writings occurs in *ep.* 20, written *c.*390 before he became a priest. See esp. *ep.* 20. 3: 'Certainly, no one who is properly concerned over the state of his own soul, and humbly desirous of seeking the will of the Lord, will fail to distinguish the one Catholic faith from any kind of schism, especially if he has the help of a good teacher' (Parsons, trans., 47 (CSEL 34. 1: 49. 1–5: 'nemo enim fere sollicitus de statu animae suae atque ob hoc sine pertinacia inquirendae uoluntatis domini intentus est, qui bono demonstratore usus non dinoscat, quid inter schisma quodlibet atque unam catholicam intersit').

[2] *ep.* 23. 5 (Parsons, trans., 63; CSEL 34. 1: 69. 21–70. 5).

[3] See *retr.* 1. 17 (16). The Council met on 8 October 393 (CCSL 149: 20).

[4] For his discussion of the schismatics see *f. et symb.* 10. 21. That Augustine is thinking principally of the Donatists is evident from a comparison of his language here and in the almost exactly contemporaneous *ps. c. Don.*

his exposition of the Sermon on the Mount (*s. dom. m.* 1. 5. 13), which he was in the process of writing at this time. Towards the end of 393 or the beginning of 394 he composed his first anti-Donatist work, the *Psalm against the Donatists*. He used the form of an alphabetical psalm[5] in order 'to familiarize the most lowly people, and especially the ignorant and uneducated, with the cause of the Donatists and to impress it on their memory',[6] in other words, to counter Donatist propaganda.[7] Although it deals with substantive issues, principally the unity, catholicity, and authority of the Church, the work has suffered comparative neglect from scholars, perhaps because they are embarrassed to see 'the delicate-minded author of the *Soliloquies* . . . descend to the doggerel of a music-hall ditty'.[8]

At about the same time, Augustine wrote a polemical treatise *Against a Letter of the Heretic Donatus* to refute the claim of Donatus the Great that true baptism was to be found only in the Donatist Church.[9] Meanwhile, his letter-writing campaign continued. In 395 or 396 he wrote to Proculeianus, the Donatist bishop of Hippo, again earnestly seeking the reconciliation of the two churches. The pastoral difficulties the schism was creating are vividly portrayed: 'Husbands and wives agree about their bed and disagree about the altar of Christ. . . . Sons share one home with their parents, but they do not share the same house of God.'[10] As in Letter 23 to Maximinus, Augustine desires above all dialogue, whether by personal conversation, a more formal conference, or any other means.[11] Unable to obtain satisfaction from Proculeianus, however, he proceeded to write to that man's superior, the Donatist bishop Eusebius, reiterating his desire to confer and iron out differences (*ep.* 34). That too seems to have been unavailing, and later in 396 he wrote again to Eusebius, complaining now in tones of growing exasperation (*ep.* 35). It would appear that the Donatists wanted to avoid having to deal with Augustine.

Also about 396 he composed *On the Christian Struggle*, an explanation of the rule of faith and of the Christian life written in a plain style for the unlearned.[12] In explaining the catholicity of the Church, Augustine contrasts the false teaching of the Donatists, which is already condemned in Scripture.[13]

Finally, throughout this period Augustine spoke out against the Donatists in his

[5] The first letter of the first line of each strophe is in alphabetical order. For analysis of the form of *ps. c. Don.* see Bonner, *St Augustine of Hippo*, 253–7, and the references given there.

[6] *retr.* 1. 20 (19), Bogan, trans., 86 (CCSL 57: 61. 2–4: 'Volens etiam causam Donatistarum ad ipsius humillimi uulgi et omnino imperitorum atque idiotarum notitiam peruenire, et eorum quantum fieri per nos posset inhaerere memoriae').

[7] Popular psalms had already been composed by the Donatists, most notably by Parmenian, bishop of Carthage (see Frend, *The Donatist Church*, 193–4).

[8] Van der Meer, *Augustine the Bishop*, 105.

[9] *retr.* 1. 21 (20). 1. It would appear from Augustine's remarks that he also discussed the primacy of Peter in this treatise, which is no longer extant.

[10] *ep.* 33. 5 (Parsons, trans., 129 (CSEL 34. 2: 21. 23–4 and 22. 2–3)).

[11] See esp. *ep.* 33. 4. Cf. *ep.* 23. 2, 6–7.

[12] *retr.* 2. 3 (29) (see esp. CCSL 57: 91. 1–3).

[13] *agon.* 29. 31.

sermons[14] and his *Expositions of the Psalms*.[15] It is clear that Augustine regarded himself as being in the midst of a campaign to bring the Donatist schism to an end. He thought continually of the account he would have to give on the Day of Judgement.[16] Despite the fact that his first major work against the Donatists, *Against the Letter of Parmenianus*, was not written until 400, Augustine's personal engagement in the Donatist controversy should be regarded as beginning not then but much earlier, with his ordination to the priesthood in 391 and his acceptance of the pastoral responsibilities that went with it.

To the evidence of Augustine's own writings we may add that of two contemporaries. Possidius, who shared the monastic life with Augustine at this time, records that as a priest Augustine opposed Donatism in books and sermons and as a newly ordained bishop he was so concerned with Donatism that he laboured continually to bring the schism to an end.[17] Augustine's reputation grew rapidly, even spreading overseas.[18] Thus Paulinus of Nola, writing in 396 to Romanianus in Rome, extols Augustine as the man destined by God to crush both Donatists and Manichees.[19] Donatist bishops were reluctant to debate with him or even to answer his letters.[20] So even at this point Augustine was regarded as a formidable adversary.[21]

When we add to the foregoing evidence an examination of the historical context from which it emerged, our view is corroborated. Frend has remarked that 'it was in [the] ten years between 388 and 398 that Donatism came nearest to achieving complete mastery in Africa'.[22] At Hippo itself and in the surrounding countryside the Donatists predominated,[23] reducing the Catholics to the status of a 'harassed minority'.[24] In this same period, however, the possibility of effecting real change was presented to the Catholics with the death *c*.391 of Parmenianus, Donatist bishop of Carthage since 363 and a powerful opponent of the Catholic Church. When he was succeeded by the tyrannical Primianus, crisis and division ensued within the Donatist Church. At almost exactly the same time, the Catholics had a momentous change for the better in their leadership, when the ineffectual Genethlius was succeeded in the see of Carthage by Aurelius, who was to prove a

[14] *ss.* 252. 4–6, 273. 2, and those Augustine refers to in *ep.* 29.

[15] *en. Ps.* 10; 21 serm. 2; 25 serm. 2. 6; 35. 9; 54. 26. For the dates of these *enarrationes* see CCSL 38: p. xv.

[16] e.g. *ep.* 23. 6: 'I am considering how I shall give an account to the Prince of all shepherds of the sheep entrusted to me' (Parsons, trans., 64 (CSEL 34. 1: 70. 18–19)). Cf. *ep.* 43. 1. 2.

[17] *Vita* 7. 1 and 9. 2.

[18] *Vita* 7. 4.

[19] Augustine, *ep.* 32. 2 (= Paulinus, *ep.* 7. 2).

[20] Possidius, *Vita* 9. 4. Cf. Augustine, *epp.* 34. 5–6 and 35. 1. (Eventually debates *were* held. See Augustine, *epp.* 43 and 44.)

[21] Monceaux, *Histoire littéraire*, vii. 13.

[22] Frend, *The Donatist Church*, 210.

[23] Augustine himself mentions how a generation earlier the Donatists had adopted a particular policy at Hippo 'because of the paucity of Catholics there' (*c. litt. Pet.* 2. 83. 184 (CSEL 52: 114. 14: 'quoniam catholicorum ibi paucitas erat')).

[24] Brown, *Augustine of Hippo*, 139.

gifted Church leader and organizer. The possibility of winning Donatists back into the Catholic fold appeared better than ever. It is not surprising therefore to find in the ecclesiastical legislation emerging from the Council of Hippo clear evidence that the Donatists were in mind, as Willis notes:

Some of the abridged canons of this council, contained in the *Codex Canonum Ecclesiae Africanae*, appear to have reference to Donatism. Thus Canon 12 of these prohibits the marriage of sons of bishops and clergy with heathens, heretics and schismatics; Canon 14 says that bishops and clergy shall not choose for their heirs those who are not Catholic Christians, even though they may be relatives; Canon 17 that no man may be ordained bishop, priest or deacon who has not first made all his household Catholic Christians; and by Canon 29 bishops and clergy are forbidden to have meals in church, except when necessary for the refreshment of guests, and then none of the laity shall be admitted. The last canon seems to have in mind the possible imitation of the riotous feasts of the Donatists. . . . Canon 37 reaffirms the old rule of the Councils, that no Donatist clerics shall be received into the Church except into lay communion, unless they can show that they have never practised rebaptism, or that they wish to come over with their whole congregation. Men baptized in infancy by the Donatists are not thereby to be deprived of the privilege of Catholic ordination.[25]

This Council is of great historical importance in itself and as the first in a long series of councils[26] under the presidency of Aurelius, bishop of Carthage and primate of Africa, who together with Augustine would play a leading role in the struggle against the Donatists.

Thus Donatism was very much on Augustine's mind during this period, even though he appears not to have written any major treatise on the subject at the time. Yet the pastoral mission Augustine undertook with regard to the Donatists—to heal the schism for the sake of Mother Church—was never merely a matter of theological treatises, but embraced and permeated the whole of his life as an ordained minister.[27]

[25] Willis, *Saint Augustine and the Donatist Controversy*, 30–1. Willis's interpretation is accepted by Bonner, *St Augustine of Hippo*, 115 n. 5. For the Latin text of the Hippo Breviary see the edition of C. Munier in CCSL 149: 22–53.

[26] Extending from 393 to 424.

[27] Cf. Baus: 'For an understanding of Augustine it is crucial to know that the central motive for his personal involvement in [the Donatist] question was the pastoral mission, perceived as a sublime responsibility, to guard those confided to him in the Church and to win back the others for the Church and the truth proclaimed by it' (Jedin and Dolan (eds.), *History of the Church*, ii. 148).

Bibliography

AUGUSTINE'S *COMMENTARY ON GALATIANS*

Latin:

AUGUSTINUS, SANCTUS AURELIUS, *Opera, Sect. IV, Pars I: Expositio Quarundam Propositionum ex Epistola ad Romanos; Epistolae ad Galatas Expositionis Liber Unus; Epistolae ad Romanos Inchoata Expositio*, ed. Johannes Divjak, CSEL 84 (Vienna: Hoelder-Pichler-Tempsky, 1971).

(For other printed editions of the Latin text, see Appendix 1 above.)

French:

PÉRONNE *et al.*, *Œuvres Complètes de Saint Augustin évêque d'Hippone*, xi (Paris: Librairie de Louis Vivès, 1871).

Italian:

IODICE, SALVATORE, *Legge e grazia in S. Agostino* (Naples: Associazione di Studi Tardoantichi, 1977).

TARULLI, VINCENZO, *Opere di Sant'Agostino: Opere esegetiche II*, NBA 10/2 (Rome: Città Nuova, 1997).

Spanish:

Obras de San Agustín, xviii, ed. Balbino Martin Pérez (Biblioteca de Autores Cristianos) (Madrid: La Editorial Católica, 1959).

OTHER LATIN TEXTS

AMBROSIASTER, *Ambrosiastri qui dicitur Commentarius in Epistulas Paulinas, Pars Tertia: In epistulas ad Galatas, etc.*, ed. H. I. Vogels, CSEL 81. 3 (Vienna: Hoelder-Pichler-Tempsky, 1969).

AUGUSTINUS, SANCTUS AURELIUS, 'Sermons inédits de saint Augustin prêchés en 397 (2ème série)', ed. F. Dolbeau, *Revue Bénédictine*, 102 (1992), 44–74.

CICERO, MARCUS TULLIUS, *Tusculanae Disputationes*, ed. M. Pohlenz (Stuttgart: Teubner, 1982 (repr. of 1918 edn.)).

DE BRUYNE, DONATIEN (ed.), *Les Fragments de Freising (épîtres de S. Paul et épîtres catholiques)*, Collectanea Biblica Latina, 5 (Rome: Bibliothèque Vaticane, 1921).

DONATUS, AEL., 'Epistula: Ael. Donatus L. Munatio Suo Salutem', in *Vitae Vergilianae Antiquae*, ed. C. Hardie (Oxford: Clarendon Press, 1957), 1.

FREDE, HERMANN JOSEF, *Ein neuer Paulustext und Kommentar*, i. *Untersuchungen*; ii. *Die Texte*, Vetus Latina: Die Reste der altlateinischen Bibel, Aus der Geschichte der lateinischen Bibel, 7–8 (Freiburg: Herder, 1973–4).

GELLIUS, AULUS, *Noctes Atticae*, ed. P. K. Marshall, Oxford Classical Texts (Oxford: Clarendon Press, 1968; rev. edn. 1990).

GREEN, R. P. H.: see under 'English Translations'.

HIERONYMUS, SANCTUS EUSEBIUS, *Commentarii in quattuor Epistolas S. Pauli: ad Galatas, ad Ephesios, ad Titum, ad Philemonem*, ed. J.-P. Migne, PL 26 (Paris, 1845), 307–618.

——*Gli Uomini Illustri/De viris illustribus*, ed. Aldo Ceresa-Gastaldo, BP 12 (Florence: Nardini, 1988).

JEROME: see under Hieronymus, Sanctus Eusebius.

LOWE, E. A., *Codices Latini Antiquiores*, pt. I (Oxford: Clarendon Press, 1934).

PELAGIUS, *Pelagius's Expositions of Thirteen Epistles of St Paul*, ii. *Text*, ed. Alexander Souter, Texts and Studies, 9 (Cambridge: Cambridge University Press, 1926).

POSSIDIUS, *Operum S. Augustini Elenchus*, ed. A. Wilmart, in *Miscellanea Agostiniana* (Rome: Tipografia Poliglotta Vaticana, 1930–1), ii. 149–233.

——*Vita Augustini*, ed. A. A. R. Bastiaensen, in Christine Mohrmann (ed.), *Vite dei Santi*, iii. *Vita di Cipriano, Vita di Ambrogio, Vita di Agostino* (Milan: Arnoldo Mondadori, 1975).

SABATIER, PIERRE, *et al.* (eds.), *Bibliorum Sacrorum Latinae versiones antiquae: seu vetus Italica, et caeterae quaecunque in codicibus mss. & antiquorum libris reperiri potuerunt: quae cum Vulgata Latina, & cum textu Graeco comparantur. Accedunt praefationes, observationes, ac notae, indexque novus ad Vulgatam e regione editam, idemque locupletissimus / opera & studio d. Petri Sabatier* (Turnhout: Brepols, 1981).

VICTORINUS, MARIUS, *Marii Victorini Opera, Pars 2: Opera Exegetica*, ed. Franco Gori, CSEL 83. 2 (Vienna: Hoelder-Pichler-Tempsky, 1986).

ENGLISH TRANSLATIONS

ARAND, LOUIS A., *St. Augustine: Faith, Hope, and Charity*, ACW 3 (Westminster, Md.: The Newman Bookshop, 1947).

BAXTER, JAMES HOUSTON, *St. Augustine: Select Letters*, Loeb Classical Library (New York: G. P. Putnam's Sons, 1930).

BETTENSON, HENRY, *Augustine: City of God* (London: Penguin, 1972).

BEYENKA, MARY MELCHIOR, *Saint Ambrose: Letters*, FC 26 (Washington, DC: Catholic University of America Press, 1967).

BOGAN, MARY INEZ, *Saint Augustine: The Retractations*, FC 60 (Washington, DC: Catholic University of America Press, 1968).

BURLEIGH, JOHN H. S., *Augustine: Earlier Writings*, LCC 6 (Philadelphia:

Westminster Press, 1953).

CHADWICK, HENRY, *Saint Augustine: Confessions* (Oxford: Oxford University Press, 1991).

CUNNINGHAM, J. C., *Letters of St. Augustin*, NPNF, 1st ser., 1 (Buffalo: Christian Literature Co., 1886), 209–593.

DE BRUYN, THEODORE S., *Pelagius' Commentary on St Paul's Epistle to the Romans*, Oxford Early Christian Studies (Oxford: Clarendon Press, 1993).

EDWARDS, MARK, *Optatus: Against the Donatists* (Liverpool: Liverpool University Press, 1997).

FREMANTLE, W. H., *et al.*, *St. Jerome: Letters and Select Works*, NPNF, 2nd ser., 6 (Grand Rapids: Eerdmans, n.d.).

GALLAGHER, DONALD A., and GALLAGHER, IDELLA J., *Saint Augustine: The Catholic and Manichaean Ways of Life*, FC 56 (Washington, DC: Catholic University of America Press, 1966).

GREEN, R. P. H. (ed. and trans.), *Augustine: De Doctrina Christiana*, Oxford Early Christian Texts (Oxford: Clarendon Press, 1995).

HILL, EDMUND, *Sermons*, WSA, 3/1–11 (Brooklyn, NY: New City Press, 1990–7).

—— *The Trinity*, WSA, 1/5 (New Rochelle, NY: New City Press, 1995).

HOARE, F. R., *The Life of St. Augustine*, by St. Possidius, Bishop of Calama, in F. R. Hoare (ed.), *The Western Fathers* (New York: Sheed & Ward, 1954), 189–244.

HRITZU, JOHN N., *Saint Jerome: Dogmatic and Polemical Works*, FC 53 (Washington, DC: Catholic University of America Press, 1965).

JEPSON, JOHN J., *St. Augustine: The Lord's Sermon on the Mount*, ACW 5 (Westminster, Md.: Newman Press, 1948).

LANDES, PAULA FREDRIKSEN, *Augustine on Romans: Propositions from the Epistle to the Romans, Unfinished Commentary on the Epistle to the Romans*, Society of Biblical Literature Texts and Translations 23, Early Christian Literature Series 6 (Chico, Calif.: Scholars Press, 1982).

LAWLESS, GEORGE: see under 'Secondary Literature'.

LEINENWEBER, JOHN, *Letters of Saint Augustine* (Liguori, Mo.: Triumph Books, 1992).

MOSHER, DAVID L., *Saint Augustine: Eighty-three Different Questions*, FC 70 (Washington, DC: Catholic University of America Press, 1982).

MULDOWNEY, MARY SARAH, 'Lying', in Roy J. Deferrari (ed.), *Saint Augustine: Treatises on Various Subjects*, FC 16 (New York: Fathers of the Church, 1952), 45–110.

PARSONS, SISTER WILFRID, *Saint Augustine: Letters*, i. *1–82*, FC 12 (New York: Fathers of the Church, 1951).

RUSSELL, ROBERT P., *Divine Providence and the Problem of Evil* (New York: Cosmopolitan Science and Art Service Co., 1942).

STOTHERT, R., *St. Augustin: Reply to Faustus the Manichaean*, NPNF, 1st ser., 4 (Grand Rapids: Eerdmans, 1989), 151–345.

TAYLOR, JOHN HAMMOND, *St. Augustine: The Literal Meaning of Genesis*, ACW

41–2 (New York: Newman Press, 1982).

TESKE, ROLAND J., *Answer to Julian* and *Answer to the Two Letters of the Pelagians*, WSA, 1/24 (Hyde Park, NY: New City Press, 1998).

—— *The Deeds of Pelagius*, WSA, 1/23 (Hyde Park, NY: New City Press, 1997).

WHITE, CAROLINNE, *The Correspondence (394–419) Between Jerome and Augustine of Hippo* (Lewiston, NY: Edwin Mellen, 1990).

SECONDARY LITERATURE

ACKROYD, P. R., and EVANS, C. F. (eds.), *The Cambridge History of the Bible*, i. *From the Beginnings to Jerome* (Cambridge: Cambridge University Press, 1963).

ALTANER, BERTHOLD, 'Augustins Methode der Quellenbenützung. Sein Studium der Väterliteratur', *Sacris Erudiri*, 4 (1952), 5–17.

Augustinus-Lexikon: see under Mayer, Cornelius (ed.).

BABCOCK, WILLIAM S., 'Augustine and the Spirituality of Desire', *Augustinian Studies*, 25 (1994), 179–99.

—— 'Augustine and Tyconius: A Study in the Latin Appropriation of Paul', *Studia Patristica*, 17/3, ed. Elizabeth A. Livingstone (Oxford: Pergamon Press, 1982), 1209–15.

—— 'Augustine on Sin and Moral Agency', *Journal of Religious Ethics*, 16 (1988), 28–55.

—— 'Augustine's Interpretation of Romans (AD 394–396)', *Augustinian Studies*, 10 (1979), 55–74.

BACCHI, LEE FRANCIS, *The Theology of Ordained Ministry in the Letters of Augustine of Hippo* (San Francisco: International Scholars Publications, 1998).

BAKHUIZEN VAN DEN BRINK, J. N. '*Mereo(r)* and *meritum* in some Latin Fathers', *Studia Patristica*, 3, ed. F. L. Cross (Berlin: Akademie, 1961), 333–40.

BAMMEL, C. P., 'The Last Ten Years of Rufinus's Life and the Date of his Move South from Aquileia', *Journal of Theological Studies*, NS 28 (1977), 372–429.

—— 'Pauline Exegesis, Manichaeism and Philosophy in the Early Augustine', in C. P. Bammel, *Tradition and Exegesis in Early Christian Writers* (Aldershot: Variorum, 1995), article 16.

BARDY, G., 'Introduction', *De diversis quaestionibus 83*, BA 10 (Paris: Desclée de Brouwer, 1952), 11–50.

BASTIAENSEN, ANTOON A. R., 'Augustin commentateur de saint Paul et l'Ambrosiaster', *Sacris Erudiri*, 36 (1996), 37–65.

—— 'Augustin et ses prédécesseurs latins chrétiens', in J. den Boeft and J. van Oort (eds.), *Augustiniana Traiectina* (Paris: Études augustiniennes, 1987), 25–57.

BAXTER, J. H., 'Ambrosiaster cited as "Ambrose" in 405', *Journal of Theological Studies*, 24 (1923), 187.

BETZ, HANS DIETER, *Galatians: A Commentary on Paul's Letter to the Churches in*

Galatia, Hermeneia (Philadelphia: Fortress, 1979).

—— 'The Literary Composition and Function of Paul's Letter to the Galatians', *New Testament Studies*, 21 (1975), 353–79.

—— 'Paul in the Mani Biography (Codex Manichaicus Coloniensis)', in L. Cirillo (ed.), *Codex Manichaicus Coloniensis*, Atti del Simposio Internazionale 1984 (Cosenza: Marra, 1986), 215–34.

BLIGH, JOHN, *Galatians: A Discussion of St Paul's Epistle* (London: St Paul Publications, 1969).

BODIN, YVON, *Saint Jérôme et l'Église* (Paris: Beauchesne, 1966).

BOEFT, J. DEN, and OORT, J. VAN (eds.), *Augustiniana Traiectina* (Paris: Études augustiniennes, 1987).

BOHLIN, TORGNY, *Die Theologie des Pelagius und ihre Genesis*, trans. Harald Buch, Uppsala universitetsårsskrift, 9 (Uppsala: A.-B. Lundequist, and Wiesbaden: Otto Harrassowitz, 1957).

BONNER, GERALD, 'Augustine as Biblical Scholar', in P. R. Ackroyd and C. F. Evans (eds.), *The Cambridge History of the Bible*, i. *From the Beginnings to Jerome*, 541–63.

—— *God's Decree and Man's Destiny* (London: Variorum Reprints, 1987).

—— *St Augustine of Hippo: Life and Controversies*, rev. edn. (Norwich: Canterbury Press, 1986.)

BOYLE, MARJORIE O'ROURKE, 'A Likely Story: The Autobiographical as Epideictic', *Journal of the American Academy of Religion*, 57 (1989), 23–51.

BROWN, PETER, *Augustine of Hippo* (Berkeley and Los Angeles: University of California Press, 1967).

—— *The Body and Society* (New York: Columbia University Press, 1988).

—— 'The Diffusion of Manichaeism in the Roman Empire', *Journal of Roman Studies*, 59 (1969), 92–103 (repr. in his *Religion and Society*).

—— 'The Patrons of Pelagius: The Roman Aristocracy between East and West', *Journal of Theological Studies*, NS 21 (1970), 56–72 (repr. in his *Religion and Society*).

—— 'Pelagius and his Supporters: Aims and Environment', *Journal of Theological Studies*, NS 19 (1968), 93–114 (repr. in his *Religion and Society*).

—— *Power and Persuasion in Late Antiquity: Towards a Christian Empire* (Madison, Wis.: University of Wisconsin Press, 1992).

—— *Religion and Society in the Age of St. Augustine* (London: Faber, 1972).

—— 'The Saint as Exemplar in Late Antiquity', *Representations*, 1 (1983), 1–25.

BROWN, RAYMOND E., *The Epistles of John*, Anchor Bible, 30 (Garden City: Doubleday, 1982).

—— and MEIER, JOHN P., *Antioch and Rome: New Testament Cradles of Catholic Christianity* (London: Geoffrey Chapman, 1983).

BUBY, B., *Mary of Galilee*, iii (New York: Alba House, 1997).

BULTMANN, RUDOLF, 'Ist voraussetzungslose Exegese möglich?', *Theologische Zeitschrift*, 13 (1957), 409–17 ('Is Exegesis Without Presuppositions Possible?',

258   *Bibliography*

in Rudolf Bultmann, *'New Testament and Mythology' and Other Basic Writings*, ed. and trans. Schubert M. Ogden (Philadelphia: Fortress, 1984), 145–53).

BULTMANN, RUDOLF, 'Das Problem der Hermeneutik', *Zeitschrift für Theologie und Kirche*, 47 (1950), 47–69 ('The Problem of Hermeneutics', in Rudolf Bultmann, *Essays Philosophical and Theological*, trans. James C. G. Greig (New York: Macmillan, 1955), 234–61).

BURGESS, THEODORE C., *Epideictic Literature* (New York and London: Garland Publishing, 1987 (reprint)).

BURNABY, JOHN, 'The "Retractations" of St. Augustine: Self-criticism or Apologia?', *Augustinus Magister* (Paris: Études augustiniennes, 1954), i. 85–92.

BURNS, J. PATOUT, 'Ambrose Preaching to Augustine: The Shaping of Faith', in Joseph C. Schnaubelt and Frederick Van Fleteren (eds.), *Collectanea Augustiniana*, 373–86.

—— *The Development of Augustine's Doctrine of Operative Grace* (Paris: Études augustiniennes, 1980).

—— 'The Interpretation of Romans in the Pelagian Controversy', *Augustinian Studies*, 10 (1979), 43–54.

BURRELL, DAVID, 'Reading the Confessions of Augustine: An Exercise in Theological Understanding', *Journal of Religion*, 50 (1970), 327–51.

CAMERON, AVERIL, *Christianity and the Rhetoric of Empire: The Development of Christian Discourse* (Berkeley and Los Angeles: University of California Press, 1991).

CAMERON, MICHAEL, 'The Christological Substructure of Augustine's Figurative Exegesis', in Pamela Bright (ed.), *Augustine and the Bible* (Notre Dame: University of Notre Dame Press, 1999), 74–103.

CAMPENHAUSEN, HANS VON, *The Fathers of the Latin Church*, trans. Manfred Hoffmann (London: A. & C. Black, 1964).

CANNING, RAYMOND, *The Unity of Love for God and Neighbour in St. Augustine* (Leuven: Augustinian Historical Institute, 1993).

CAVALLERA, FERDINAND, *Saint Jérôme: Sa vie et son œuvre*, Spicilegium Sacrum Lovaniense: Études et documents, 1 (2 vols.; Louvain and Paris: Champion, 1922).

CHADWICK, HENRY, 'The Ascetic Ideal in the History of the Church', in W. J. Sheils (ed.), *Monks, Hermits and the Ascetic Tradition*, Studies in Church History, 22 (Padstow: Basil Blackwell, 1985), 1–23.

—— *Augustine* (Oxford: Oxford University Press, 1986).

—— *Early Christian Thought and the Classical Tradition* (New York: Oxford University Press, 1966).

—— *The Early Church* (Harmondsworth: Penguin Books, 1967).

—— 'The Enigma of St Paul', Ethel M. Wood Lecture (London: Athlone Press, 1969).

—— 'History and Symbolism in the Garden at Milan', in F. X. Martin and J. A. Richmond (eds.), *From Augustine to Eriugena: Essays on Neoplatonism and*

Christianity in Honor of John O'Meara (Washington, DC: Catholic University of America Press, 1991).

CIPRIANI, NELLO, 'Agostino lettore dei commentari paolini di Mario Vittorino', *Augustinianum*, 38 (1998), 413–28.

——'L'autonomia della volontà umana nell'atto di fede: le ragioni di una teoria prima accolta e poi respinta da S. Agostino', in L. Alici *et al.* (eds.), *Il mistero del male e la libertà possibile: linee di antropologia agostiniana*, Atti del VI Seminario del Centro di Studi Agostiniani di Perugia (Rome: Institutum Patristicum Augustinianum, 1995), 7–17.

CLARK, ELIZABETH A., *The Origenist Controversy: The Cultural Construction of an Early Christian Debate* (Princeton: Princeton University Press, 1992).

COLE-TURNER, RONALD S., 'Anti-Heretical Issues and the Debate over Galatians 2: 11–14 in the Letters of St. Augustine to St. Jerome', *Augustinian Studies*, 11 (1980), 155–66.

COMEAU, MARIE, *Saint Augustin exégète du Quatrième Évangile* (Paris: Beauchesne, 1930).

CONTE, GIAN BIAGIO, *Latin Literature: A History*, trans. J. B. Solodow (Baltimore: Johns Hopkins University Press, 1994).

COOPER, STEPHEN A., '*Narratio* and *Exhortatio* in Galatians According to Marius Victorinus Rhetor', *Zeitschrift für die neutestamentliche Wissenschaft*, 91 (2000), 107–35.

——*Understanding Spiritually: The Commentary of Marius Victorinus on Paul's Letter to the Galatians*, Oxford Early Christian Studies (Oxford: Clarendon Press, forthcoming).

COURCELLE, PIERRE, *Late Latin Writers and Their Greek Sources*, trans. H. E. Wedeck (Cambridge, Mass.: Harvard University Press, 1969).

——*Recherches sur les Confessions de saint Augustin* (Paris: Boccard, 1950).

COYLE, JOHN KEVIN, *Augustine's 'De Moribus Ecclesiae Catholicae'* (Fribourg: Fribourg University Press, 1978).

CRANZ, F. EDWARD, 'The Development of Augustine's Ideas on Society Before the Donatist Controversy', *Harvard Theological Review*, 47 (1954), 255–316.

CROSS, F. L., 'History and Fiction in the African Canons', *Journal of Theological Studies*, NS 12 (1961), 227–47.

DE BRUYN, THEODORE S., 'Constantius the *Tractator*: Author of an Anonymous Commentary on the Pauline Epistles?', *Journal of Theological Studies*, NS 43 (1992), 38–54.

DECRET, F., *L'Afrique manichéenne (IVe–Ve siècles)* (2 vols.; Paris: Études augustiniennes, 1978).

——*Aspects du manichéisme dans l'Afrique romaine* (Paris: Études augustiniennes, 1970).

DELAROCHE, BRUNO, *Saint Augustin Lecteur et Interprète de Saint Paul* (Paris: Études augustiniennes, 1996).

DI BERARDINO, ANGELO (ed.), *Patrology*, iv, trans. Placid Solari (Westminster,

Md.: Christian Classics, 1986).

DIVJAK, JOHANNES, 'Zur Textüberlieferung der augustinischen *Expositio in epistolam ad Galatas*', *Studia Patristica*, 14, ed. Elizabeth A. Livingstone (Berlin: Akademie-Verlag, 1976), 402–9.

DOIGNON, JEAN, ' "Nos bons hommes de foi": Cyprien, Lactance, Victorin, Optat, Hilaire (Augustin, *De doctrina christiana*, IV, 40, 61)', *Latomus*, 22 (1963), 795–805.

DOLBEAU, F., 'Sermons inédits de saint Augustin prêchés en 397 (2ème série)': see under Augustinus, Sanctus Aurelius, in 'Other Latin Texts'.

DOULL, JAMES A., 'Augustinian Trinitarianism and Existential Theology', *Dionysius*, 3 (1979), 111–59.

DUNN, JAMES D. G., *The Epistle to the Galatians*, Black's New Testament Commentaries (London: A. & C. Black, 1993).

ENO, ROBERT B., 'Some Patristic Views on the Relationship of Faith and Works in Justification', *Recherches augustiniennes*, 19 (1984), 3–27.

ERDT, WERNER, *Marius Victorinus Afer, der erste lateinische Pauluskommentator: Studien zu seinen Pauluskommentaren im Zusammenhang der Wiederentdeckung des Paulus in der abendländischen Theologie des 4. Jahrhunderts* (Frankfurt am Main: Peter D. Lang, 1980).

FERRARI, LEO CHARLES, 'Augustine's "Discovery" of Paul (*Confessions* 7. 21. 27)', *Augustinian Studies*, 22 (1991), 37–61.

——'Truth and Augustine's Conversion Scene', in Joseph C. Schnaubelt and Frederick Van Fleteren (eds.), *Collectanea Augustiniana*, 9–19.

FITZGERALD, ALLAN D. (ed.), *Augustine through the Ages: An Encyclopedia* (Grand Rapids: Eerdmans, 1999).

FREDRIKSEN, PAULA, 'Apocalypse and Redemption in Early Christianity', *Vigiliae Christianae*, 45 (1991), 151–83.

——'Augustine's Early Interpretation of Paul', Ph.D. diss., Princeton University, 1979.

——*Augustine on Romans*: see under Landes, Paula Fredriksen, in 'English Translations'.

——'Beyond the Body/Soul Dichotomy: Augustine on Paul against the Manichees and the Pelagians', *Recherches augustiniennes*, 23 (1988), 87–114.

——'*Excaecati Occulta Justitia Dei*: Augustine on Jews and Judaism', *Journal of Early Christian Studies*, 3/3 (1995), 299–324.

——'Paul and Augustine: Conversion Narratives, Orthodox Traditions, and the Retrospective Self', *Journal of Theological Studies*, NS 37 (1986), 3–34.

FREND, W. H. C., *The Donatist Church: A Movement of Protest in Roman North Africa* (Oxford: Clarendon Press, 1952).

FROEHLICH, KARLFRIED, 'Fallibility Instead of Infallibility? A Brief History of the Interpretation of Galatians 2:11–14', in Paul C. Empie *et al.* (eds.), *Teaching Authority and Infallibility in the Church* (Minneapolis: Augsburg, 1980), 259–69 and 351–7.

GILSON, ÉTIENNE, *The Christian Philosophy of Saint Augustine*, trans. L. E. M. Lynch (New York: Random House, 1960).

GORDAY, PETER, *Principles of Patristic Exegesis: Romans 9–11 in Origen, John Chrysostom, and Augustine*, Studies in the Bible and Early Christianity, 4 (New York: Edwin Mellen, 1983).

GORE, CHARLES, 'Victorinus Afer', in *Dictionary of Christian Biography*, 4 (London: 1887) 1129–38.

GRABOWSKI, STANISLAUS J., *The Church: An Introduction to the Theology of St. Augustine* (London: Herder, 1957).

GUITTON, JEAN, *Le Temps et l'éternité chez Plotin et saint Augustin*, 3rd, rev. edn. (Paris: Librairie Philosophique J. Vrin, 1959).

HADOT, PIERRE, 'L'Image de la Trinité dans l'âme chez Victorinus et chez saint Augustin', *Studia Patristica*, 6, ed. F. L. Cross, TU 81 (Berlin: Akademie-Verlag, 1962), 409–42.

——*Marius Victorinus: Recherches sur sa vie et ses œuvres* (Paris: Études augustiniennes, 1971).

HAGENDAHL, HARALD, *Latin Fathers and the Classics* (Göteborg: Almqvist & Wiksell, 1967).

HALPORN, BARBARA C., 'Johann Amerbach's Collected Editions of St. Ambrose, St. Augustine, and St. Jerome', Ph.D. diss., Indiana University, 1988.

HAMMOND BAMMEL, C. P.: see under Bammel, C. P.

HANSON, A. T., *The Pastoral Epistles*, New Century Bible Commentary (Grand Rapids: Eerdmans, 1982).

HARNACK, ADOLPH, *History of Dogma*, v, trans. Neil Buchanan from 3rd German edn. (New York: Dover, 1961).

——*Der kirchengeschichtliche Ertrag der exegetischen Arbeiten des Origenes*, TU 42 (Leipzig: J. C. Hinrichs', 1918–19).

HARRISON, CAROL, *Augustine: Christian Truth and Fractured Humanity* (Oxford: Oxford University Press, 2000).

HAYS, RICHARD B., 'Christology and Ethics in Galatians: The Law of Christ', *Catholic Biblical Quarterly*, 49 (1987), 268–90.

——*The Moral Vision of the New Testament* (San Francisco: HarperSanFrancisco, 1996).

HEFELE, CHARLES JOSEPH, *A History of the Councils of the Church*, ii. *A.D. 326 to A.D. 429*, trans. H. N. Oxenham (Edinburgh: T. & T. Clark, 1896).

HENNINGS, RALPH, *Der Briefwechsel zwischen Augustinus und Hieronymus und ihr Streit um den Kanon des Alten Testaments und die Auslegung von Gal. 2,11–14*, Supplements to Vigiliae Christianae, 21 (New York; Leiden; Cologne: E. J. Brill, 1994).

HENRY, PAUL, and HADOT, PIERRE (eds.), *Marius Victorinus: Traités théologiques sur la Trinité*, 1, SC 68 (Paris: Les Éditions du Cerf, 1960).

HOLTZ, LOUIS, *Donat et la tradition de l'enseignement grammatical: Étude sur l'Ars Donati et sa diffusion (IVe–IXe siècle) et édition critique* (Paris: Centre National de la Recherche Scientifique, 1981).

JEANROND, WERNER G., *Theological Hermeneutics: Development and Significance* (New York: Crossroad, 1991).

JEDIN, HUBERT, and DOLAN, JOHN (eds.), *History of the Church*, 2 (New York: Seabury Press, 1980).

KASTER, ROBERT A., *Guardians of Language: The Grammarian and Society in Late Antiquity*, The Transformation of the Classical Heritage, 11 (Berkeley: University of California Press, 1988).

KELLY, J. N. D., *Jerome: His Life, Writings, and Controversies* (New York: Harper & Row, 1975).

LA BONNARDIÈRE, A.-M., 'Jérôme "informateur" d'Augustin au sujet d'Origène', *Revue des études augustiniennes*, 20 (1974), 42–52.

——'Le Verset paulinien *Rom.*, V. 5 dans l'œuvre de saint Augustin', *Augustinus Magister* (Paris: Études augustiniennes, 1954), ii. 657–65.

LADNER, GERHART B., *The Idea of Reform: Its Impact on Christian Thought and Action in the Age of the Fathers* (Cambridge, Mass.: Harvard University Press, 1959).

LAW, VIVIEN, 'St Augustine's *De grammatica*: Lost or Found?', *Recherches augustiniennes*, 19 (1984), 155–83.

LAWLESS, GEORGE, 'Augustine of Hippo and His Critics', in Joseph T. Lienhard *et al.* (eds.), *Augustine: Presbyter Factus Sum*, 3–28.

——*Augustine of Hippo and his Monastic Rule* (Oxford: Clarendon Press, 1987).

LIENHARD, JOSEPH T., MULLER, EARL C., and TESKE, ROLAND J. (eds.), *Augustine: Presbyter Factus Sum* (New York: Peter Lang, 1993).

LIEU, SAMUEL N. C., *Manichaeism in the Later Roman Empire and Medieval China*, 2nd edn. (Tübingen: Mohr, 1992).

LIGHTFOOT, J. B., 'J. B. Lightfoot and New Testament Interpretation: An Unpublished Manuscript of 1855', edited with an introduction by B. N. Kaye and G. R. Treloar, *Durham University Journal*, 82 (1990), 161–75.

——*Saint Paul's Epistle to the Galatians*, 10th edn. (London: Macmillan, 1902).

LOHSE, BERNHARD, 'Beobachtungen zum Paulus-Kommentar des Marius Victorinus und zur Wiederentdeckung des Paulus in der lateinischen Theologie des vierten Jahrhunderts', in Adolf Martin Ritter (ed.), *Kerygma und Logos: Beiträge zu den geistesgeschichtlichen Beziehungen zwischen Antike und Christentum* (Göttingen: Vandenhoeck & Ruprecht, 1979), 351–66.

LONGENECKER, R. N., *Galatians*, Word Biblical Commentary, 41 (Dallas: Word, 1990).

LUNEAU, A., *L'Histoire du salut chez les Pères de l'Église: La Doctrine des âges du monde* (Paris: Beauchesne, 1964).

MANDOUZE, ANDRÉ, *Prosopographie de l'Afrique chrétienne (303–533)* (Paris: Centre National de la Recherche Scientifique, 1982).

MARA, MARIA GRAZIA, 'Commentaries on the Pauline Epistles', in Angelo Di Berardino (ed.), *Encyclopedia of the Early Church*, trans. Adrian Walford (New

York: Oxford University Press, 1992), 658–9.

—— 'Il significato storico-esegetico dei commentari al corpus paolino dal IV al V secolo', *Annali di Storia dell'Esegesi*, 1 (1984), 59–74.

—— 'Note sulla *Expositio epistulae ad Galatas* di Agostino', in *Memoriam sanctorum venerantes: Miscellanea in onore di Monsignor Victor Saxer*, Studi di antichità cristiana, 48 (Città del Vaticano: Pontificio Istituto di Archeologia Cristiana, 1992), 539–45.

—— 'Storia ed esegesi nella *Expositio epistulae ad Galatas* di Agostino', *Annali di Storia dell'Esegesi*, 2 (1985), 93–102.

MARGERIE, BERTRAND DE, *An Introduction to the History of Exegesis*, iii. *Saint Augustine*, trans. Pierre de Fontnouvelle (Petersham, Mass.: Saint Bede's Publications, 1991).

MARKUS, ROBERT, *Conversion and Disenchantment in Augustine's Spiritual Career*, The Saint Augustine Lecture 1984 (Villanova: Villanova University Press, 1989).

—— *The End of Ancient Christianity* (Cambridge: Cambridge University Press, 1990).

—— 'Marius Victorinus and Augustine', *The Cambridge History of Later Greek and Early Medieval Philosophy*, pt. 5, ed. A. H. Armstrong (Cambridge: Cambridge University Press, 1967), 331–421.

—— 'Paganism, Christianity and the Latin Classics in the Fourth Century', in J. W. Binns (ed.), *Latin Literature of the Fourth Century* (London: Routledge & Kegan Paul, 1974), 1–21.

—— 'St. Augustine on Signs', *Phronesis*, 2 (1957), 60–83.

MARROU, HENRI IRÉNÉE, *Saint Augustin et la fin de la culture antique* (Paris: Boccard, 1938); *Retractatio* (Paris: Boccard, 1949).

MARTYN, J. LOUIS, *Galatians*, Anchor Bible 33A (New York: Doubleday, 1997).

MATTER, E. ANN, 'Conversion(s) in the *Confessiones*', in Joseph C. Schnaubelt and Frederick Van Fleteren (eds.), *Collectanea Augustiniana*, 21–8.

MAYER, CORNELIUS (ed.), *Augustinus-Lexikon* (Basle/Stuttgart: Schwabe & Co. AG, 1986–).

MENDOZA, MARIO, 'Introduzione al *Commento della Lettera ai Galati*', in NBA, 10/2 (Roma: Città Nuova, 1997), 479–87.

METZGER, BRUCE M., *The Early Versions of the New Testament: Their Origins, Transmission, and Limitations* (Oxford: Clarendon Press, 1977).

MISCH, GEORG, *A History of Autobiography in Antiquity*, ii. trans. E. W. Dickes (London: Routledge & Kegan Paul, 1950).

MONCEAUX, PAUL, *Histoire littéraire de l'Afrique chrétienne* (7 vols.; Paris: Ernest Leroux, 1901–23).

MOHRMANN, CHRISTINE, 'The *Confessions* as a Literary Work of Art', in Christine Mohrmann, *Études sur le latin des Chrétiens*, i. 371–81.

—— *Études sur le latin des Chrétiens* (Rome: Edizioni di Storia e Letteratura, 1958), i.

—— 'Saint Augustine and the "Eloquentia"', in Christine Mohrmann, *Études sur le latin des Chrétiens*, i. 351–70.

NAUTIN, PIERRE, 'La Date des commentaires de Jérôme sur les épîtres pauliniennes', *Revue d'histoire ecclésiastique*, 74 (1979), 5–12.

NEWMAN, JOHN HENRY, *An Essay on the Development of Christian Doctrine*, 7th edn. (London: Sheed & Ward, 1960).

O'CONNELL, ROBERT J., *The Origin of the Soul in St. Augustine's Later Works* (New York: Fordham University Press, 1987).

O'DONNELL, JAMES J., 'Augustine's Classical Readings', *Recherches augustiniennes*, 15 (1980), 144–75.

—— *Augustine: Confessions* (3 vols; Oxford: Clarendon Press, 1992).

O'DONOVAN, OLIVER, '*Usus* and *Fruitio* in Augustine, *De Doctrina Christiana* 1', *Journal of Theological Studies*, NS 33 (1982), 361–97.

O'MEARA, JOHN J., '"Arripui, aperui, et legi"', in *Augustinus Magister* (Paris: Études augustiniennes, 1954), i. 59–65.

—— 'Augustine and Neoplatonism', *Recherches augustiniennes*, 1 (1958), 91–111.

—— 'Augustine's *Confessions*: Elements of Fiction', in J. McWilliam (ed.), *Augustine: From Rhetor to Theologian* (Waterloo, Ontario: Wilfred Laurier University Press, 1992), 77–95.

—— 'The Historicity of the Early Dialogues of Saint Augustine', *Vigiliae Christianae*, 5 (1951), 150–78.

—— *The Young Augustine: The Growth of St. Augustine's Mind up to His Conversion* (London: Longmans, Green & Co., 1954).

PARKES, M. B., *Pause and Effect: An Introduction to the History of Punctuation in the West* (Berkeley and Los Angeles: University of California Press, 1993).

PELLEGRINO, MICHELE, *The True Priest: The Priesthood as Preached and Practised by St Augustine*, trans. Arthur Gibson (New York: Philosophical Library, 1968).

PERLER, OTHMAR, 'Das Datum der Bischofsweihe des heiligen Augustinus', *Revue des études augustiniennes*, 11 (1965), 25–37.

—— *Les Voyages de saint Augustin* (Paris: Études augustiniennes, 1969).

PINCHERLE, ALBERTO, *La formazione teologica di Sant'Agostino* (Rome: Edizioni Italiane, n.d. [1947]).

PLUMER, ERIC, 'The Influence of Marius Victorinus on Augustine's *Commentary on Galatians*', *Studia Patristica*, 33, ed. Elizabeth A. Livingstone (Leuven: Peeters, 1997), 221–8.

POLMAN, A. D. R., *The Word of God According to St. Augustine*, trans. A. J. Pomerans (Grand Rapids: Eerdmans, 1961).

PORTALIÉ, EUGÈNE, *A Guide to the Thought of Saint Augustine*, trans. R. J. Bastian (Chicago: Henry Regnery, 1960).

PRENDIVILLE, J. G., 'The Development of the Idea of Habit in the Thought of St. Augustine', *Traditio*, 28 (1972), 29–99.

QUASTEN, JOHANNES, '"Vetus Superstitio et Nova Religio": The Problem of *Refrigerium* in the Ancient Church of North Africa', *Harvard Theological*

Review, 33 (1940), 253–66.

REYNOLDS, L. D., and WILSON, N. G., *Scribes and Scholars: A Guide to the Transmission of Greek and Latin Literature*, 3rd edn. (Oxford: Clarendon Press, 1991).

RICŒUR, PAUL, 'Preface to Bultmann', trans. P. McCormick, in Lewis S. Mudge (ed.), *Paul Ricœur, Essays on Biblical Interpretation* (Philadelphia: Fortress, 1980).

RIES, JULIEN, 'La Bible chez saint Augustin et chez les manichéens', *Revue des études augustiniennes*, 7 (1961), 231–43; 10 (1964), 309–29.

ROUSSELET, JEAN, 'A propos d'un édition critique: pour mieux lire les Commentaires d'Augustin sur les Epîtres aux Romains et aux Galates', *Revue des études augustiniennes*, 18 (1972), 233–47.

SANDERS, E. P., *Paul, the Law, and the Jewish People* (London: SCM Press, 1985).

SCANLON, MICHAEL J., 'Augustine and Theology as Rhetoric', *Augustinian Studies*, 25 (1994), 37–50.

SCHATKIN, MARGARET A., 'The Influence of Origen upon St. Jerome's Commentary on Galatians', *Vigiliae Christianae*, 24 (1970), 49–58.

SCHMID, R., 'Marius Victorinus und seine Beziehungen zu Augustin', diss., Kiel, 1895.

SCHNACKENBURG, RUDOLF, *The Moral Teaching of the New Testament*, trans. J. Holland-Smith and W. J. O'Hara (New York: Herder & Herder, 1965).

SCHNAUBELT, JOSEPH C., and VAN FLETEREN, FREDERICK (eds.), *Collectanea Augustiniana* (New York: Peter Lang, 1990).

SELBY, ROBIN C., *The Principle of Reserve in the Writings of John Henry Cardinal Newman* (London: Oxford University Press, 1975).

SIMONETTI, MANLIO, *Biblical Interpretation in the Early Church: An Historical Introduction to Patristic Exegesis*, trans. John A. Hughes (Edinburgh: T. & T. Clark, 1994).

SMITH, ALFRED J., 'The Latin Sources of the Commentary of Pelagius on the Epistle of St Paul to the Romans', *Journal of Theological Studies*, 19 (1917–18), 162–230; 20 (1918–19), 55–65, 127–77.

—— 'Pelagius and Augustine', *Journal of Theological Studies*, 31 (1929–30), 21–35.

SOLIGNAC, A. (ed.), *Les Confessions*, BA 13–14 (Paris: Desclée de Brouwer, 1962).

SOMERS, H., 'Image de Dieu: Les Sources de l'exégèse augustinienne', *Revue des études augustiniennes*, 7 (1961), 105–25.

SOUTER, ALEXANDER, *The Earliest Latin Commentaries on the Epistles of St. Paul* (Oxford: Clarendon Press, 1927).

—— *A Glossary of Later Latin to 600 A.D.* (Oxford: Clarendon Press, 1949).

SPARKS, H. F. D., 'Jerome as Biblical Scholar', in P. R. Ackroyd and C. F. Evans (eds.), *The Cambridge History of the Bible*, i. *From the Beginnings to Jerome*, 510–41.

STARNES, COLIN, *Augustine's Conversion: A Guide to the Argument of* Confessions *I–IX* (Waterloo, Ontario: Wilfrid Laurier University Press, 1990).

STENDAHL, KRISTER, 'The Apostle Paul and the Introspective Conscience of the

West', *Harvard Theological Review*, 56 (1963), 199–215.

STRAW, CAROLE E., 'Augustine as Pastoral Theologian: The Exegesis of the Parables of the Field and Threshing Floor', *Augustinian Studies*, 14 (1983), 129–51.

SUMRULD, WILLIAM A., *Augustine and the Arians: The Bishop of Hippo's Encounters with Ulfilan Arianism* (Selinsgrove, Pa.: Susquehanna University Press, 1994).

TESELLE, EUGENE, *Augustine the Theologian* (New York: Herder & Herder, 1970).

——'Serpent, Eve, and Adam: Augustine and the Exegetical Tradition', in Joseph T. Lienhard *et al.* (eds.), *Augustine: Presbyter Factus Sum*, 341–61.

TILLEY, MAUREEN A., *The Bible in Christian North Africa: The Donatist World* (Minneapolis: Fortress, 1997).

TRACY, DAVID, 'Charity, Obscurity, Clarity: Augustine's Search for a True Rhetoric', in Mary Gerhart and Anthony C. Yu (eds.), *Morphologies of Faith: Essays in Religion and Culture in Honor of Nathan A. Scott, Jr.*, AAR Studies in Religion, 59 (Atlanta: Scholars Press, 1990), 123–43.

TRENCH, RICHARD CHENEVIX, *Exposition of the Sermon on the Mount Drawn from the Writings of St. Augustine, with an Introductory Essay on Augustine as an Interpreter of Scripture*, 4th edn., rev. (London: Kegan Paul, Trench, & Co., 1886).

TROUT, DENNIS E., 'The Dates of the Ordination of Paulinus of Bordeaux and of his Departure for Nola', *Revue des études augustiniennes*, 37 (1991), 237–60.

VAN BAVEL, TARSICIUS J., 'Parallèles, Vocabulaire et Citations Bibliques de la "Regula Sancti Augustini": Contribution au problème de son authenticité', *Augustiniana*, 9 (1959), 12–77.

——*Recherches sur la christologie de saint Augustin: L'Humain et le divin dans le Christ d'après saint Augustin*, Paradosis, 10 (Fribourg: Éditions Universitaires, 1954).

——*The Rule of Saint Augustine*, trans. R. Canning (Garden City: Doubleday, 1986).

VAN DER LOF, L. J., 'De invloed van Marius Victorinus Rhetor op Augustinus', *Nederlands Theologisch Tijdschrift*, 5 (1950–1), 287–307.

VAN DER MEER, F., *Augustine the Bishop: The Life and Work of a Father of the Church*, trans. Brian Battershaw and G. R. Lamb (London: Sheed & Ward, 1961).

VAN FLETEREN, FREDERICK, 'St. Augustine's Theory of Conversion', in Joseph C. Schnaubelt and Frederick Van Fleteren (eds.), *Collectanea Augustiniana*, 65–80.

VERHEIJEN, LUC, *La Règle de saint Augustin*, i. *Tradition manuscrite*; ii. *Recherches historiques* (Paris: Études augustiniennes, 1967).

——*Saint Augustine: Monk, Priest, Bishop* (Villanova: Villanova University Press, 1978).

——*Saint Augustine's Monasticism in the Light of Acts 4.32–35* (Villanova: Villanova University Press, 1979).

——'The Straw, The Beam, The Tusculan Disputations and The Rule of Saint Augustine—on a Surprising Augustinian Exegesis', *Augustinian Studies*, 2

(1971), 17–36.

VESSEY, MARK, 'Conference and Confession: Literary Pragmatics in Augustine's "*Apologia contra Hieronymum*"', *Journal of Early Christian Studies*, 1/2 (1993), 175–213.

——'Jerome's Origen: The Making of a Christian Literary *Persona*', *Studia Patristica*, 28, ed. E. A. Livingstone (Leuven: Peeters Press, 1993), 135–45.

WETZEL, JAMES, *Augustine and the Limits of Virtue* (Cambridge: Cambridge University Press, 1992).

WILCKENS, ULRICH, 'Zur Entwicklung des paulinischen Gesetzesverständnisses', *New Testament Studies*, 28 (1982), 154–90.

WILES, MAURICE F., *The Divine Apostle: The Interpretation of St Paul's Epistles in the Early Church* (Cambridge: Cambridge University Press, 1967).

WILLIAMS, ROWAN, 'Language, Reality and Desire in Augustine's *De Doctrina*', *Journal of Literature and Theology*, 3/2 (1989), 138–50.

WILLIS, GEOFFREY GRIMSHAW, *Saint Augustine and the Donatist Controversy* (London: SPCK, 1950).

ZUMKELLER, ADOLAR, *Augustine's Ideal of the Religious Life*, trans. Edmund Colledge (New York: Fordham University Press, 1986).

Index of Biblical References

Index of Ancient Authors

Index of Augustine's Works

6. 5. 7–8 11
6. 5. 7 10 n.29
6. 6. 9 243 n.11, 243 n.12, 245 n.24
6. 7. 11–10. 16 247 n.43
6. 7. 12 13–14 n.46, 66 n.41
6. 8. 13 247 n.44
6. 11. 18 10 n.26, 11
6. 11. 19 13, 13 n.45
6. 14. 24 72 n.77
7. 1. 1–7. 11 11
7. 1. 1 10 n.26
7. 6. 8–10 82 n.123
7. 7. 11 91 n.14
7. 9. 13–14 245 n.28
7. 9. 13 12
7. 9. 14 11, 12 n.35, 97 n.47
7. 9. 15 17 n.62, 17 n.63, 243 n.14
7. 10. 16–11. 17 11
7. 10. 16 146 n.51
7. 12. 18–13. 19 11
7. 14. 20 243 n.14
7. 16. 22 11
7. 17. 23 11, 146 n.51
7. 18. 24–19. 25 245 n.28
7. 18. 24 12
7. 19. 25–20. 26 12
7. 20. 26 97 n.48
7. 21. 23 16
7. 21. 24–7 97 n.45
7. 21. 27 12, 97 nn.47, 49, 244 n.21
8. 1. 1 12
8. 1. 2 12, 14 n.49
8. 2. 3 12, 13, 15 n.57, 16, 17 n.63, 245 n.24
8. 2. 4 13, 14 n.47
8. 4. 9 13 n.46, 15 n.54, 17 n.64
8. 5. 10–6. 14 14 n.49
8. 5. 10–12 246 n.32
8. 5. 10 13
8. 6. 14–15 73 n.79
8. 7. 17 10 n.26, 13–14 n.46
8. 7. 18 14 n.49
8. 11. 27 216 n.239
8. 12. 29 9 n.22, 14 n.47, 83 n.130
8. 12. 30 14 n.49
9. 1. 1 13 n.42
9. 2. 3 13 n.43
9. 4. 7 17, 73 n.81
9. 5. 13 73 n.80
9. 7. 15 70 n.67
9. 8. 17 73 n.82
9. 8. 18 247 n.45
9. 13. 37 244 n.17

10. 3. 4 244 n.17
10. 4. 3–4. 5 248 n.47
10. 4. 5 244 n.17
10. 4. 6 245 n.27
10. 5. 7 247 n.39
10. 8. 12 247 n.35
10. 29. 40 207 n.219
10. 32. 48 247 n.39
10. 36. 59–38. 63 228 n.269
10. 36. 59 247 n.41
10. 40. 65 247 nn.35, 41
10. 41. 66 247 n.39
10. 43. 68 245 n.27
11. 1. 1 244 n.17
11. 2. 3 247 n.37, 247 n.40
12. 1. 1 132 n.17
12. 16. 23 173 n.124
13. 9. 10 210 n.226
13. 14. 15 244 n.21
13. 29. 44 90, 90 n.12
13. 38. 53 132 n.17

cons. eu., 1. 35. 54 246 n.29

cont., 7. 18 63 n.12, 208 nn.223–4

Cresc., 3. 80. 92 248 n.46

diu. qu. 19, 74, 76
   35. 2 204 n.211
   40 246 n.33
   66–75 76
   66. 3–7 209 n.225
   66. 6 213 n.233
   67. 6 173 n.124
   69. 1 70 n.69
   70 208 n.223
   71 76–7, 98 n.50, 226 n.265

doctr. chr. 19, 118–19
   1. 26. 27 96 n.40
   1. 36. 40 96 n.40
   1. 36. 41 104 n.74
   1. 37. 41 87 n.147, 91 n.13
   1. 40. 44 96 n.40
   2. 7. 10 96 n.40
   2. 11. 16 53 n.295, 240 n.2
   2. 14. 21–15. 22 101 n.62
   2. 16. 23 53 n.296
   2. 21. 32–22. 34 82 n.123, 120 n.12
   2. 23. 35 218 n.245
   2. 40. 60–1 16–17, 119 n.6
   2. 40. 60 39 n.215

General Index

authority (*cont.*)
see also leadership, spiritual

Babcock, William S. 208 n.224
Bammel, C. P. 6 n.9
baptism 15, 111, 173
  and Cyprian 32, 51–2
  and Donatism 70, 84, 249–50
Bardy, G. 19 n.83, 25 n.125, 76 n.102
Bastiaensen, Antoon A. R. 54 nn.303, 307,
  55 n.311
Baus, Karl 252 n.27
Baxter, J. H. 26
beauty, physical and spiritual 79, 215–17
Berlin Görres 97 (ii) MS 238 n.10
Betz, Hans Dieter 62 n.6, 89 nn.2–3, 115
  n.93, 126 n.9, 140 n.35, 230 n.277
Bible
  allusions to 69, 79, 132 n.17, 245 n.24
  Augustine's knowledge of xi, 18–19, 23,
    83, 99
  authority ix, 48–51, 84–5, 87, 95, 119
  and Creed 70, 99–101
  ignorance of 81–2
  inspiration 50, 65, 90–5, 195
  and Jesus as Word 101, 103, 246
  Old Latin version 240–1
  and revelation 102–3
  text of 101–4
  as unity 65, 95–9, 118, 227 n.268
  see also interpretation
Bligh, John 47 n.271, 196 n.190
Bodin, Yvon 45
Bonner, Gerald 32 n.161, 62 n.4, 68 n.47,
  75, 242 n.2, 243 n.8, 250 n.5, 252 n.25
Boyle, Marjorie O'Rourke 243 n.10
Brown, Peter 5 n.1, 9, 18 n.80, 83 n.130,
  118, 174 n.126, 243 n.7
  and Augustine's monastic life 73–4, 81
    n.121
  and Augustine's study of Scripture 19
    n.87, 20 n.88
  and Council of Hippo 23 n.115
  and Donatism 24 n.120, 251 n.24
  and human will 246
  and Jerome 43 n.241
  and Manichees 19 n.85
  and sexual desire 216 n.241
Brown, Raymond E. 197 n.191
Brown, Raymond E. and Meier, J. P. 89, 98
  n.51
Buby, B. 134 n.21
Budapest commentator 6, 56–7, 59 n.334

Bultmann, Rudolf 90, 96, 97 n.44, 102 n.66
Burgess, Theodore C. 243 n.9
Burnaby, J. 247 n.38
Burns, J. Patout 11 n.30, 182 n.150

calendar, Jewish 186 nn.157–8, 187–9
Campenhausen, Hans von 36 n.190, 41
Carthage, Councils 3, 32, 240 n.5, 244 n.18
Cassiciacum dialogues 9 n.22, 17, 62, 73
catholicity of the Church 68–9, 119, 250
Cavallera, Ferdinand 35 n.180, 42 n.234
Chadwick, Henry 10 n.27, 16 n.60, 18 n.72,
  39 n.214, 63 n.14, 69 n.53, 90 n.12, 94
  n.33, 243 n.11, 246 n.30
Chaldeans 184–5 n.155, 185
Christology
  of Augustine 106, 110, 119, 165 n.102
  Manichean 62
Church
  authority of 31–2, 45, 86, 91, 94
  as body of Christ 111, 117, 175
  catholicity 68–9, 119, 250
  Christ as head 8, 111, 175
  Gentile churches 143, 171
  Jewish churches 137
  reform of North African Church 85–6
  unity 8, 32, 51, 69, 87, 108, 111–12,
    141–3, 173–5, 179
Cicero, Marcus Tullius
  and Augustine 9, 17–18
  and Jerome 40
  and Victorinus 43
Cipriani, Nello 7 n.12, 16 n.49, 29, 55 n.313
circumcision
  and dispute between Peter and Paul 60,
    107–8, 110, 127, 139, 143–5
  of Gentiles 60, 105, 107–8, 129–31, 155,
    199, 231–3
  and Manicheism 65
  as sacramental work of the law 110, 129,
    153–7
  and salvation 29, 108, 113, 116, 125, 139,
    143–5, 169, 199–203, 221, 231–3
  of Timothy 49–50, 66, 91, 113, 116, 139,
    199, 233
Clark, Elizabeth A. 35 n.180
Claudius of Turin 238
Codex Andegavensis 159 238
Codex Bruxellensis 1058 238
Codex Parisinus Latinus 2700 238
Codex Parisinus Latinus 12225 238
Codex Vaticanus Latinus 491 157 n.81, 238
Cole-Turner, Ronald S. 32 n.159, 50, 51–2

290 General Index

Jesus Christ (*cont.*)
  humanity of 12, 181, 235
  and humility 12, 97–8, 103, 106, 110–11,
    115, 117–18, 131–3, 145, 165–7, 171,
    245
  as indwelling 109, 151, 191–3, 211
  and the law 179
  as mediator 12, 110, 164 n.101, 165–75,
    235
  proscription 8 n.18, 28, 109, 150 n.62,
    151–3, 199–201
  as Son of God 100, 151, 165, 173, 177,
    179–81
  and truth of the Bible 90–1
  virginal conception 67, 107, 111
  as wholly God after resurrection 127–9,
    233–5
  as Word of God 12, 100–1, 103, 246
journey, life as 111, 175
Jovinian 134 n.21
Judaism
  and the gospel 181
  and the law 106, 111, 113, 125–7, 133–5,
    171–3, 231
  Matthew, 10: 5–6 181
  and Paul 133–5
  and use of Hebrew Bible 98
Judaizers 124 n.5, 139, 143–7, 153–5, 221
  and apostolic authority of Paul 60
  and circumcision of Gentiles 105, 107–8,
    129–31, 155, 199, 231–3
  and humility 98
  and James, brother of Jesus 108, 144
    n.48, 145
  and the law 105, 125–35, 185
Judas Iscariot 82, 110, 161
Julian of Eclanum 247 n.45
justification by faith 8, 26, 80, 97, 110,
    147–9, 151, 153, 157–65
Justina, Empress 70

Kaster, Robert A. 13 n.44, 39 n.212
Kelly, J. N. D. 6 n.7, 35 nn.176,178, 38
    n.202, 40, 42 n.234, 238
Ker, I. T. 7 n.15
Kunzelmann, A. 79 n.113

La Bonnardière, A.-M. 53 n.297, 79 n.113,
    154 n.74
Lactantius
  as influence on Augustine 17, 119
  and Jerome 40

Latin church
  and the commentary 5–6
  and interest in Pauline letters 5
Lausberg, H. 148 n.53
law
  as benefit to Jews 171–3
  as disciplinarian 111, 114 n.91, 149, 172
    n.118, 173–9
  and gospel 109
  and grace 60, 66, 109–11, 114, 125,
    147–55, 171, 201, 211–13
  and Judaizers 125–35, 185
  and Manichees 106, 133 n.20, 152 n.67,
    198 n.196
  new versus old 30, 93–4, 105, 106
  and Paul 45
  and Peter 46
  see also circumcision; fear; sin; slavery;
    works of the law
Law, Vivien 18 nn.71-2
Lawless, George 3 n.6, 18, 71, 72 nn.75, 78,
    73 nn.83, 89, 77 nn.105-6, 78 n.108,
    79 nn.111,115, 81 n.119
leadership, spiritual 79–80, 85–6, 89, 118,
    144–5, 190–1, 202–3
Lieu, Samuel N. C. 62 n.4, 82 n.123
life, four stages 113–14, 192 n.176, 193,
    209–11, 229
Lightfoot, J. B. 46 n.267, 134 n.21, 138
    n.33, 170 n.109, 230 n.277
  and Augustine 72
  and biblical interpretation 90
  and Jerome 34
  and Victorinus 21, 22 n.103, 31 n.158
Lohse, Bernhard 5 n.1
longing, temporal 211
love
  and Christian fellowship 78, 88, 103–5,
    106–7, 209
  compared with fornication 217–19
  and correction 78, 87, 109, 115, 225–7
  and faith x, 113, 125, 167, 201, 229–31
  and fear 110, 112, 113, 115, 145 n.49,
    155, 161–3, 201, 205
  as fulfilment of law 207–9
  of God and neighbour x, 76, 96–7,
    103–4, 113, 115, 155, 205–9, 227
  as hermeneutical key 96–8
  and hope 231–3
  and humility 97, 118, 145
  Latin words for 204 n.211, 217 n.244
  as motive of Christian action 69, 116, 145
    n.49